Pam

May 8, 2007

2007 STANDARD CATALOG OF®

WINCHESTER FIREARMS

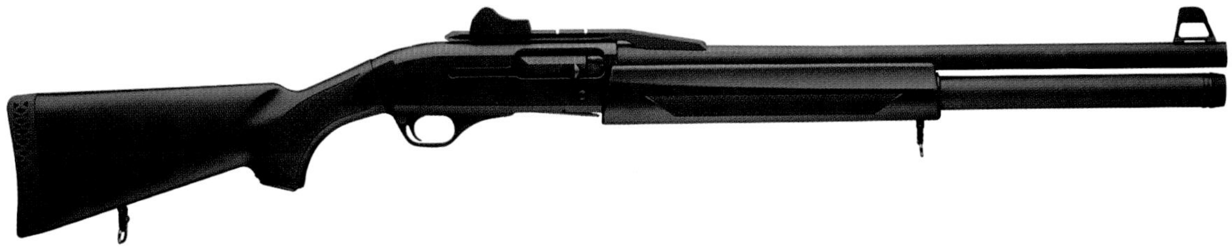

by JOSEPH MADDEN CORNELL, CMA, ASA, ISA

Photography by Paul Goodwin
unless otherwise noted
with the generous assistance of
Little John Auction Service of Orange, California

Published by

Gun Digest® Books
An imprint of F+W Publications
700 East State Street • Iola, WI 54990-0001
715-445-2214 • 888-457-2873
www.gundigestbooks.com

Our toll-free number to place an order or obtain
a free catalog is (800) 258-0929.

Library of Congress Control Number: 2007924546

ISBN-13: 978-0-89689-535-5
ISBN-10: 0-89689-535-1

Designed by Elizabeth Krogwold
Edited by Dan Shideler

Printed in China

DEDICATION

To My Father, F. R. Cornell. He's the one who got me started with guns, and everything else.

PHOTO CREDITS

Except as otherwise noted, all photos in this book were originally taken by Paul Goodwin. The Editor would also like to thank, and endorse, one of the nation's premier auction houses

LITTLE JOHN AUCTION SERVICE
1740 W. La Veta Ave. Orange, CA 92868
714.939.1170; www.littlejohnsauctionservice.com

for their generous assistance in assembling the following photos used in this book:

Jennings rifle; Volcanic rifles; Henry brass & iron frame rifles; Model 1886; Model 1866; Model 1873, Model 1876; Hotchkiss rifle; Model 1885; Model 1866; Model 71; Model 1892; Model 1894; Model 55; Model 64; Model 1895; Winchester-Lee Straight Pull Rifle; Model 1890; Model 1906; Model 61; Model 62; Model 62A; Model 1903; Model 63; Model 1907; Model 55 Rimfire Rifle; Model 74; Model 100; Model 1900; Model 1902; Model 1904; Model 43; Model 52; Model 57; Model 60; Model 60A; Model 68; Model 70; Model 75; Model 250; Model 63; Model 94; Model 9422; New Model 1892; Model 1897; Model 12; Model 21; Model 42; Model 120 Ranger; Model 1200; Super X Model 1; Model 23 Golden Quail; Model 101 Quail Special; and all commemorative rifles and carbines.

CONTENTS

Model 1300 NWTF Short Turkey.

Model 21 Grand American, Closeup of Receiver.

INTRODUCTION

By Joseph Madden Cornell, CMA, ASA, ISA

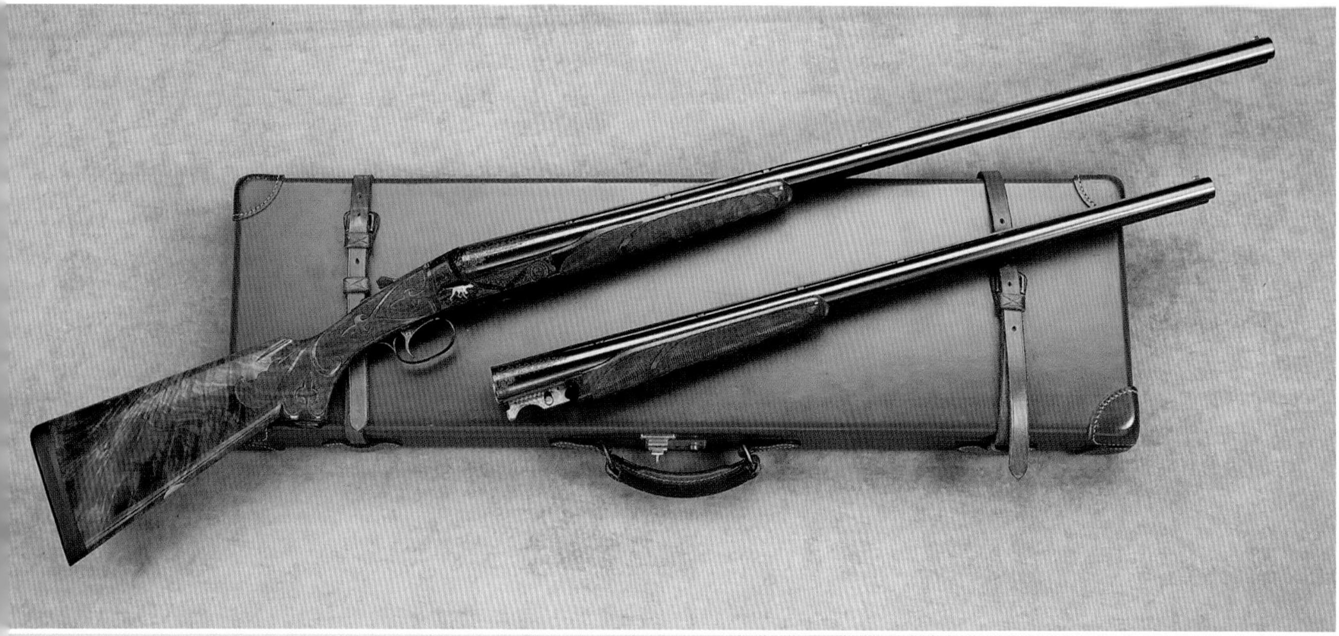

Model 21 Grand American Two-Barrel Set.

This book represents our continuing commitment to follow the tradition of the Standard Catalog® of Firearms, which is to produce the very best informational/informative book available to help those interested in firearm research, pricing information, and identification. We are dedicated to supplying the best in firearm information, well thought out, knowledgeable opinions as to pricing, and pertinent descriptions along with pictures intended to help our readers identify particular firearms they find in the marketplace.

We intend to provide general as well as specific information about Winchester and Winchester firearms. Information is power, and it is our never-ending intention to supply our readers with as much quality, accurate information – and therefore power – as is reasonably possible. It is our intention to provide a maximum number of pictures of various Winchesters. This is because we believe that while a picture may not be worth a thousand words, pictures can and do provide valuable information that the written word is ill-suited to accomplish. (Our sincere compliments and thanks go out to Paul Goodwin, who provided most of the photographs appearing in this book.)

We wish for our readers to recognize that purchasing this book is an excellent investment as it provides them with real knowledge – and therefore real power – that has real practical value as they pursue their involvement in the firearm marketplace. In short, we have endeavored to be the best source for pricing information, research, and identification available today in the United States. This is a tall order, and while we realize perfection is impossible, we intend on doing our very best.

While pricing information is important, we see ourselves as being able to provide the collector with valuable information when it comes to identifying the various Winchesters and their variations with which the collector comes in contact. Winchester made many models, and while manufacturing these various models the company made many changes to them during the time they were being produced. These variations provide much of the basis for the collector interest in Winchester firearms. Certainly, one of our main objectives is to help collectors identify these variations within the same model. In addition, we endeavor to deal with these variations in a manner that will provide the collector with the maximum amount of information as to how the dissimilarity of weapons within the same model can, and does, result in dramatic variations in

"Other than condition, nothing causes more interest in the Winchester collector community than factory special order enhancements."

price. We want to give our readers an advantage in the highly sophisticated and competitive arena that surrounds the collection of Winchester firearms.

We should take a moment and discuss a few of the factors that influence value:

Condition. For many models, condition is everything, and is oftentimes more important than any other single factor.

Rarity. Rarity can have monumental effects on value – but also, in some cases, rarity can have little relative effect on value. For instance, all condition factors being equal, a rare one-of-a-kind Winchester single shot .22 will not be, relatively speaking, be as valuable or as desirable as a rare one-of-a-kind Winchester Model 1886.

Collector Interest. Some models have very low collector interest, while other models have very high collector interest. There are many reasons for variations in the desirability of the different Winchester models, e.g., history, mystique, notoriety, interesting variations within the model, period of manufacture, cinematic exposure, obscurity, celebrity association, "sex appeal," reputation in the firearms industry and among firearm collectors, etc.

Availability. Some models and variations of those models, while manufactured in large numbers, seem, for one reason or another, to lack availability in the marketplace. In order to have mass collector appeal, large numbers of a particular model must be available in the marketplace so that many people can become interested in it.

Factory or Aftermarket Enhancements. Other than condition, nothing causes more interest in the Winchester collector community than factory special order enhancements. Special aftermarket enhancements, such as being engraved by or for some famous personage, can also dramatically increase the value of a firearm.

Provenance. Proven ownership by famous individuals, or an association with historical events, can vastly increase the value of a firearm.

Super X3 Composite. Photo Courtesy U. S. Repeating Arms Company.

Pricing differs from value. This book is a price guide inasmuch as it tends to reflect prices realized for firearms in given conditions. It does not intend to offer appraisal information or be a substitute for a professionally prepared appraisal. Strictly speaking, values are quite different from prices. Values require appraisals. Appraisals are formal written documents that must contain, in order to be credible, 22 separate elements. An appraiser finds for as many as 13 separate values, depending upon the situation. For example, replacement value is used in insurance matters. Fair Market Value is used in situations such as divorces and/or where courts are involved. This can all become quite complicated. For example, neither of these values has anything to say about what the item is actually worth in the relevant marketplace or about how an item should be priced in the marketplace, or about what a collector should expect to pay for an item in the marketplace.

The competent appraiser is expected to provide the apposite value – in other words, the suitable or relevant value – of the item being appraised. Pricing is more subjective. Because the market for firearms is very fluid, pricing information supplied in any price guide can be somewhat obsolete by the date of publication. We are what we say we are: we are a price guide, and by that we mean that we offer

Model 42, Standard Grade.

our opinion as to pricing trends within the firearm marketplace. We are in the firearms market on an almost daily basis, and we will do our very best to offer our very best thoughts as to proper pricing strategies. Our pricing recommendations come from a variety of forms: retail gun stores, individuals collectors, gun shows, auction houses, and personal research/participation in the marketplace. We intend to keep this book as simple as possible and to breed as little confusion as possible, and to help our readers sort out pricing dilemmas as they appear within the collector market.

Manufacturers often offer pricing recommendations in terms of MSRP, but as we all know, dealers are often willing to deviate from MSRP depending on what they think the local market will bear. Some automobile dealers ask more than MSRP on extremely desirable models when they first come out, while on other models they are willing to negotiate down from MSRP. It's all a matter of developing a feel for the marketplace and developing a strategy for balancing the maximization of profits with planned cash turnaround times.

A marketplace, whether it deals with autos or Winchester firearms, has several different levels: wholesale and retail are but two of these levels. The pricing information we provide in this book is always at retail. We try, in this book, to provide our opinion as to what price a willing buyer and a willing seller would agree upon to transact and consummated a sale between the parties. (In determining certain types of values, especially in cases dealing with the IRS, auction values are not highly regarded. Consequently, in establishing our pricing guidelines we use auction results sparingly and only then with the application of our experience, training, education, collaboration with others, and market knowledge.

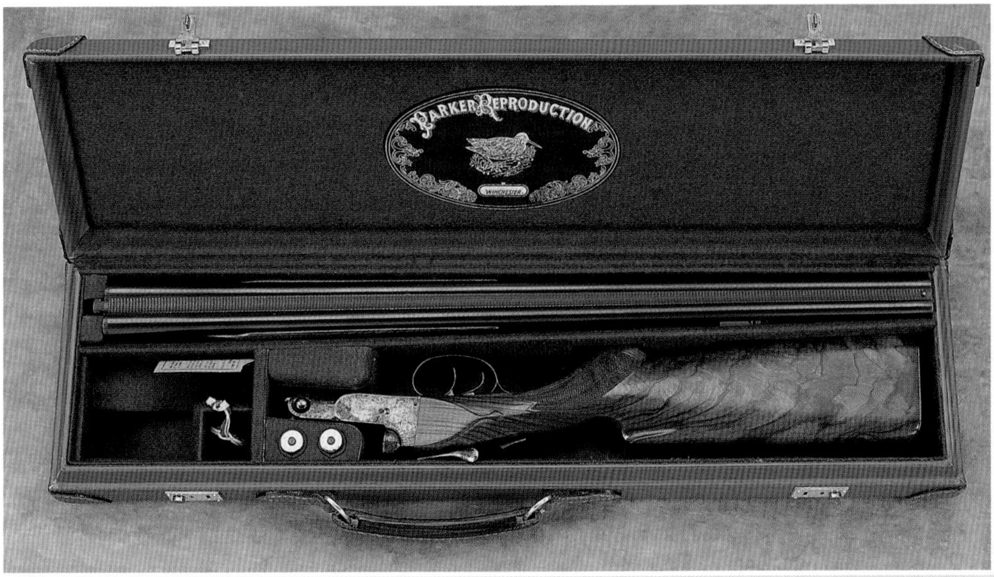

Model 91 Parker VHE Reproduction.

THE BROWNING CONNECTION

Some clarification should be made about the future of Winchester and the manufacture of Winchester firearms. In August of 2006, Winchester announced a long-term licensing agreement between themselves and Browning for the manufacture and distribution of Winchester rifles and shotguns. In Winchester's announcement of this deal, the company said: "With this new agreement, Winchester is confident Browning will produce innovative firearms worthy of the Winchester name, continuing a tradition that people around the world associate with the Winchester brand." Richard Hammett, president of Winchester ammunition, went on to say: "We are proud of our heritage as 'The Gun The One the West' and consider this arrangement as entering a new era for the legendary Winchester firearms brand."

This agreement was announced approximately four months after the closing of the US Repeating Arms Company manufacturing facility in New Haven, Connecticut. The company apparently failed in its major attempt to reopen its plant, and to stop the sale of its equipment, which was due in late September. For more than 10 years, Browning has handled the sales and marketing of Winchester firearms and other associated products. This new agreement provides many additional opportunities and advantages for the legendary Winchester brand.

The president of Browning, Charles Guevremont, said: "We are more committed today than ever before to the development of exciting new Winchester firearms designs. We will continually strive to build the quality products that generations of loyal Winchester customers have come to expect and will be proud to own and use for decades to come."

In an attempt to demonstrate its new commitment to state-of-the-art design, Winchester introduced in 2007 additions to its over and under shotgun lines, updates and redesigns to the Super X Rifle, and added variations to the .22 bolt-action Wildcat. In addition, Winchester released a statement that they expect to have many more new guns available in 2008. In addition, they said that it was going to be their intention to be very aggressive in their introduction of Winchester guns.

The Winchester saga, it appears, is far from over. Now let's get on with the show!

GRADING SYSTEM

In the opinion of the editor, all grading systems are subjective. It is our task to offer the collector and dealer a measurement that most closely reflects a general consensus on condition. The system we present seems to come closest to describing a firearm in universal terms. We strongly recommend that the reader acquaint himself with this grading system before attempting to determine the correct price for a particular firearm's condition. Remember, in most cases condition determines price.

NIB—NEW IN BOX

This category can sometimes be misleading. It means that the firearm is in its original factory carton with all of the appropriate papers. It also means the firearm is new; that it has not been fired and has no wear. This classification brings a substantial premium for both the collector and shooter.

EXCELLENT

Collector quality firearms in this condition are highly desirable. The firearm must be in at least 98 percent condition with respect to blue wear, stock or grip finish, and bore. The firearm must also be in 100 percent original factory condition without refinishing, repair, alterations or additions of any kind. Sights must be factory original as well. This grading classification includes both modern and antique (manufactured prior to 1898) firearms.

VERY GOOD

Firearms in this category are also sought after both by the collector and shooter. Modern firearms must be in working order and retain approximately 92 percent original metal and wood finish. It must be 100 percent factory original, but may have some small repairs, alterations, or non-factory additions. No refinishing is permitted in this category. Antique firearms must have 80 percent original finish with no repairs.

GOOD

Modern firearms in this category may not be considered to be as collectable as the previous grades, but antique firearms are considered desirable. Modern firearms must retain at least 80 percent metal and wood finish, but may display evidence of old refinishing. Small repairs, alterations, or non-factory additions are sometimes encountered in this class. Factory replacement parts are permitted. The overall working condition of the firearm must be good as well as safe. The bore may exhibit wear or some corrosion, especially in antique arms. Antique firearms may be included in this category if their metal and wood finish is at least 50 percent original factory finish.

FAIR

Firearms in this category should be in satisfactory working order and safe to shoot. The overall metal and wood finish on the modern firearm must be at least 30 percent and antique firearms must have at least some original finish or old refinish remaining. Repairs, alterations, nonfactory additions, and recent refinishing would all place a firearm in this classification. However, the modern firearm must be in working condition, while the antique firearm may not function. In either case the firearm must be considered safe to fire if in a working state.

POOR

Neither collectors nor shooters are likely to exhibit much interest in firearms in this condition. Modern firearms are likely to retain little metal or wood finish. Pitting and rust will be seen in firearms in this category. Modern firearms may not be in working order and may not be safe to shoot. Repairs and refinishing would be necessary to restore the firearm to safe working order. Antique firearms will have no finish and will not function. In the case of modern firearms their principal value lies in spare parts. On the other hand, antique firearms in this condition may be used as "wall hangers" or as an example of an extremely rare variation or have some kind of historical significance.

PRICING SAMPLE FORMAT

NIB	EXC.	V.G.	GOOD	FAIR	POOR
550	450	400	350	300	200

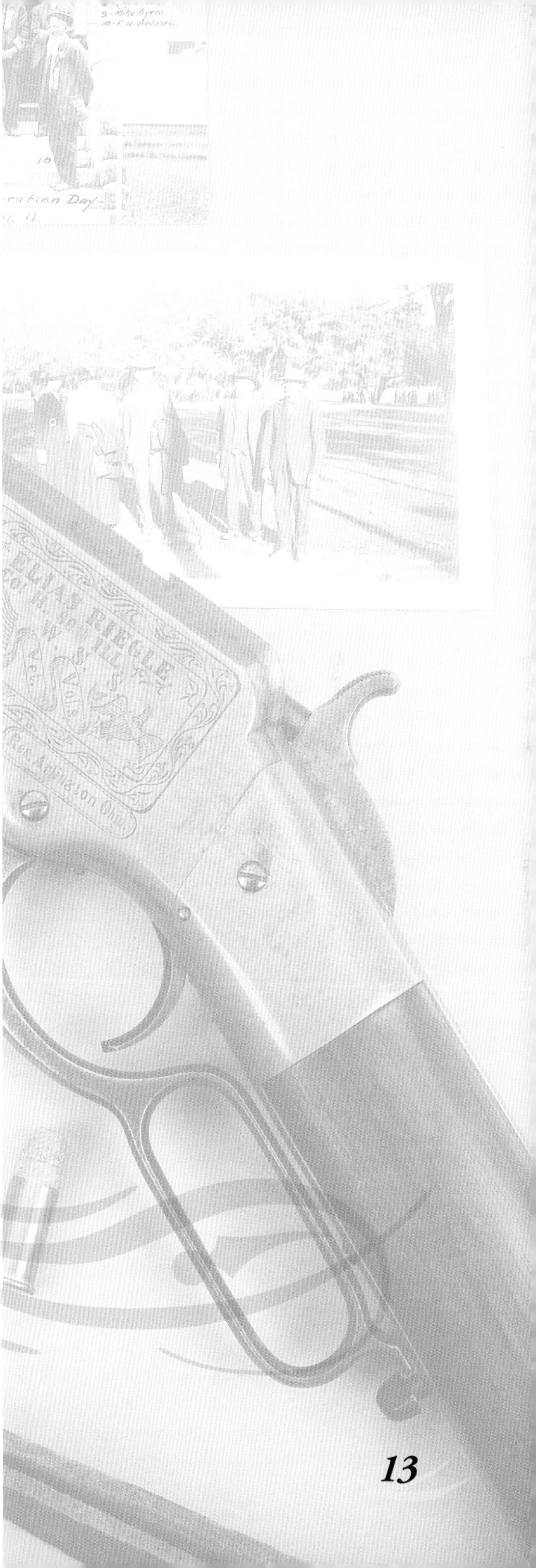

HOW TO USE THIS BOOK

When Winchester began the naming or numbering of their models, they most likely never contemplated that someone would, someday, be responsible for attempting to catalog them in some manner that would make logical sense. The naming of the various Winchester models was certainly never done on a scientific basis, or on a basis that lends itself well to chronicling or organizing the various models for study, particularly by those who are unfamiliar with the various Winchester models and their years of manufacture.

Recognizing that no system is perfect, the author has made an attempt to organize these Winchester firearms into 10 sections. The author has decided that the only method that makes sense for the intended reader is to list each weapon according to whether it is a rifle or shotgun, and then to dividing these broad types into subsections according to the number of digits in model numbers – for

Model 21 Grand American, Cased.

example, Model 75, Model 101, Model 1894, etc. – or by name rather than a number for those unnumbered models: Select, Supreme, etc. Ultimately, this methodology requires ten sections.

Trying to make this is easy as possible, the Author has tried to make it so that that Reader will have to know only three things in order to find a particular weapon: the gun's type, its model number or name, and whether it is a standard production, commemorative or Government-purchased weapon.

In any case, we recommend using the index to find the weapon you are researching, and then going to the proper page number. We sincerely hope that our struggle with this problem will be rewarded by our readers having as easy time as possible in finding the weapon they wish to research – but when dealing with a system as complex as Winchester's, again, nothing is perfect.

THOUGHTS ON COLLECTING WINCHESTER FIREARMS

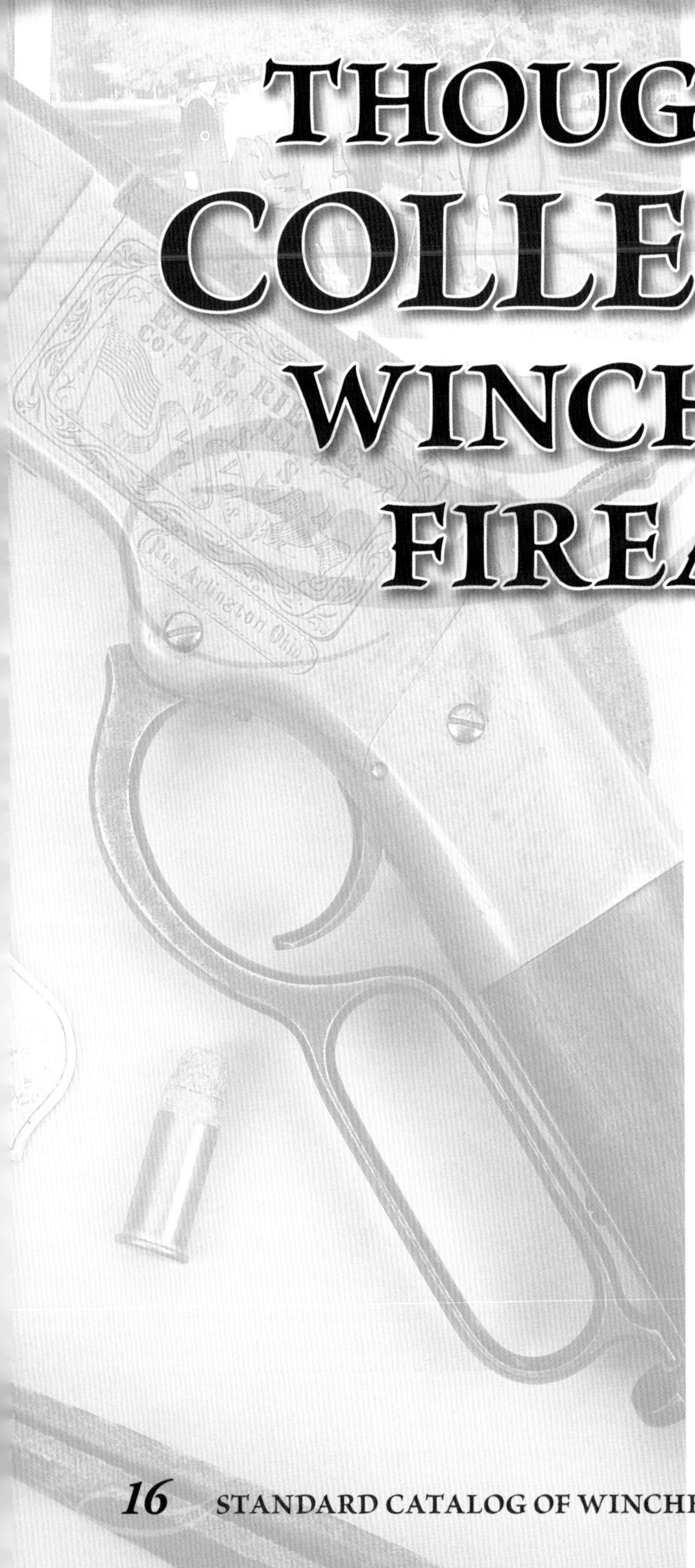

By Joseph Madden Cornell, CMA, ASA, ISA

As the only certified, accredited and designated firearm appraiser in the United States, I am often asked about collecting firearms. It is a subject that is near and dear to my heart, and it is a subject that I have been familiar with for over 50 years. It has also been my life's obsession.

Before I get started with this discussion, I need to clarify one point: there is a difference between collecting and accumulating. Collecting takes place in an organized fashion, usually with specific goals in mind. Accumulating guns means buying particular guns because of specific interest, or, as often occurs, because the opportunity presented itself and the price was right. Some people, including myself, do both: they buy specific guns as part of a collecting plan, and they buy guns because of opportunity and price. Both are worthy pastimes, and both are noble endeavors, but collecting, as far as I'm concerned, is much more interesting and ultimately, much more rewarding. Besides, willy-nilly accumulation of Winchester firearms, usually, means that sooner or later you're going to have to build an addition on to your home, and that might not make for marital bliss. In addition, hiding a medium-size collection from one's spouse is much easier than hiding a vast accumulation of miscellaneous Winchester firearms.

Another thing I've noticed is that firearm accumulators buy all kinds of guns, e.g., Remingtons, Marlins, Colts, and usually in large numbers. Collectors, on the other hand, tend to have a few other weapons but mostly concentrate on the acquisition of weapons within their collecting purview.

"I trust to my own eyes," Baron Duveen, a very famous international art dealer, once testified in explaining the basis on which his firm, Duveen Brothers, reached decisions as to the merits of art objects. He went on to say, "I view each with an eye stored with the recollected visions of all the finest examples studied in over 40 years." Whether an individual is going to collect or accumulate a few firearms, or is much more ambitious and wants a whole houseful, Mr. Duveen's statement is worthy of consideration. If a collector/accumulator starts to acquire firearms without some standards or methodology, most purchases are likely to be far from supplying long-term satisfaction. There is no question that "an eye stored with recollected vision" will benefit the collector/accumulator time and time again. There is no substitute whatsoever for knowing what you are looking at and having the confidence to know that you know it.

Consequently, if you decide to buy firearms, whether or not you are collecting them or just accumulating them, know what it is you're doing, do what it is you know, and always strive to know more. By following this philosophy you will have begun your education and become enrolled in a course of study that can be taken as far as you

Model SXR Super X Rifle. Photo Courtesy U. S. Repeating Arms Company.

"There is no substitute for a well-trained eye, as it will save you time and time again from making mistakes that you will later regret!"

might like. Please do not believe that all there is to know about firearms has already been learned, or for that matter written about. The truth lies in the contrary!

Individual taste in collecting and or accumulating firearms is the most important factor in making good choices – not necessarily choices that will please everyone, but choices that you will be satisfied with long after you have made them. In this way, collecting is a lot like or ordering dinner at a very nice restaurant: everyone doesn't like the same thing. There is no substitute for a well-trained eye, as it will save you time and time again from making mistakes that you will later regret!

Firearms can usually be judged by using one's educated eye, but not always. Sometimes, it takes a magnifying glass, and other times it takes the opinion of an expert. Always know your own limitations, and always be willing to seek whatever help you might need in making the right determinations about a firearm before you make a purchasing decision. Haste, more often than not, will make waste! Knowledge and the skills of a good investigator in gathering information about a potential purchase are the stock in trade of all successful collector/accumulators. Every piece has a story to tell, and upon examination each will testify whether it is real, a fake, or carefully refinished to look like the real thing. With careful inspection, a firearm will tell its story to you if you will only listen. It will never perjure itself, because all the evidence is there for the trained eye to read. Learn to detect the genuine as well as the fraud. Make an item prove that it is what it purports to be. Never assume it is what it purports to be.

At cost of modern labor, only the best pieces will warrant the expenditure of the great deal of time and money necessary to fool the knowledgeable buyer, but it does happen, and it happens more than we would like to think. There are many dealers who make a good living "helping" firearms be something they are not, or be something they used to be. These dealers are unscrupulous and most have been exposed to the experts in the firearms industry. Asked around about a dealer and his reputation before you buy something from him that looks too good to be true, which usually it is. Such Philistines are guilty of the worst kinds of these unfortunate crimes against amateur and less than knowledgeable collector/accumulators. After three thousand years, caveat emptor – let the buyer beware – is still a good rule.

Normal signs of wear are a great help in judging a firearm. An immutable rule is that a genuine firearm will most probably have seen some use. The battle scars of this use should be most apparent and consistent throughout the entire firearm. The edges might be dulled; the finish might be somewhat faded; miscellaneous dents and some scratches will most probably exist. Look them over; they are part of the story the firearm has to tell you. Use will have left its traces. Be aware of the stories told you by dealers, but rely on the story the weapon tells, not on sales hype. Oftentimes dealers, often most innocently, will tell the most astounding untruths regarding the firearm you're holding in your hand and the one they want you to buy.

I want to tell my readers about one of my prejudices. Yes, I am prejudiced...very prejudiced. Rarity is important to me, but only if it comes with condition, quality and originality. I recommend that only weapons that are 100% original, are very high-quality, and are in excellent or better condition should be purchased by "collectors." On the other hand, accumulators can purchase weapons irrespective of condition or originality. Economically, however, one is always ahead purchasing weapons that have a lot of condition, are of high quality, and are 100% original. Weapons that do not have condition, are of poor quality, and are not original, in my opinion, are not collectible. I know that this is a very controversial philosophy, and that many, probably most, collectors will reject this idea as been too "pure." But I am a purist, and with over 50 years experience, I can promise you that this philosophy has been rewarding on many different levels: pride in my collection; growth of my investment; making my collection highly fungible; and putting smiles on other people's faces, when they see my collection, or parts of it. (I have in my collection of model 62s, one weapon that has much less condition than I would like. It has a two-digit serial number, and was put together with a 1890 nickeled expert receiver and other nickeled 1890 expert parts, but it is numbered as a 62 and it is stamped "Model 62.")

Collectors are a breed of human beings unto themselves. It's almost as if they are a subspecies. Some are quiet and methodical as they go about putting together their collections. Others are boisterous, loud and very aggressive. Some work with huge budgets where price isn't a particularly significant issue; others work with very limited budgets, where price is a central issue. Neither is nobler than the other. However, from my experience, I believe that individuals who are working on a limited budget are more careful about their collecting, more circumspect about their purchases. They seem to be more careful about what they buy; certainly they are more careful about what an item costs.

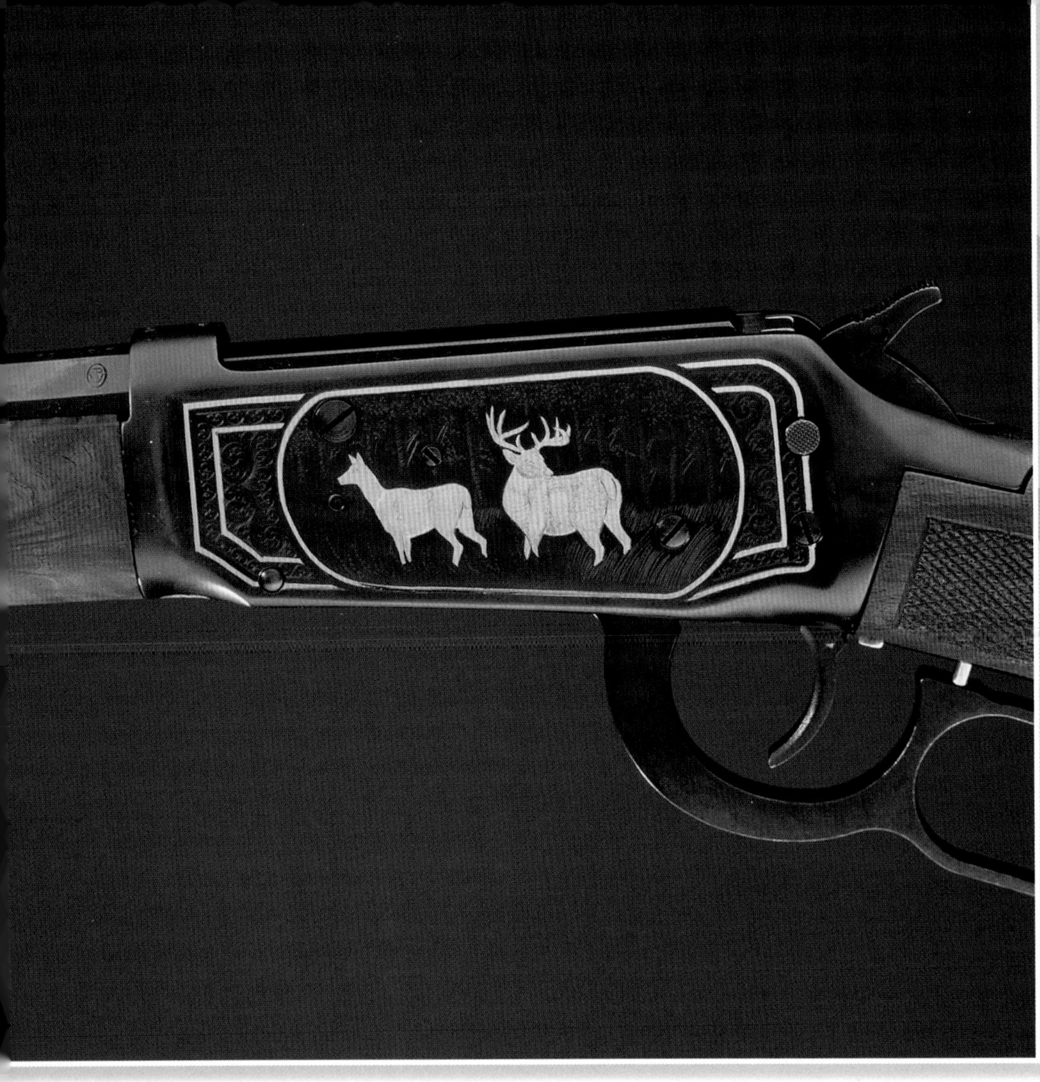

Model 94 1 of 1000, Closeup of Left Receiver. Photo Courtesy U. S. Repeating Arms Company.

When one decides to become a collector of Winchesters, he is entering a world where, most think, stiff competition is everywhere. This isn't always true; it all depends what Winchesters a person decides to collect. If you're going to collect the early lever actions, competition exists everywhere. If you're going to collect some of the later models, little or moderate competition is what you will find. In addition, Winchester prices have a great deal to do with condition and factory originality, not always rarity. For example, a Winchester model 255 is quite rare, but no one seems to care. On the other hand, a standard early Winchester model 1886 is much more common than the model 255, but everyone seems to care about 1886s. An extremely nice 1886, with just a few value-adding features, can cost as much as a brand new sports car. A mint condition model 255 Winchester usually costs less than a one-night stay at a fancy hotel.

Over the years, I have come to view some of the dichotomies in Winchester collecting – e.g., the difference in prices between Winchester Model 1886s and Winchester Model 71s – to be very interesting. The Winchester model 71 was created in the early 1930s using model 1886 Winchester receiver designs, with improvements, so that the rifle could handle an improved cartridge, the .348. With a little looking around, a deluxe Winchester model 71 in very nice condition can be purchased for the very modest price of under $2500. A deluxe Winchester Model 1886, depending on value-adding features to be found on the weapon, can cost 25 to 50 times more. These are the types of interesting paradoxes one finds in the world of the Winchester collector. Even though there are some very real differences between these two rifles, I see many more deluxe Winchester model 1886s for sale than I see deluxe Winchester model 71s for sale. Mechanically speaking, and except for a couple of the 1886s calibers, it's much easier to find ammunition for the Model 71 than for the 1886, and in terms of hunting, the Model 71 has it hands down over the model 1886. However, this is what makes collecting Winchesters so fascinating, and so compelling.

Every serious Winchester collector dreams of that moment when the phone rings, and on the line is a neighbor, or someone at work, telling him that a relative has passed away and that they found a Winchester Model 1886 in the closet. They then ask him if he would like to buy the weapon for $1000, because that's what a neighbor told him it was worth. The Winchester collector's heart rate will increase by a minimum of 20 beats a minute then and there. If, upon inspection, the rifle's receiver shows bright case color, the telltale band of a take-down rifle is there, the wood on the rifle is checkered, and the caliber is one of the more rare ones, the collector just might be in danger of having a heart attack.

Such is the collector's dream – except for the heart attack part – and it happens in real life with more regularity than most people might suspect. In the mid-1980s, I purchased seven mint model 1876 rifles, of which all are different, and all were deluxe models, one being a 1 of 100 model and one being a 1 of a 1000 model. I paid a total of $5000 for the seven rifles. When I think back to those glorious moments, even today, I get excited. I still have these rifles, and they give me great pleasure and satisfaction, and I realize how lucky I was then, and how fortunate I am now.

Winchester, or U.S. Repeating Arms, closed its doors in New Haven, Connecticut effective March 31, 2006. Collectors and dealers alike, have already started to accumulate recently manufactured examples of that Model 94 rifles and carbines. Many

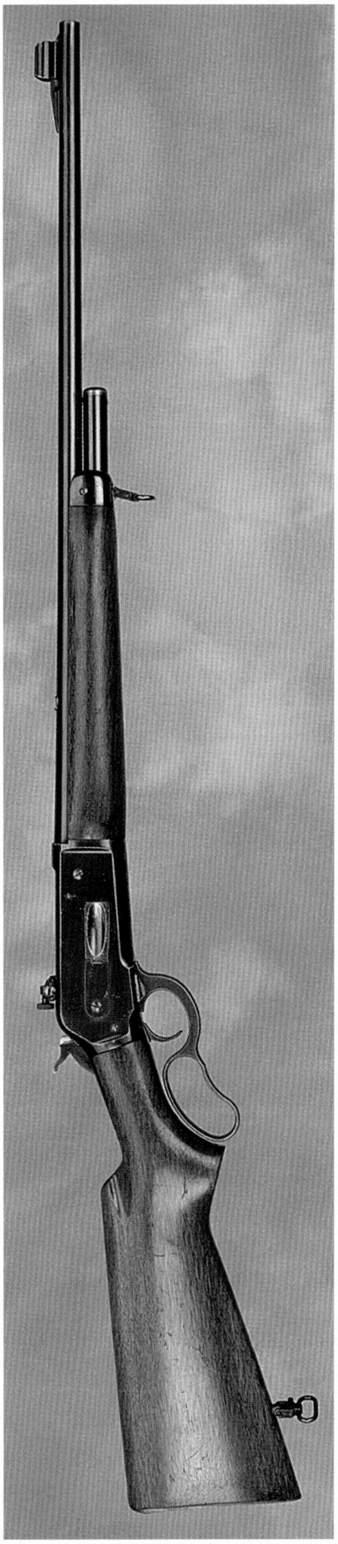

Model 71
Standard Rifle.

Model 94 Heritage 1 of 1000. Photo Courtesy U. S. Repeating Arms Company.

of these later weapons have been selling for as much as 50% over retail value. This may represent an opportunity for investment, or for collecting weapons that exist in the marketplace in rather large numbers, but, for the most part, are still very affordable. Beware, production of these rifles may, at some point in time, recur – and if it does, it's likely that prices will recede to approximate recent levels.

Collecting Winchester rifles is something to which each collector should give a lot of thought as to budget, goal, collecting parameters, storage, insurance, etc. Most collectors I know of started off just accumulating weapons with no well-thought-out collecting philosophy. This is okay, but it probably doesn't make a lot of sense, as what one ends up with if this is what happens is an accumulation of weapons, without order, and without continuity.

If you want to become a collector, rather than an accumulator, you should begin to develop a "collector's philosophy." You may want to collect a particular model, or you may want to collect a particular "type" of weapon, e.g., US-marked weapons, weapons of a particular caliber or configuration, or a broader category of weapons such as bolt action .22 rimfire rifles. There are so many interesting collections that can be assembled that it would take a whole book to just discuss the possibilities.

To give the reader a little something to think about, I would like to give you a little story about my collecting history. When I first graduated from university, I was mostly broke. I loved guns, and couldn't stay away from other gun people, nor was I able to stay away from the gun shows. But I couldn't afford to buy the guns I really wanted, which were the guns that everyone else wanted: Winchester lever action rifles. Consequently, I looked around for something to buy, and I came up with the idea of collecting High Standard pistols. I did so for seven reasons: 1) they were very inexpensive, 2) there were lots of variations,) there were lots of them around, 4) they were in a caliber, .22 long rifle, that I could afford to shoot, 5) no one seemed to know much about them, 6) they were very well-made, and 7) no one cared about them. In the next few years, I put together a very nice collection of about 50 guns, most of them either in the box or in mint condition, and one that included all of the extremely rare examples.

As my financial situation improved and I found out that I could, for the most part, finance my collecting with buying and selling, I got into collecting Winchesters. As time went on, I became fascinated with almost every Winchester rifle that was hand-fitted and had a machined receiver. However, at one time, I became very interested in the little high-quality .22 bolt action rifles that Winchester made in the 1920s through the 1950s. They are very interesting, and there are a lot of them, and once again, I could accumulate them very inexpensively, because no one else cared. I had a lot of fun with that, and in no way did it interfere with my primary pursuit.

Once, in the late 1970s, I went to a gun show and saw an elderly gentleman selling off his collection of Model 62 and 61 Winchesters. I could not afford to buy them all, but I bought the rarest ones, but only if they were in mint or better condition. Eventually, I was able to fill in the ones I didn't have, but because I had many of the more rare ones, it was easy and it could be done economically.

I share with you this event because it demonstrates how a person can begin a collection of particular Winchester rifles and in the long run end up with something that provides a lot of pleasure and at the same time is an excellent investment vehicle. At no time, however, did I merely "accumulate" Winchesters. Each of my areas of interest was well-defined.

I believe there are many opportunities for the would-be Winchester collector. With the changes that have recently occurred at United States Repeating Arms/Winchester, it is my opinion that these changes provide interesting opportunities for novice collectors who do not want to, or perhaps cannot afford to, start purchasing $10,000 rifles or shotguns. All one has to do is look over this book and decided on weapons that one can afford, and weapons that are interesting. This is a way to get started. It's not difficult, and it doesn't have to be expensive.

It can, however, be your obsession.

"I believe there are many opportunities for the novice Winchester collector."

MY PERSONAL COLLECTING PHILOSOPHY

By Joseph Madden Cornell, CMA, ASA, ISA

If one is going to be a collector of guns, or even an accumulator of weapons, I think it important that the individual develop a philosophy so that his acquisitions make sense and fit into some type of organized and well-thought-out plan. Personally, I have been both a collector and an accumulator, but as I get older I have become more of a collector. I found out a long time ago it's much easier to buy firearms than it is to sell them at a price that I believe reflects their worth. It's easy to find bargains at almost any gun show, if one has an encyclopedic memory and is more of an accumulator than a collector. Remember, one can always sell all the firearms that one owns at wholesale or below almost as quickly as one can unload them from your vehicle at a gun show. Myself, I would much prefer to be very active; I am always on the hunt for something that I want. Right now, for example, I have an interest in purchasing higher grade 101 Winchesters in 28 gauge or 410 gauge. So, for me, collecting allows me to continue to be active, aggressive, and involved, but at the same time it allows me to curtail and to control my purchasing.

Because I'm sure that there are at least as many philosophies involved in the collection of Winchesters as there are collectors, I feel I should explain my personal philosophy about collecting. I believe that it will be somewhat instructive to the novice, because he or she can take my ideas and, using them, develop an individual pathway. I also believe that accumulators can use this same philosophy to develop their own hybrid purchasing philosophy. The elements, or central ideas, are approximately the same for both.

THE FIRST THING THAT A COLLECTOR SHOULD DO IS FORMULATE HIS OWN GOALS, BOTH SHORT-TERM AND LONG-TERMS. MY COLLECTING GOALS ARE THESE:

1) I want my collection to be something that I can be proud of owning. In this regard, I guess that I'm a purist and certainly an elitist. Over the years, I have seen collections that consist of unoriginal weapons, weapons of poor condition, weapons that make me wonder, "Why would anyone want to own something like this?" But, if originality and condition are not important to you, then one should feel free to buy anything without regard to originality or condition. Personally, I would rather own one exquisite example than a whole gun case of "junk." I realize that's just me, and I hope that such a statement does not alienate my readership. On the other hand, I have seen collections that make me salivate and make my knees weak. These are the collections that, for me, increase my blood pressure by at least 30 points.
2) I want my collection to be a good investment and to increase in value. I would think that this would be an almost universal goal for almost every collector; however, based upon what I have observed, I'm not sure.
3) I want to be able to own, someday, a complete collection of whatever it is I'm trying to collect. I like order and simplicity and eventual closure; therefore, I want my collection to follow some logical course; to make sense to observers and more importantly, to myself.

Years ago, in the early eighties, I decided to collect pre-'64 model 70s. Using Roger Rule's book and his list of what he thought it would take to have a complete collection, I began purchasing model 70s to that end. However, in order to have a complete collection – and because there are an inexhaustible and innumerable number

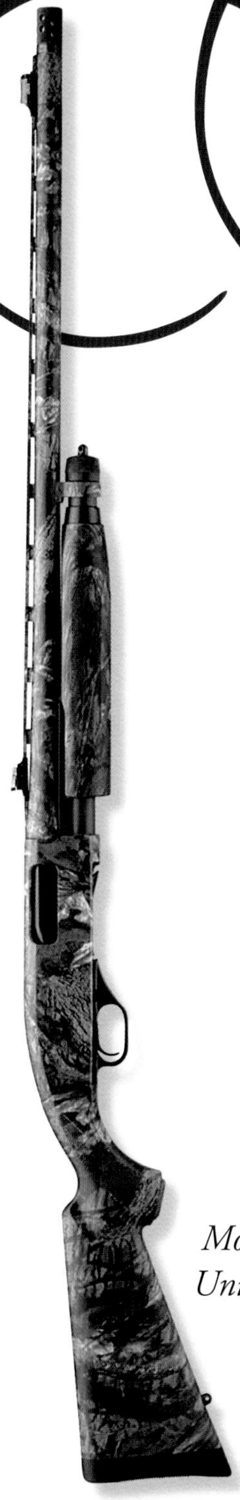

Model 1300 Universal Hunter.

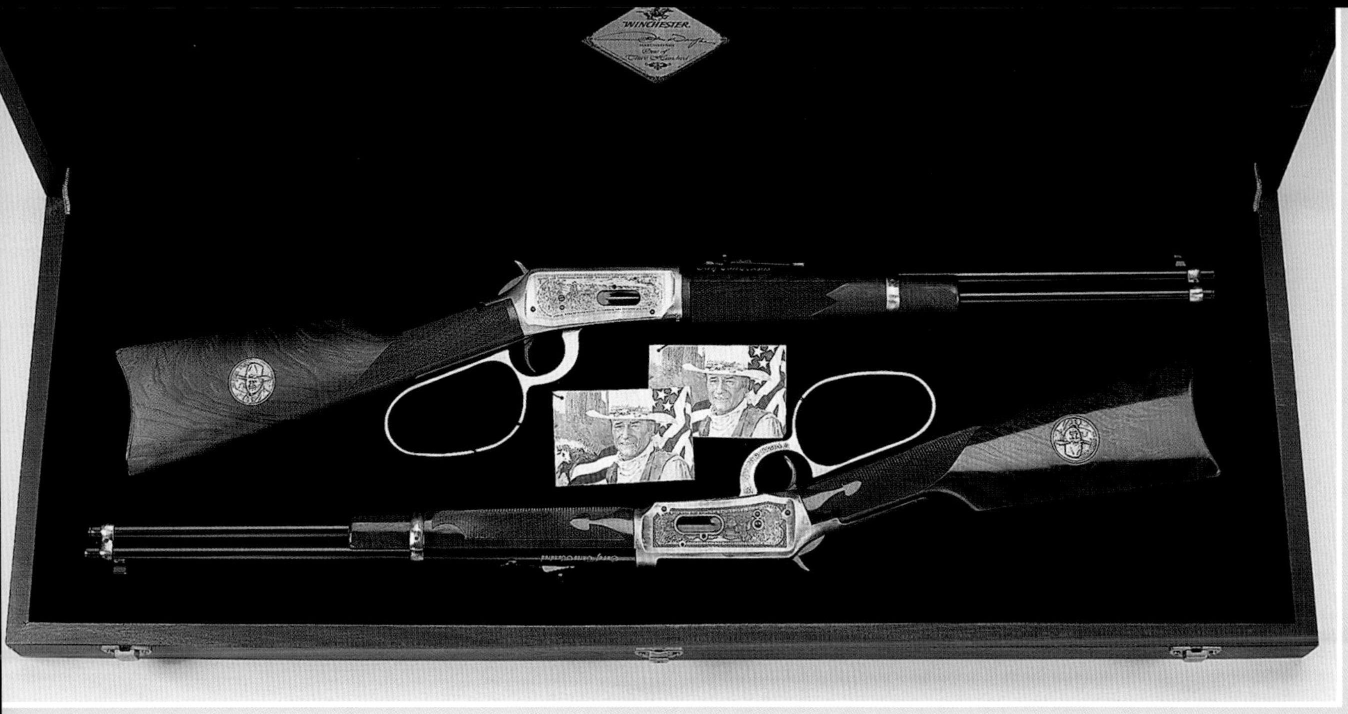

1981 John Wayne Commemorative Matched Set.

of prototypes, uncatalogued specimens, one-of-a-kind, special order, and custom shop guns – I limited my collection to only Winchester catalogued listed guns and their variations. This worked out very well, and within a few years I had a complete, self-limited collection of these magnificent rifles.

4) I want to be able to own every Winchester that I need in order to complete my collection. This precludes me from collecting many different models of Winchesters, e.g., Henrys, 1866s, 1886s, engraved Model 21 Winchesters, etc. Consequently, I choose to collect within an area in which, if I see something I need or want, I can afford to buy it. To me, this make sense. Why collect something that you cannot afford to collect? I own some factory special order 1886 rifles in exquisite condition, but I do not collect them; I have accumulated/invested in them. In this regard, I might be inclined to trade one of them, or, more if the situation warranted, for something that I really want to own, if it would help me fill in a collection that I was involved in completing. I am married only to those things I collect, not the things I have accumulated.

Let's talk about the investment aspect of collecting Winchester weapons. As the only accredited, certified, designated firearm appraiser in the United States, I am continually, on an everyday basis, involved in the market for Winchester firearms and have been for over 30 years. This gives me a special insight into firearm values, including Winchesters, because I see and appraise the best guns in United States. Because of this involvement, I have developed some exacting theories on what makes the best firearm investment. Allow me, to share some of this with you:

- Always buy condition. Never buy junk. Within any collecting category, those properties that have the highest degree of condition will be among the most desirable and, without question, the best investments.
- Always buy originality. Never buy cobbled-up/refinished weapons; they are not collectible. Within any collecting category, those properties that are 100% original will be amongst the most desirable, and, without question, will be the best investments.
- Rarity is good, but it pales in importance when compared to condition and originality. If one is concerned about mak-

ing a good investment, even rare items should have condition and originality.

- Exceptional, well-documented, and historical weapons with market-acceptable provenance usually make good investments. The exception to this is if the weapon in question lacks condition, and/or originality. The investment potential of such pieces is limited when compared to other similar pieces with condition and originality.
- Look for Winchesters that are not undergoing accumulation. As every Winchester enthusiast knows, the market more enthusiastically pursues some models of Winchesters at different times than others. At one time, Model 70 pre-'64 Winchesters were among the hottest collectible Winchesters in the marketplace. At another time, Model 12 pre-'64 Winchesters were among the hottest. It still another time, Model 21 Winchesters were hot. A few years ago, Model 42 Winchesters were being pursued by almost the entire Winchester marketplace. Try to avoid starting a collection during these hot periods unless you have very deep pockets.

The opposite of accumulation is distribution. Often times, Winchesters that are not under accumulation or distribution may be being "held" by the marketplace. They are neither being accumulated nor distributed, in market terms. However, there are always models of Winchesters that are undergoing distribution; this means that they are being sold in unusual numbers and that collector/accumulators are converting them to either cash or in trade.

Right now, there are more high-grade Winchester lever actions on the market than I have ever seen before. I believe these models, or at least some of them, are undergoing distribution. In the beginning of any period of distribution for any highly desirable Winchester, there is a type of market frenzy that takes place. It's very interesting to someone like myself who is so involved on a daily basis with such an active marketplace as we see with Winchester firearms. High prices and market frenzy often create large numbers of particular models of Winchesters to be released onto the market. I never buy weapons at high prices when they are undergoing distribution except at the very end of a distribution cycle, when prices usually decline.

In short, my collecting philosophy is to buy that which I can afford and need to complete my collection: weapons with condition, originality, and rarity – weapons that, I believe, will, within a reasonable time, undergo accumulation and a resulting increase in value.

That's my collecting philosophy. What's yours?

A BRIEF COLLECTER'S HISTORY

OF THE WINCHESTER REPEATING ARMS COMPANY OF NEW HAVEN, CONNECTICUT

By Joseph Madden Cornell, CMA, ASA, ISA

For firearm collectors, and for people interested in American history, the name "Winchester" is truly magical. It conjures up pictures of movie stars engaged in life-and-death struggles, conducting shootouts with bad guys and Indians. Novelists of years past made Winchester-toting heroes the idol of every one reading their books. The Winchester name is synonymous with American frontier heroes and antiheroes alike, and as such was a part of every cowboy and Indian scenario played out in the backyards of American youth. The Winchester name is inextricably tied with the 19th-century philosophy of "Manifest Destiny," which the intellectual basis for Americans moving West. It can be argued that without Winchester rifles, America's move West would have been much more difficult and taken much longer.

Winchester rifles and shotguns are prized for their collectibility and investment potential, as well as for their historical significance. If one tracks the stock market, the market for art – gold, antiques, real estate, almost any other investment vehicle – one finds serious market fluctuations and ups and downs. When one tracks the value of original Winchester firearms, especially those of high condition, one can see that original Winchester firearms have consistently showed a steady increase in value. One of the more remarkable things about original Winchester firearms, and original firearms in general, is their amazing fungibility.

Firearms, very much like gold, are quickly, almost instantaneously, easily converted to cash. Original Winchesters, especially those of high condition, are among the most fungible of all firearms. So, not only have Winchester buyers been interested in acquiring these weapons for purposes of collection, but also, financially speaking, Winchester firearms have made great investments. With banks paying interest rates of 3% to 5%, collectors find that, if they can find a Winchester firearm reasonably priced, an investment in an original Winchester will is often times more profitable than money in the bank. But as always, THE BUYER MUST BEWARE because not all deals are good deals!

Today, as we view of the firearm market, we can see some interesting changes taking place. Highly desirable pieces in pristine condition are bringing astronomical prices. That's interesting, because that's what I was saying 25 years ago. Less desirable pieces in moderate condition are increasing in value, but certainly not at the rate of increases enjoyed by the more desirable models, especially weapons with unusually high condition. This au-

"Winchester rifles and shotguns are prized for their collectibility and investment potential, as well as for their historical significance."

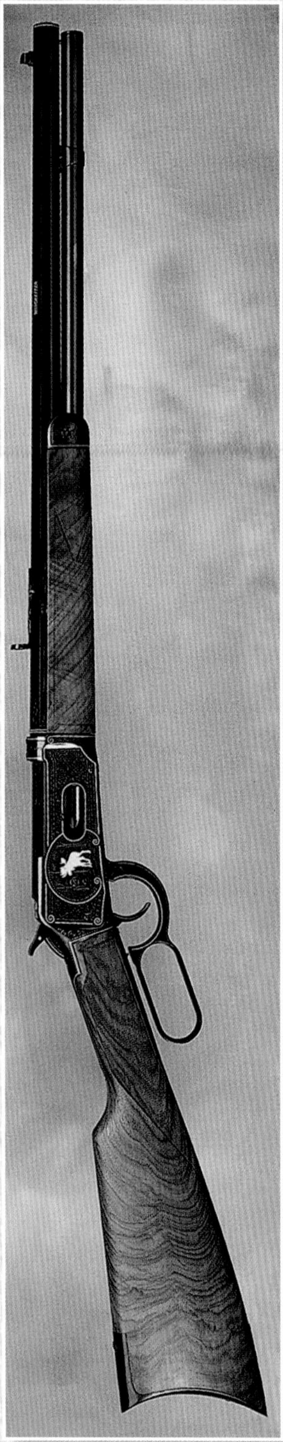

1991 Winchester 125th Anniversary Commemorative, Full View.

thor is involved in the firearm market on almost a daily basis, and the prices being paid for original Winchester firearms, especially those of high condition, are on the rise with no sign whatsoever of moderation.

With any discussion of Winchester firearms, one should talk about Winchester firearms that were owned by famous people. The proper term for the association of an item with a famous personage or significant historical event is called provenance. Provenance can have a very dramatic effect on the firearm's value, e.g., a Winchester firearm associated with Custer's Last Stand, or one owned by Teddy Roosevelt will be worth dramatically more than a very similar firearm without such association.

The Winchester Repeating Arms Company was formally established by Oliver F. Winchester on February 20, 1866, and the first model to bear the name of the company was the Model 1866 lever-action rifle chambered for the .44 caliber rimfire cartridge. As with any enterprise it is helpful to study the background and beginnings of the Winchester company so as to better understand the chronological sequence of various rifles and pistols that preceded the Winchester Model 1866.

The story begins with Walter Hunt of New York City who, in 1848, developed the Rocket Ball and Volition Repeater, a unique lever-action, breechloading, underbarrel magazine tube repeater. This rifle was the origin for future concepts. Hunt's business partner, George Arrowsmith, had as his machinist a man named Lewis Jennings, who improved and simplified Walter Hunt's original concept. Jennings's improvements were granted a U.S. patent in 1849. Th resulting 25-shot repeating rifle was promoted by Arrowsmith, who found a willing investor in Courtland Palmer, a Connecticut merchant. Palmer bought both the Hunt and Jennings patents and had 5,000 Jennings rifles built by Robbins and Lawrence in Vermont in 1850. The foreman at Robbins and Lawrence was Benjamin

Tyler Henry, a man who would play an important role in future repeating rifle developments.

By 1851 two additional individuals would enter the Hunt-Jennings story: Daniel Wesson and Horace Smith. These two men improved on Lewis Jennings' design, and Smith was granted a patent in 1851, which he assigned to Palmer. Despite the initial achievements with the Jennings rifle, the action proved too complex and the cartridges too light for successful marketability.

In 1854 Horace Smith and Daniel Wesson were granted a U.S. patent for a repeating firearm similar to earlier Horace Smith design. Courtland Palmer funded the experimental work on the new pistol, which featured a 4" barrel and a full-length underbarrel magazine. Palmer, Smith and Wesson formed a partnership incorporating the Hunt, Jennings, Smith, and new Smith & Wesson patents. The pistols were made in Norwich, Connecticut, under the name of Smith & Wesson. B. Tyler Henry was an employee of the new firm.

Only about 1,000 of these pistols were produced before the company name was changed to Volcanic Repeating Arms Company, an incorporated firm, in 1855. The new company was formed by Palmer, Smith, and Wesson with the additional financial assistance of Oliver F. Winchester. Winchester was at the time a successful manufacturer of men's clothing in New Haven, Connecticut. The new company bought out Palmer and Smith, while Daniel Wesson stayed on as shop foreman to work on his metallic rimfire cartridge. Volcanic pistols and rifles were first built at the original Smith & Wesson factory in Norwich until 1856, when a new plant was located at New Haven. In 1857 the majority of stock in the Volcanic Repeating Arms Company was owned by Oliver Winchester

The New Haven Arms Company was structured in April 1857 to assume the business of Volcanic Repeating Arms Company. This new company continued the production of Volcanic pistols and rifles, but these were now marked as "NEW HAVEN CONN. PATENT FEB. 14, 1854." These Volcanics received favorable reports as to their ra-

1991 Winchester 125th Anniversary Commemorative, Closeup of Left Receiver.

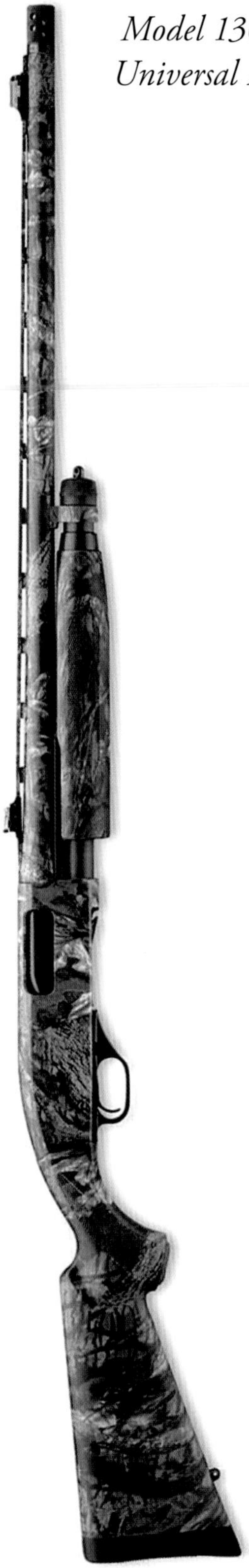

Model 1300 Universal Hunter.

pidity of fire and ease of operation, but they suffered from low velocity, energy, and small calibers. These difficulties affected sales, which remained slow. Perhaps this would be the end of the story had it not been for B. Henry Tyler, who was the shop foreman at New Haven Arms Company after the departure of Daniel Wesson. Tyler had been involved with the predecessors for the past 10 years and he received a patent in 1860 for the improvement in magazine firearms.

The success of Henry's new design was twofold: first, the development of a new, more powerful .44-caliber metallic rimfire cartridge that was sufficiently potent enough to compete with the single-shot rifles of the day; and, second, the advancement in the firing pin design, the addition of an extractor, and improvements in the bolt and feeding mechanisms. All of these improvements helped to make the Henry rifle a success. The first production Henry rifles were delivered in 1862. In 1866 the New Haven Arms Company name was changed to Winchester Repeating Arms Company.

The subsequent models offered by Winchester are highly prized by collectors. Winchester Repeating Arms Company went on to establish itself as one of the world's leading firearms manufacturers. Winchester will forever have a place as the company that built the guns that "Won the West." By the beginning of World War I, 1914, Winchester was the leading domestic firearms producer in the United States and also exported guns around the world.

After World War I ended and beginning in the early 1920s, the company began to lose its dominant position in the firearms industry. The decade of the 1920s marked a difficult financial period for Winchester, with the company finally being forced into receivership by the end of the decade. In 1931, Winchester was purchased by the Western Cartridge Company, which was owned by the Olin family. Because of the changing times, the company's focus was now on sporting arms and the drive for new models and manufacturing techniques came from the vision and foresight of John M. Olin.

From 1931 until 1963, Winchester Repeating Arms regained and retained its reputation for quality firearms, and the rifles and shotguns produced during this period in the company's history are as collectible as those guns that preceded it. In 1964, the company could no longer afford to mass-produce firearms that in reality were hand-fitted and hand-machined. Production changes were implemented that reflected the mass-production psychology that was becoming so commonplace in American industry. This streamlining, which many consumers viewed as nothing more than ill-advised cost-cutting, resulted in the "pre-'64 is good, post-'64 is bad" mentality that is still quite common in collecting circles today.

Some notable exceptions to the prevailing view of post-'64 Winchesters are the Model 21 shotgunsand a few other select models of Winchester firearms which continued after 1964 and are considered handfitted and hand-machined. In 1981 Winchester Repeating Arms Company sold its firearms division to U.S. Repeating Arms Company, a third-party manufacturing concern.

The Winchester legend lives on, and Winchester guns are collected and respected by many. For several decades it has been the opinion of diehard and recalcitrant Winchester collectors, often of previous generations, that Winchester weapons manufactured after 1964 are not collectible. This is rapidly changing. With changes at the Winchester factory that occurred in 2005 and 2006, post-1964 Winchester rifles, irrespective of date of manufacture, are considered by a growing number of individuals to be collectible. Also, with the accelerating values of original Winchesters manufactured prior to 1964, many individuals are collecting post-1964 production original Winchesters because they are the only Winchesters they can afford.

In many cases, collecting pre-1964 Winchesters

"In many cases, collecting pre-1964 Winchesters has become a rich man's game, especially if the collectors are interested in high-quality guns."

has become a rich man's game, especially if the collectors are interested in high-quality guns. One of the reasons that post-1964 Winchesters are considered by many to be highly collectible is that Winchester continued to manufacture interesting models with many variations. The Winchester name has been magical enough to create collector interest, and the numerous interesting variations of models and variations within those models has been sufficient to help sustain collector interest.

Along with Browning's, Winchester's corporate offices are located in Morgan, UT. During the time Winchester was under Olin Corp. management, Winchester manufactured shotguns and rifles at the Olin Kodensha Plant, which closed in 1989. This manufacturing facility was located in Tochigi, Japan, but had subsidiaries in Europe. In 1992, GIAT (Groupement des Industries de l'Armée de Terre, now known as Nexter) which is located in France and partly owned by the French government, acquired Winchester. In late 1997, both Browning and U.S. Repeating Arms were acquired by Belgian interests.

The prices given in the following pages concern, for the most part, standard original guns without optional features that were so often furnished by the factory. These optional or extra-cost features are too numerous to list and can affect the price of a shotgun or rifle to an enormous degree. In some cases these options are one of a kind. Collectors and those interested in Winchester firearms have the benefit of some of the original factory records. These records are now stored in the Cody Firearms Museum, Buffalo Bill Historical Center, P.O. Box 1000, Cody, Wyoming (307) 587-4771. For a $25 fee the museum will provide factory letters containing the original specifications of certain Winchester models using the original factory records. CAUTION: Buyers should confirm by Cody letter any special-order feature on any Winchester within the Cody record range before paying a premium for a scarce feature, or particularly valuable piece.

Unfortunately, due to the high prices now commanded by many Winchester models, especially those having unusually high condition, we are finding more and more counterfeit Winchester firearms. In addition, we are finding that many Winchester firearms have been "helped." In this case, the entire firearm has not been counterfeited, but only certain parts of it have been changed, "helped," in order to make the gun appear more rare, or in original condition, or in better condition than prior to undergoing such changes. We strongly recommend that before buying an expensive Winchester firearms that buyers seek expert council and help. The problem with this is that even the experts are often fooled. The Rule: The Buyer Must Beware!

Collectors of firearms are continually confronted with making decisions as to whether or not the weapon they are buying or selling is factory original, and as to the firearm's condition. In this book, our values are for weapons that are factory original. Often times, the author has encountered collections of mostly altered Winchester firearms, firearms which are not factory original. The value of nonoriginal Winchester firearms can be a mere percentage of factory original firearms, especially if the nonoriginal firearm is also in less than pristine condition, e.g., refinished.

There are some individuals in the United States who are very accomplished in refinishing Winchester firearms, but their numbers are few. Unfortunately, even the work of one of these experts seriously diminishes the value of a like-conditioned factory original Winchester. Their work can seemingly restore the looks of an old Winchester to approximately original condition, but their work does not restore the value of an original old Winchester. Serious collectors will usually NEVER buy a reconditioned or refinished Winchester, or for that matter, any Winchester that is not completely 100% factory original. These refinished/refurbished/restored guns, call them what you will, are bought by people who want to shoot them or by people who just don't know any better. One of the aims of this book is to reduce the population of the latter group to the extent possible.

Winchester, or more properly U.S. Repeating Arms, closed its doors in New Haven, Connecticut, effective March 31, 2006. Collectors and dealers alike have already started to accumulate recently manufactured examples of the sainted Model 94 rifles and carbines. Many of these later weapons have been selling for as much as 50% over retail value. This may represent an opportunity for investment, or for collecting weapons that exist in the marketplace in rather large numbers, but, for the most part, they are still very affordable. Beware that production of these rifles may at some point in time resume, and if it does, it's likely that prices will recede to approximate recent levels. In this book, we do not supply values based on speculation, but rather upon observed retail pricing ("street pricing").

The Winchester manufacturing facilities in North America may have closed, but one of the relatively few certainties in firearms collecting is that the lustre of the Winchester name will go on, even if only in the hearts of Winchester collectors. To them, Winchester is not only a reminder of the golden days of American expansion, but the stuff of legend.

SECTION I

EARLY RIFLES WITH MODEL NAMES DESIGNATIONS; NOT NUMBERS, EG, JENNINGS, LEE

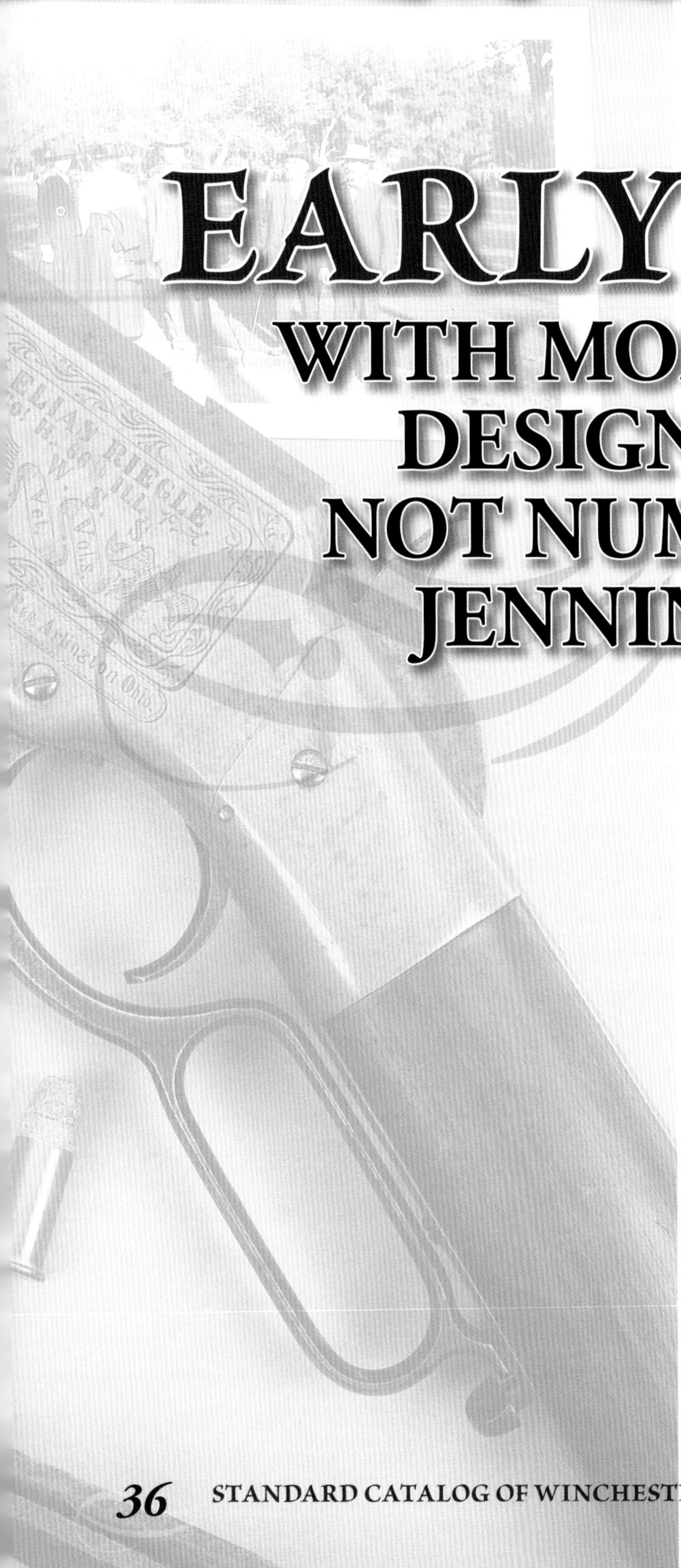

HUNT REPEATING RIFLE

Walter Hunt described his repeating rifle as the Volition Repeater. Hunt was granted U.S. patent number 6663 in August of 1849 for a repeating rifle that was to pave the way for future generations of Winchester repeating rifles. Hunt's rifle design was unique and innovative as was his patent number 5701 for a conical lead bullet that was to be fired in his rifle. This ingenious bullet had a hole in its base filled with powder and closed by a disc with an opening in the middle to admit the ignition from an independent priming source that used priming pellets made of fulminate of mercury. The rifle actually worked but only the patent model was built; it is now in the Cody Firearms Museum.

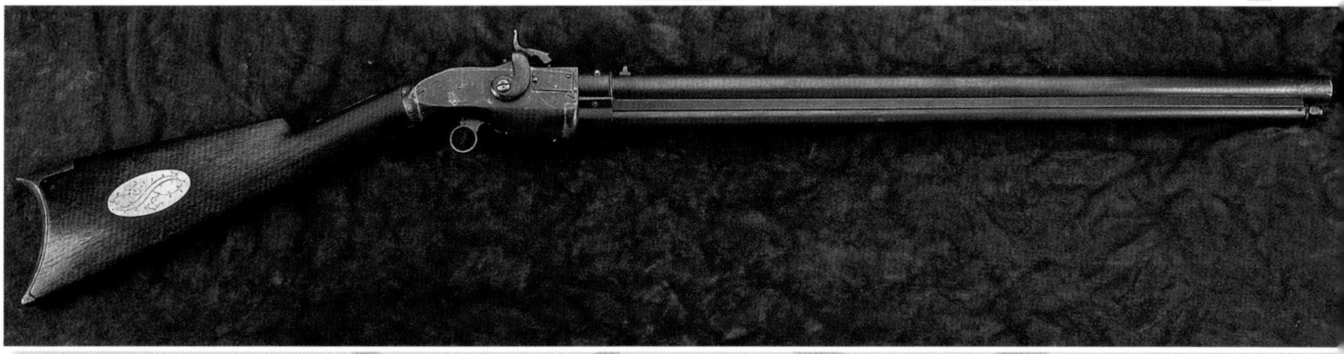

2nd Model Jennings Rifle, Right View.

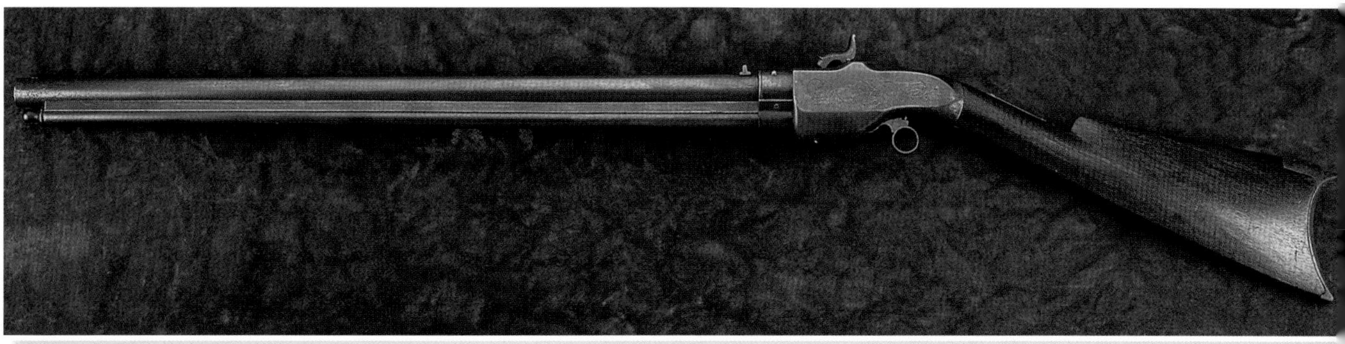

2nd Model Jennings, Left View.

JENNINGS

Second in the evolutionary line of Winchester rifles is the Jennings. Made by Robbins & Lawrence of Windsor, Vermont, this rifle incorporated the original concept of the Hunt design with the additional improvements utilized by Lewis Jennings. The Jennings rifle is important not only as a link in the chain of repeating-rifle development but also because it introduced Benjamin Henry Tyler to the concept of the tubular magazine lever-action repeating rifle. The Jennings rifle was built in three separate and distinct models. While total production of the three types was contracted for 5,000 guns, it is probable that only about 1,000 were actually produced.

FIRST MODEL

The First Model Jennings was built in a .54 caliber, breech-loading, single-shot configuration with a ring trigger, oval trigger guard, and 26" barrel. A ramrod was fixed to the underside of the barrel as well. This variation was made from 1850 to 1851.

EXC.	V.G.	GOOD	FAIR	POOR
-	-	4000	1750	700

SECOND MODEL

The Second Model Jennings was produced adopting the improvements made by Horace Smith. This Second Model is a breech-loading repeating rifle with an under barrel magazine tube and a 26" barrel. The frame is sculptured, unlike the First Model. The ring trigger is still present, but the trigger guard was removed as part of the design change. The caliber remained a .54, and the rifle was fitted with a 25" barrel. The Second Model was produced in 1851 and 1852.

EXC.	V.G.	GOOD	FAIR	POOR
-	-	8000	4000	1500

Volcanic Repeating Arms Company Pistol With Shoulder Stock.

THIRD MODEL

The Third Model represents an attempt by investors to use the remaining parts and close out production. The .54 caliber Third Model was a muzzleloading rifle with a ramrod mounted under the barrel and a 26-1/2" barrel. The frame was the same as that used on the First Model, but the trigger was more of the conventional type. The trigger guard had a bow in the middle giving this model a distinctive appearance. This variation was produced in 1852 and marks the end of the early conceptual period in repeating rifle development.

EXC.	V.G.	GOOD	FAIR	POOR
-	-	9500	4500	1500

SMITH & WESSON VOLCANIC FIREARMS

An interesting connection in the evolution of the lever-action repeating firearm is found in the production of a small group of pistols and rifles built in Norwich, Connecticut, by Horace Smith and Daniel Wesson under the firm name of Smith & Wesson. The company built two types of Volcanic pistols. One was a large-frame model with an 8" barrel and chambered in .41 caliber. About 500 of these large frames were produced. The other pistol was a small-frame version with a 4" barrel chambered in .31 caliber. Slightly more of these small-frame pistols were built, about 700, than the large-frame version. In both variations the barrel, magazine, and frame were blued. Smith & Wesson also produced a lever-action repeating rifle. These rifles are exceedingly rare with fewer than 10 having been built. They were chambered for the .528 caliber and were fitted with 23" barrels. Because of the small number of rifles built, no value is offered. These weapons are extremely rare and the advice of an expert should be retained prior to purchasing. Unfortunately, in recent years, we have seen an increase in weapons that have been "helped," or are outright frauds. The buyer must beware.

8" PISTOL

EXC.	V.G.	GOOD	FAIR	POOR
-	-	13000	6000	1500

4" PISTOL

EXC.	V.G.	GOOD	FAIR	POOR
-	-	11000	4000	1000

VOLCANIC FIREARMS (VOLCANIC REPEATING ARMS COMPANY)

With the incorporation of the Volcanic Repeating Arms Company, a new and important individual was introduced who would have an impact on the American arms industry for the next 100 years: Oliver F. Winchester. This new company introduced the Volcanic pistol using the improvements made by Horace Smith and Daniel Wesson. Volcanic firearms are marked on the barrel, "THE VOLCANIC REPEATING ARMS CO. PATENT NEW HAVEN, CONN. FEB. 14, 1854."

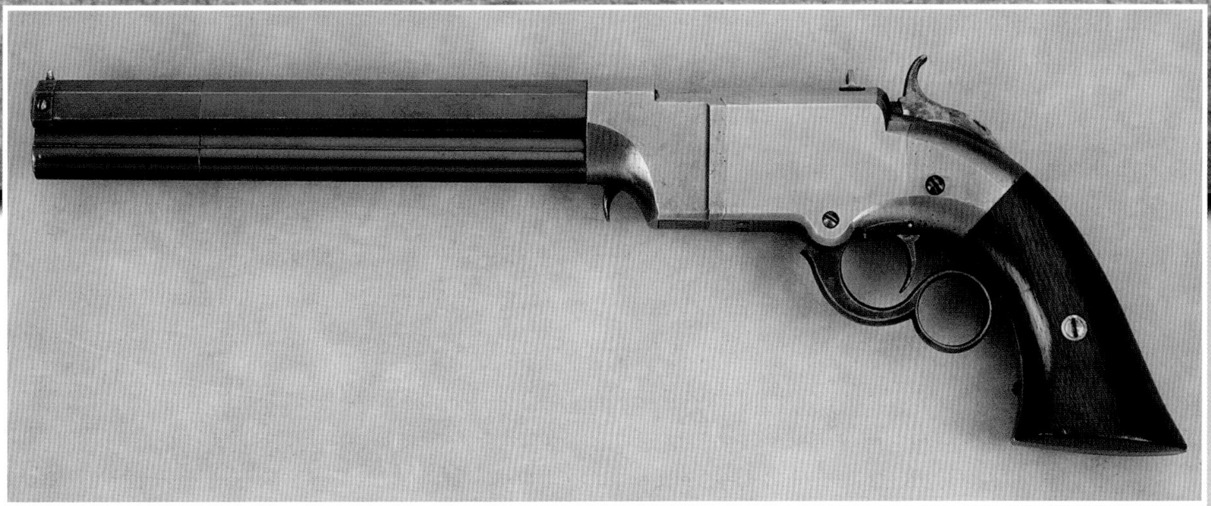

New Haven Arms Company Volcanic Pistol, Left View.

The Volcanic was offered as a .38 caliber breech-loading tubular magazine repeater with blued barrel and bronze frame. These pistols were available in three barrel lengths. These weapons are extremely rare and the advice of an expert should be retained prior to purchasing. Unfortunately, in recent years, we have seen an increase in weapons that have been "helped," or are outright frauds. The buyer must beware.

6" BARREL

EXC.	V.G.	GOOD	FAIR	POOR
-	-	7000	3500	1500

8" BARREL

EXC.	V.G.	GOOD	FAIR	POOR
-	-	7000	3500	1500

16" BARREL

EXC.	V.G.	GOOD	FAIR	POOR
-	-	14000	5500	2500

NOTE: A few Volcanic pistols were produced with detachable shoulder stocks. These are considered quite rare. For original guns with this option, the prices listed should be increased by 25 percent.

VOLCANIC FIREARMS (NEW HAVEN ARMS COMPANY)

In 1857 the New Haven Arms Company was formed to continue the production of the former Volcanic Repeating Arms Company. Volcanic firearms continued to be built but were now marked on the barrel, "NEW HAVEN, CONN. PATENT FEB. 14, 1854." The Volcanic pistols produced by the New Haven Arms Company were built in .30 caliber and used the same basic frame as the original Volcanic. These pistols were produced in 3-1/2" and 6" barrel lengths. These weapons are extremely rare and the advice of an expert should be retained prior to purchasing. Unfortunately, in recent years, we have seen an increase in weapons that have been "helped," or are outright frauds. The buyer must beware; even "experts" can be fooled by unscrupulous individuals, who have mastered the art of creating fraudulent guns.

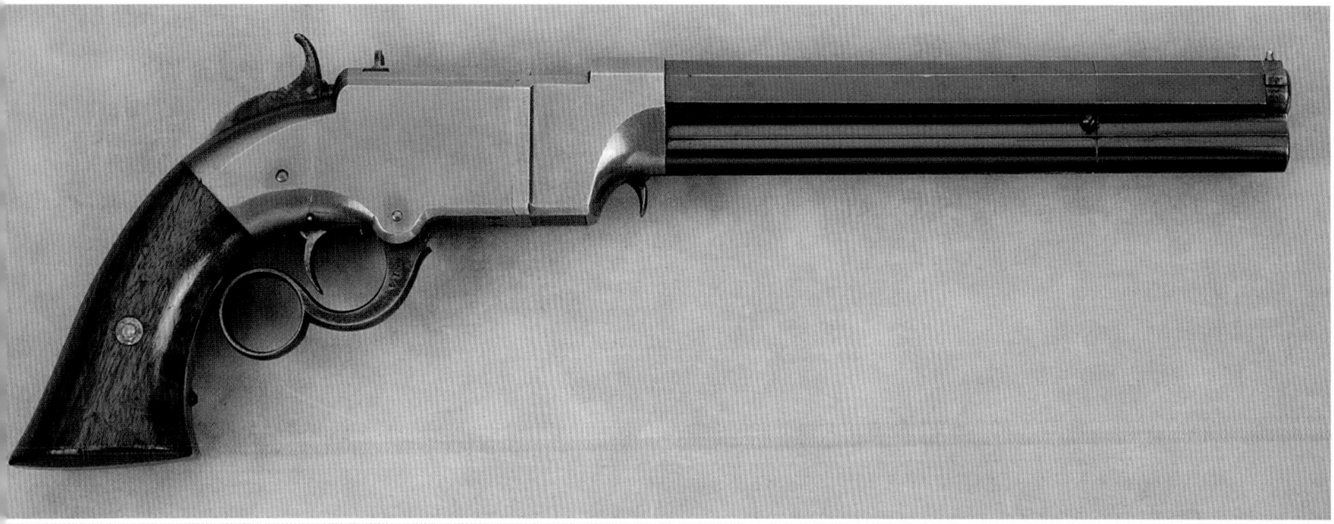

New Haven Arms Company Volcanic Pistol, Right View.

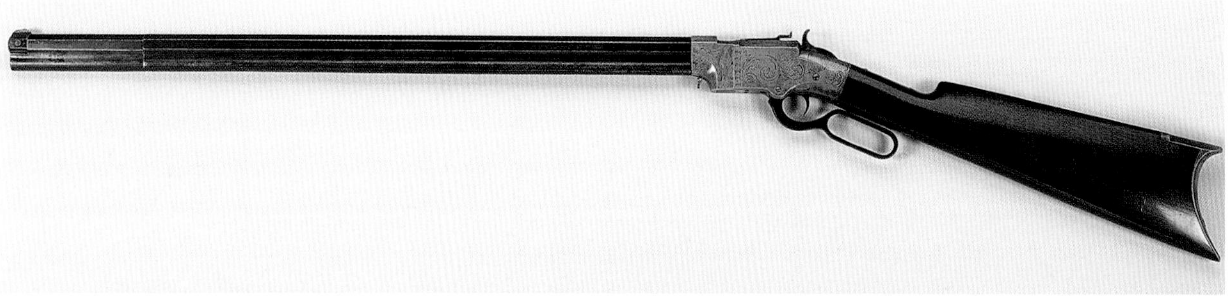

Volcanic Lever Action Carbine.

3-1/2" BARREL

EXC.	V.G.	GOOD	FAIR	POOR
-	-	5000	2500	1500

6" BARREL

EXC.	V.G.	GOOD	FAIR	POOR
-	-	5750	3000	1500

LEVER ACTION CARBINE

New Haven Arms introduced, for the first time, a Volcanic rifle that featured a full-length slotted magazine tube with a spring- activated thumbpiece follower that moved along the entire length of the magazine tube. These rifles were chambered for a .38 caliber cartridge and were offered in three barrel lengths: 16", 20", and 24". These weapons are extremely rare and the advice of an expert should be retained prior to purchasing. Unfortunately, in recent years, we have seen an increase in weapons, which have been "helped," or are outright frauds. The buyer must beware; even "experts" can be fooled by unscrupulous individuals who have mastered the art of creating fraudulent guns.

16" BARREL

EXC.	V.G.	GOOD	FAIR	POOR
-	-	15000	6000	2000

20" BARREL

EXC.	V.G.	GOOD	FAIR	POOR
-	-	18000	8000	3000

24" BARREL

EXC.	V.G.	GOOD	FAIR	POOR
-	-	22500	10000	3000

Iron-Framed Henry Rifle.

HENRY RIFLE

With the development of B. Tyler Henry's improvements in the metallic rimfire cartridge and his additional improvements in the Volcanic frame, the direct predecessor to the Winchester lever-action repeater was born. The new cartridge was the .44 caliber rimfire, and the Henry rifle featured a 24" octagon barrel with a tubular magazine holding 15 shells. The rifle had no forearm, but was furnished with a walnut buttstock with two styles of buttplates: an early rounded heel crescent shape seen on guns produced from 1860 to 1862 and the later sharper heel crescent butt found on guns built from 1863 to 1866. The early models, produced from 1860 to 1861, were fitted with an iron frame, and the later models, built from 1861 to 1866, were fitted with brass frames. About 14,000 Henry rifles were made during the entire production period; only about 300 were iron frame rifles. These weapons are extremely rare and the advice of an expert should be retained prior to purchasing. Unfortunately, in recent years, we have seen an increase in weapons that have been "helped," or are outright frauds. The buyer must beware; even "experts" can be fooled by unscrupulous individuals who have mastered the art of creating fraudulent guns.

IRON FRAME RIFLE

EXC.	V.G.	GOOD	FAIR	POOR
-	-	85000	30000	-

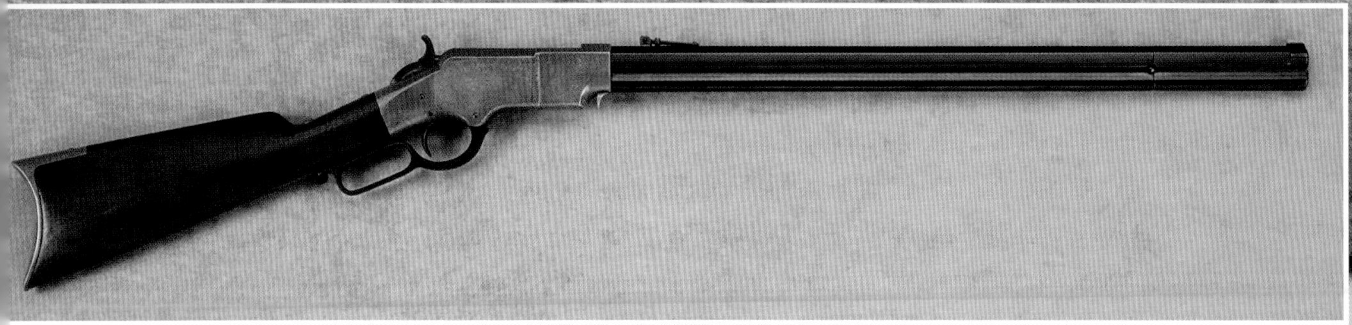

Brass-Framed Henry Rifle.

BRASS FRAME RIFLE

EXC.	V.G.	GOOD	FAIR	POOR
-	-	37500	17500	9000

MARTIALLY INSPECTED HENRY RIFLES

Beginning in 1863 the Federal Government ordered 1,730 Henry Rifles for use in the Civil War. Most of these government- inspected rifles fall into serial number range 3000 to 4000 while the balance are close to this serial-number range. They are marked "C.G.C." for Charles G. Chapman, the government inspector. These Henry rifles were used under actual combat conditions and for that reason it is doubtful that there are any rifles that would fall into the Excellent condition category. Therefore no price is given. These weapons are extremely rare and the advice of an expert should be retained prior to purchasing. Unfortunately, in recent years, we have seen an increase in weapons that have been "helped," or are outright frauds. The buyer must beware; even "experts" can be fooled by unscrupulous individuals, who have mastered the art of creating fraudulent guns.

EXC.	V.G.	GOOD	FAIR	POOR
-	-	60000	25000	12000

WINCHESTER'S IMPROVEMENT CARBINE

Overall length 43-1/2"; barrel length 24"; caliber .44 rimfire. Walnut stock with a brass buttplate; the receiver and magazine cover/forend of brass; the barrel and magazine tube blued. The magazine loading port is exposed by sliding the forend forward. This design was protected by O.F. Winchester's British Patent Number 3285 issued December 19, 1865. Unmarked except for internally located serial numbers. Approximately 700 manufactured in December of 1865 and early 1866, the majority of which were sold to Emperor Maximilian of Mexico. Prospective purchasers are strongly advised to secure an expert appraisal prior to acquisition. These weapons are extremely rare and the advice of an expert should be retained prior to purchasing. Unfortunately, in recent years, we have seen an increase in weapons that have been "helped," or are outright frauds. The buyer must beware; even "experts" can be fooled by unscrupulous individuals who have mastered the art of creating fraudulent guns.

EXC.	V.G.	GOOD	FAIR	POOR
-	-	35000	12500	9000

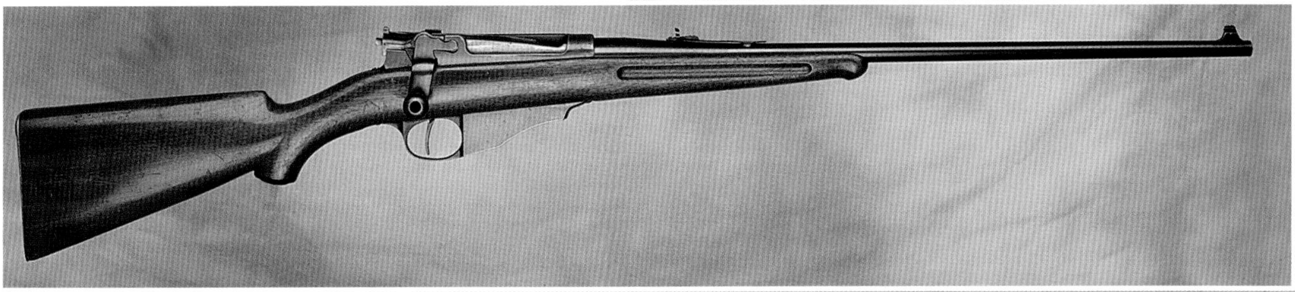

Winchester-Lee Straight Pull Sporting Rifle.

WINCHESTER-LEE STRAIGHT PULL RIFLE

This rifle was a military firearm that Winchester built for the U.S. Navy in 1895. The Navy version was a musket type with a 28" round barrel and musket style forearm and plain walnut pistol grip stock. In 1897, Winchester offered a commercial musket version for public sale as well as a Sporting Rifle. All of these guns were chambered for the 6mm Lee (.236 Caliber) cartridge. The Sporting Rifle featured a 24" round barrel with plain walnut pistol grip stock and finger grooves in the forearm. Built from 1895 to 1905, Winchester sold about 20,000 Lee rifles; 15,000 were sold to the U.S. Navy, 3,000 were sold in the commercial version, and 1,700 were Sporting Rifles.

U.S. NAVY MUSKET

EXC.	V.G.	GOOD	FAIR	POOR
2500	2000	1500	700	500

COMMERCIAL MUSKET

EXC.	V.G.	GOOD	FAIR	POOR
2500	2000	1500	700	500

SPORTING RIFLE

EXC.	V.G.	GOOD	FAIR	POOR
2500	2000	1500	700	500

SECTION II

EARLY MODELS
HAVING FOUR-DIGIT NUMBERS FOR THEIR MODEL DESIGNATION

MODEL 1866

In 1866 the New Haven Arms Company changed its name to the Winchester Repeating Arms Company. The first firearm to be built under the Winchester name was the Model 1866. This first Winchester was a much-improved version of the Henry. A new magazine tube developed by Nelson King, Winchester's plant superintendent, was a vast improvement over the slotted magazine tube used on the Henry and its predecessor. The old tube allowed dirt to enter through the slots and was weakened because of it. King's patent, assigned to Winchester, featured a solid tube that was much stronger and reliable. His patent also dealt with an improved loading system for the rifle. The rifle now featured a loading port on the right side of the receiver with a spring-loaded cover. The frame continued to be made from brass. The Model 1866 was chambered for the .44 caliber Flat Rimfire or the .44 caliber Pointed Rimfire. Both cartridges could be used interchangeably. These weapons are extremely rare and the advice of an expert should be retained prior to purchasing. Unfortunately, in recent years, we have seen an increase in weapons, which have been "helped," or are outright frauds. The buyer must beware; even "experts" can be fooled by unscrupulous individuals who have mastered the art of creating fraudulent guns.

The barrel on the Model 1866 was marked with two different markings. The first, which is seen on early guns up to serial number 23000, reads "HENRY'S PATENT-OCT. 16, 1860 KING'S PATENT-MARCH 29, 1866." The second marking reads, "WINCHESTER'S-REPEATING-ARMS. NEW HAVEN, CT. KING'S-IMPROVEMENT-PATENTED MARCH 29, 1866 OCTOBER 16, 1860." There are three basic variations of the Model 1866:

1) Sporting Rifle round or octagon barrel. Approximately 28,000 were produced.
2) Carbine round barrel. Approximately 127,000 were produced.
3) Musket round barrel. Approximately 14,000 were produced.

The rifle and musket held 17 cartridges, and the carbine had a capacity of 13 cartridges. Unlike the Henry, Model 1866s were fitted with a walnut forearm. The Model 1866 was discontinued in 1898 with approximately 170,000 guns produced.

The Model 1866 was sold in various special order configurations, such as barrels longer or shorter than standard, including engraved guns. The prices listed represent only standard-model 1866s. For guns with special-order features, an independent appraisal from an expert is highly recommended.

FIRST MODEL

This first style has both the Henry and King patent dates stamped on the barrel, a flat-loading

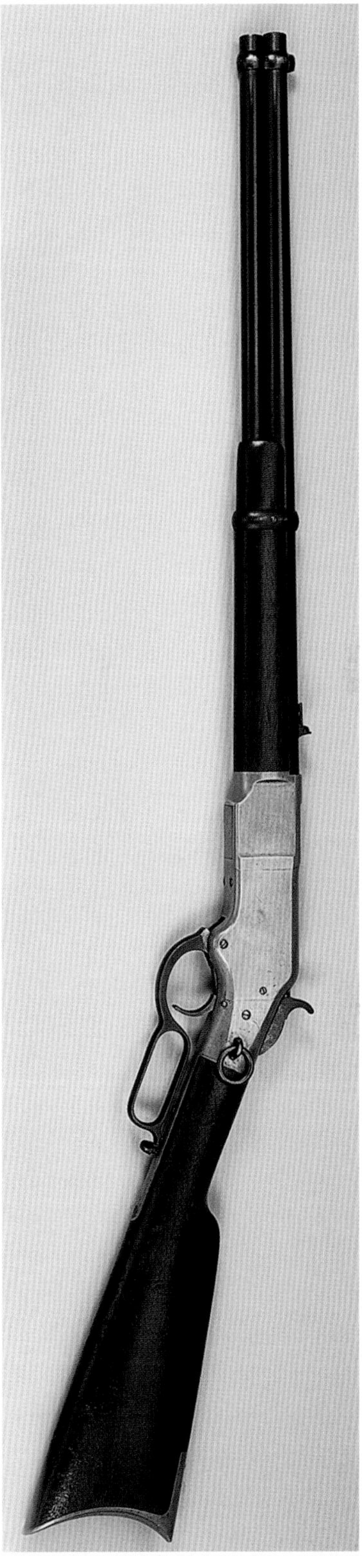

Model 1866 Brass-Frame Carbine, 1st Model.

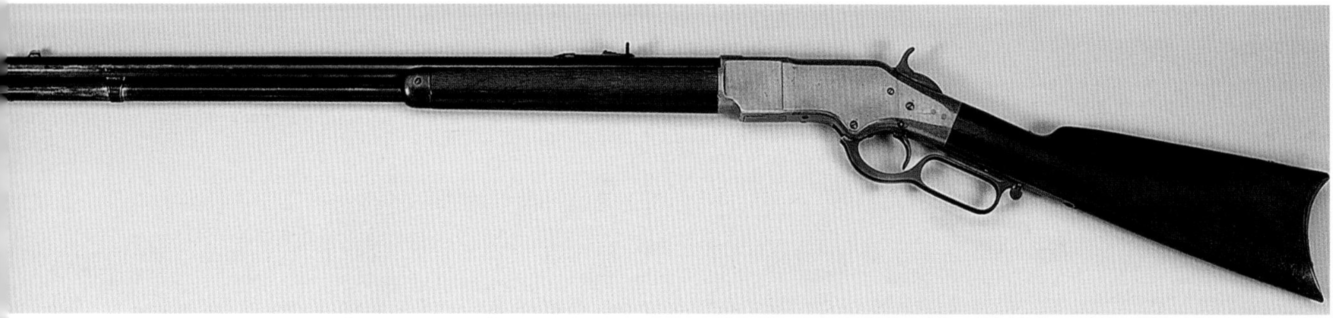

Model 1866 Rifle, 4th Model.

port cover, and a two-screw upper tang. Perhaps the most distinctive feature of the First Model is the rapid drop at the top rear of the receiver near the hammer. This is often referred to as the "Henry Drop," a reference to the same receiver drop found on the Henry rifle. First Models will be seen up through the 15000 serial number range.

RIFLE

EXC.	V.G.	GOOD	FAIR	POOR
-	27500	17500	8500	4000

CARBINE

EXC.	V.G.	GOOD	FAIR	POOR
-	25000	14000	7500	5000

SECOND MODEL

The second style differs from the first most noticeably in its single screw upper tang and a flare at the front of the receiver to meet the forearm. The Second Model also has a more gradual drop at the rear of the receiver than the First Model. The Second Style Model 1866 appears through serial number 25000.

RIFLE

EXC.	V.G.	GOOD	FAIR	POOR
-	22500	12500	7000	4000

CARBINE

EXC.	V.G.	GOOD	FAIR	POOR
-	17500	12000	8500	3500

THIRD MODEL

The third style's most noticeable characteristic is the more moderately curved receiver shape at the rear of the frame. The serial number is now stamped in block numerals behind the trigger, thus allowing the numbers to be seen for the first time without removing the stock. The barrel marking is stamped with the Winchester address. The Third Model is found between serial numbers 25000 and 149000. For the first time, a musket version was produced in this serial-number range.

RIFLE

EXC.	V.G.	GOOD	FAIR	POOR
-	16000	11000	6000	3500

CARBINE

EXC.	V.G.	GOOD	FAIR	POOR
-	12000	9500	5500	3500

MUSKET

EXC.	V.G.	GOOD	FAIR	POOR
-	11000	8000	3500	2500

FOURTH MODEL

The fourth style has an even less pronounced drop at the top rear of the frame, and the serial number is stamped in script on the lower tang under the lever. The Fourth Model is seen between serial number 149000 and 170100 with the late guns having an iron buttplate instead of brass.

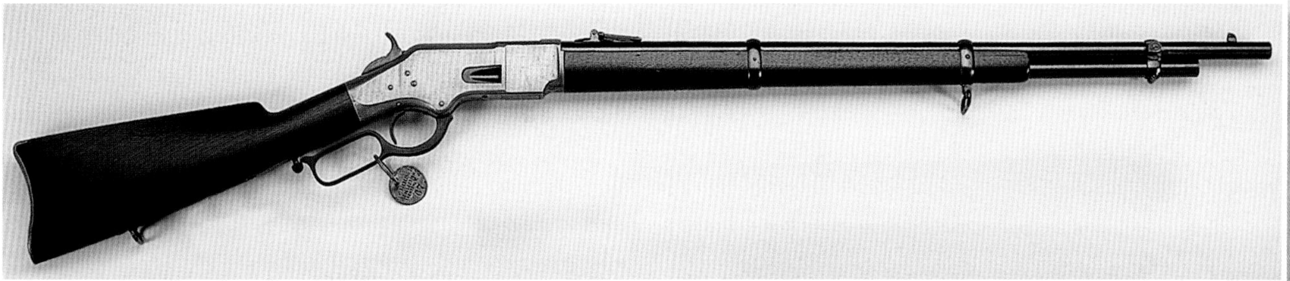

Model 1866 Brass-Frame Rifled Musket.

RIFLE

EXC.	V.G.	GOOD	FAIR	POOR
-	14000	8500	5000	3500

CARBINE

EXC.	V.G.	GOOD	FAIR	POOR
-	11000	9000	3500	2500

MUSKET

EXC.	V.G.	GOOD	FAIR	POOR
-	12000	9000	3500	2500

MODEL 1866 IRON FRAME RIFLE MUSKET

Overall length 54-1/2"; barrel length 33-1/4"; caliber .45 centerfire. Walnut stock with casehardened furniture, barrel burnished bright, the receiver casehardened. The finger lever catch mounted within a large bolster at the rear of the lever. Unmarked except for serial numbers that appear externally on the receiver and often the buttplate tang. Approximately 25 made during the early autumn of 1866. Prospective purchasers are strongly advised to secure an expert appraisal prior to acquisition. Due to the recent identification of this model, pricing schedules have yet to be established.

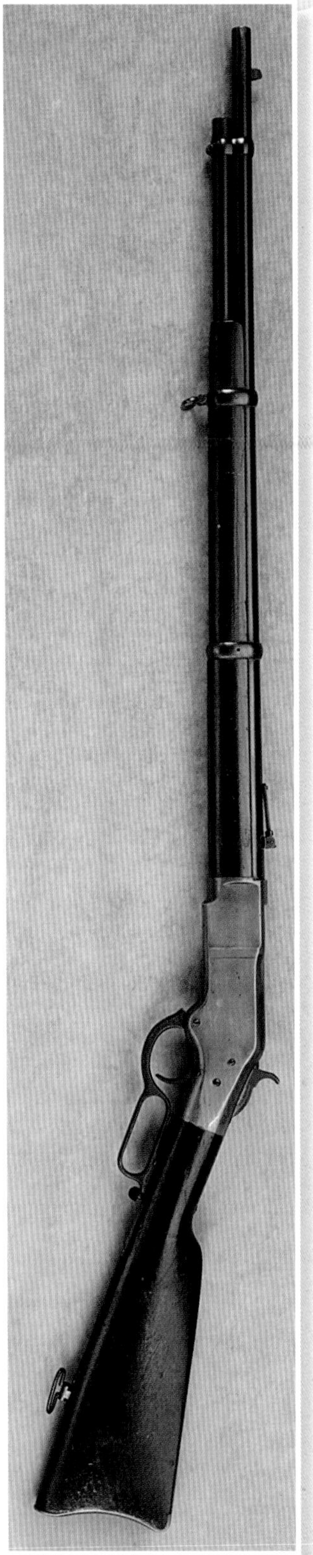

Model 1866 Iron Frame Musket.

MODEL 1866 IRON FRAME SWISS SHARPSHOOTERS RIFLE

As above, but in .41 Swiss caliber and fitted with a Scheutzen style stock supplied by the firm of Weber Ruesch in Zurich. Marked Weber Ruesch, Zurich on the barrel and serial numbered externally. Approximately 400 to 450 manufactured in 1866 and 1867. Prospective purchasers are strongly advised to secure an expert appraisal prior to acquisition. Due to the recent identification of this model pricing schedules have yet to be established.

MODEL 1867 IRON FRAME CARBINE

Overall length 39-1/4"; barrel length 20"; caliber .44 rimfire. Walnut stock with casehardened furniture; the barrel and magazine tube blued; the receiver casehardened. The finger lever catch mounted within the rear curl of the lever. Unmarked except for serial numbers that appear externally on the receiver and often the buttplate tang. Approximately 20 manufactured. Prospective purchasers are strongly advised to secure an expert appraisal prior to acquisition. Due to the recent identification of this model pricing schedules have yet to be established.

MODEL 1868 IRON FRAME RIFLE MUSKET

Overall length 49-1/2" (.455 cal.), 50-1/2" or 53" (.45 and .47 cal.); barrel length 29-1/2" (.455 cal.) and 30-1/4" or 33" (.45 and .47 cal.); calibers .45, .455, and .47 centerfire. Walnut stock with casehardened or burnished bright (.45 and .47 cal.) furniture; the barrel burnished bright; the receiver casehardened or burnished bright (.45 and .47 cal.). The finger lever catch mounted on the lower receiver tang. The rear of the finger lever machined with a long flat extension on its upper surface. Unmarked except for serial number. Approximately 30 examples made in .45 and .455 caliber and 250 in .47 caliber. Prospective purchasers are strongly advised to secure an expert appraisal prior to ac-

quisition. Due to the recent identification of this model pricing schedules have yet to be established.

MODEL 1868 IRON FRAME CARBINE

Overall length 40"; barrel length 20"; caliber .44 centerfire. Walnut stock with casehardened furniture; barrel and magazine tube blued; the receiver casehardened. The finger lever catch as above. Unmarked except for serial numbers (receiver and buttplate tang). Approximately 25 manufactured. These weapons are extremely rare and the advice of an expert should be retained prior to purchasing. Unfortunately, in recent years, we have seen an increase in weapons that have been "helped" or are outright frauds. The buyer must beware; even "experts" can be fooled by unscrupulous individuals who have mastered the art of creating fraudulent guns.

MODEL 1873

This Winchester rifle was one of the most popular lever-actions the company ever produced. This is the "gun that won the West" and with good reason. It was chambered for the more powerful centerfire cartridge, the .44-40. Compared to the .44 Henry, this cartridge was twice as good. With the introduction of the single-action Colt pistol in 1878, chambered for the same cartridge, the individual had the convenience of a pistol for protection and the accuracy of the Winchester for food and protection. The .44-40 was the standard cartridge for the Model 1873. Three additional cartridges were offered but were not as popular as the .44. The .38-40 was first offered in 1879 and the.32-20 was introduced in 1882. In 1884 the Model 1873 was offered in .22 caliber rimfire, with a few special order guns built in .22 extra long rimfire. Approximately 19,552 .22 caliber Model 1873s were produced. These weapons are extremely rare and the advice of an expert should be retained prior to purchasing. Unfortunately, in recent years, we have seen an increase in weapons that have been "helped," or are outright frauds. The buyer must beware, as even "experts" can be fooled by unscrupulous individuals who have mastered the art of creating fraudulent guns.

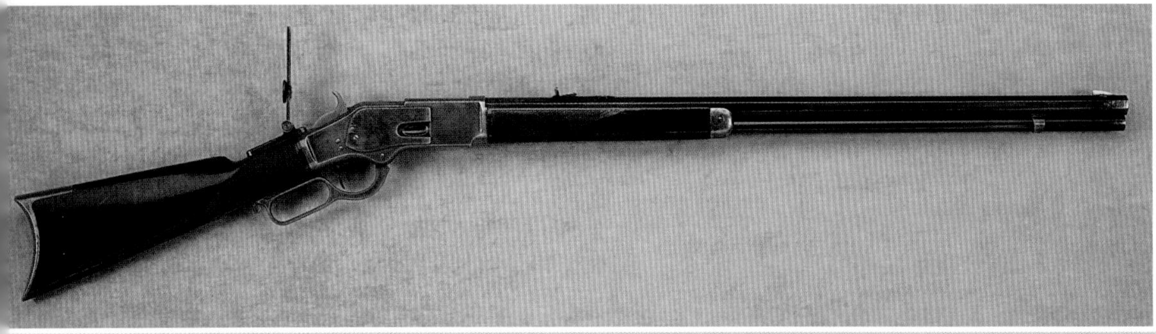

Model 1873 Rifle, 1 of 1000, Right View.

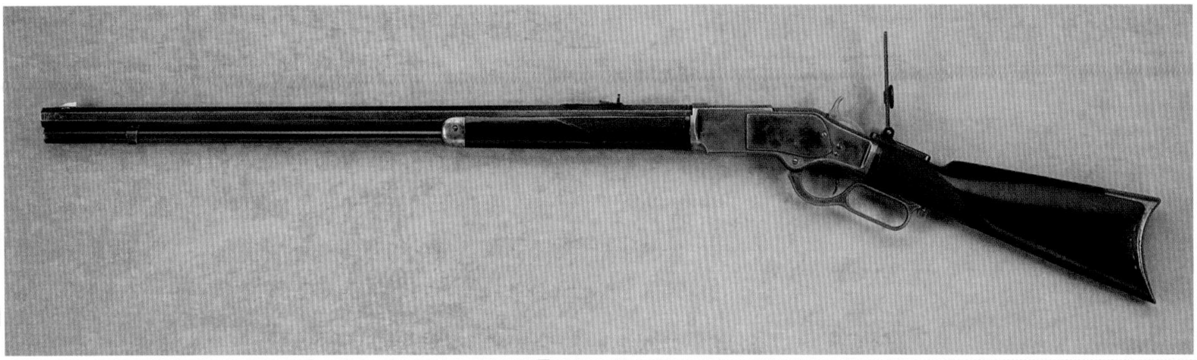

Model 1873 Rifle, 1 of 1000, Left View.

Early Model 1873s were fitted with an iron receiver until 1884, when a steel receiver was introduced. The Model 1873 was offered in three styles:

1) Sporting Rifle, 24" round, octagon, or half-octagon barrel. Equipped standard with a crescent iron buttplate, straight-grip stock and capped forearm.
2) Carbine, 20" round barrel. Furnished standard with a rounded iron buttplate, straight-grip stock, and carbine style forend fastened to the barrel with a single barrel band.
3) Musket, 30" round barrel. Standard musket is furnished with a nearly full-length forearm fastened to the barrel with three barrel bands. The buttstock has a rounded buttplate.

The upper tang was marked with the model designation and the serial number was stamped on the lower tang. Caliber stampings on the Model 1873 are found on the bottom of the frame and on the breech end of the barrel. Winchester discontinued the Model 1873 in 1919, after producing about 720,000 guns.

The Winchester Model 1873 was offered with a large number of extra-cost options that greatly affect the value of the gun. For example, Winchester built two sets of special Model 1873s: the 1-of-100 and the 1-of-1000. Winchester sold only eight 1-of-100 Model 1873s, and 136 of the 1-of-1000 guns that were built. In 2006 a few of these special guns were sold at auction and brought prices exceeding $240,000. The prices listed here are for standard guns only. For Model 1873 with special features, it is best to secure an expert appraisal. Model 1873s with case colored receivers will bring a premium.

FIRST MODEL

The primary difference between the various styles of the Model 1873 is found in the appearance and construction of the dust cover. The First Model has a dust cover held in place with grooved guides

Model 1873 Saddle Ring Carbine, 1st Model.

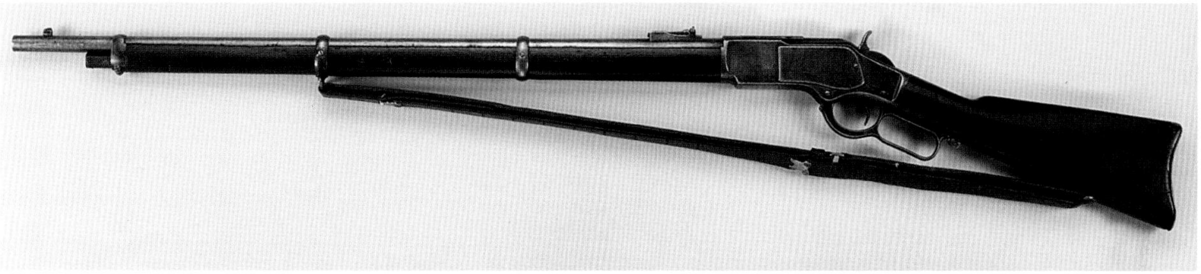

Model 1873 Musket, 1st Model.

on either side. A checkered oval finger grip is found on top of the dust cover. The latch that holds the lever firmly in place is anchored into the lower tang with visible threads. On later First Models, these threads are not visible. First Models appear from serial number 1 to about 31000.

RIFLE

EXC.	V.G.	GOOD	FAIR	POOR
17500	9000	4750	3000	1400

CARBINE

EXC.	V.G.	GOOD	FAIR	POOR
25000	17500	9000	4000	2500

MUSKET

EXC.	V.G.	GOOD	FAIR	POOR
-	4750	2500	1800	1000

SECOND MODEL

The dust cover on the Second Model operates on one central guide secured to the receiver with two screws. The checkered oval finger grip is still used, but on later Second Models this is changed to a serrated finger grip on the rear of the dust cover.

Model 1873 Trapper's Model Carbine.

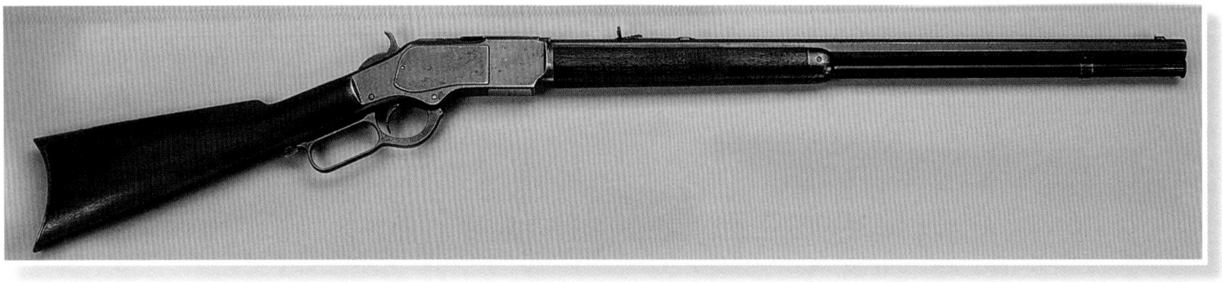

Model 1873 .22 Rimfire Rifle.

Second Models are found in the 31000 to 90000 serial number range.

RIFLE

EXC.	V.G.	GOOD	FAIR	POOR
16000	8500	4000	3000	1250

CARBINE

EXC.	V.G.	GOOD	FAIR	POOR
17000	9000	6000	3000	1000

MUSKET

EXC.	V.G.	GOOD	FAIR	POOR
7500	4000	2000	1250	900

THIRD MODEL

The central guide rail is still present on the Third Model, but it is now integrally machined as part of the receiver. The serrated rear edges of the dust cover are still present on the Third Model.

RIFLE

EXC.	V.G.	GOOD	FAIR	POOR
11500	7500	4000	2000	750

CARBINE

EXC.	V.G.	GOOD	FAIR	POOR
14000	9000	5000	2000	800

MUSKET

EXC.	V.G.	GOOD	FAIR	POOR
6000	3500	1250	850	500

MODEL 1873 .22 RIMFIRE RIFLE

Winchester's first .22 caliber rifle and the first .22 caliber repeating rifle made in America was introduced in 1884 and discontinued in 1904. Its drawback was the small caliber. The general preference during this period of time was for the larger-caliber rifles. Winchester sold a little more than 19,000 .22 caliber Model 1873s.

EXC.	V.G.	GOOD	FAIR	POOR
12500	6500	3000	1700	750

MODEL 1876

Winchester's Model 1876, sometimes referred to as the Centennial Model, was the company's response to the public's demand for a repeater rifle ca-

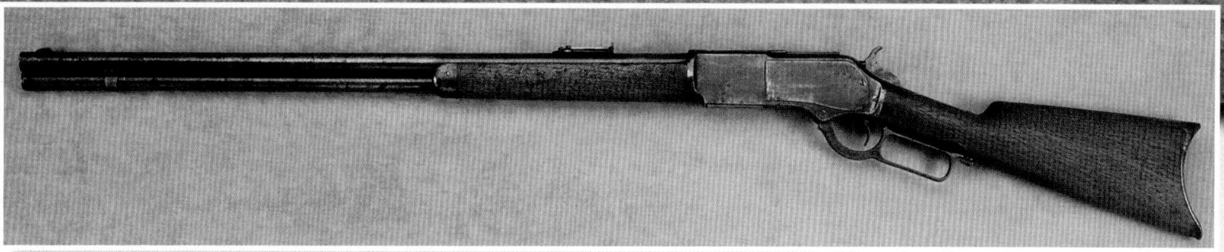

Model 1876, 1st Model.

pable of handling larger and more potent calibers. Many single-shot rifles were available at this time to shoot more powerful cartridges, and Winchester redesigned the earlier Model 1873 to answer this need. The principal changes made to the Model 1873 were a larger and stronger receiver to handle more powerful cartridges. Both the carbine and the musket had their forearms extended to cover the full length of the magazine tube. The carbine barrel was increased in length from 20" to 22", and the musket barrel length was increased from 30 to 32". The Model 1876 was the first Winchester to be offered with a pistol-grip stock on its special Sporting Rifle. The Model 1876 was available in these calibers: .45-77 W.C.F., .50-95 Express, .45-60 W.C.F., .40-60 W.C.F. These weapons are extremely rare and the advice of an expert should be retained prior to purchasing. Unfortunately, in recent years, we have seen an increase in weapons that have been "helped," or are outright frauds. The buyer must beware, as even "experts" can be fooled by unscrupulous individuals who have mastered the art of creating fraudulent guns.

The Model 1876 was offered in four different styles:

1) Sporting Rifle, 28" round, octagon, or half-octagon barrel. This rifle was fitted with a straight-grip stock with crescent iron buttplate. A special sporting rifle was offered with a pistol-grip stock.
2) Express Rifle, 26" round, octagon, or half-octagon barrel. The same sporting rifle stock was used.
3) Carbine, 22" round barrel with full length forearm secured by one barrel band and straight-grip stock.
4) Musket, 32" round barrel with full-length forearm secured by one barrel band and straight-grip stock.

Stamped on the barrel is the Winchester address with King's patent date. The caliber marking is stamped on the bottom of the receiver near the magazine tube and the breech end of the barrel. Winchester also furnished the Model 1876 in 1-of-100 and 1-of-1000 special guns. Only 8 1-of-100 Model 1876s were built and 54 1-of-1000 76s were built. In 2006 a few of these special guns were sold at auction and brought prices exceeding $250,000. Approximately 64,000 Model 1876s were built by Winchester between 1876 and 1897. As with other Winchesters, the prices given are for standard guns.

FIRST MODEL

As with the Model 1873, the primary difference in model types lies in the dust cover. The First Model has no dust cover and is seen between serial number 1 and 3000.

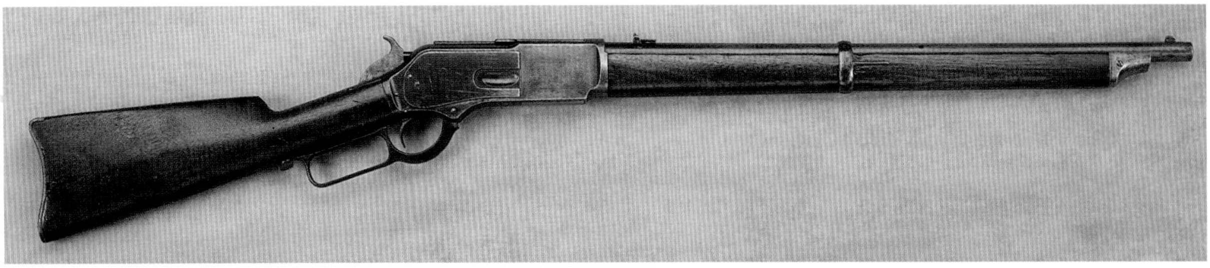

Model 1876 Saddle Ring Carbine, 2nd Model.

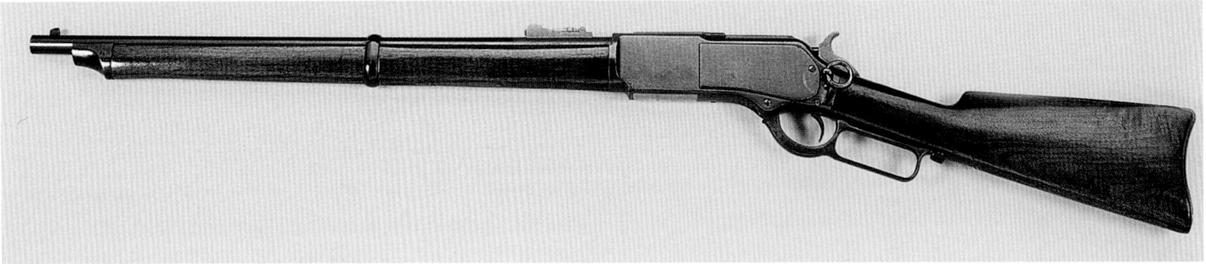

Model 1876 NorthWest Mounted Police Carbine.

RIFLE

EXC.	V.G.	GOOD	FAIR	POOR
12000	8500	4500	2750	1000

CARBINE

EXC.	V.G.	GOOD	FAIR	POOR
10000	7500	5000	2500	1000

MUSKET

EXC.	V.G.	GOOD	FAIR	POOR
15000	12000	6500	3000	1500

SECOND MODEL

The Second Model has a dust cover with guide rail attached to the receiver with two screws. On the early Second Model an oval finger guide is stamped on top of the dust cover while later models have a serrated finger guide along the rear edge of the dust cover. Second Models range from serial numbers 3000 to 30000.

RIFLE

EXC.	V.G.	GOOD	FAIR	POOR
11000	7500	4000	2000	1000

CARBINE

EXC.	V.G.	GOOD	FAIR	POOR
9000	6000	4250	2000	1200

MUSKET

EXC.	V.G.	GOOD	FAIR	POOR
18000	9000	5000	1750	1000

NORTHWEST MOUNTED POLICE CARBINE

The folding rear sight is graduated in meters instead of yards.

EXC.	V.G.	GOOD	FAIR	POOR
15000	9000	4500	2000	1250

NOTE: Deduct 50 percent from prices if factory records do not confirm NPW use. A Model

1876 NWP in excellent condition is very rare. Proceed with caution.

THIRD MODEL

The dust cover guide rail on Third Model 76s is integrally machined as part of the receiver with a serrated rear edge on the dust cover. Third Model will be seen from serial numbers 30000 to 64000.

RIFLE

EXC.	V.G.	GOOD	FAIR	POOR
10000	6500	3250	1500	750

CARBINE

EXC.	V.G.	GOOD	FAIR	POOR
10000	6500	3000	2000	1250

MUSKET

EXC.	V.G.	GOOD	FAIR	POOR
9500	4750	3000	1250	1000

MODEL 1883 OR MORE COMMONLY KNOWN AS THE HOTCHKISS BOLT-ACTION RIFLE

This model is also known as the Hotchkiss Magazine Gun or the Model 1883. This rifle was designed by Benjamin Hotchkiss in 1876, and Winchester acquired the manufacturing rights to the rifle in 1877. In 1879 the first guns were delivered for sale. The Hotchkiss rifle was a bolt-action firearm designed for military and sporting use. It was the first bolt-action rifle made by Winchester. The rifle was furnished in .45-70 Government, and although the 1884 Winchester catalog lists a .40- 65 Hotchkiss as being available, no evidence exists that such a chamber was ever actually furnished. The Model 1883 was available in three different styles:

1) Sporting Rifle, 26" round, octagon, or half-octagon barrel fitted with a rifle-type stock that included a modified pistol grip or straight-grip stock.
2) Carbine, 24" round or 22-1/2" round barrel with military-style straight-grip stock.
3) Musket, 32" or 28" round barrel with almost full-length military-style straight-grip stock.

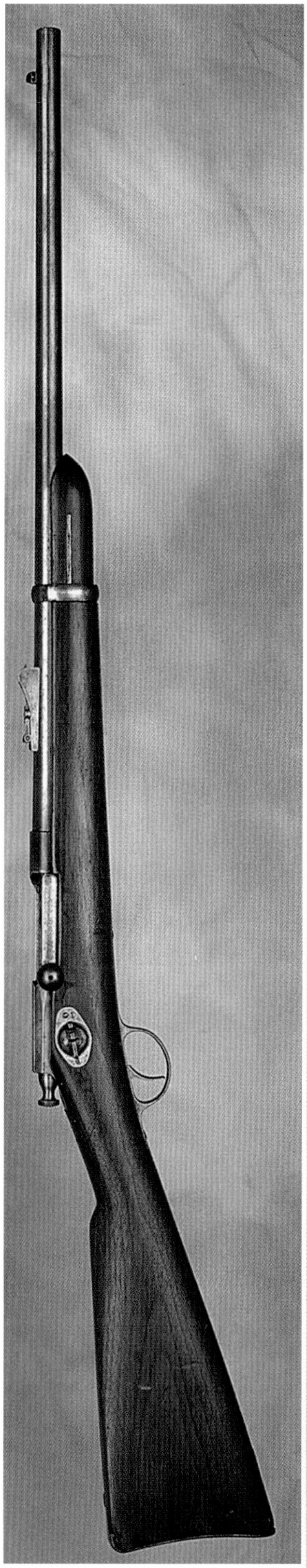

1st Model Hotchkiss.

2nd Model Hotchkiss.

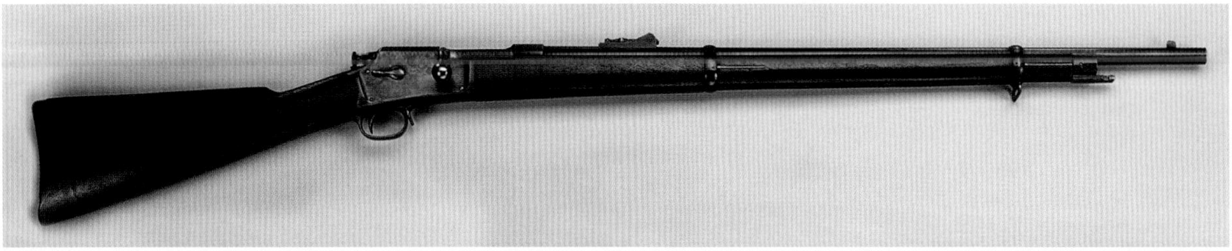

3rd Model Hotchkiss.

Winchester produced the Model 1883 until 1899, having built about 85,000 guns.

FIRST MODEL

This model has the safety and a turn button magazine cut-off located above the trigger guard on the right side. The Sporting Rifle is furnished with a 26" round or octagon barrel while the carbine has a 24" round barrel with a saddle ring on the left side of the stock. The musket has a 32" round barrel with two barrel bands, a steel forearm tip, and bayonet attachment under the barrel. The serial number range for the First Model is between 1 and about 6419.

SPORTING RIFLE

EXC.	V.G.	GOOD	FAIR	POOR
5500	2500	1500	900	500

CARBINE

EXC.	V.G.	GOOD	FAIR	POOR
5500	2500	1500	900	500

MUSKET

EXC.	V.G.	GOOD	FAIR	POOR
5500	2500	1500	900	500

SECOND MODEL

On this model the safety is located on the top left side of the receiver, and the magazine cutoff is located on the top right side of the receiver to the rear of the bolt handle. The sporting rifle remains unchanged from the First Model with the above exceptions. The carbine has a 22-1/2" round barrel with a nickeled forearm cap. The musket now has a 28" barrel. Serial number range for the Second Model runs from 6420 to 22521.

SPORTING RIFLE

EXC.	V.G.	GOOD	FAIR	POOR
4500	2500	1000	750	500

CARBINE

EXC.	V.G.	GOOD	FAIR	POOR
4500	2250	1000	750	500

MUSKET

EXC.	V.G.	GOOD	FAIR	POOR
4500	2250	1000	750	500

THIRD MODEL

The Third Model is easily identified by the two-piece stock separated by the receiver. The specifications for the sporting rifle remain the same as before, while the carbine is now fitted with a 20" barrel with saddle ring and bar on the left side of the frame. The musket remains unchanged from the Second Model with the exception of the two-piece stock. Serial numbers of the Third Model range from 22552 to 84555.

SPORTING RIFLE

EXC.	V.G.	GOOD	FAIR	POOR
4250	2500	1000	750	500

CARBINE

EXC.	V.G.	GOOD	FAIR	POOR
4250	2500	1000	700	400

MUSKET

EXC.	V.G.	GOOD	FAIR	POOR
4250	2500	750	500	300

MODEL 1885 (SINGLE-SHOT)

The Model 1885 marks an important development between Winchester and John M. Browning. The Single-Shot rifle was the first of many Browning patents that Winchester would purchase and provided the company with the opportunity to diversify its firearms line. The Model 1885 was the first single-shot rifle built by Winchester. The company offered more calibers in this model than any other. A total of 45 centerfire calibers were offered from the .22 extra long to the 50-110 Express, as well as 14 rimfire calibers from .22 B.B. cap to the .44 Flat Henry. Numerous barrel lengths, shapes, and weights were available as were stock configurations, sights, and finishes. These rifles were also available in solid frame and takedown styles. One could almost argue that each of the 139,725 Model 1885s built is unique. Many collectors of the Winchester Single-Shot specialize in nothing else. For this reason it is difficult to provide pricing that will cover most of the Model 1885s that the collector will encounter. However the prices given here are for standard guns in standard configurations.

The Model 1885 was offered in two basic frame types:

1) The High Wall was the first frame type produced and is so called because the frame covers the breech and hammer except for the hammer spur.
2) The breech and hammer are visible on the Low Wall frame with its low sides. This frame type was first introduced around the 5000 serial number range.

Both the High Wall and the Low Wall were available in two type frame profiles: the Thickside and the Thinside. The Thickside frame has flat sides that do not widen out to meet the stock. The Thickside is more common on the low wall rifle and rare on the High Walls. The Thinside frame has shallow milled sides that widen out to meet the stock. Thinside frames are common on High Wall guns and rare on Low Wall rifles.

NOTES:

- The standard High Wall rifle was available with octagon or round barrel with length determined by caliber. The butt stock and forearm were plain walnut with crescent buttplate and blued frame.
- The standard Low Wall featured a round or octagon barrel with length determined by caliber and a plain walnut stock and forearm with crescent buttplate.
- The High Wall musket most often had a 26" round barrel chambered for the .22 caliber cartridge. Larger calibers were available as were different barrel lengths. The High Wall Musket featured an almost full length forearm fastened to the barrel with a single barrel band and rounded buttplate.
- The Low Wall musket is most often referred to as the Winder Musket named after the distinguished marksman, Colonel C.B. Winder. This model features a Lyman receiver sight and was made in .22 caliber.
- The High Wall Schuetzen rifle was designed for serious target shooting and was available with numerous extras including a 30" octagon

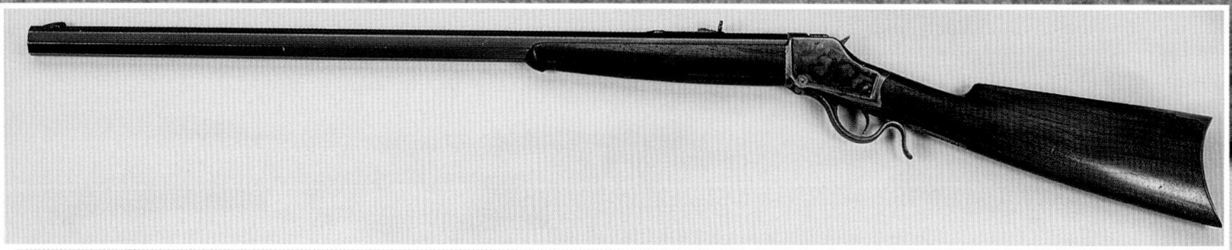

Model 1885 Standard High Wall Rifle.

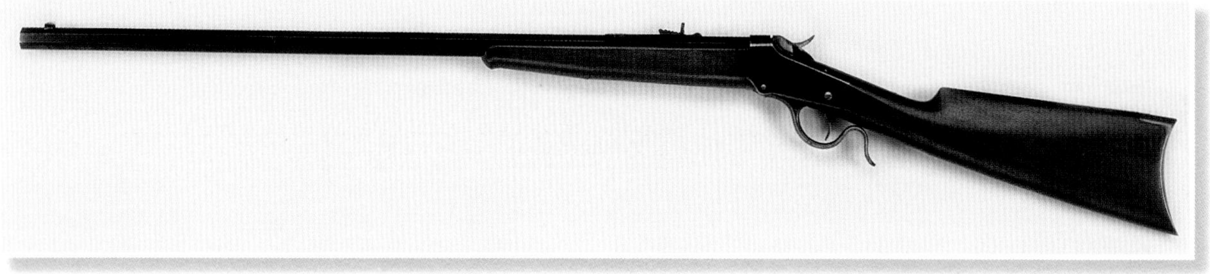

Model 1885 Standard Low Wall Rifle.

barrel medium weight without rear sight seat; fancy walnut checkered pistol grip Schuetzen- style cheekpiece; Schuetzen-style buttplate; checkered forearm; double set triggers; spur finger lever, and adjustable palm rest.

- The Low Wall carbine was available in 15", 16", 18", and 20" round barrels. The carbine featured a saddle ring on the left side of the frame and a rounded buttplate.
- The Model 1885 was also available in a High Wall shotgun in 20 gauge with 26" round barrel and straight-grip stock with shotgun style rubber buttplate. The Model 1885 was manufactured between 1885 and 1920 with a total production of about 140,000 guns.

NOTE ON CALIBERS:

As stated above it is difficult to provide pricing on specific rifles, especially chamberings, because of the wide range of variables. However, the collector may find it useful to know that the most common rimfire calibers were the .22 Short, .22 WCF, and .22 Long, in that order, with the .22 Long Rifle a distant fourth. The most common centerfire chambers were the .32 WCF and the .32-40. Other popular centerfire calibers were the .38-55, .25-20, .44 WCF, .32 Long WCF, and the .45-70. There were a number of chamberings that are extremely rare. It is strongly recommended that research is done prior to purchasing a Model 1885 chambered for one of these odd calibers to determine whether it is original.

STANDARD HIGH WALL RIFLE

EXC.	V.G.	GOOD	FAIR	POOR
6500	4000	3250	1500	950

STANDARD LOW WALL RIFLE

EXC.	V.G.	GOOD	FAIR	POOR
5000	3500	2250	1400	900

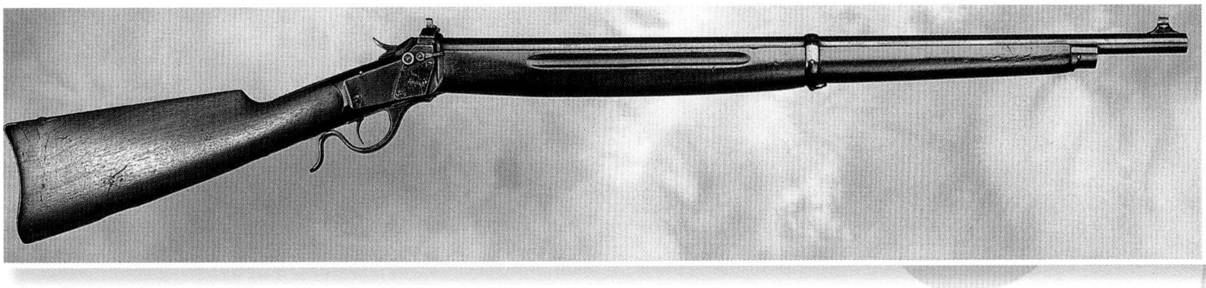

Model 1885 Winder Musket.

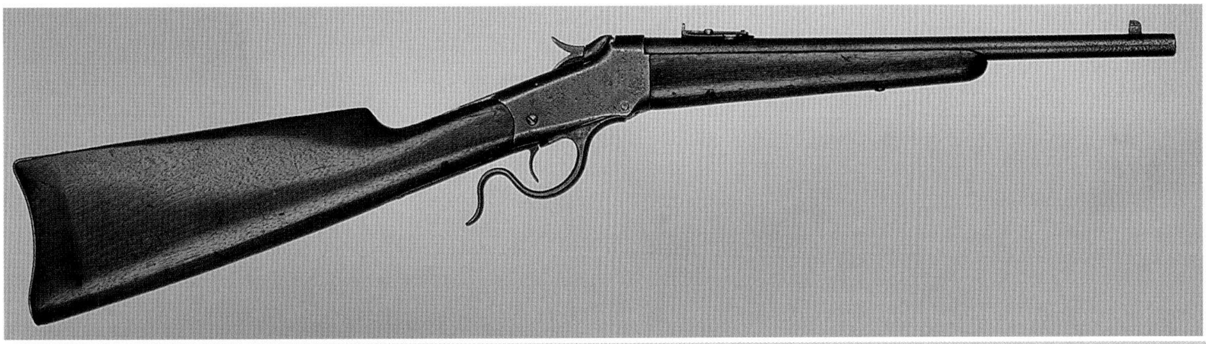

Model 1885 Low Wall Carbine.

HIGH WALL MUSKET

EXC.	V.G.	GOOD	FAIR	POOR
4000	3000	2000	1500	900

LOW WALL MUSKET (WINDER MUSKET)

EXC.	V.G.	GOOD	FAIR	POOR
3500	2000	1200	750	400

HIGH WALL SCHUETZEN RIFLE

EXC.	V.G.	GOOD	FAIR	POOR
17500	12000	6000	4000	2500

LOW WALL CARBINE

EXC.	V.G.	GOOD	FAIR	POOR
17500	10000	7000	3000	1500

HIGH WALL SHOTGUN

EXC.	V.G.	GOOD	FAIR	POOR
4500	3000	2250	1250	850

NOTE: Model 1885s with casecolored frames bring a premium of 25% over guns with blued frames. Model 1885s in calibers .50-110 and .50-100 will bring a premium depending on style and configuration.

MODEL 1886

This model, due to a variety of factors, has become, in the author's opinion, the most popular early Winchester lever action firearm. This is the first Winchester lever action firearm for which larger caliber modern ammunition is still available.

Based on a John Browning patent, the Model 1886 was one of the finest and strongest lever-actions ever utilized in a Winchester rifle. Winchester introduced the Model 1886 in order to take advantage of the more powerful centerfire cartridges of the time. These weapons are extremely rare and the advice of an expert should be retained prior

> *"The Model 1886 was produced from 1886 to 1935 with about 160,000 in production."*

to purchasing. Unfortunately, in recent years, we have seen an increase in weapons that have been "helped," or are outright frauds. The buyer must beware, as even "experts" can be fooled by unscrupulous individuals who have mastered the art of creating fraudulent guns.

Model 1886 rifles and carbines were furnished with walnut stocks, casehardened frames, and blued barrels and magazine tubes. In 1901 Winchester discontinued the use of casehardened frames on all its rifles and used blued frames instead. For this reason, casehardened Model 1886 rifles will bring a premium.

Winchester provided a large selection of extra cost options on the Model 1886, and for rifles with these options, a separate valuation should be made by a reliable source. The Model 1886 was produced from 1886 to 1935 with about 160,000 in production.

The rifle was available in 10 different chamberings:

- .45-70 U.S. Government
- .45-90 W.C.F.
- .40-70 W.C. F.
- .40-82 W.C.F.
- .38-70 W.C. F.
- .40-65 W.C.F.
- .50-100-450
- .38-56 W.C.F.
- .33 W.C. F.
- .50-110 Express

The most popular caliber was the .45-70 Government. Prices of the Model 1886 are influenced by caliber, with the larger calibers bringing a premium. The 1886 was available in several different configurations.

1) Sporting Rifle, 26", round, octagon, or half-octagon barrel, full or half magazine and straight-grip stock with plain forearm.
2) Fancy Sporting Rifle, 26", round or octagon barrel, full or half magazine and fancy checkered walnut pistol-

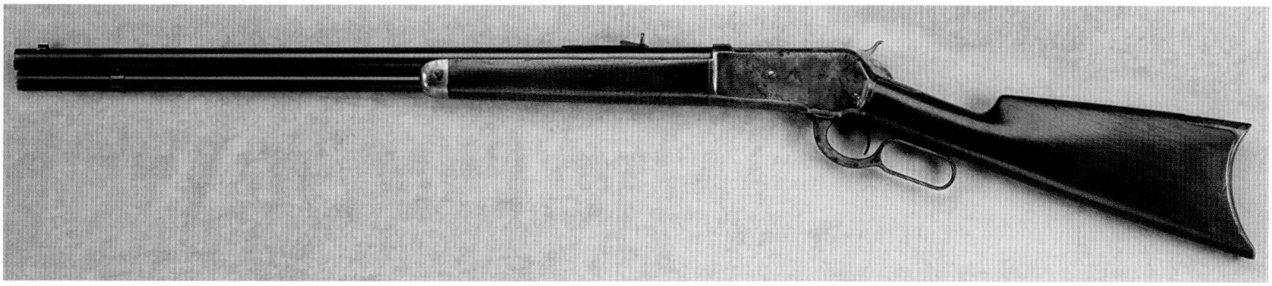

Model 1886 Sporting Rifle.

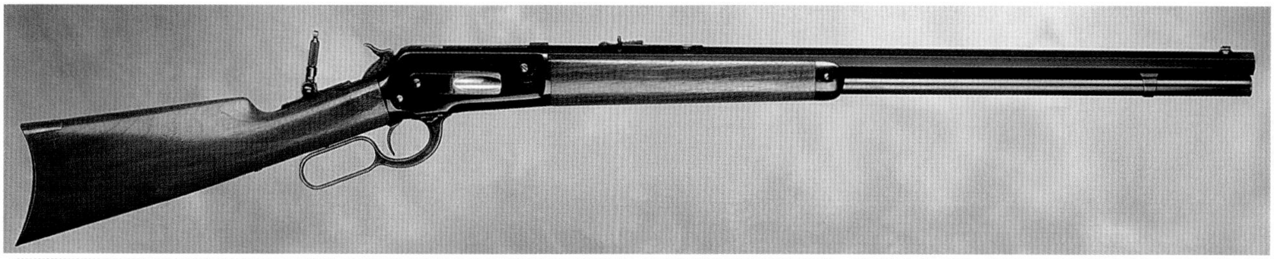

Model 1886 Express Rifle in .50-100 Express.

grip stock with checkered forearm.

3) Takedown Rifle, 24" round barrel, full or half magazine with straight-grip stock fitted with shotgun rubber buttplate and plain forearm.
4) Extra Lightweight Takedown Rifle, 22" round barrel, full or half magazine with straight-grip stock fitted with shotgun rubber buttplate and plain forearm.
5) Extra Lightweight Rifle, 22" round barrel, full or half magazine with straight-grip stock fitted with a shotgun rubber buttplate and plain forearm.
6) Carbine, 22" round barrel, full or half magazine, with straight-grip stock and plain forearm.
7) Musket, 30" round barrel, musket-style forearm with one barrel band. Military-style sights. About 350 Model 1886 Muskets were produced.

SPORTING RIFLE

EXC.	V.G.	GOOD	FAIR	POOR
15000	10000	7500	5000	2500

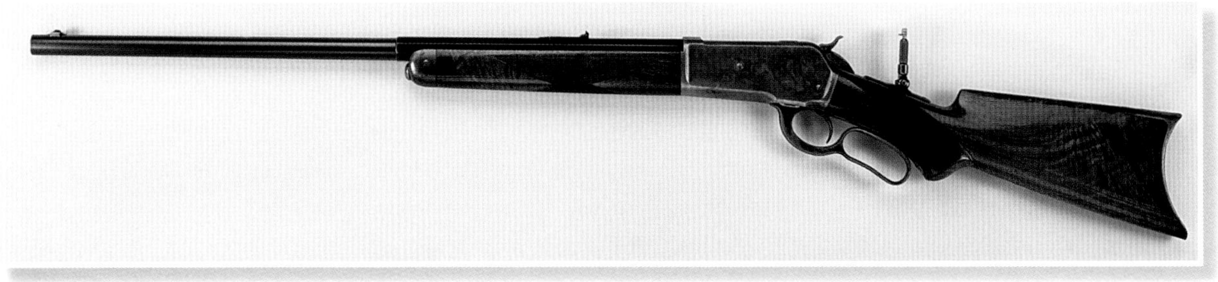

Model 1886 Fancy Sporting Rifle.

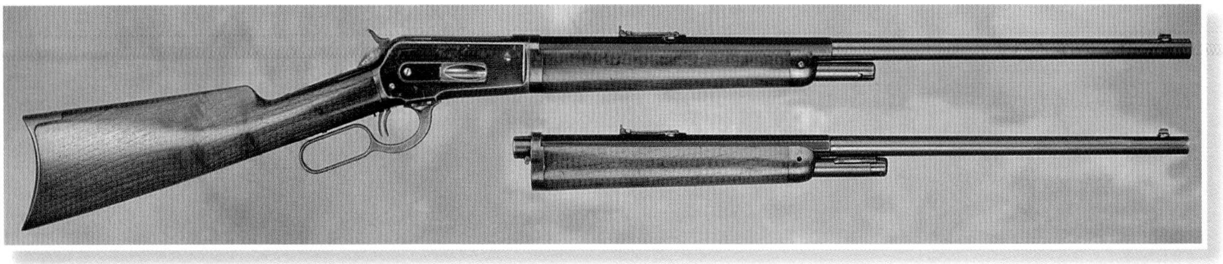

Model 1886 Takedown Rifle with Extra Barrel.

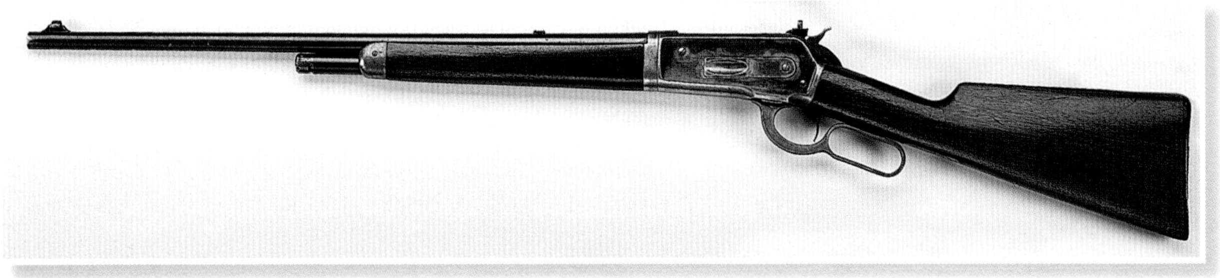

Model 1886 Extra Lightweight Takedown Rifle in .33 Winchester.

FANCY SPORTING RIFLE

EXC.	V.G.	GOOD	FAIR	POOR
25000	14000	8000	6000	3000

TAKEDOWN RIFLE-STANDARD

EXC.	V.G.	GOOD	FAIR	POOR
12500	8500	4200	2000	700

TAKEDOWN RIFLE-DELUXE

EXC.	V.G.	GOOD	FAIR	POOR
17000	13000	8700	6500	3000

EXTRA LIGHTWEIGHT TAKEDOWN RIFLE-.33 CALIBER

EXC.	V.G.	GOOD	FAIR	POOR
4500	3000	1500	750	400

EXTRA LIGHTWEIGHT TAKEDOWN RIFLE-OTHER CALIBERS

EXC.	V.G.	GOOD	FAIR	POOR
7750	5500	1800	1250	500

EXTRA LIGHTWEIGHT RIFLE-.33 CALIBER

EXC.	V.G.	GOOD	FAIR	POOR
5000	3500	1800	1000	500

EXTRA LIGHTWEIGHT RIFLE-OTHER CALIBERS

EXC.	V.G.	GOOD	FAIR	POOR
7750	5500	2250	950	500

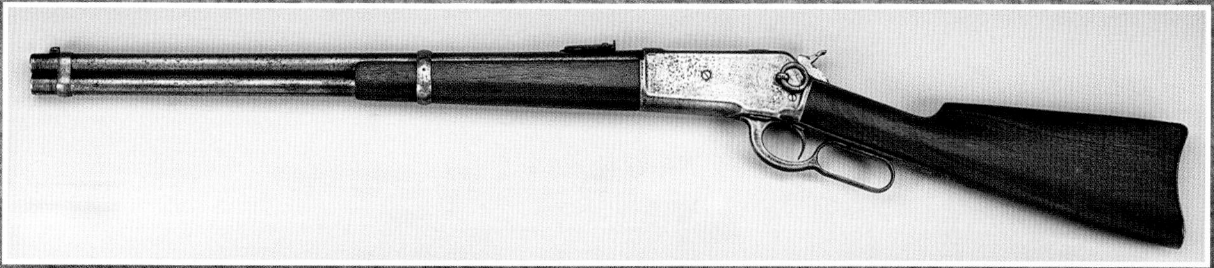

Model 1886 Carbine.

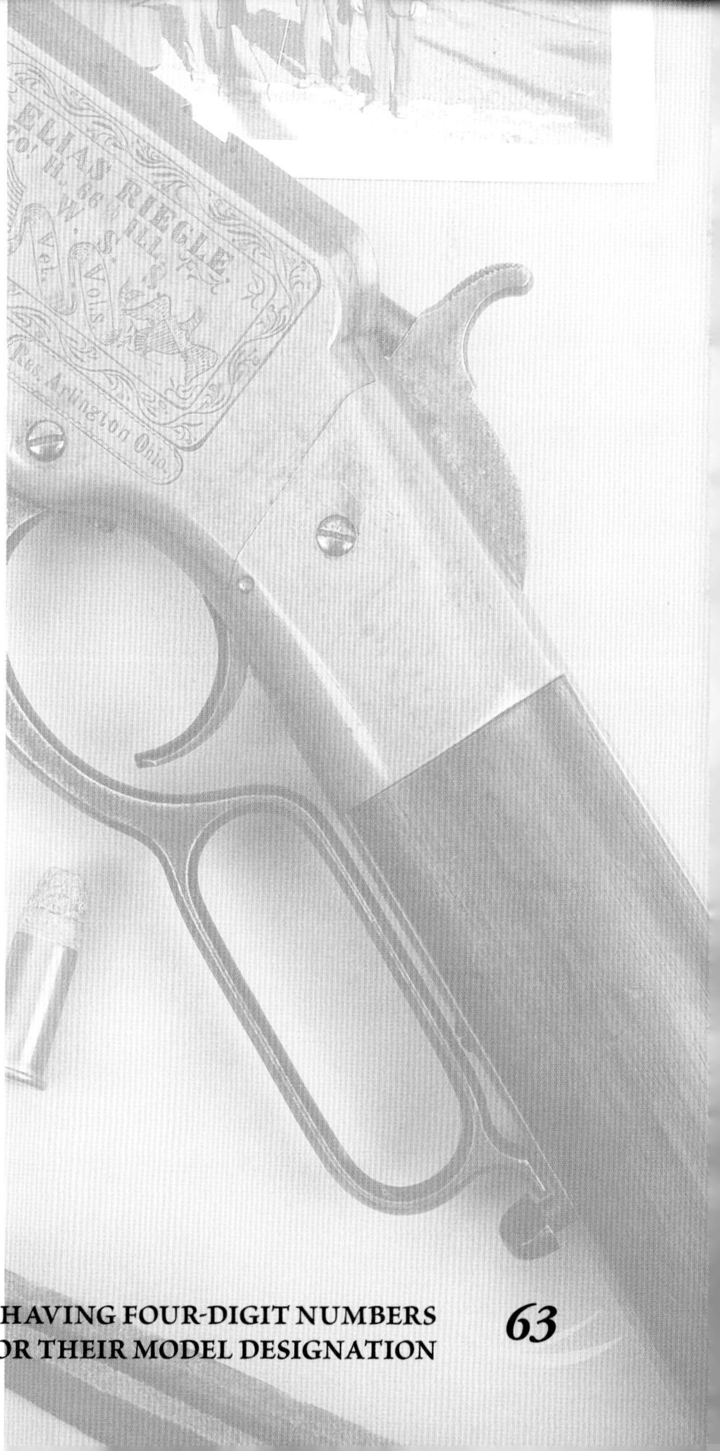

CARBINE

Model 1886 carbine barrels are 22". A few were Trappers with 20" barrels. Add 50 percent if Trapper.

EXC.	V.G.	GOOD	FAIR	POOR
25000	15000	9000	4500	2000

MUSKET

EXC.	V.G.	GOOD	FAIR	POOR
-	18000	9000	3500	1500

NOTE: For .50 Express add a premium of 50 percent. Case colored Model 1886s will bring a premium of 25 percent. These very large bore rifles are very rare, and exceedingly desirable, as they seem to have a mystique all their own.

MODEL 1890

The Model 1890 was the first slide-action rifle ever produced by Winchester. Designed by John and Matthew Browning, this rifle was chambered for the .22 Short, Long, and Winchester Rimfire cartridges (the WRF cartridge was developed by Winchester specifically for the Model 1890) but not on an interchangeable basis. In 1919 the .22 LR cartridge was offered as well.

The rifle was a slide-action top ejecting rifle with an 18" underbarrel magazine tube. All standard Model 1890s were furnished standard with

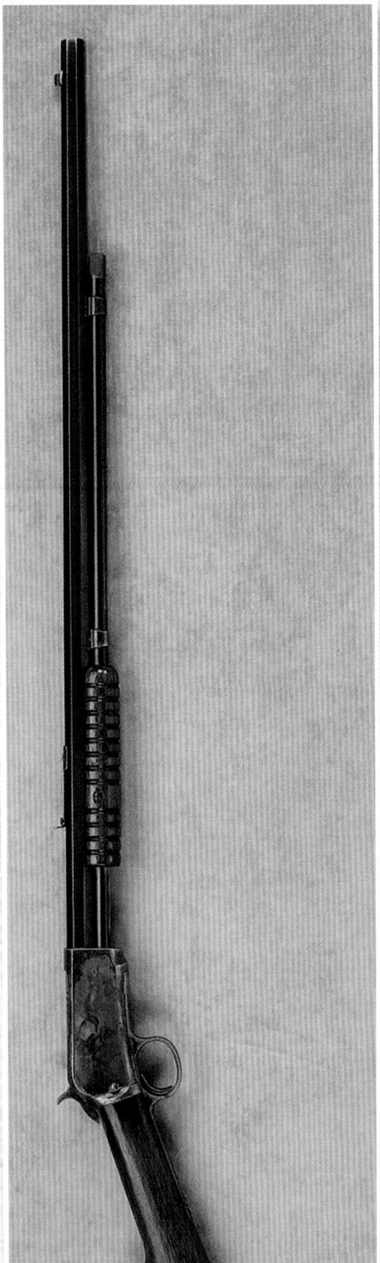

Model 1890, 2nd Model with Case-Hardened Frame.

plain walnut straight stocks with crescent buttplate and 12 groove slide handle. This rifle was one of the company's best selling small caliber firearms and was in worldwide use. Even though several hundred thousand of these Winchesters were manufactured, original model 1890 22 rifles are extremely desirable in the collector's market – especially casecolored examples. They have a special appeal to young and old Winchester lovers alike. The Model 1890 came in three separate and distinct variations that greatly affect its value:

1) First Model, solid frame, 24" octagon barrel, casehardened frame, and fixed rear sight. Approximately 15,552 of these First Model guns were produced, and their distinctive feature is concealed locking lugs and solid frame. Serial numbered on the lower tang only. Built from 1890 to 1892.
2) Second Model, takedown, 24" octagon barrel, casehardened frame, and adjustable rear sight. Serial numbered from 15553 to 112970 (on lower tang only) these Second Model guns feature the same concealed locking lugs but with the added takedown feature. A Deluxe version was offered with fancy walnut checkered straight- or pistol-grip stock and grooved slide handle.
   a. Second Model (blued frame variation), same as above but with blued frame. Serial numbered from 112971 to 325250 (on lower tang until 232328, then also on bottom front end of receiver) these blued frame Second Models are much more numerous than the casehardened variety. A Deluxe version was offered with fancy walnut checkered straight- or pistol-grip stock and grooved slide handle.
3) Third Model, takedown, 24" octagon barrel, blued frame, adjustable rear sight. Serial numbered from 325251 to as high

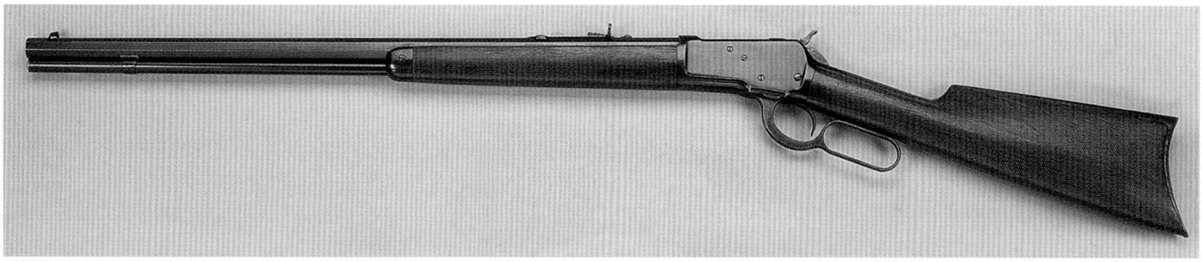

Model 1892 Sporting Rifle.

as 853000 (numbered on both the lower tang and bottom front of receiver) the distinctive feature of the Third Model is the locking cut made on the front top of the receiver to allow the breech bolt to lock externally. A Deluxe version was offered with fancy walnut checkered stock, straight or pistol grip with grooved slide handle.

Winchester offered many extra-cost options for this rifle that will greatly affect the value. Secure an expert appraisal before proceeding. The Model 1890 was produced from 1890 to 1932 with approximately 775,000 guns sold.

FIRST MODEL-STANDARD GRADE

EXC.	V.G.	GOOD	FAIR	POOR
9000	5000	2500	1250	750

SECOND MODEL-CASE-HARDENED FRAME

STANDARD

EXC.	V.G.	GOOD	FAIR	POOR
5500	3500	2000	1000	500

DELUXE

EXC.	V.G.	GOOD	FAIR	POOR
10000	7000	3500	2000	1000

SECOND MODEL-BLUED FRAME

STANDARD

EXC.	V.G.	GOOD	FAIR	POOR
3000	2000	1500	750	250

DELUXE

EXC.	V.G.	GOOD	FAIR	POOR
7500	5500	3000	1500	750

THIRD MODEL

STANDARD

EXC.	V.G.	GOOD	FAIR	POOR
2500	1500	900	450	250

DELUXE

EXC.	V.G.	GOOD	FAIR	POOR
6500	4000	2000	1000	750

NOTE: For Third Models chambered for .22 LR add 25 percent premium.

MODEL 1892

The Model 1892 was an updated successor to the Model 1873 using a scaled-down version of the Model 1886 action. The rifle was chambered for the popular smaller cartridges of the day, namely the .25-20, .32-20, .38-40, .44-40, and the rare .218 Bee. The rifle was available in several different configurations:

1) Sporting Rifle, solid frame or take-down (worth an extra premium of about 20 percent), 24" round, octagon, or half- octagon barrel with 1/2, 2/3, or full magazines. Plain straight-grip walnut stock with capped forearm.
2) Fancy Sporting Rifle, solid frame or take-down (worth 20% premium), 24" round,

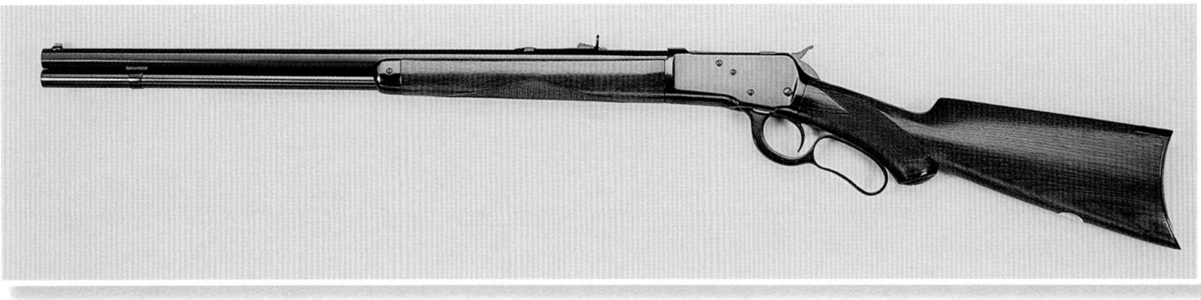

Model 1892 Fancy Sporting Rifle.

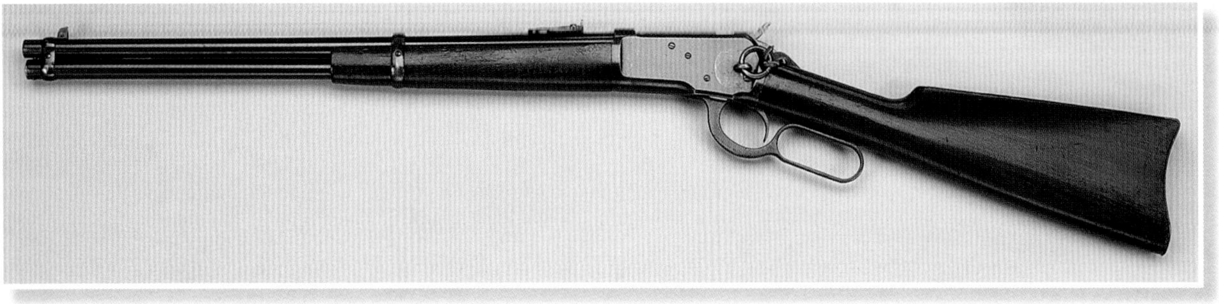

Model 1892 Saddle Ring Carbine.

octagon, or half-octagon barrel with 1/2, 2/3, or full magazine. Checkered walnut pistol-grip stock with checkered capped forearm.

3) Carbine, 20" round barrel, full or half magazine, plain walnut straight-grip stock with one barrel band forearm. Carbines were offered only with solid frames.
4) Trapper's Carbine, 18", 16", 15", or 14" round barrel with the same dimensions of standard carbine. Federal law prohibits the possession of rifles with barrel lengths shorter than 16". The Model 1892 Trapper's Carbine can be exempted from this law as a curio and relic with a federal permit providing the gun is original and left the factory with the short Trapper barrel.
5) Musket, 30" round barrel with full magazine. Almost full-length forearm held by two barrel bands. Buttstock is plain walnut with straight grip.

The Model 1892 was built between 1892 and 1932 with slightly more than 1 million sold. The Model 1892 carbine continued to be offered for sale until 1941.

NOTE: Antique Winchester Model 1892s (pre-1898 manufacture) will bring a premium of 15 percent. In addition, Winchester model 1892s in 38-40 caliber and 44-40 caliber will bring a premium of 15% and 25% respectively.

SPORTING RIFLE

EXC.	V.G.	GOOD	FAIR	POOR
5000	3500	1250	700	350

FANCY SPORTING RIFLE

EXC.	V.G.	GOOD	FAIR	POOR
12000	7500	4000	2500	1000

CARBINE

EXC.	V.G.	GOOD	FAIR	POOR
5000	4000	2000	1200	600

Model 1892 Trapper's Carbine, Closeup of Receiver, Right View.

Model 1892 Trapper's Carbine, Closeup of Receiver, Left View.

TRAPPER'S CARBINE

EXC.	V.G.	GOOD	FAIR	POOR
12000	8500	4000	2500	1250

NOTE: Add 20% for 15" barrel. Add 50% for carbines chambered for .25-20 cartridge.

MUSKET

EXC.	V.G.	GOOD	FAIR	POOR
-	9500	4500	2500	1500

MODEL 1894

Based on a John M. Browning patent, the Model 1894 was the most successful centerfire rifle Winchester ever produced. This model was in production until 2005, a record of longevity unequalled by any other American sporting arm. The values given here reflect those rifles produced before 1964, or around serial number 2550000.

The Model 1894 was the first Winchester developed especially for smokeless powder and was chambered for these cartridges: .32-40, .38-55, .25-35 Winchester, .30-30 Winchester, and the .32 Winchester Special. The rifle was available in several different configurations:

1) Sporting Rifle, 26" round, octagon, or half-octagon barrel, in solid frame or takedown. Full, 2/3 or 1/2 magazines were available. Plain walnut straight or pistol-grip stock with crescent buttplate and plain capped forearm.
2) Fancy Sporting Rifle, 26" round, octagon, or half-octagon barrel, in solid frame or takedown. Full, 2/3, or 1/2 magazines were available. Fancy walnut checkered straight or pistol-grip stock with crescent buttplate and checkered fancy capped forearm.
3) Extra lightweight Rifle, 22" or 26" round barrel with half magazine. Plain walnut straight-grip stock with shotgun buttplate and plain capped forearm.
4) Carbine, 20" round barrel, plain walnut straight-grip stock with carbine style buttplate. Forearm was plain walnut uncapped with one barrel band. Carbines were available with solid frame only. Carbines made prior to 1925 were fitted with a saddle ring on the left side of receiver and worth a premium over carbines without saddle ring.

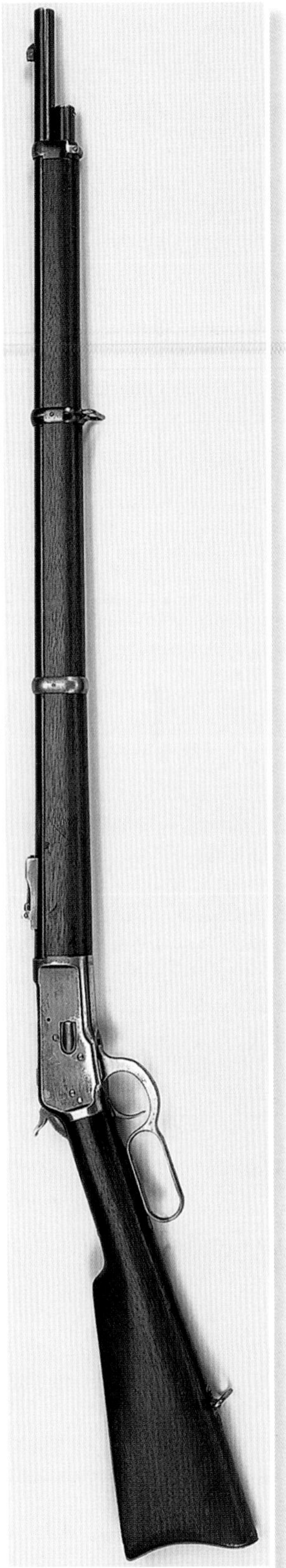

Model 1892 Musket.

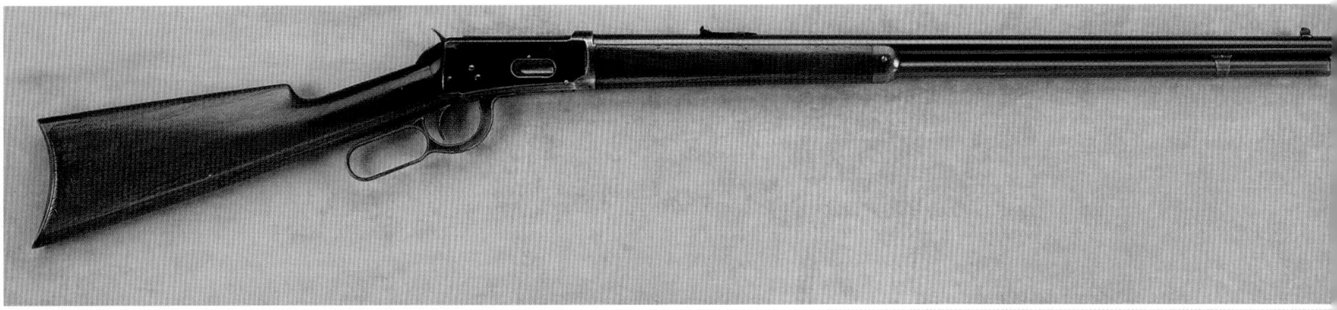

Model 1894 Sporting Rifle, Right View.

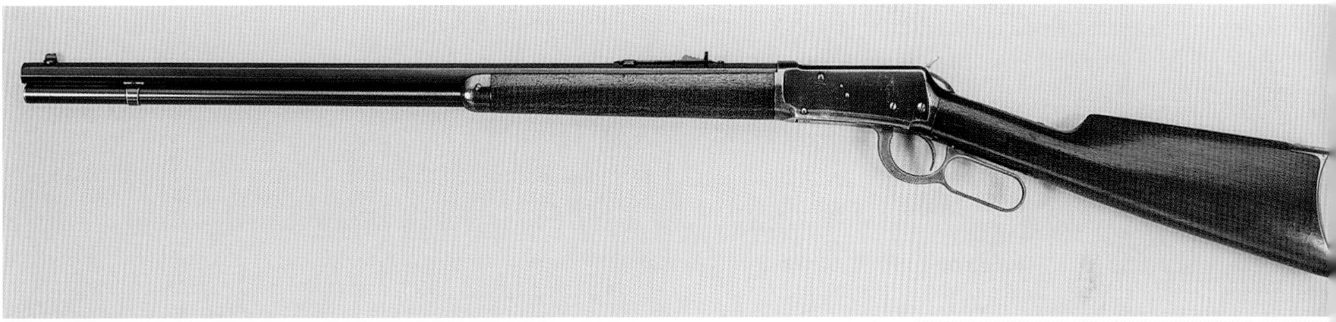

Model 1894 Sporting Rifle, Left View.

5) Trapper's Carbine, 18", 16", 15", or 14". Buttstock, forearm, and saddle ring specifications same as standard carbine.

All Model 1894s were furnished with blued frames and barrels, although casehardened frames were available as an extra-cost option. Casecolored Model 1894s are rare and worth a considerable premium, perhaps as much as 1,000%. Guns with extra-cost options should be evaluated by an expert to determine proper value.

Between 1894 and 1963, approximately 2,550,000 Model 1894s were sold.

NOTE: Antique Winchester Model 1894s (pre-1898 manufacture) will bring a premium of 10 percent. First year production guns, October 1894 to December 1894, documented by the Cody Museum will command a 100% premium. Winchester Model 1894s in 25-35 caliber will bring a premium of approximately 15%, while the caliber 38-55 will bring a premium of approximately 25%. Ammunition is readily available for many of the calibers for which this rifle is chambered.

FIRST MODEL SPORTING RIFLE

Very early model that incorporates a screw entering the receiver over the loading port from the outside. Rare.

EXC.	V.G.	GOOD	FAIR	POOR
8500	4000	2000	1250	500

SPORTING RIFLE

EXC.	V.G.	GOOD	FAIR	POOR
4000	3000	1500	850	450

NOTE: Takedown versions are worth approximately 20 percent more.

FANCY SPORTING RIFLE

EXC.	V.G.	GOOD	FAIR	POOR
12000	7500	3500	2000	900

NOTE: Takedown versions are worth approximately 20% more. Fancy Sporting Rifles were also engraved at the customer's request. Check factory where possible and proceed with caution. Factory engraved Model 1894s are extremely valuable.

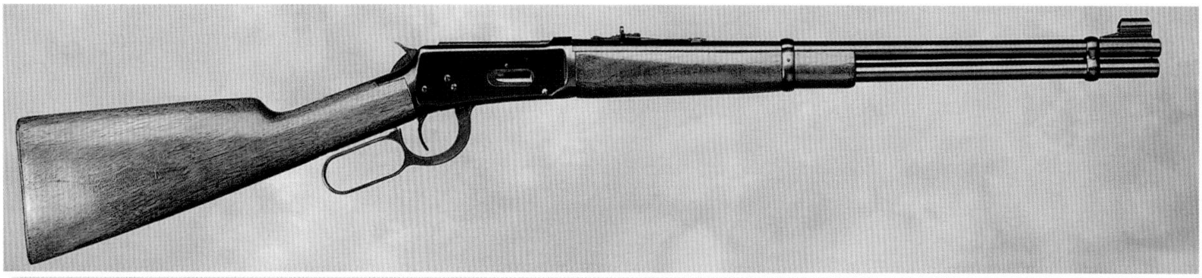

Model 1894 Eastern Carbine.

Model 1894 Saddle Ring Carbine.

EXTRA LIGHTWEIGHT RIFLE

EXC.	V.G.	GOOD	FAIR	POOR
5500	4000	1500	1000	450

CARBINE

EXC.	V.G.	GOOD	FAIR	POOR
3000	2000	600	400	200

NOTE: The above values are for guns with saddle rings. For carbines without saddle rings deduct 35%. Add 25% for carbines chambered in .25-35 or .38-55.

TRAPPER'S CARBINE

EXC.	V.G.	GOOD	FAIR	POOR
6500	4250	2500	1500	700

NOTE: Add 30% for carbines chambered for .25-35 or .38-55 calibers.

MODEL 1895

For a myriad of reasons, this model of early Winchester lever action rifles, with the exception of weapons chambered in the .405 caliber, .30-06 caliber, .30-03 caliber, or models with the takedown feature, is the least popular of the early Winchester lever action rifles. The Model 1895 was the first nondetachable box magazine rifle offered by Winchester. Built on a John M. Browning patent, this rifle was introduced by Winchester to meet the demand for a rifle that could handle the new high-power, smokeless hunting cartridges of the period.

The Model 1895 was available in these calibers:

- .30-40 Krag
- .38-72 Winchester
- .40-72 Winchester
- .303 British
- .35 Winchester
- .405 Winchester (rare)
- 7.62 Russian
- .30-03 (desirable)
- .30-06 (desirable)

The rifle gained fame as a favorite hunting rifle of Theodore Roosevelt. Because of its box magazine, the Model 1895 has a distinctive look like no other Winchester lever-action rifle. The rifle was available in several different configurations:

1) Sporting Rifle, 28" or 24" (depending on caliber) round barrel, plain walnut straight-grip stock with plain forend. The first 5,000 rifles were manufactured with flat-sided receivers, and the balance of production were built with

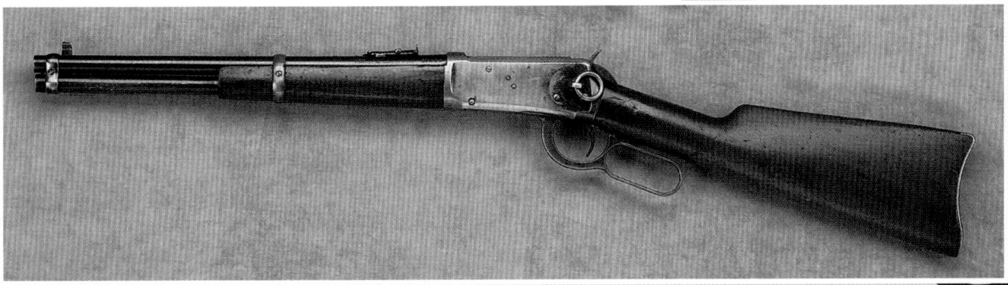

Model 1894 Trapper's Saddle Ring Carbine.

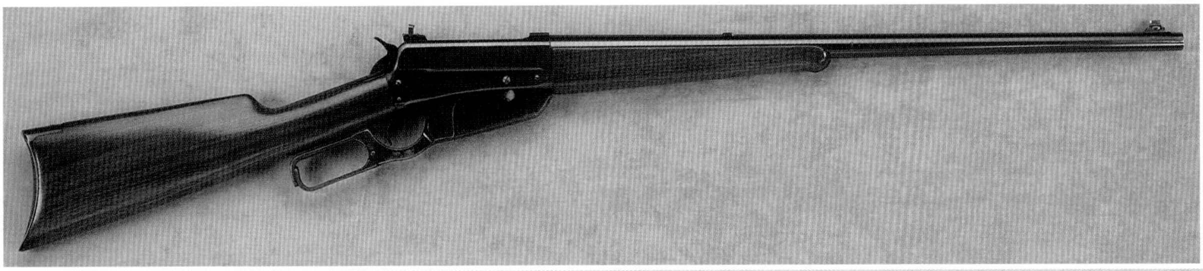

Model 1895 Sporting Rifle.

the receiver sides contoured. After serial-number 60000, a takedown version was available.

2) Fancy Sporting Rifle, 28" round barrel, fancy walnut checkered straight-grip stock and fancy walnut checkered forearm. Rifles with serial numbers below 5000 had flat sided frames.

3) Carbine, 22" round barrel, plain walnut straight-grip stock with military-style hand guard forend. Some carbines are furnished with saddle rings on left side of receiver.

4) Musket

- Standard Musket, 28" round, plain walnut straight-grip stock with musket style forend with two barrel bands.
- U.S. Army N.R.A. Musket, 30" round barrel, Model 1901 Krag-Jorgensen rear sight. Stock similar to the standard musket. This musket could be used for "Any Military Arm" matches under the rules of the National Rifle Association.
- N.R.A. Musket, Models 1903 and 1906, 24" round barrel with special buttplate. Also eligible for all matches under "Any Military Arm" sponsored by the NRA. This musket was fitted with the same stock as listed above.
- U.S. Army Musket, 28" round barrel chambered for the .30-40 Krag. Came equipped with or without knife bayonet. These muskets were furnished to the U.S. Army for use during the Spanish-American War and are "US" marked on the receiver.
- Russian Musket, similar to standard musket but fitted with clip guides in the top of the receiver and with bayonet. Approximately 294,000 Model 1895 Muskets were sold to the Imperial Russian Government between 1915 and 1916. The first 15,000 Russian Muskets had 8" knife bayonets, and the rest were fitted with 16" bayonets.

The Model 1895 was produced from 1895 to 1931 with about 426,000 sold.

NOTE: Add a 10% premium for rifles built before 1898.

SPORTING RIFLE

EXC.	V.G.	GOOD	FAIR	POOR
5000	3000	1200	700	300

NOTE: Flat-side rifles will bring a premium of 100%. Takedown rifles will add an additional 15%.

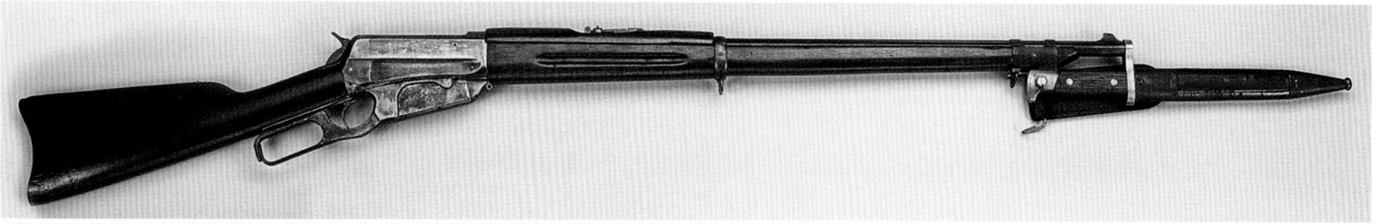

Model 1895 NRA Musket.

Model 1895 Russian Musket.

FANCY SPORTING RIFLES

EXC.	V.G.	GOOD	FAIR	POOR
6500	4500	1500	1100	500

NOTE: Flat-side rifles will bring a premium of 100%. Takedown rifles will add an additional 15%.

CARBINE

EXC.	V.G.	GOOD	FAIR	POOR
3000	1750	1050	600	300

STANDARD MUSKET

EXC.	V.G.	GOOD	FAIR	POOR
3000	1750	1050	600	300

U.S. ARMY N.R.A. MUSKET

EXC.	V.G.	GOOD	FAIR	POOR
4500	2000	1200	800	400

N.R.A. MUSKET, MODEL 1903 AND 1906

EXC.	V.G.	GOOD	FAIR	POOR
5500	2500	1200	800	400

U.S. ARMY MUSKET

EXC.	V.G.	GOOD	FAIR	POOR
-	3000	1500	850	450

RUSSIAN MUSKET

EXC.	V.G.	GOOD	FAIR	POOR
4000	2500	1000	500	250

MODEL 1900

This single-shot bolt-action .22 caliber rifle was based on a John M. Browning design. It was furnished with an 18" round barrel and chambered for the .22 Short and Long interchangeably. The stock was a one-piece plain gumwood straight grip without a buttplate. The rifle was not serial numbered. It was produced from 1899 to 1902 with about 105,000 sold.

EXC.	V.G.	GOOD	FAIR	POOR
2500	1250	450	300	200

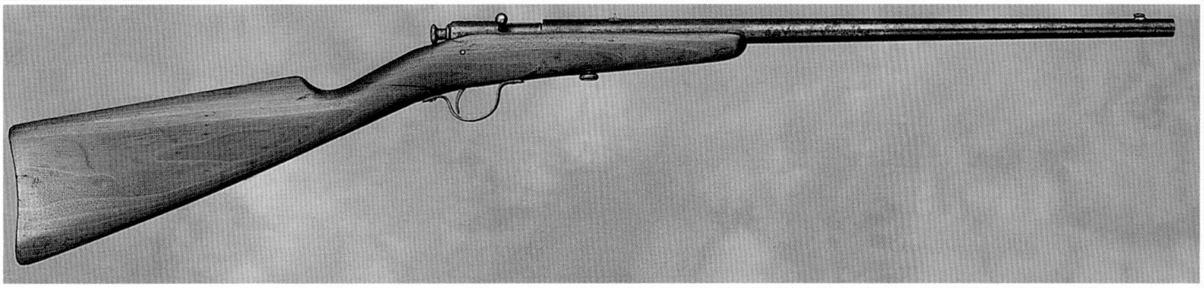

Model 1900.

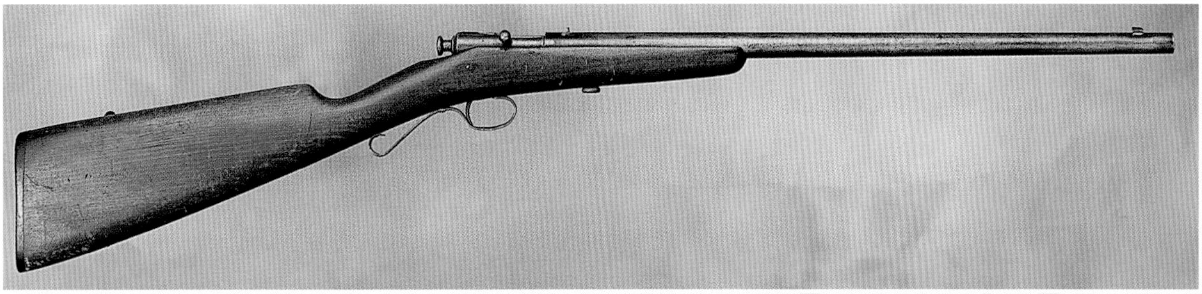

Model 1902.

MODEL 1902

Also a single-shot, this model was of the same general design as the Model 1900 with several improvements: a special shaped metal trigger guard was added, a shorter trigger pull, a steel buttplate, a rear peep sight, and the barrel was made heavier at the muzzle. The rifle was chambered for the .22 Short and Long cartridges until 1914 when the .22 Extra Long was added. In 1927 the .22 Extra Long was dropped in favor of the more popular .22 LR. All of these cartridges were interchangeable. The stock was a one-piece plain gumwood with straight grip (the metal trigger guard added a pistol grip feel) and steel buttplate, which was changed to composition in 1907. This model was not serial numbered. About 640,000 Model 1902s were sold between 1902 and 1931 when it was discontinued.

EXC.	V.G.	GOOD	FAIR	POOR
1000	750	400	225	125

MODEL 99 OR THUMB TRIGGER

NOTE: The Model 99 does not strictly qualify for this section because it has a two-digit, rather than a four-digit, model number. However, the editor is willing to fudge things a bit because the Model 1904 is so closely based on the Model 1902 (see above). Besides, it doesn't fit anywhere else in the book.

This rifle was a modification of the Model 1902 without a traditional trigger. The rifle was fired by depressing the trigger with the thumb, which was part of the sear and extractor located behind the bolt. The rifle was chambered for the .22 Short and Long until 1914 when it was also chambered for the .22 Extra Long. All cartridges could be shot interchangeably. The stock was the same as the Model 1902, Gumwood stained walnut, without the trigger or trigger guard. This model was not serial numbered. Built between 1904 and 1923. Winchester sold about 76,000 rifles.

EXC.	V.G.	GOOD	FAIR	POOR
3000	1250	600	300	200

MODEL 1903

The first semi-automatic rifle produced by Winchester was designed by T. C. Johnson. This rifle was offered in a takedown version only and was available in a 20" round barrel chambered for the .22 Winchester Automatic Rimfire. This ammunition is produced on an irregular basis by a few specialty manufacturers and tends to be expensive. The tubular magazine is located in the buttstock and holds 10 cartridges. The rifle was available in two different configurations:

1) Standard Rifle, 20" round barrel, plain walnut straight-grip stock with plain forend. Steel crescent butt was standard.
2) Deluxe Rifle, 20" round barrel, fancy checkered walnut pistol-grip stock with checkered forearm. Manufactured from 1903 to 1932, about 126,000 were sold.

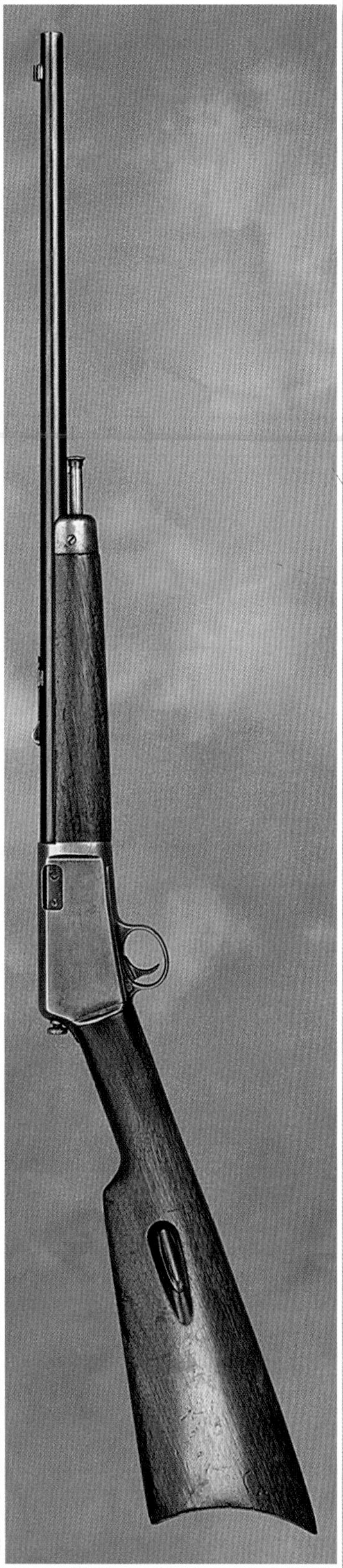

Model 1903.

STANDARD RIFLE

EXC.	V.G.	GOOD	FAIR	POOR
850	550	325	200	100

DELUXE RIFLE

EXC.	V.G.	GOOD	FAIR	POOR
2250	1000	700	500	250

NOTE: The first 5,000 guns were built without safeties, and the first 15,000 guns were furnished with bronze firing pins instead of steel. These early Model 1903s will bring a premium of 30%.

MODEL 1904

This model was a slightly more expensive version of the Model 1902. It featured a 21" round barrel, a one-piece plain gumwood straight-grip stock (the metal trigger guard gave the rifle a pis-

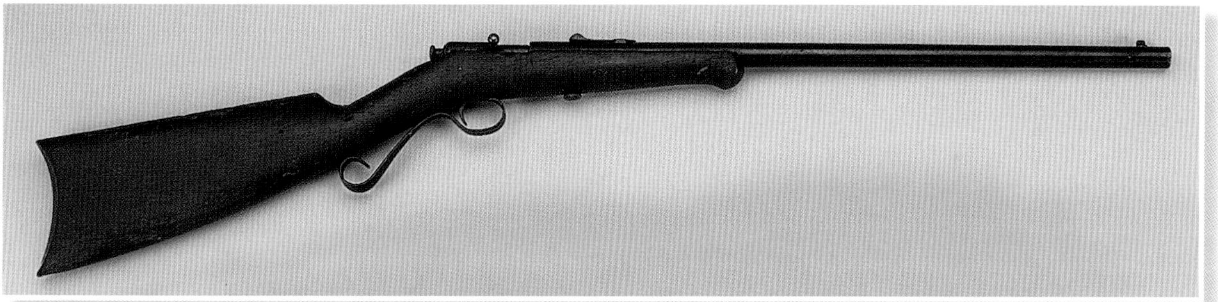

Model 1904.

Model 1905.

tol grip feel) with a small lip on the forend. Rifle was chambered for the .22 Short and Long until 1914 when the .22 Extra Long was added. The .22 LR cartridge was added in place of the Extra Long in 1927. This model was not serial numbered. Produced between 1904 and 1931, about 303,000 rifles were sold.

EXC.	V.G.	GOOD	FAIR	POOR
850	600	350	200	100

MODEL 1905

The Model 1905 was a larger version of the Model 1903, developed by T.C. Johnson to handle the more powerful centerfire cartridges. It was chambered for the .32 Winchester Self Loading (WSL) and .35 Winchester Self Loading cartridges, loaded by means of a detachable box magazine. Available in takedown only, this model was offered in two different styles:

1) Sporting Rifle, 22" round barrel, plain walnut straight grip (changed to pistol grip in 1908) stock with plain forend.
2) Fancy Sporting Rifle, 22" round barrel, fancy walnut checkered pistol-grip stock with checkered forend. This model was the first Winchester semi-automatic rifle to fire centerfire cartridges. Produced from 1905 to 1920 with about 30,000 rifles sold.

SPORTING RIFLE

EXC.	V.G.	GOOD	FAIR	POOR
500	350	250	175	125

FANCY SPORTING RIFLE

EXC.	V.G.	GOOD	FAIR	POOR
600	400	300	200	150

MODEL 1906

In 1906 Winchester decided to offer a lower-cost version of the Model 1890. The Model 1906 used the same receiver but was fitted with a 20" round barrel and plain gumwood straight-grip stock. When the Model 1906 was first introduced, it sold for two-thirds of the price of the Model 1890.

For the first two years the gun was chambered for the .22 Short cartridge only. In 1908 the rifle

Model 1906.

was modified to shoot .22 Short, Long, and LR cartridges interchangeably. This modification ensured the Model 1906's success, and between 1906 and 1932 about 800,000 were sold. All Model 1906s were of the takedown variety.

An interesting fact about this weapon is that 1906 Winchesters are rarely found in excellent condition, partly because, for some reason, the blue finish slips/flakes away easily. The Model 1906 is available in three important variations:

1) 22 Short Only, 20" round barrel, straight-grip gumwood stock and smooth slide handle. These were built from serial number 1 to around 113000.
2) Standard Model 1906, 20" round barrel, straight-grip gumwood stock with 12 groove slide handle. Serial numbered from 113000 to 852000.
3) Model 1906 Expert, 20" round barrel, pistol-grip gumwood stock with fluted smooth slide handle. Expert was available from 1918 to 1924 and was offered in three different finishes regular blued finish, half nickel (receiver, guard, and bolt), and full nickel (receiver, guard, bolt, and barrel nickeled). These weapons are extremely rare and the advice of an expert should be retained prior to purchasing. Unfortunately, in recent years, we have seen an increase in weapons which have been "helped," or are outright frauds. The buyer must beware, as even "experts" can be fooled by unscrupulous individuals who have mastered the art of creating fraudulent guns.

MODEL 1906 .22 SHORT ONLY

EXC.	V.G.	GOOD	FAIR	POOR
3500	1750	750	500	200

STANDARD MODEL 1906

NIB	EXC.	V.G.	GOOD	FAIR	POOR
4250	2000	1000	650	400	200

MODEL 1906 EXPERT

EXC.	V.G.	GOOD	FAIR	POOR
3500	1850	950	500	300

NOTE: Prices are for half-nickel Experts. Add 10% for blued guns and 100% for full nickel.

MODEL 1907

The Model 1907 was an improved version of the Model 1905 and chambered for the new .351 Winchester Self Loading (WSL) cartridge. Its outward appearance was the same as Model 1905 except for its 20" round barrel. This rifle was available in three different styles:

1) Sporting Rifle, 20" round barrel, plain walnut pistol-grip stock with plain forend. Discontinued in 1937.
2) Fancy Sporting Rifle, 20" round barrel, fancy walnut checkered pistol-grip stock and checkered forend.
3) Police Rifle, 20" round barrel, plain walnut pistol-grip stock and beavertail forend. This version was fitted with a leather sling and with

Model 1907.

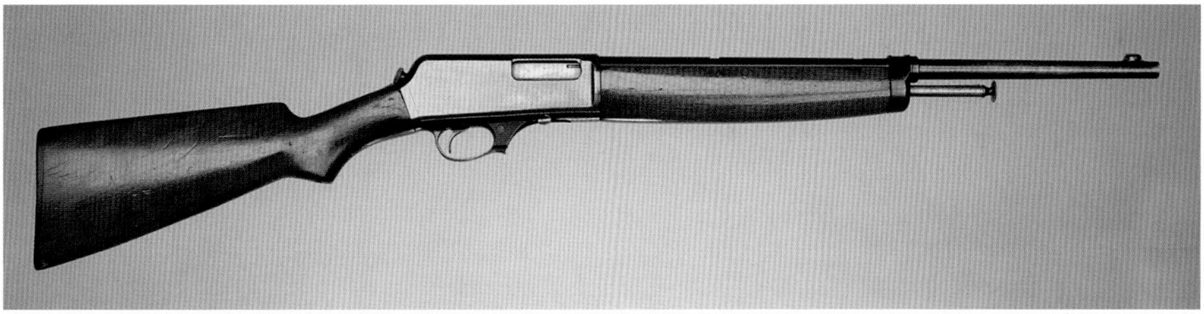

Model 1910.

or without knife bayonet. First introduced in 1937. Winchester discontinued this model in 1957 after having sold about 59,000 guns.

SPORTING RIFLE

EXC.	V.G.	GOOD	FAIR	POOR
550	300	250	175	125

FANCY SPORTING RIFLE

EXC.	V.G.	GOOD	FAIR	POOR
750	550	350	200	150

POLICE RIFLE

EXC.	V.G.	GOOD	FAIR	POOR
550	350	275	200	150

MODEL 1910

This model was similar to the Model 1907 but the action was made stronger to handle the new Winchester .401 Self Loading (WSL) cartridge. The specifications for this model are the same as the Model 1907. Built between 1907 and 1936, only about 21,000 of these guns were sold.

SPORTING RIFLE

EXC.	V.G.	GOOD	FAIR	POOR
400	300	250	175	125

FANCY SPORTING RIFLE

EXC.	V.G.	GOOD	FAIR	POOR
550	400	300	200	150

MODEL 1917 OR MODEL D MILITARY RIFLE

Overall length 46-3/8"; barrel length 26"; caliber 7.62mm. Walnut stock with blued barrel, receiver, magazine housing and furniture. Receiver ring over barrel breech stamped with serial number and Winchester proofmark. A total of 500 Model D Rifles were shipped to Russia for trial in March of 1917.

Prospective purchasers are strongly advised to secure an expert appraisal prior to acquisition. Due to the recent identification of this model pricing schedules have yet to be established.

SECTION III

LATER (POST-'64) MODEL HAVING FOUR-DIGIT NUMBERS IN THEIR MODEL NAME

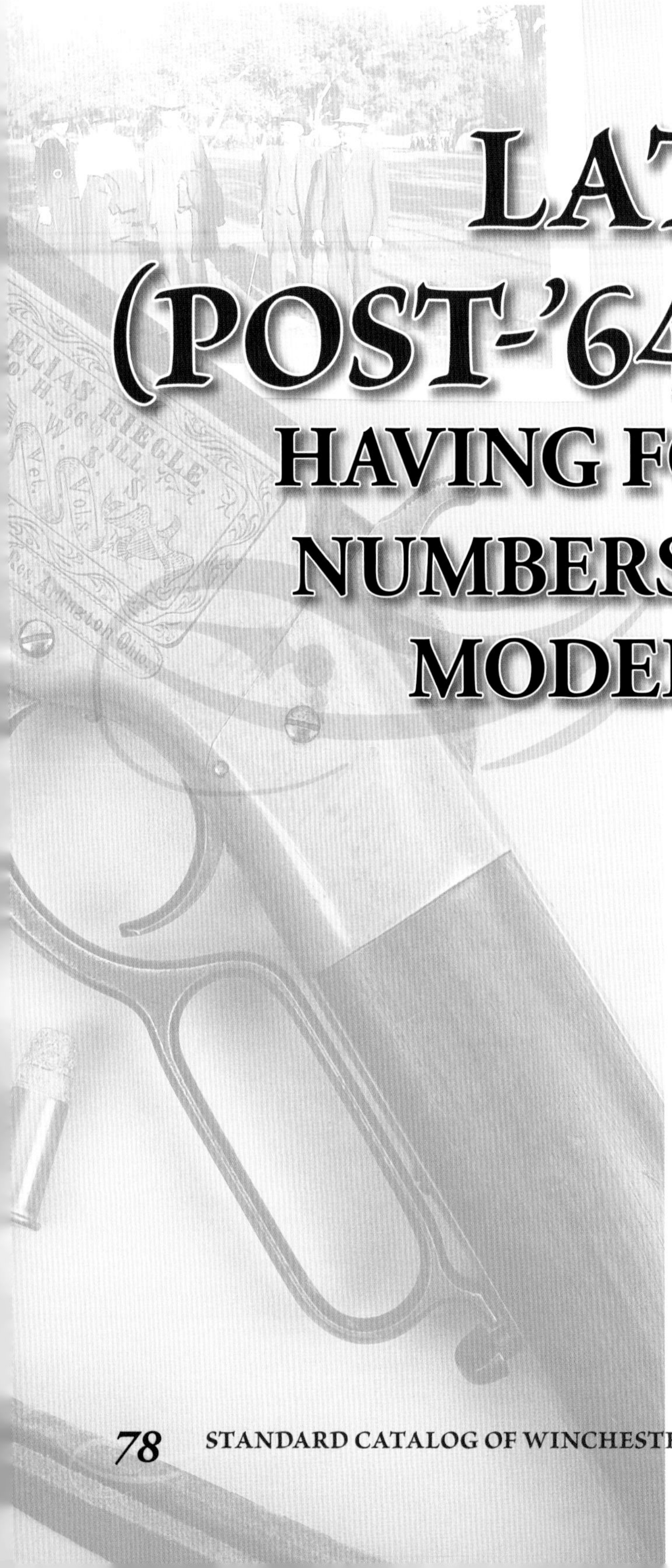

MODEL 1885 LOW WALL

Introduced in fall of 1999 this single-shot model is chambered for the .22 LR cartridge. It is fitted with a 24.5" half octagon barrel with leaf rear sight. Drilled and tapped for a tang sight. Crescent steel buttplate. Walnut stock. Weight is about 8 lbs. Limited to 2,400 rifles.

GRADE I

NIB	EXC.	V.G.	GOOD	FAIR	POOR
875	725	600	500	—	—

HIGH GRADE

NIB	EXC.	V.G.	GOOD	FAIR	POOR
1225	925	—	—	—	—

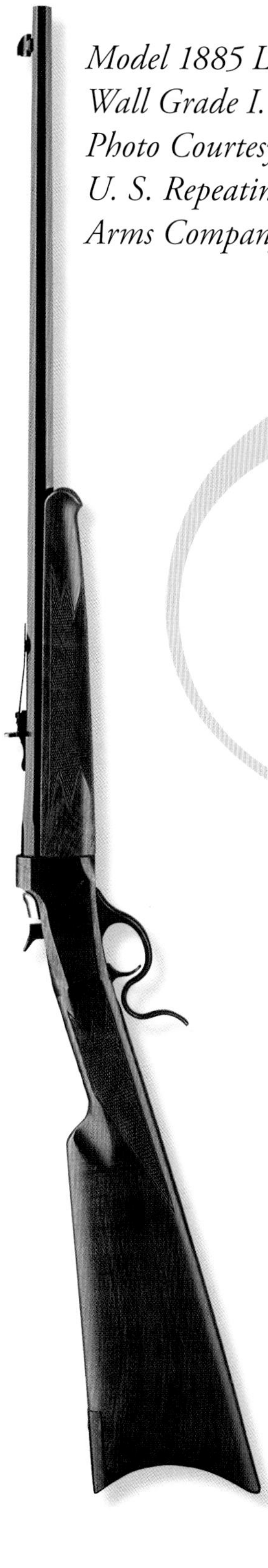

Model 1885 Low Wall Grade I. Photo Courtesy U. S. Repeating Arms Company.

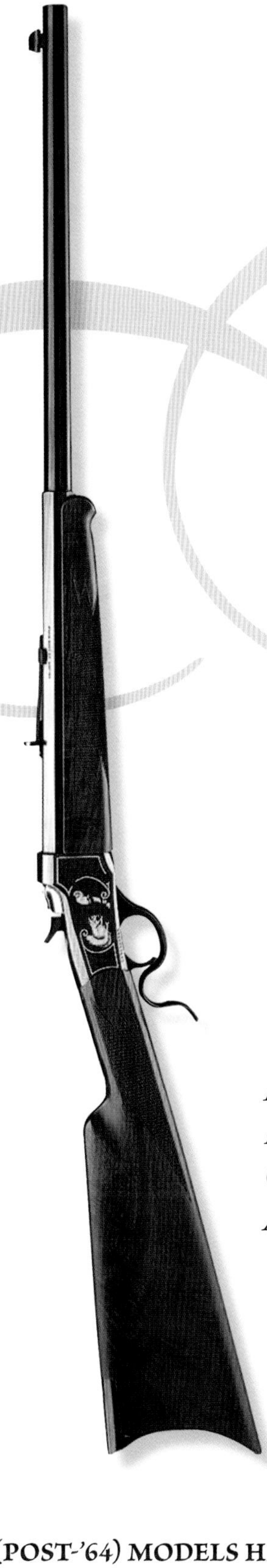

Model 1885 Low Wall Rifle, High Grade. Photo Courtesy U. S. Repeating Arms Company.

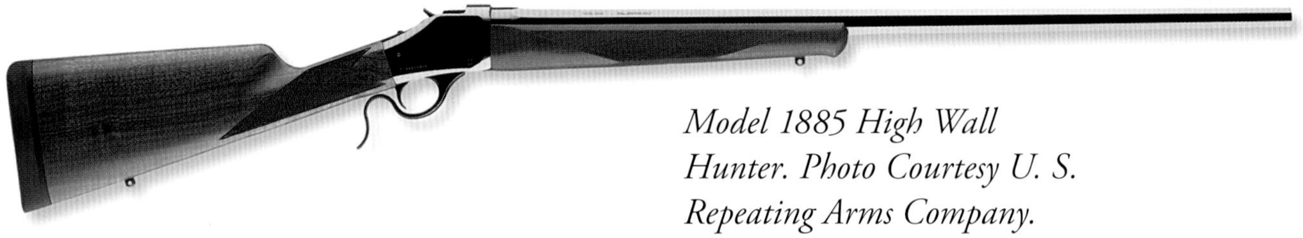

Model 1885 High Wall Hunter. Photo Courtesy U. S. Repeating Arms Company.

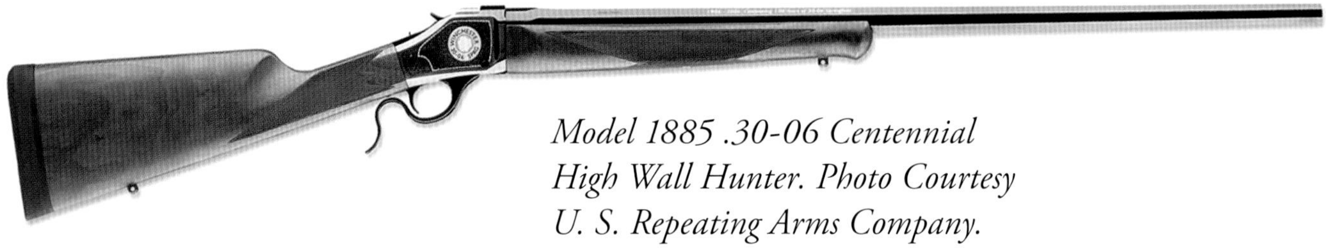

Model 1885 .30-06 Centennial High Wall Hunter. Photo Courtesy U. S. Repeating Arms Company.

MODEL 1885 HIGH WALL HUNTER

Single-shot; patterned after original Model 1885 designed by John Browning. Calibers: .223, .22-250, .270 WSM, 7mm WSM, .300 WSM, .325 WSM. Stock: Checkered walnut. Barrel: 28-inch blued, sightless octagon with Pachmayr pad. Weight: 8-1/2 lbs.

NIB	EXC.	V.G.	GOOD	FAIR	POOR
875	725	600	500	—	—

MODEL 1885 .30-06 CENTENNIAL HIGH WALL HUNTER

Similar to Model 1885 High Wall Hunter but with premium wood and gold inlay on receiver. Commemorates centennial of .30-06 cartridge. Introduced 2006.

NIB	EXC.	V.G.	GOOD	FAIR	POOR
1600	1250	600	500	—	—

MODEL 1885 LOW WALL CLASSIC

This single-shot rifle is chambered for the .17 HMR cartridge and fitted with a 24" octagon barrel. Checkered walnut stock with straight grip and schnabel forend. Adjustable sights. Weight is about 8 lbs. Introduced in 2003. In 2005 the .17 Mach 2 caliber was offered in this model.

NIB	EXC.	V.G.	GOOD	FAIR	POOR
1025	825	700	—	—	—

MODEL 1885 LOW WALL 17 MACH 2

Similar to Model 1885 High Wall but with low-profile receiver, crescent buttplate, and 24-inch barrel. Chambered for 17 Mach 2 rimfire cartridge. Introduced 2006.

NIB	EXC.	V.G.	GOOD	FAIR	POOR
1025	825	700	—	—	—

MODEL 1886

Introduced to the Winchester line in 1997, this was a noncatalogued item. This model features a 26" octagon barrel, semi-pistol grip, and crescent buttplate.

GRADE I

2,500 rifles blued receiver.

NIB	EXC.	V.G.	GOOD	FAIR	POOR
1000	800	-	-	-	-

HIGH GRADE

1,000 rifles with gold accents on receiver.

NIB	EXC.	V.G.	GOOD	FAIR	POOR
1575	1300	-	-	-	-

MODEL 1886 TAKE DOWN CLASSIC

Introduced in 1999, this model is chambered for the .45-70 cartridge and features a 26" barrel with takedown feature. Walnut stock with pistol grip and crescent butt. Magazine capacity is 8 rounds. Weight is about 9.25 lbs.

NIB	EXC.	V.G.	GOOD	FAIR	POOR
1140	950	-	-	-	-

MODEL 1886 EXTRA LIGHT

This model is similar to the Model 1886 Classic but fitted with a 22" round tapered barrel and half magazine. Chambered for the .45-70 cartridge. Shotgun butt. Weight is about 7.25 lbs. Limited edition. Introduced in 2000.

GRADE I (3,500)

NIB	EXC.	V.G.	GOOD	FAIR	POOR
1150	950	-	-	-	-

HIGH GRADE (1,000)

NIB	EXC.	V.G.	GOOD	FAIR	POOR
1350	1050	-	-	-	-

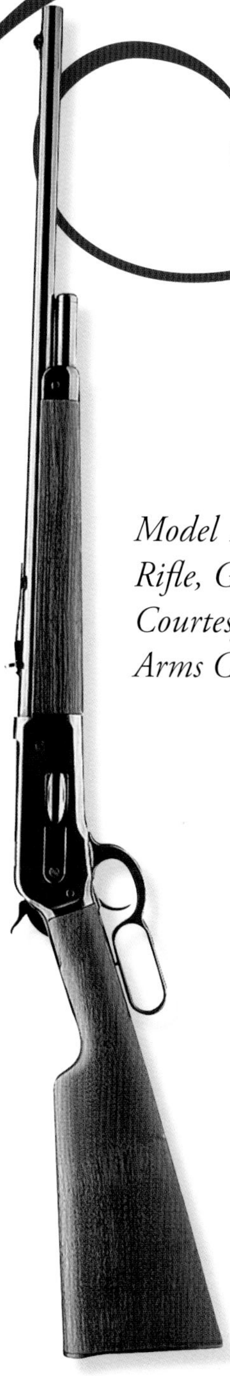

Model 1886 Extra-Light Rifle, Grade I. Photo Courtesy U. S. Repeating Arms Company.

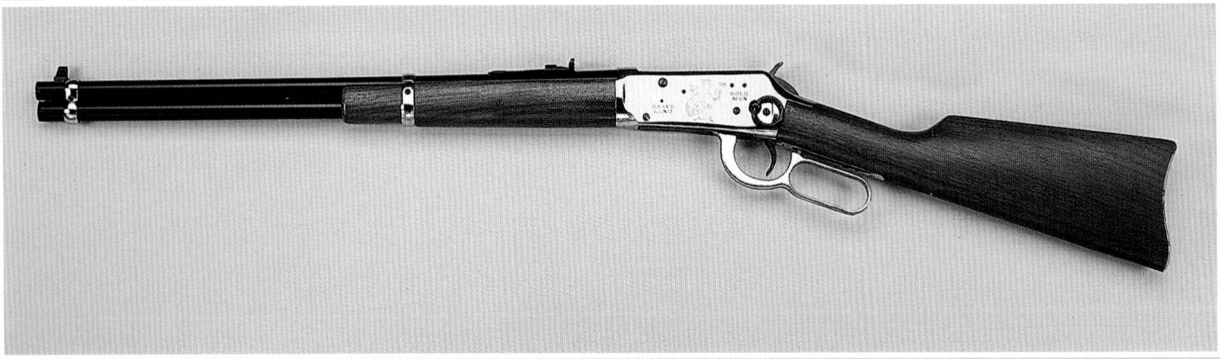

Model 1892.

Model 1892 Short Rifle. Photo Courtesy U. S. Repeating Arms Company.

MODEL 1892

Introduced in mid-1997 this model is chambered for the .45 Colt cartridge, the .357 Magnum, and the 44-40 WCF. It features a straight grip, full magazine, and crescent buttplate, 24" inch barrel, similar to the early Model 1892, round barrel, straight grip, only in blue finish.

GRADE I

2,500 RIFLES WITH ENGRAVED RECEIVER.

NIB	EXC.	V.G.	GOOD	FAIR	POOR
625	475	-	-	-	-

SHORT-BARRELED VERSION WITH 20-INCH BARREL.

NIB	EXC.	V.G.	GOOD	FAIR	POOR
675	500	-	-	-	-

HIGH GRADE

1,000 RIFLE WITH GOLD ACCENTS AND GAME SCENE.

NIB	EXC.	V.G.	GOOD	FAIR	POOR
1200	1050	-	-	-	-

MODEL 1895

Introduced in 1995 this reproduction of the famous Model 1895 is offered in .30-06 caliber with 24" barrel. Magazine capacity is 4 rounds. Weight is approximately 8 lbs. Available in two grades, each limited to 4,000 rifles.

GRADE I

Values are for .270 or .30-06 calibers

NIB	EXC.	V.G.	GOOD	FAIR	POOR
900	700	-	-	-	-

Add $50 for .405 caliber; subtract $100 for Limited Edition with uncheckered wood.

HIGH GRADE

Values for 30-06, engraved, with multiple gold inlays, high-grade checkered wood.

NIB	EXC.	V.G.	GOOD	FAIR	POOR
1300	1000	-	-	-	-

Add $150 for .405 Winchester caliber.

Model 1895 Grade I. Photo Courtesy U. S. Repeating Arms Company.

Model 9422 Standard.

MODEL 1895: LIMITED EDITION FOR THE YEAR 2000

Same as above but chambered for the .405 Win. cartridge. Introduced in 2000.

GRADE I

NIB	EXC.	V.G.	GOOD	FAIR	POOR
1150	800	-	-	-	-

HIGH GRADE

NIB	EXC.	V.G.	GOOD	FAIR	POOR
1550	1150	-	-	-	-

MODEL 9422

Introduced in 1972, this model is chambered for the .22 LR or .22 Magnum rimfire cartridges. It is fitted with a 20.5" barrel, front ramp sight with hood, and adjustable semi-buckhorn rear sight. The tubular magazine holds 21 Shorts, 17 Longs, and 15 LR cartridges. The Magnum version holds 11 cartridges. Weight is about 6.25 lbs. Two-piece American walnut stock with no checkering. Between 1972 and 1992 approximately 750,000 Model 9422s were produced.

NIB	EXC.	V.G.	GOOD	FAIR	POOR
470	375	250	200	150	100

MODEL 9422 XTR

This is a deluxe lever-action rifle chambered for the .22 rimfire cartridge. It is a takedown rifle with a 20.5", round barrel and a tubular magazine. The finish is blued with a checkered, high-gloss, straight-grip walnut stock. It was introduced in 1978. A .22 Magnum version is also available and would be worth approximately $10 additional.

NIB	EXC.	V.G.	GOOD	FAIR	POOR
450	350	250	200	125	100

MODEL 9422 XTR CLASSIC

This version is similar to the standard Model 9422 XTR except that it features a 22.5" barrel and a satin-finished, plain, pistol-grip walnut stock. It was manufactured between 1985 and 1987.

NIB	EXC.	V.G.	GOOD	FAIR	POOR
600	500	350	250	200	125

Model 9422 Traditional. Photo Courtesy U. S. Repeating Arms Company.

MODEL 9422 TRADITIONAL

This weapon was manufactured in .22 Long Rifle or .22 Magnum calibers. It has an 11- or 15-shot tubular magazine, grooved receiver, 20" round barrel, straight checkered stock or weather resistant satin finish. It was manufactured from 1972 to 2004. Add $35 for .22 Magnum caliber and $35 for large loop lever. Rifles manufactured toward the beginning of the production run will command a 10% premium.

EXC.	V.G.	GOOD	FAIR	POOR
400	300	200	–	–

MODEL 9422 WINTUFF

This model features an uncheckered laminated wood stock that is brown in color and is chambered for both the .22 Rimfire and the .22 Winchester Magnum Rimfire. Weighs 6.25 lbs. Other features are the same as the standard Model 9422.

NIB	EXC.	V.G.	GOOD	FAIR	POOR
350	275	225	165	100	75

MODEL 9422 WINCAM

This model is chambered only for the .22 Winchester Magnum Rimfire. The laminated stock is a green color. Weighs 6.25 lbs.

NIB	EXC.	V.G.	GOOD	FAIR	POOR
375	280	225	165	100	75

MODEL 9422 TRAPPER

Introduced in 1996 this model features a 16.5" barrel but is similar in other respects to the standard 9422. It has an overall length of 33". Weight is 5.5 lbs.

NIB	EXC.	V.G.	GOOD	FAIR	POOR
375	300	250	200	150	100

Model 9422 Traditional 20" Carbine. Photo Courtesy U. S. Repeating Arms Company.

Model 9422 Trapper. Photo Courtesy U. S. Repeating Arms Company.

Model 9422 25th Anniversary.

MODEL 9422 HIGH GRADE

This variation of the Model 9422 series features a specially engraved receiver and fancy wood stock. Barrel length is 20.5". Weight is about 6 lbs.

NIB	EXC.	V.G.	GOOD	FAIR	POOR
500	400	300	250	175	125

MODEL 9422 25TH ANNIVERSARY RIFLE

Introduced in 1997 this model features 20.5" barrel. Limited quantities.

GRADE I

Engraved receiver.

NIB	EXC.	V.G.	GOOD	FAIR	POOR
600	475	-	-	-	-

HIGH GRADE

Engraved receiver with silver border.

NIB	EXC.	V.G.	GOOD	FAIR	POOR
1350	1100	-	-	-	-

MODEL 9422 LEGACY

This model has a semi-pistol-grip stock of checkered walnut. Will shoot .22 caliber LR, L, or S cartridges interchangeably. Fitted with a 16" barrel. Weight is about 6 lbs. Introduced in 1998.

NIB	EXC.	V.G.	GOOD	FAIR	POOR
500	400	325	250	-	-

MODEL 9422 LARGE LOOP & WALNUT

Introduced in 1998 this model features a walnut stock with large loop lever. Large loop offered on .22 LR, L, or S model. Standard lever on .22 WMR version. Fitted with 16" barrel. Weight is about 6 lbs.

NIB	EXC.	V.G.	GOOD	FAIR	POOR
400	300	-	-	-	-

MODEL 9422 HIGH GRADE SERIES II

This model features a high-grade walnut stock with cut checkering. Its receiver is engraved with dogs and squirrels. Fitted with 16" barrel. Weight is about 6 lbs. Introduced in 1998.

NIB	EXC.	V.G.	GOOD	FAIR	POOR
500	400	-	-	-	-

MODEL 9417 TRADITIONAL

Introduced in 2003, this model is chambered for the .17 HMR cartridge and fitted with a 20.5" barrel. Adjustable sights. Checkered walnut stock with straight grip. Weight is about 6 lbs.

NIB	EXC.	V.G.	GOOD	FAIR	POOR
500	400	-	-	-	-

Model 9422 Legacy. Photo Courtesy U. S. Repeating Arms Company.

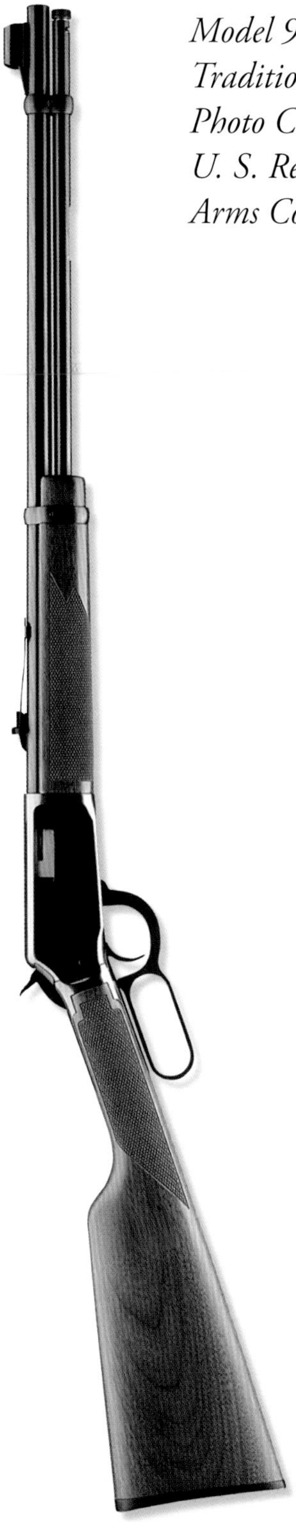

Model 9417 Traditional. Photo Courtesy U. S. Repeating Arms Company.

MODEL 9417 LEGACY

Similar to the Model 9417 Traditional but fitted with a 22.5" barrel and checkered walnut with pistol grip. Weight is about 6 lbs. Introduced in 2003.

NIB	EXC.	V.G.	GOOD	FAIR	POOR
535	425	-	-	-	-

MODEL 9422 TRIBUTE SERIES

Production of the Model 9422 ended in 2005. The final production Model 9422s were limited to a total production of 9,422 rifles. Each rifle has the Winchester Horse and Rider on one side and the Model 9422 tribute logo on the other.

MODEL 9422 HIGH GRADE TRADITIONAL TRIBUTE

This model features a 20.5" barrel with high grade checkered walnuty stock. Blued receiver with high-relief silver inlay on both sides of the receiver.

NIB	Exc.	V.G.	Good	Fair	Poor
1050	775	-	-	-	-

MODEL 9422 HIGH GRADE LEGACY TRIBUTE

Similar to the model above but with semi-pistol grip and 22.5" barrel.

NIB	EXC.	V.G.	GOOD	FAIR	POOR
1085	800	-	-	-	-

MODEL 9422 CUSTOM TRADITIONAL TRIBUTE

This model is fitted with a 20.5" barrel, high grade checkereed walnut stock. High-relief scroll engraved receiver with gold logos on both sides. Limited to 222 rifles.

NIB	EXC.	V.G.	GOOD	FAIR	POOR
2310	1750	-	-	-	-

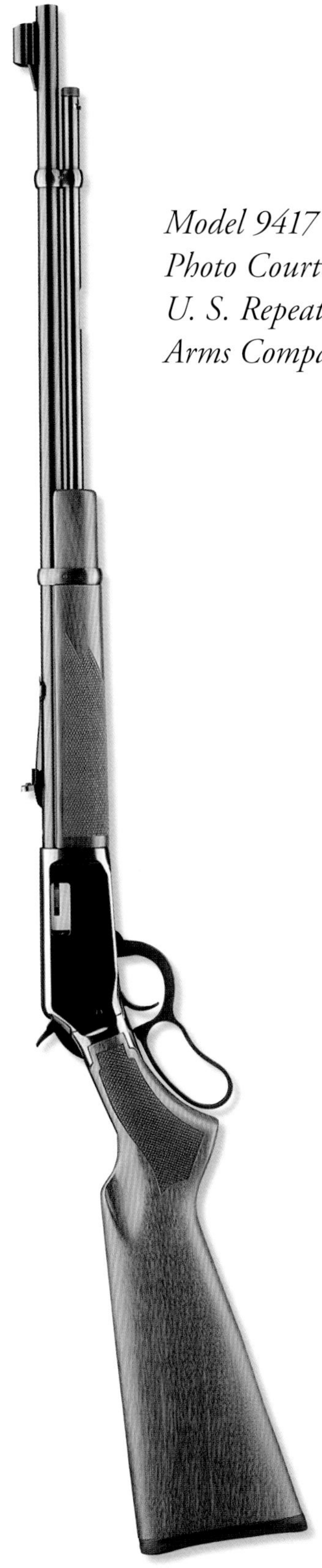

Model 9417 Legacy. Photo Courtesy U. S. Repeating Arms Company.

Model 9422 High Grade Traditional Tribute. Photo Courtesy U. S. Repeating Arms Company.

Model 9422 High Grade Legacy Tribute. Photo Courtesy U. S. Repeating Arms Company.

Model 9422 Custom Traditional Tribute Rifle with Closeup of Receiver. Photo Courtesy U. S. Repeating Arms Company.

MODEL 9422 SPECIAL EDITION TRADITIONAL TRIBUTE

This model has a 20.5" barrel with checkered walnut straight grip stock and engraved blued receiver. Engraved logos appear on both sides of the receiver.

NIB	EXC.	V.G.	GOOD	FAIR	POOR
515	400	-	-	-	-

MODEL 9422 SPECIAL EDITION LEGACY TRIBUTE

This model has a 22.5" barrel, checkered semi-pistol grip stock, and blued receiver with engraved logos on both sides.

NIB	EXC.	V.G.	GOOD	FAIR	POOR
550	400	-	-	-	-

Model 9422 Special Edition Traditional Tribute. Photo Courtesy U. S. Repeating Arms Company.

Model 9422 Special Edition Legacy Tribute. Photo Courtesy U. S. Repeating Arms Company.

SECTION IV

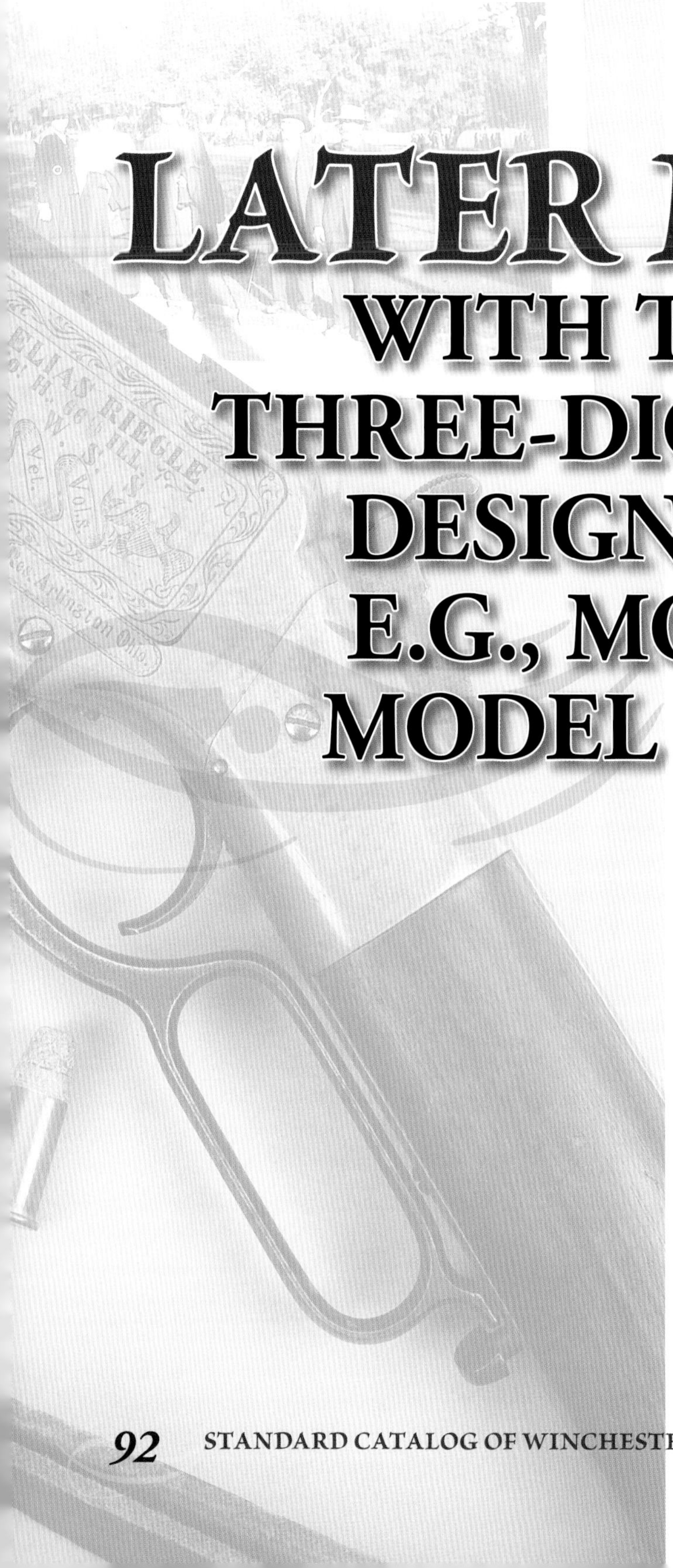

LATER MODELS WITH TWO- OR THREE-DIGIT MODEL DESIGNATIONS, E.G., MODEL 64, MODEL 100, ETC.

MODEL 43

Introduced in 1949, this rifle was chambered for the .218 Bee, .22 Hornet, .25-20 Winchester, and the .32-20 Winchester. The rifle was a bolt-action with detachable box magazine, fitted with a 24" round barrel and front sight ramp forged integrally with barrel. This model was not drilled and tapped for scope blocks except for a few late rifles. This model was available in two styles:

1) Standard Rifle, 24" round barrel, plain walnut pistol-grip stock and forend. One inch sling swivels are standard.

2) Special Rifle, 24" round barrel, select walnut checkered pistol-grip stock and checkered forend. Furnished with either open sporting rear sight or Lyman 57A micrometer receiver sight.

The Model 43 was produced from 1949 to 1957 with about 63,000 sold.

STANDARD RIFLE

EXC.	V.G.	GOOD	FAIR	POOR
650	550	400	300	200

SPECIAL RIFLE OR DELUXE

EXC.	V.G.	GOOD	FAIR	POOR
750	650	550	250	175

NOTE: For rifles chambered for .25-20 and .32-20 add a 50 percent premium. For rifles with non-factory drilled and tapped scope holes deduct 40 percent.

MODEL 47

This model was a single-shot bolt-action rifle chambered for the .22 Short, Long, and LR interchangeably. The rifle was furnished with a 25" round barrel, plain walnut pistol-grip stock and forend. The bolt, bolt handle, and trigger are chrome plated. This model has a special bolt with a post on the underside. This moves into the safety position when the bolt is closed.This model was not serial numbered. Produced between 1948 and 1954, Winchester sold about 43,000 guns.

EXC.	V.G.	GOOD	FAIR	POOR
450	350	250	200	150

MODEL 47 TARGET RIFLE

Fitted with a 28" round standard weight or heavyweight barrel, plain walnut modified pistol-grip stock with correct bolt.

EXC.	V.G.	GOOD	FAIR	POOR
650	500	350	250	150

NOTE: Add 10 percent premium for Model 47 with factory peep sight.

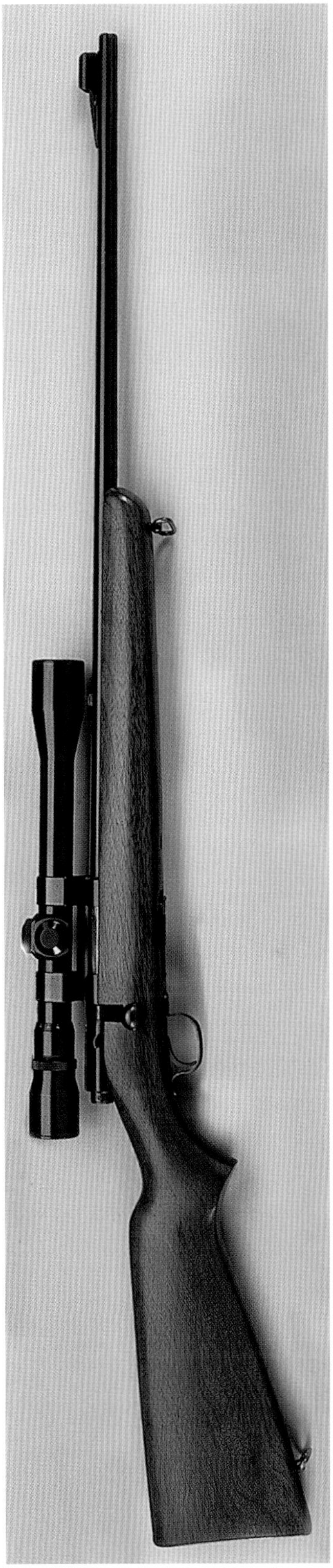

Model 43. Scope not original.

"One of the finest small-caliber bolt-action rifles ever built, the Model 52 was Winchester's answer to the increased demand for a military-style target rifle following WWI."

MODEL 51 IMPERIAL BOLT-ACTION MAGAZINE RIFLE

Designed by T.C. Johnson, approximately 25 of these rifles were made during 1919 and 1920 in two different styles and three calibers. The takedown variation has an overall length of 42-1/4", barrel length 22" and was made in .27, .30-06 and .35 Newton calibers. The solid frame version is identical in form, dimensions and calibers. Sight configurations and markings vary. To0 rare to price.

MODEL 52

Editor's Comment: According to Winchester factory records, Model 52 barrels were "originally drilled and tapped for Winchester telescope bases designed for use with the Winchester 3A, 5A, and Lyman telescopes." These bases had a 6.2" center-to-center spacing ... a change in the bases and the spacing to be used was authorized on January 11, 1933. These new bases had a specially shaped Fecker-type notch added on the right-hand side of both bases. They are known as Winchester Combination Telescope Sight Bases and are satisfactory for use with Winchester, Lyman, Fecker, and Unertl telescopes. Bases are spaced 7.2" center to center. All Model 52 targets were factory drilled for scope mounting but only the "C" series Sporters were factory drilled for scopes.

One of the finest small-caliber bolt-action rifles ever built, the Model 52 was Winchester's answer to the increased demand for a military-style target rifle following WWI. The Model 52 was a well-made quality-built bolt-action rifle. The rifle was chambered for the .22 LR cartridge. Designed by T.C. Johnson, this rifle was built in several different configurations over its production life:

1) Model 52 with finger groove in forend and one barrel band. Produced from 1920 to 1929.
2) Model 52 Target Rifle, same as above but without finger groove in forend and has first speed lock. Made from 1929 to 1932.

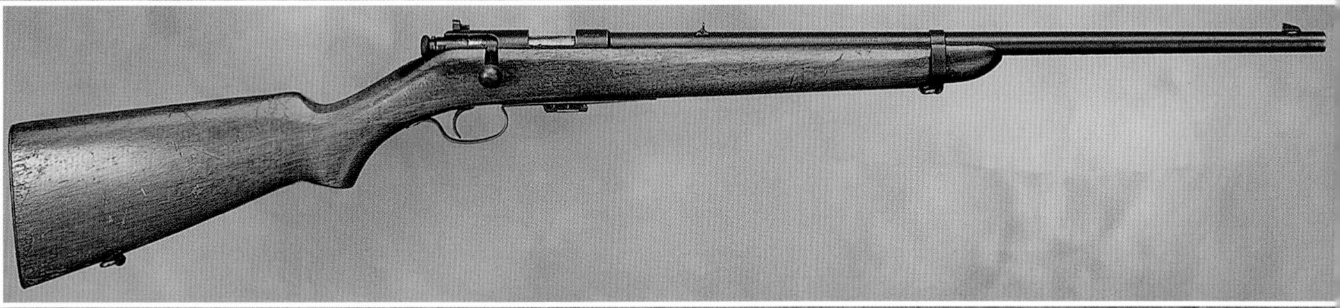

Model 52 Target.

3) Model 52A Target Rifle, same as above with addition of reinforced receiver and locking lug. Made from 1932 to 1935.
4) Model 52B Target Rifle, same as above with addition of adjustable sling swivel and single-shot adaptor. Made from 1935 to 1947.
5) Model 52C Target Rifle, same as above with addition of an easily adjustable vibration-free trigger mechanism. Made from 1947 to 1961.
6) Model 52D Target Rifle, this is a single-shot rifle with free-floating barrel and new design stock with adjustable hand-stop channel.
7) Model 52 Bull Gun, same as target rifle but fitted with extra heavyweight barrel. Made from 1939 to 1960. The Bull Barrel measures 1.125" at the receiver juncture while the heavyweight measures 1". Both barrels measure .875" at the muzzle.
8) Model 52 International Match, a free-style stock with thumb hole and adjustable buttstock and forend introduced in 1969. International Prone model with no thumb hole or adjustable buttplate and forend was introduced in 1975. Both discontinued in 1980.
9) Model 52 Sporter, 24" round barrel, select walnut checkered pistol-grip stock with cheekpiece and forend with black plastic tip. Pistol grip was furnished with hard-rubber grip cap. The Model 52 Sporter was introduced in 1934 and discontinued in 1958. It went through the same improvements as the Target Rifle, thus the designation Model 52A Sporter, etc.

MODEL 52 STANDARD

EXC.	V.G.	GOOD	FAIR	POOR
750	600	450	350	200

MODEL 52 TARGET

EXC.	V.G.	GOOD	FAIR	POOR
1250	1100	850	700	350

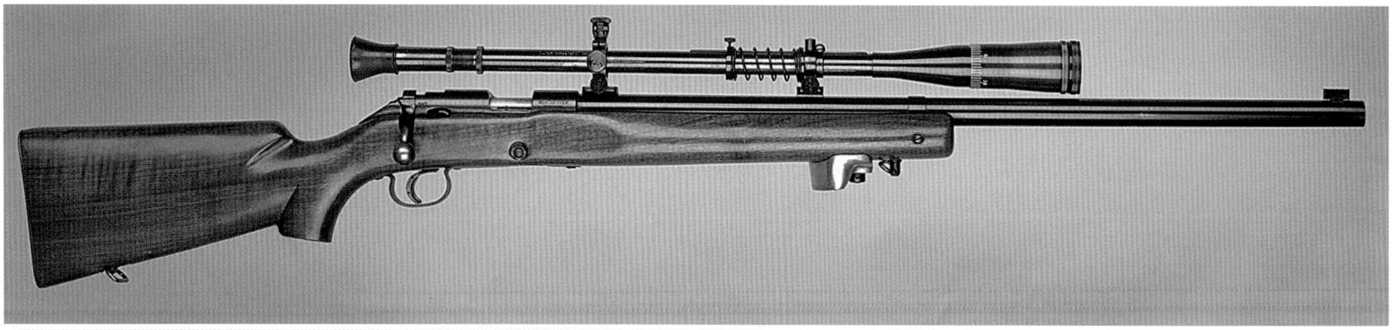

Model 52B Target Heavy Barrel.

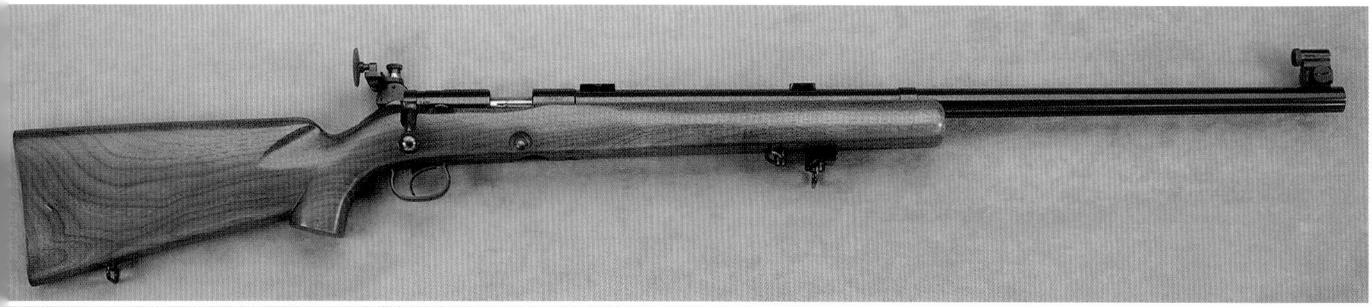

Model 52 Target, Bull Barrel.

MODEL 52 TARGET-SPEED LOCK

EXC.	V.G.	GOOD	FAIR	POOR
1200	1000	750	600	350

MODEL 52A TARGET HEAVY BARREL-RARE

EXC.	V.G.	GOOD	FAIR	POOR
1200	1000	750	600	350

MODEL 52B TARGET HEAVY & STANDARD BARREL

EXC.	V.G.	GOOD	FAIR	POOR
1000	900	650	500	300

MODEL 52B TARGET BULL BARREL

EXC.	V.G.	GOOD	FAIR	POOR
1200	1000	900	700	500

MODEL 52C TARGET

EXC.	V.G.	GOOD	FAIR	POOR
1200	1000	750	600	400

MODEL 52D TARGET

EXC.	V.G.	GOOD	FAIR	POOR
1300	1100	1000	850	400

MODEL 52B BULL GUN

EXC.	V.G.	GOOD	FAIR	POOR
1300	1100	1000	850	400

MODEL 52C BULL GUN

EXC.	V.G.	GOOD	FAIR	POOR
1300	1100	1000	850	500

MODEL 52 INTERNATIONAL MATCH

Approximately 300 manufactured.

FREE STYLE

EXC.	V.G.	GOOD	FAIR	POOR
3250	2500	1750	1000	500

PRONE

EXC.	V.G.	GOOD	FAIR	POOR
1100	950	850	600	500

MODEL 52 SPORTER-B & C MODELS

EXC.	V.G.	GOOD	FAIR	POOR
3600	3000	2000	1600	900

NOTE: Add 50 percent to above prices for "A" or pre-"A" series sporters. These are very rare early models in the Sporter Series.

MODEL 52B SPORTING RIFLE

A 1993 limited-edition rifle (6,000 guns) that is a faithful reproduction of the famous Winchester Model 52 Sporter. Equipped with a 24" barrel, adjustable trigger, and "B" style cheekpiece. This model was reissued in 1997 and limited to 3,000 rifles.

NIB	EXC.	V.G.	GOOD	FAIR	POOR
1100	750	500	375	250	150

MODEL 54

The Model 54 was to centerfire cartridges what the Model 52 was to rimfire cartridges. The Model 54 was also a quality-made bolt-action rifle with a nondetachable box magazine and was chambered for a variety of calibers: .270, .30-06, .30- 30, 7mm, 7.65, 9.mm, .250-3000, .22 Hornet, .220 Swift, and .257 Roberts. This was Winchester's

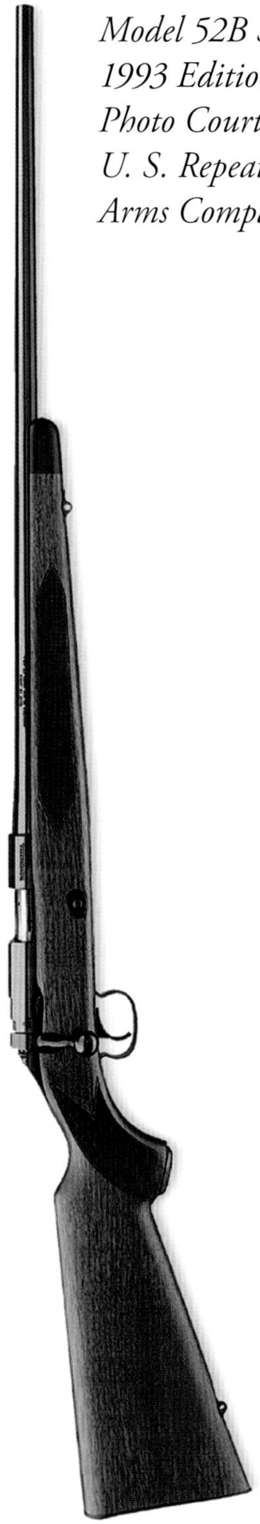

Model 52B Sporter, 1993 Edition. Photo Courtesy U. S. Repeating Arms Company.

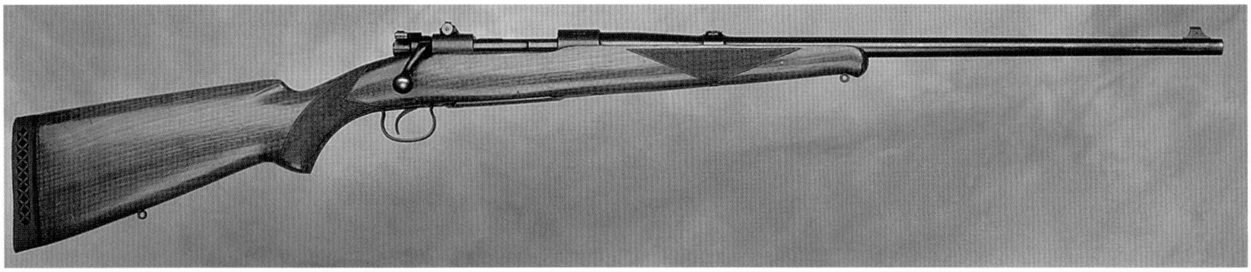

Model 54.

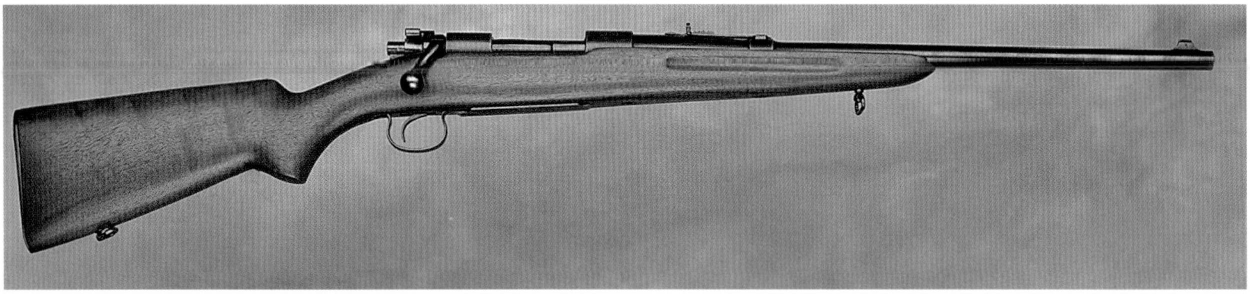

Model 54 Carbine.

first bolt-action rifle built for heavy, high velocity ammunition. The rifle was available in several different styles:

1) Standard Rifle, 24" or 20" round barrel (except .220 Swift, which was 26"), plain walnut checkered pistol-grip stock and forend.
2) Carbine, 20" round barrel, plain walnut pistol-grip stock with finger groove on each side of forend.
3) Sniper's Rifle, 26" round heavyweight barrel, plain walnut pistol-grip stock and forend.
4) N.R.A. Rifle, 24" round barrel, select walnut checkered pistol-grip stock and forend.
5) Super Grade Rifle, 24" round barrel, select walnut checkered pistol-grip stock with cheekpiece and checkered forend with black plastic tip. Pistol grip was capped with hard rubber cap. Super Grade was equipped with 1" detachable sling swivels.
6) Target Rifle, 24" round heavyweight barrel, plain walnut checkered pistol-grip stock and forend.
7) National Match Rifle, 24" round barrel, plain walnut special target stock and forend.

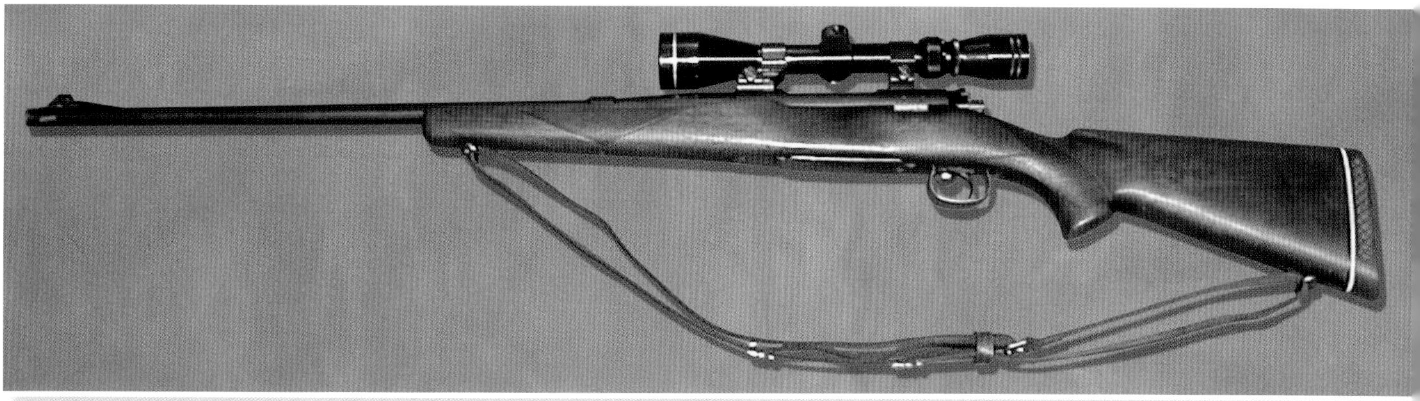

Model 54. Scope, sling and buttpad not origional.

The Model 54 was introduced in 1925 and was discontinued in 1936 with about 50,000 guns sold.

STANDARD RIFLE

EXC.	V.G.	GOOD	FAIR	POOR
650	550	400	300	225

CARBINE

EXC.	V.G.	GOOD	FAIR	POOR
700	600	450	350	275

SNIPER'S RIFLE

EXC.	V.G.	GOOD	FAIR	POOR
900	750	600	500	350

N.R.A. RIFLE

EXC.	V.G.	GOOD	FAIR	POOR
900	750	600	500	350

SUPER GRADE RIFLE

EXC.	V.G.	GOOD	FAIR	POOR
900	750	600	450	375

TARGET RIFLE

EXC.	V.G.	GOOD	FAIR	POOR
900	750	600	450	375

NATIONAL MATCH RIFLE

EXC.	V.G.	GOOD	FAIR	POOR
900	750	600	450	375

NOTE: The rare calibers are the 7mm, 7.65mm and the 9mm, which bring considerable premiums (in some cases as much as 250 percent) over standard calibers. Popular calibers such as .22 Hornet, .220 Swift, .30-30, and .257 Roberts will also bring a premium. Proceed with caution on Model 54s with rare caliber markings.

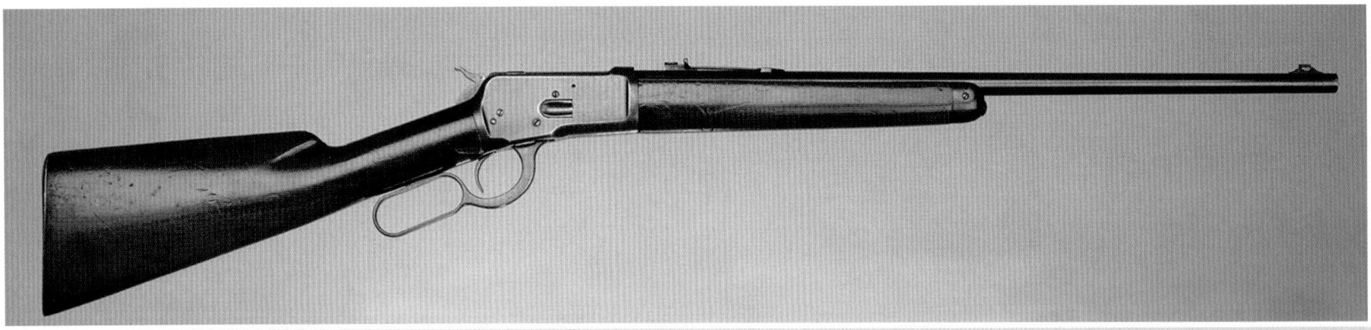

Model 53.

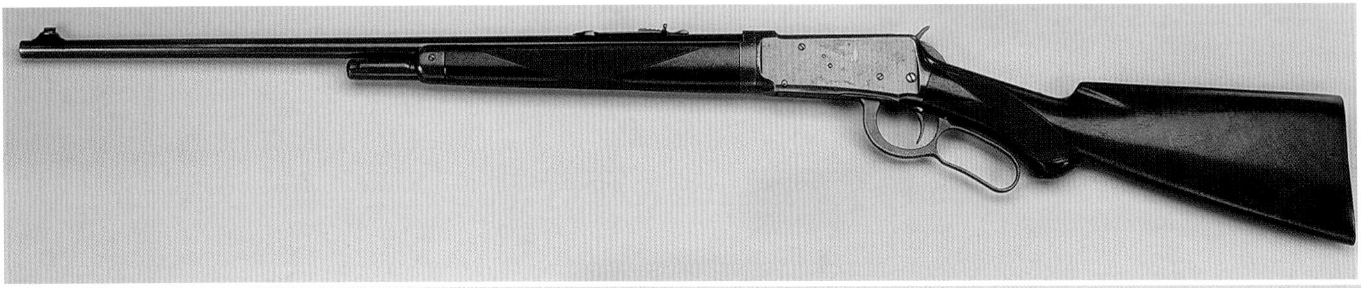

Model 55 Deluxe Takedown Rifle.

MODEL 53

This model was in fact a slightly more modern version of the Model 1892 offered in these calibers: .25-20, .32-20, and the .44-40. It was available in only one style: the Sporting Rifle, 22" round barrel, half magazine, straight- or pistol-grip plain walnut stock with shotgun butt. It was available in solid frame or takedown with blued frame and barrel. The Model 53 was produced from 1924 to 1932 with about 25,000 built.

SPORTING RIFLE

EXC.	V.G.	GOOD	FAIR	POOR
3500	2500	1000	500	300

NOTE: Add 10 percent for takedown model. Add 40 percent for rifles chambered for .44-40 cartridge. A few of these rifles were fitted with stainless steel barrel in the early 1930s. If the black paint on these barrels is in good condition, they will bring a substantial premium.

MODEL 55

This model was a continuation of the Model 1894 except in a simplified version. Available in the same calibers as the Model 1894, this rifle could be ordered only with a 24" round barrel, plain walnut straight-grip stock with plain forend and shotgun butt. Frame and barrel were blued with solid or takedown features. This model was produced between 1924 and 1932 with about 21,000 sold. Serial numbers for the Model 55 were numbered separately until about serial number 4500; then the guns were numbered in the Model 1894 sequence.

STANDARD RIFLE

EXC.	V.G.	GOOD	FAIR	POOR
1500	1000	650	450	200

NOTE: .25-35 caliber will bring about a 60 percent premium. Add 10 percent for models with solid frame.

MODEL 55 RIMFIRE RIFLE

Not to be confused with the lever-action model, this .22 caliber rifle was a semi-automatic single-shot with a 22" round barrel. Fitted with a plain walnut pistol-grip one-piece stock and forend. The safety goes on when each cartridge is inserted into the chamber. This model was not serial numbered and was produced from 1957 to 1961 with about 45,000 guns sold.

STANDARD RIFLE

EXC.	V.G.	GOOD	FAIR	POOR
250	200	125	100	60

MODEL 56

This model was designed to be a medium-priced bolt-action rimfire rifle. It featured a detachable box magazine and was chambered for the .22 Short or .22 LR cartridges. The rifle was offered in two styles:

1) Sporting Rifle, 22" round barrel, plain walnut pistol-grip stock and forend.
2) Fancy Sporting Rifle, 22" round barrel, fancy walnut checkered pistol-grip stock and forend.

Both styles had a forend with a distinctive lip on the forend tip. The rifle was introduced in 1926 and was discontinued in 1929 with about 8,500 rifles sold.

SPORTING RIFLE

EXC.	V.G.	GOOD	FAIR	POOR
1500	1000	750	525	400

FANCY SPORTING RIFLE

Very rare, use caution.

EXC.	V.G.	GOOD	FAIR	POOR
3000	2000	1500	900	750

NOTE: Add a 50 percent premium for rifles chambered for .22 Short only.

Model 55 Rimfire Rifle.

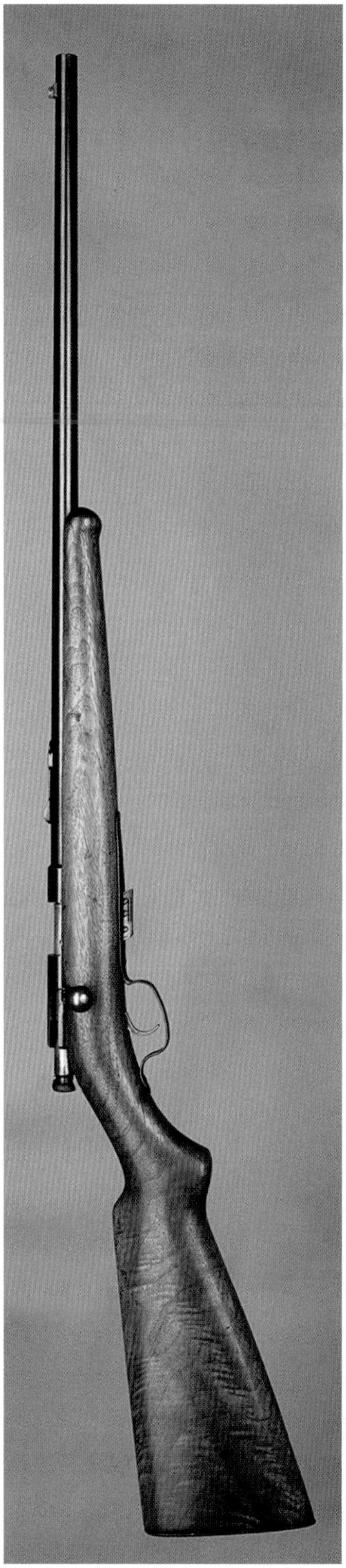

Model 57 Sporting Rifle.

MODEL 57

The Model 57 was close in appearance to the Model 56 with the addition of a heavier stock, target sights, and swivel bows attached to the stock. The rifle was chambered for the .22 Short or .22 LR and featured a 22" round barrel with detachable box magazine. The stock was plain walnut with pistol grip and plain forend. The rifle was introduced in 1927 and dropped from the Winchester line in 1936 having sold only about 19,000 guns.

EXC.	V.G.	GOOD	FAIR	POOR
750	600	450	325	250

NOTE: Add 20 percent premium for web sling.

MODEL 58

This model was an attempt by the company to market a low-priced .22 caliber rimfire rifle in place of its Models 1902 and 1904. This was a single-shot bolt-action, cocked by pulling the firing pin head to the rear. It had an 18" round barrel and was chambered for the .22 Short, Long, and LR interchangeably. The stock was a one-piece plain wood with straight grip. This model was not serial-numbered. The Model 58 was introduced in 1928 and discontinued in 1931. About 39,000 were sold.

EXC.	V.G.	GOOD	FAIR	POOR
2000	1000	425	250	125

MODEL 59

The Model 59 was essentially a Model 58 with the addition of a pistol-grip stock and a 23" round barrel. Introduced in 1930, it was dropped from the product line in the same year with a total sales of about 9,000 guns.

EXC.	V.G.	GOOD	FAIR	POOR
2000	1000	400	200	125

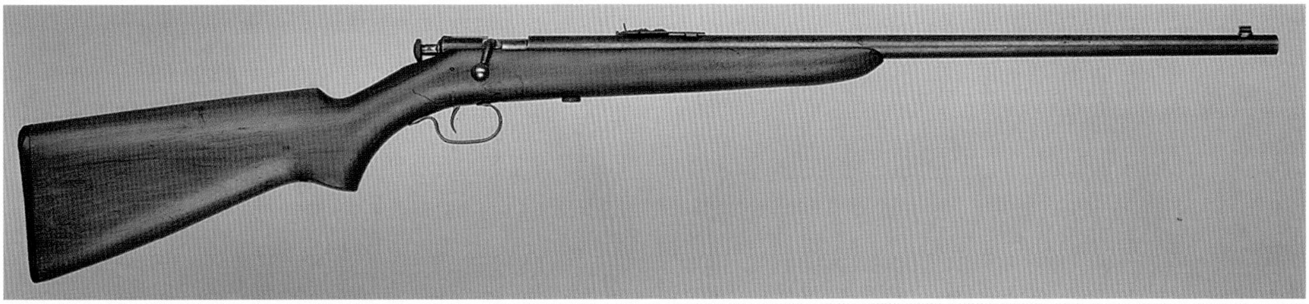

Model 60.

MODEL 60 AND 60A

This rifle used the same action as that of the Model 59. When the rifle was first introduced in 1931, it was furnished with a 23" round barrel which was changed to 27" in 1933. Several other mechanical improvements were included with this model; perhaps the most noticeable were the chrome-plated bolt, bolt handle, and trigger. The stock was plain wood with pistol grip. In 1933 the Model 60A was added, which was the same rifle but in a target configuration. The front sight was a square top military blade with a Lyman 55W receiver sight. The Model 60 was discontinued in 1934 with about 166,000 rifles sold. The Model 60A was dropped in 1939 with only about 6,100 rifles sold.

MODEL 60

EXC.	V.G.	GOOD	FAIR	POOR
400	250	200	150	100

MODEL 60A

EXC.	V.G.	GOOD	FAIR	POOR
400	300	250	150	100

MODEL 61

Winchester developed the Model 61 in an attempt to keep pace with its competitors' hammerless .22 rifles. The Model 61 featured a 24" round or octagonal barrel and could be ordered by the customer in a variety of configurations, and is often considered to be the best hammerless pump 22 rifle ever manufactured. Collector interest in this rifle is high because of its quality and the fairly large number of variations. The Model 61 is often considered a companion to the Winchester Model 12 and Model 42 shotguns.The following is a list of chamber and barrel variations found in this model:

- 1.24" round barrel, .22 Short, Long, LR
- 2.24" octagonal barrel, .22 Short only add 200 percent.
- 3.24" octagonal barrel, .22 LR only add 200 percent.
- 4.24" octagonal barrel, .22 W.R.F. only add 200 percent.
- 5.24" round barrel, .22 LR Shot only add 300 percent.

- 5A.24" round barrel, shot only Routledge bore add 300 percent.
- 6.24" round barrel, .22 W.R.F. only add 200 percent.
- 7.24" round barrel, .22 LR only add 200 percent.
- 8.24" round barrel, .22 Winchester Magnum add 200 percent.
- 9.24" round barrel, .22 Short only add 200 percent.

The Model 61 was fitted with a plain walnut pistol-grip stock with grooved slide handle. All Model 61s were of the take down variety. Prewar models will have a short slide handle. Manufactured between 1932 and 1963, approximately 342,000 guns were sold.

PRE-WAR MODEL 61

NIB	EXC.	V.G.	GOOD	FAIR	POOR
2500	1500	800	600	325	200

NOTE: Single caliber models will command a premium of 50 percent depending on caliber. Octagon barrel models will command a premium of 75 percent. .22 LR shot only models will bring a premium of 250 percent.

POST-WAR MODEL 61

NIB	EXC.	V.G.	GOOD	FAIR	POOR
1750	800	550	450	250	150

MODEL 61 MAGNUM

NIB	EXC.	V.G.	GOOD	FAIR	POOR
1950	950	775	600	400	250

NOTE: This variation (Model 61 Magnum) was produced from 1960 to 1963.

MODEL 62 AND 62A

When the Model 1890 and Model 1906 were dropped from the Winchester product line in 1932, the company introduced the Model 62 to take their place. An updated version of the earlier slide-action .22 rifles, the Model 62 was fitted with a 23" round barrel and was capable of shooting .22 Short, Long, and LR cartridges interchangeably. Winchester of-

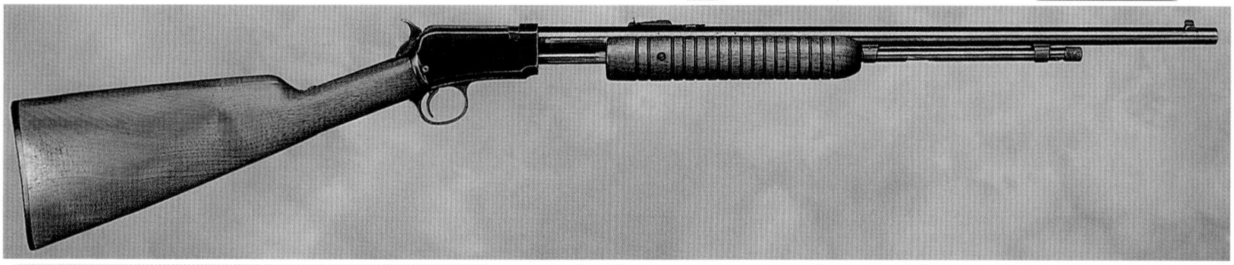

Model 62.

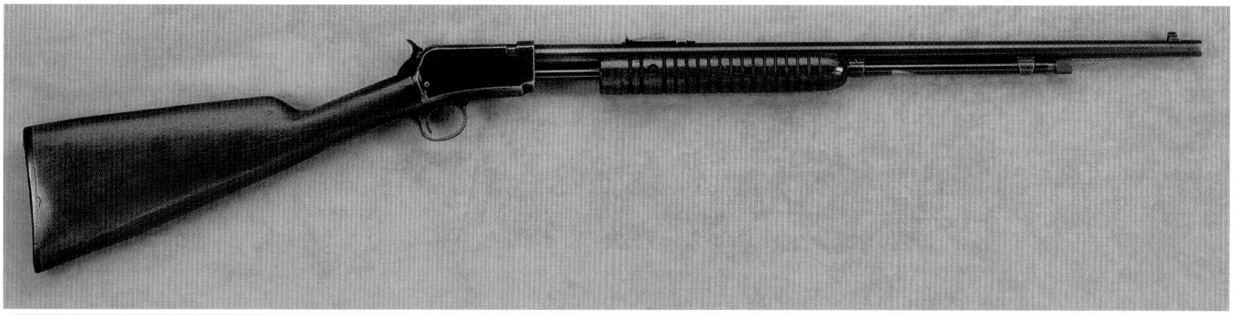

Model 62A.

fered a Gallery version of the Model 62 that was chambered for .22 Short only. Some of these Gallery guns have "Winchester" stamped on the left side of the receiver. Winchester Model 62 Gallery rifles have a triangular loading port on the loading tube that the standard models did not have. A change in the breech bolt mechanism brought about a change in the name designation from Model 62 to Model 62A. This occurred around serial number 98000. The letter "A" now appears behind the serial number. This model stayed in production until 1958, and collectors will concede a premium for guns built prior to WWII with small slide handles. The stock was of plain walnut with straight grip and grooved slide handle. Both the receiver and barrel were blued. All Model 62 and 62As were takedown. Approximately 409,000 guns were sold.

PRE-WAR MODEL 62 WITH THE WINCHESTER LOGO ON THE TOP TANG.

NIB	EXC.	V.G.	GOOD	FAIR	POOR
3000	1250	850	400	250	150

PRE-WAR MODEL 62 WITHOUT THE WINCHESTER LOGO ON THE TOP TANG.

NIB	EXC.	V.G.	GOOD	FAIR	POOR
2500	1000	650	400	250	150

NOTE: Barrels marked with Model 62 are worth more than barrels marked with Model 62A by approximately 25 percent. Gallery models will bring a premium of 300 percent.

POST-WAR MODEL 62

NIB	EXC.	V.G.	GOOD	FAIR	POOR
1500	750	450	325	225	125

MODEL 62 GALLERY

.22 Short only with triangular loading port & "winchester" stamped on side of receiver.

NIB	EXC.	V.G.	GOOD	FAIR	POOR
5000	2000	1000	650	400	200

NOTE: A Model 62 with "winchester" stamped on the side of the receiver is more desirable than one without the stamping. Deduct 10 percent for Gallery rifles without this stamping.

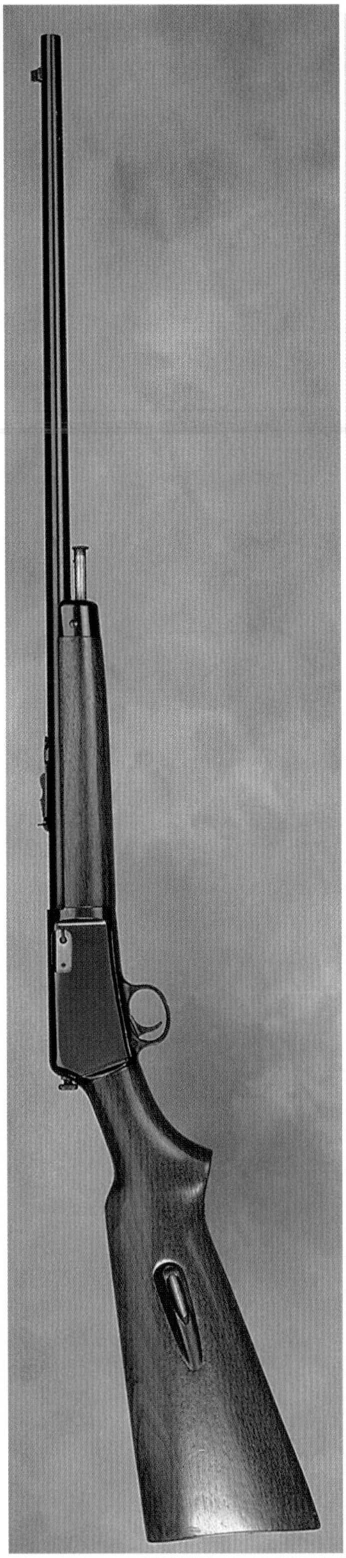

Model 63.

MODEL 63

The Model 63 took the place of the Model 1903 in 1933 in an attempt by Winchester to solve the problem of having to use a special .22 caliber cartridge in the gun to operate the blowback system. It is a very high quality semi-automatic rifle. Many collectors and shooters considered it the best rimfire semi-automatic rifle ever produced.The Model 63 was chambered for the .22 LR cartridge and was available in a 20" barrel for the first four years or until about serial number 9800. Thereafter, the model was offered with a 23" round barrel for the remainder of the production period. The gun was fitted with a plain walnut pistol-grip stock and forearm. The tubular magazine was located in the buttstock that came with a steel buttplate. The last 10,000 Model 63s were sold with a grooved receiver top to make the addition of a scope easier. Manufactured between 1933 and 1958, about 175,000 guns were sold.

20" BARREL

These weapons are extremely rare and the advice of an expert should be retained prior to purchasing.

NIB	EXC.	V.G.	GOOD	FAIR	POOR
2750	1600	1000	500	400	250

23" BARREL

NIB	EXC.	V.G.	GOOD	FAIR	POOR
1750	900	550	600	400	200

NOTE: Grooved top receivers command a premium of 20 percent.

POST-1964 MODEL 63

Introduced in 1997, this is a re-creation of the famous Model 63 .22 caliber auto. Fitted with a 23" barrel and 10-round tubular magazine. the receiver top is grooved for scope mounting.

GRADE I

NIB	EXC.	V.G.	GOOD	FAIR	POOR
675	525	-	-	-	-

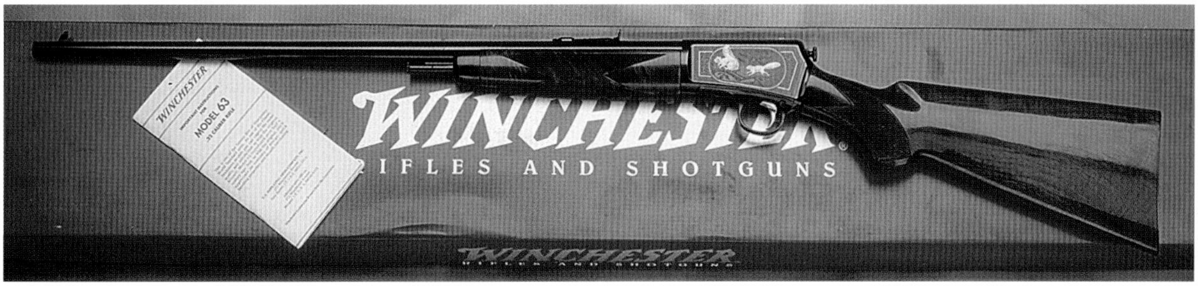

Post-64 Model 63 High Grade Rifle.

Model 63 High Grade Rifle, Closeup of Receiver, Right View.

Model 63 High Grade Rifle, Closeup of Receiver, Left View.

Model 64 Standard Rifle.

MODEL 64

An improved version of the Model 55, this gun featured a larger magazine, pistol-grip stock, and forged front sight ramp. The trigger pull was also improved. Frame and barrel were blued. Chambered for the .25-35 Win., .30-30 Win., .32 Win. Special, and the .219 zipper added in 1938 (and discontinued in the Model 64 in 1941). Serial number of the Model 64 was concurrent with the Model 1894. Built between 1933 and 1957, approximately 67,000 were sold. This model was reintroduced in 1972 and discontinued in 1973.

STANDARD RIFLE

EXC.	V.G.	GOOD	FAIR	POOR
1200	900	500	300	200

CARBINE

20" barrel.

EXC.	V.G.	GOOD	FAIR	POOR
1550	1000	650	500	250

NOTE: For Deluxe model add 50 percent to above prices. For Carbine model add 50 percent to above prices. For rifles chambered for the .219 Zipper and .25-35 cartridges add 50 percent. Add 10 percent for bolt peep sight. Model 64s in .219 Zipper left the factory with bolt peep sights as original equipment.

POST-1964 MODEL 64

This is a post-1964 version of the lever-action Model 64. It is chambered for the .30-30 cartridge and has a 24" round barrel with open sights and a 5-round, 2/3-length tubular magazine. The finish is blued with a plain walnut pistol-grip stock. It was manufactured between 1972 and 1974.

EXC.	V.G.	GOOD	FAIR	POOR
300	250	190	125	100

MODEL 65

This model was a continuation of the Model 53 and was offered in three calibers: .25-20, .32-20, and .218 Bee. It had several improvements over the Model 53, namely the magazine capacity was increased to seven cartridges, forged ramp for front sight, and a lighter trigger pull. The Model 65 was

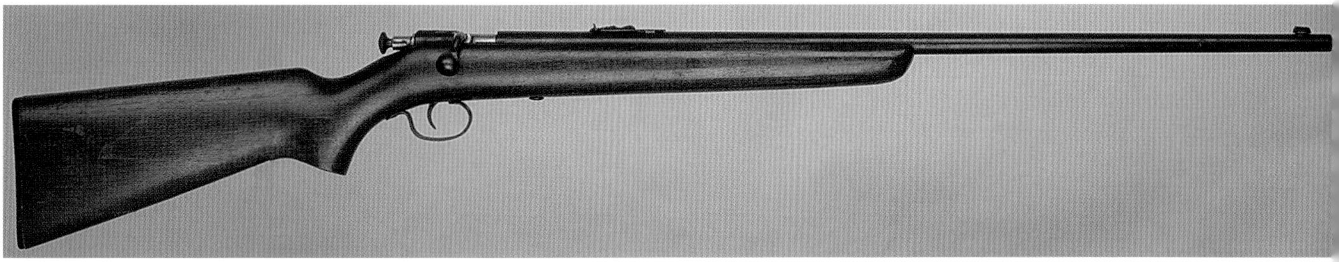

Model 67.

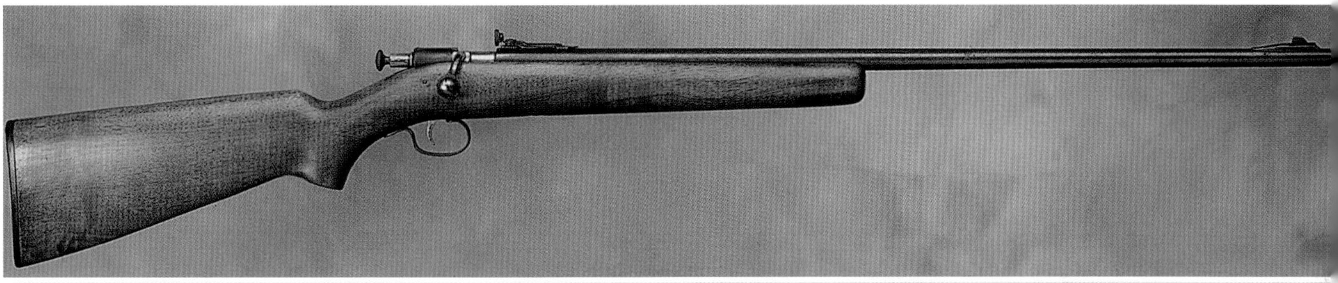

Model 67, Late Production.

available only in solid blued frame with blued barrel and pistol grip with plain walnut stock. Only about 5,700 of these rifles were built between 1933 and 1947.

STANDARD RIFLE

EXC.	V.G.	GOOD	FAIR	POOR
3500	2500	1000	550	250

NOTE: Add 10 percent for bolt peep sight. Model 65s in .218 Bee left the factory with bolt peep sights as original equipment.

MODEL 67

Winchester again upgraded and improved the Model 60 with an expansion of the styles offered to the shooting public. The standard chambering for the rifle was .22 Short, Long, and LR interchangeably, with the W.R.F. added in 1935. The Model 67 was available in four styles:

1) Sporting Rifle, 27" round barrel, stock similar to the Model 60.
2) Smoothbore Rifle, 27" barrel, chambered for the .22 long shot or .22 LR shot.
3) Junior Rifle, 20" round barrel and shorter stock.
4) Rifle with miniature target boring, 24" round barrel, chambered for .22 LR shot.

Model 67s were not serial numbered for domestic sales but were numbered for foreign sales. Introduced in 1934 the gun was dropped from the line in 1963 having sold about 384,000. Many of these models were fitted at the factory with telescopes, and the bases were mounted on the rifle and the scope was packed separately.

SPORTING RIFLE

EXC.	V.G.	GOOD	FAIR	POOR
200	150	125	100	75

SMOOTHBORE RIFLE

EXC.	V.G.	GOOD	FAIR	POOR
800	600	400	250	200

JUNIOR RIFLE

EXC.	V.G.	GOOD	FAIR	POOR
250	200	175	150	125

MINIATURE TARGET RIFLE

This model is marked "for shot only" and has beads instead of standard iron rifle sights.

EXC.	V.G.	GOOD	FAIR	POOR
1200	900	700	400	300

MODEL 68

Another takeoff on the Model 67, this model differed only in the sight equipment offered. Winchester fitted this rifle with its own 5-power telescopes. First sold in 1934 the Model 68 was dropped in 1946 with sales of about 101,000.

WITH SCOPE

EXC.	V.G.	GOOD	FAIR	POOR
750	500	300	200	150

WITHOUT SCOPE

EXC.	V.G.	GOOD	FAIR	POOR
300	225	150	100	75

NOTE: Rifles with factory scopes and no sights add 50 percent. For rifles with factory scopes and no sights chambered for .22 WRF add 200 percent.

MODEL 69 AND 69A

This model was designed by Winchester to answer the demand for a medium-priced hunting and target .22 rimfire bolt- action rifle. The rifle had a detachable box magazine, and many were offered with factory-installed telescopes in 2-3/4 and 5 power. The stock was plain walnut with pistol grip and plain forend. This model was not serial numbered. The 69A version was introduced in 1937 and featured an improved cocking mechanism. Introduced in 1935 as the Model 69, this gun was dropped in 1963 with sales of about 355,000 guns.

EXC.	V.G.	GOOD	FAIR	POOR
450	375	300	200	100

NOTE: Add 25 percent for Target Model. Add 20 percent for grooved receiver.

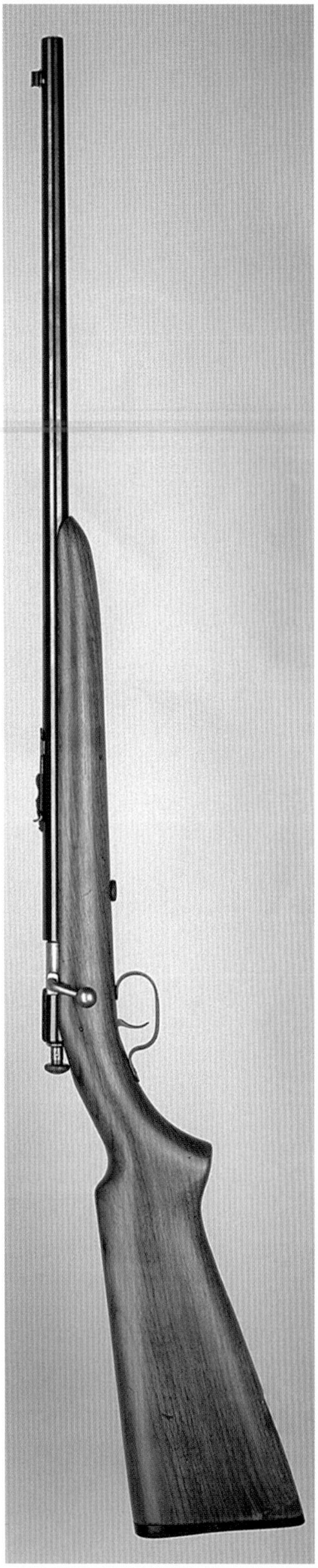

Model 67 Junior Rifle.

MODEL 70

Considered by many as the finest bolt-action rifle ever built in the United States, the pre-1964 Model 70 is highly sought after by shooters and collectors alike. Its smooth, strong action has no peer. It is often referred to as "The Riflemen's Rifle." The Model 70 is an updated and improved version of the Model 54 and features a hinged floorplate, new speed locks, new safety design that does not interfere with telescope, manually releasable bolt stop, more attractive buttstock and forend, and forged steel trigger guard. Like many Winchesters, the Model 70 was available with several extra-cost options that should be evaluated by an expert. The values listed are given for pre-1964 Model 70s with serial numbers from 1 to 581471. This rifle was available in several different styles:

1) Standard Grade, 24" round barrel (except 26" round barrel for .220 Swift and .300 H&H Magnum-25" round barrel for .375 H&H Magnum after 1937), plain walnut checkered pistol stock and forend. Built from 1936 to 1963.
2) Standard Grade Carbine, 20" round barrel, chambered for .22 Hornet, .250-3000, .257 Roberts, .270, 7mm, and .30- 06, same stock as Standard Grade. Built from 1936 to 1946.
3) Super Grade Rifle, same barrel and calibers as Standard Grade, select walnut checkered and capped pistol-grip stock with cheekpiece and checkered forend with plastic tip. Built from 1936 to 1960.
4) Featherweight, 22" round barrel chambered for .243, .264, .270, .308, .30-06, and .358. Fitted with aluminum trigger guard, aluminum buttplate, and aluminum floor plate. Later versions with plastic buttplate. Built from 1952 to 1963.
5) Featherweight Super Grade, same as above except not chambered for the .358 cartridge, but fitted with Super Grade stock. Built from 1952 to 1963.

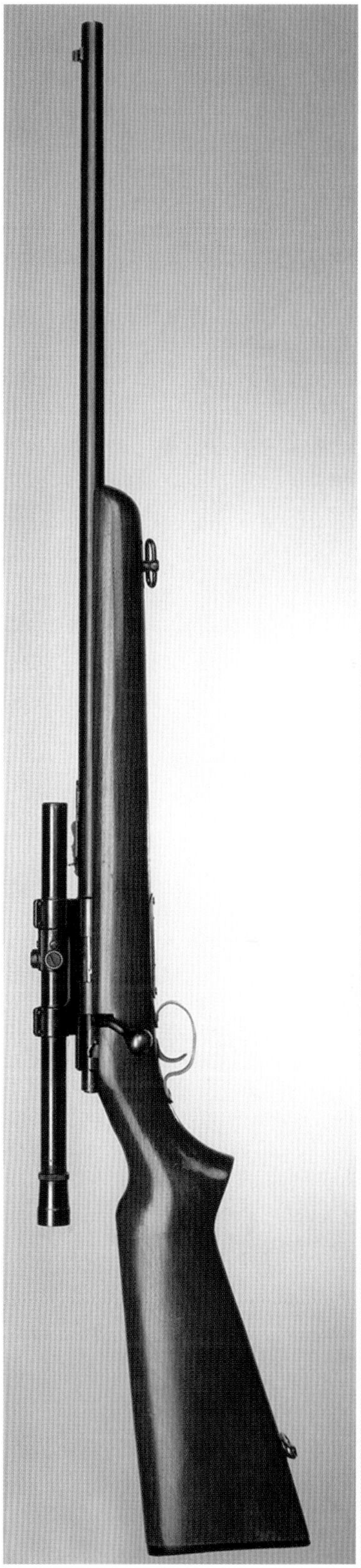

Model 69. Scope not original

Extremely rare Model 70 Sniper's Rifle as used by United States Marine Corps. Too rare to Price.

6) National Match, same as Standard Grade but fitted with target type stock and telescope bases. Chambered for .30- 06 only. Discontinued in 1960.
7) Target, 24" round medium-weight barrel with same stock as National Match in .243 and .30-06 calibers. Discontinued in 1963.
8) Varmint, 26" round heavy barrel, with heavier varmint stock, chambered for .243 and the rare .220 Swift. Built from 1956 to 1963.
9) Westerner, 26" round barrel with Standard Grade stock, chambered for .264 Winchester Magnum. Built from 1960 to 1963. Fitted with a solid rubber pad for early production guns and a vented pad for later guns.
10) Alaskan, 25" round barrel, with Standard Grade stock, chambered for .338 Winchester Magnum and .375 H&H Magnum. Built from 1960 to 1963. Fitted with a solid rubber pad marked Winchester for early production guns and a vented pad both marked Winchester for later guns.
11) Bull Gun, 28" round barrel, same stock as National Match, chambered for .30-06 and .300 H&H Magnum. Built from 1936 to 1963.

The standard calibers offered for the Model 70 are these, in order of rarity: .300 Savage, .35 Rem., .458 Win Magnum, 7mm, .358 Win., .250-3000 Savage, .300 Win Magnum, .338 Win. Magnum, .375 H&H Magnum, .257 Roberts, .220 Swift, .22 Hornet, .264 Win. Magnum, .300 H&H Magnum, .308 Win., .243 Win., .270 W.C.F., .30-06.

NOTE: Prices for the Model 70 are, in many cases, based on the caliber of the rifle; the rarer the caliber, the more premium the gun will command. Many pre-1964 Model 70s are still available in new condition in the original box with all papers. Add 100 percent if the box is serial numbered to the gun. Use caution prior to purchase of NIB guns due to fake boxes and papers.

Model 70. "The Rifleman's Rifle."

PRICING NOTE: The asterisk (*) signifies the value of the rifle with respect to a usable action. Model 70 unaltered receivers bring $500 regardless of the condition of the barrel and stock. If the receiver is unusable then the rifle is worth the value of its usable parts, i.e., about $500-$850.

For Model 70s with "X" or "D" prefex add a collector premium of 10 percent. These letters indicate that there were two rifles mistakenly stamped with the same serial number.

STANDARD RIFLE

.30-06 Springfield (1937-1963).

PRE-WAR

EXC.	V.G.	GOOD	FAIR	POOR
2250	1650	800	500*	500*

POST-WAR

EXC.	V.G.	GOOD	FAIR	POOR
1150	925	600	500*	500*

.270 WIN. (1937-1963)

PRE-WAR

EXC.	V.G.	GOOD	FAIR	POOR
2250	1650	800	500*	500*

POST-WAR

EXC.	V.G.	GOOD	FAIR	POOR
1250	1000	600	500*	500*

.243. WIN. (1955-1963)

EXC.	V.G.	GOOD	FAIR	POOR
2750	2000	1000	500*	500*

.300 H&H MAGNUM (1937-1963)

PRE-WAR

EXC.	V.G.	GOOD	FAIR	POOR
3000	2750	1350	800	500*

POST-WAR

EXC.	V.G.	GOOD	FAIR	POOR
1850	1450	900	750	500*

.264 WIN. MAGNUM (1959-1963)

EXC.	V.G.	GOOD	FAIR	POOR
2450	1450	900	750	500*

.22 HORNET (1937-1958)

PRE-WAR

EXC.	V.G.	GOOD	FAIR	POOR
3500	2750	2000	1000	500*

POST-WAR

EXC.	V.G.	GOOD	FAIR	POOR
2250	1900	1150	750	500*

.220 SWIFT (1937-1963)

PRE-WAR

EXC.	V.G.	GOOD	FAIR	POOR
2750	2000	1250	900	500*

POST-WAR

EXC.	V.G.	GOOD	FAIR	POOR
1700	1150	900	650	500*

.257 ROBERTS (1937-1959)

PRE-WAR

EXC.	V.G.	GOOD	FAIR	POOR
3350	2950	1650	950	500*

POST-WAR

EXC.	V.G.	GOOD	FAIR	POOR
1950	1600	1000	750	500*

.375 H&H MAGNUM (1937-1963)

PRE-WAR

EXC.	V.G.	GOOD	FAIR	POOR
3900	3400	2000	1350	500*

POST-WAR

EXC.	V.G.	GOOD	FAIR	POOR
2500	2000	1350	900	500*

.338 WIN. MAGNUM (1959-1963)

EXC.	V.G.	GOOD	FAIR	POOR
2750	2250	1350	900	500*

.300 WIN. MAGNUM (1962-1963)

EXC.	V.G.	GOOD	FAIR	POOR
2250	1950	1000	750	500*

.250-3000 SAVAGE (1937-1949)

EXC.	V.G.	GOOD	FAIR	POOR
4000	3000	1650	950	500*

7MM (1937-1949)

EXC.	V.G.	GOOD	FAIR	POOR
5500	4500	2500	1700	700

.35 REM. (1944-1947)

EXC.	V.G.	GOOD	FAIR	POOR
8500	5750	3500	2000	950

.300 SAVAGE (1944-1950S?)

EXC.	V.G.	GOOD	FAIR	POOR
9000	8000	3600	2000	950

.458 AFRICAN (BUILT IN SUPER-GRADE ONLY, 1956-1963)

EXC.	V.G.	GOOD	FAIR	POOR
7000	5250	4000	2750	1350

FEATHERWEIGHT

EXC.	V.G.	GOOD	FAIR	POOR
1800	1150	875	700	450

NOTE: Add 100 percent for .358 Win. For .264 and .270 calibers add 25 percent.

FEATHERWEIGHT SUPER GRADE

EXC.	V.G.	GOOD	FAIR	POOR
5000	4000	3000	1650	1000

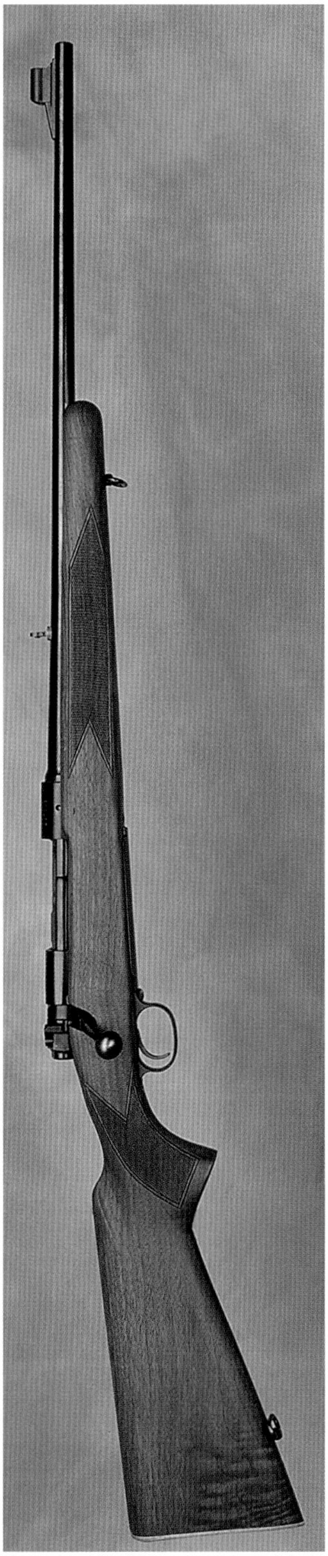

Model 70 Featherweight.

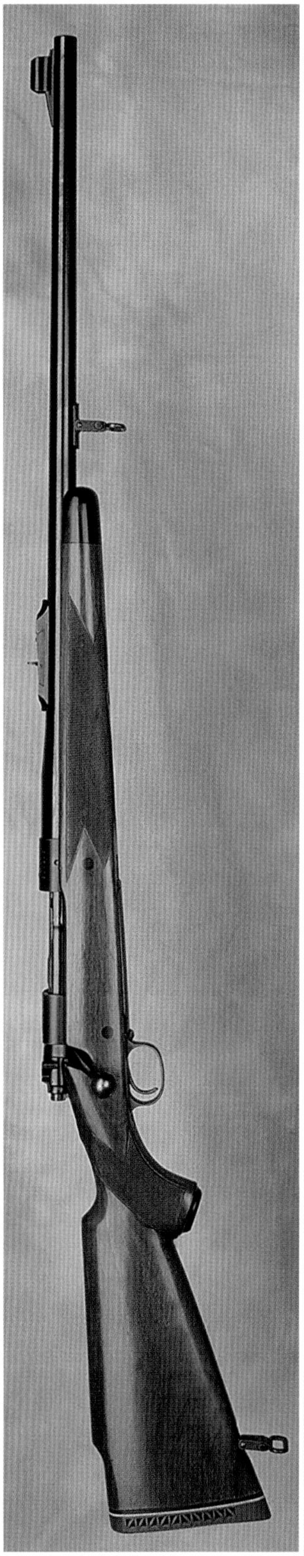

Model 70 African Super Grade .458 Magnum.

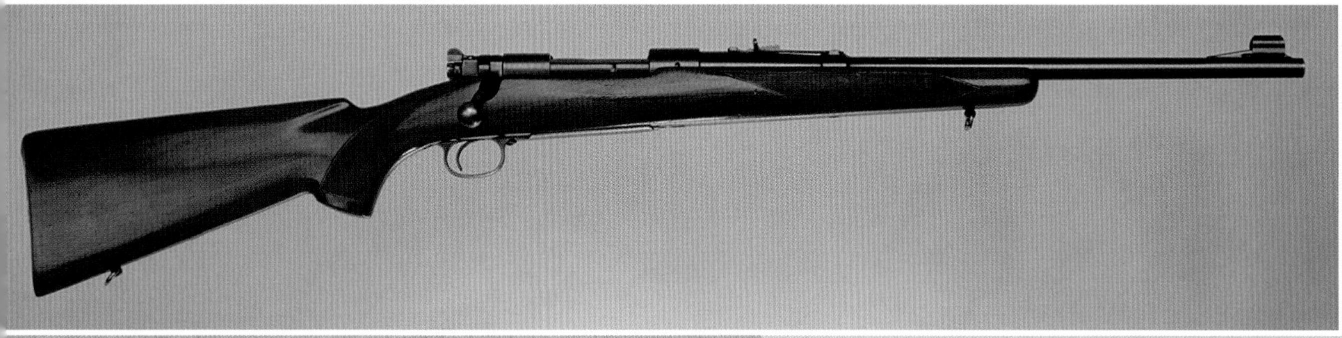

Model 70 Carbine.

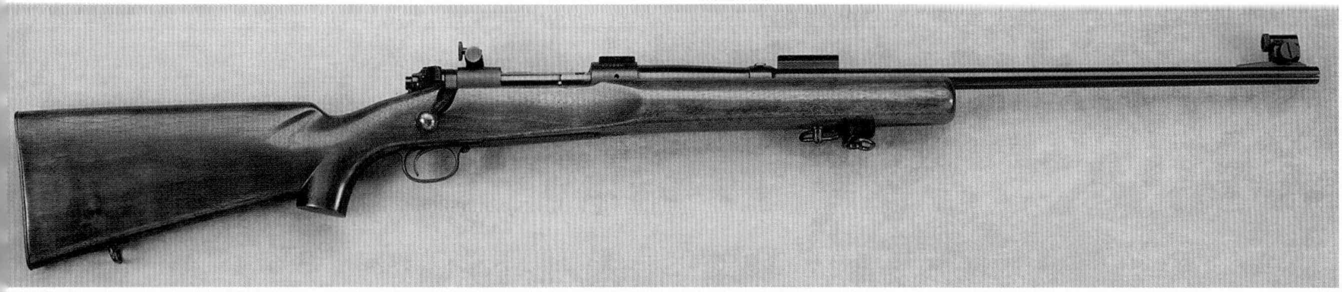

Model 70 National Match.

STANDARD GRADE CARBINE

EXC.	V.G.	GOOD	FAIR	POOR
4500	3500	1500	950	650

NOTE: For Supergrade rifles add 100 percent.

NATIONAL MATCH

EXC.	V.G.	GOOD	FAIR	POOR
3000	2250	1650	950	600

TARGET

EXC.	V.G.	GOOD	FAIR	POOR
2250	1800	950	750	550

VARMINT

EXC.	V.G.	GOOD	FAIR	POOR
1950	1650	750	600	375*

NOTE: Add 40 percent premium for .220 Swift.

BULL GUN

EXC.	V.G.	GOOD	FAIR	POOR
3500	2900	2250	850	600

POST-1964 MODEL 70 RIFLES

Winchester, or U.S. Repeating Arms, closed its doors in New Haven, Connecticut effective March 31, 2006. Collectors and dealers alike have already started to accumulate recently manufactured examples of these rifles. Many of these later weapons have been selling for as much as 50% over retail value. This may represent an opportunity for investment or for collecting weapons that exist in the marketplace in rather large numbers, but, for the most part, are still very affordable. Beware: production of these rifles may, at some point in time, reoccur, and if it does, it's likely that prices will recede to approximate recent levels. Also, please note that these rifles are not usually considered to be rare.

MODEL 70 FEATHERWEIGHT ULTRA GRADE

Limited to 1,000 rifles, this model is profusely engraved with game scene and gold line inlaid. Serial number inlaid in gold. Offered in .270 caliber with very fine-figured walnut stock with fine line checkering. Mahogany fitted case. Strongly suggest a qualified appraisal before sale.

NIB	EXC.	V.G.	GOOD	FAIR	POOR
5000	-	-	-	-	-

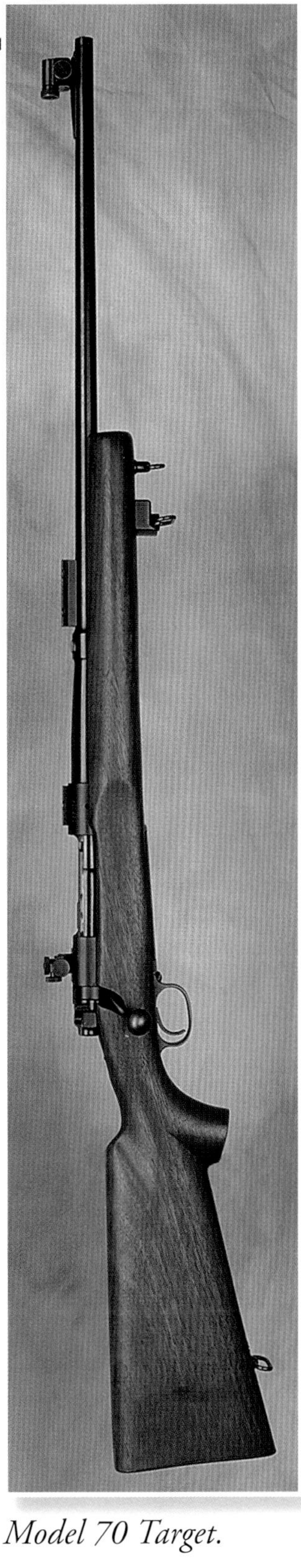

Model 70 Target.

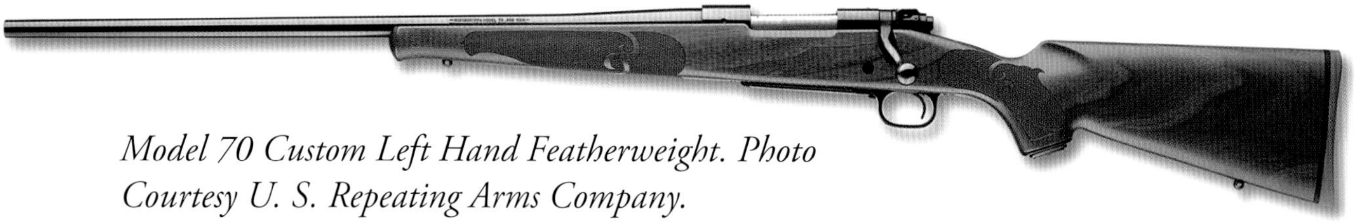

Model 70 Custom Left Hand Featherweight. Photo Courtesy U. S. Repeating Arms Company.

Model 70 Classic Custom Featherweight. Photo Courtesy U. S. Repeating Arms Company.

MODEL 70 CLASSIC CUSTOM FEATHERWEIGHT

Introduced in 2003 this rifle is chambered for the .270, 7mm Win. Mag., or the .30-06. Fitted with a 22" barrel. Semi-fancy walnut stock with schnabel forend. Offered in blued or stainless steel finish in either right- or left-hand models. Weight is about 7.25 lbs.

NIB	EXC.	V.G.	GOOD	FAIR	POOR
2700	-	-	-	-	-

MODEL 70 CUSTOM SHARPSHOOTER

A U.S.R.A. Custom Shop gun. This model is fitted with a stainless steel Schneider barrel with hand-honed action and hand fitted. The stock is a custom McMillan A-2 glass bedded stock. Offered in .223 Rem., .22-250 Rem., .308 Win. and .300 Win. Mag. Comes from the factory with a hard case.

NIB	EXC.	V.G.	GOOD	FAIR	POOR
1300	950	750	500	300	150

MODEL 70 CUSTOM CLASSIC SHARPSHOOTER II

Same as above but introduced in 1996 with an H-S heavy target stock, a pre-1964 action stainless steel H-S barrel. Weight is about 11 lbs. Offered in .22-250, .308, .30-06, and .300 Win. Mag.

NIB	EXC.	V.G.	GOOD	FAIR	POOR
1800	1400	-	-	-	-

MODEL 70 CUSTOM SPORTING SHARPSHOOTER

Essentially a take-off on the Custom Sharpshooter but configured for hunting. Fitted with a McMillan sporter-style gray stock and Schneider stainless steel barrel. Offered in .270 Win., .300 Win., and 7mm STW. Introduced in 1993.

NIB	EXC.	V.G.	GOOD	FAIR	POOR
1250	900	750	-	-	-

MODEL 70 CUSTOM CLASSIC SPORTING SHARPSHOOTER II

Introduced in 1996 this is an updated version of the model above. It features a pre-1964 action with H-S special fiberglass stock and stainless steel barrel. Available in 7mm STW, .300 Win. Mag. Weight is about 8.5 lbs.

NIB	EXC.	V.G.	GOOD	FAIR	POOR
1700	1400	-	-	-	-

MODEL 70 CLASSIC CUSTOM CARBON

This rifle features a stainless steel action with Shilen barrel wrapped in graphite epoxy. Fitted with a black composite stock. Chambered for the .270 WSM, 7mm WSM, .300 WSM, .25-06 Rem., or the .338 Win. Mag. cartridge. Fitted with a 24" barrel on all calibers but the .338 (26"). Weight is about 6.5 lbs. on the WSM calibers and 7 lbs. of the others. Magazine capacity is three rounds. Introduced in 2003.

NIB	EXC.	V.G.	GOOD	FAIR	POOR
3230	2450	-	-	-	-

MODEL 70 CUSTOM GRADE

This custom built Model 70 is hand finished, polished, and fitted in the Custom Shop. Internal parts are hand honed while the barrel is lead lapped. The customer can order individual items to his or her own taste, including engraving, special stock dimensions and carvings, etc. Each Custom Grade Model 70 should be priced on an individual basis.

MODEL 70 CUSTOM EXPRESS

Also built in the Custom Shop this model features figured walnut, hand-honed internal parts, bolt and follower are engine turned. A special 3-leaf rear sight is furnished also. Offered in .375 H&H Mag., .375 JRS, .416 Rem. Mag., .458 Win. Mag., and .470 Capstick.

NIB	EXC.	V.G.	GOOD	FAIR	POOR
1850	1550	1000	-	-	-

Model 70 Classic Custom Carbon. Photo Courtesy U. S. Repeating Arms Company.

Model 70 Custom African Express. Photo Courtesy U. S. Repeating Arms Company.

Model 70 Custom Safari Express. Photo Courtesy U. S. Repeating Arms Company.

MODEL 70 CUSTOM AFRICAN EXPRESS

Introduced in 1999 this model is chambered for the .340 Wby., .358 STA, .375 H&H, .416 Rem. Mag., and the .458 Win. Mag. Fitted with a 24" barrel and a magazine capacity of 4 rounds. Express sights. Weight is about 9.75 lbs. Ebony pistol grip cap, and select walnut stock.

NIB	EXC.	V.G.	GOOD	FAIR	POOR
3850	3000	-	-	-	-

MODEL 70 CUSTOM SAFARI EXPRESS

This model has a figured walnut stock with the bolt and follower engine turned. Express sights. Chambered in .340 Wby., .358 STA, .375 H&H, .416 Rem. Mag., and .458 Win. Mag. Barrel length is 24". Weight is about 9.5 lbs. Introduced in 1999.

NIB	EXC.	V.G.	GOOD	FAIR	POOR
2395	1750	-	-	-	-

Model 70 Custom Ultra Light Mannlicher Stock. Photo Courtesy U. S. Repeating Arms Company.

Model 70 Custom Ultimate Classic. Photo Courtesy U. S. Repeating Arms Company.

MODEL 70 CUSTOM "ULTRA LIGHT" MANNLICHER

This model features a full-length stock of figured walnut with smooth tapered barrel and blued action. Chambered for .260 Rem., .308 Win., and 7mm-08. Fitted with a 19" barrel with optional open sights. Weight is about 6.75 lbs. Introduced in 1999.

NIB	EXC.	V.G.	GOOD	FAIR	POOR
2475	1850	-	-	-	-

MODEL 70 ULTIMATE CLASSIC

This model features a number of special options as standard. Included is a pre-1964 action, choice of round, round fluted, 1/2 octagon 1/2 round barrel, full tapered octagon barrel, blued or stainless steel barrel actions, fancy American walnut stock, special Custom Shop serial numbers and proof stamp, inletted swivel bases, red recoil pad, fine cut checkering, and a hard case. Offered in a wide variety of calibers from .25-06 to .338 Win. Mag. Weight is about 7.5 to 7.75 lbs. depending on caliber. Also available in stainless steel.

NIB	EXC.	V.G.	GOOD	FAIR	POOR
2450	1950	1500	-	-	-

NOTE: In 1997 this model was introduced in a left-hand version.

Model 70 Custom Takedown Rifle. Photo Courtesy U. S. Repeating Arms Company.

MODEL 70 CUSTOM TAKEDOWN

Introduced in 1998 this composite stock rifle has a special take down feature. Chambered for .375 H&H, .416 Rem. Mag., .300 Win Mag., 7mm STW. Magazine capacity is 3 rounds. Barrel length is 26". Weight is between 8.5 and 9 lbs. Offered in fluted barrel in .300 Win. Mag. and 7mm STW.

NIB	EXC.	V.G.	GOOD	FAIR	POOR
3300	2500	-	-	-	-

MODEL 70 CUSTOM SHORT ACTION

This custom shop model is fitted with a 22" match-grade barrel Controlled feed. Chambered for short-action calibers from .243 to .358. Semi-fancy walnut stock. Hand-cut checkering. Supplied with hard case. Weight is about 7.5 lbs. Introduced in 2000. In 2003 this model was offered in a left-hand version. Like all Model 70s, now discontinued.

NIB	EXC.	V.G.	GOOD	FAIR	POOR
2700	1950	-	-	-	-

MODEL 70 CUSTOM EXTREME WEATHER

This custom shop model is fitted with a round or fluted 24" match-grade barrel. Both barrel and action are stainless steel. McMillan fiberglass stock with cheekpiece. Chambered in calibers from .25-06 to .338 Win. Mag. Weight is about 7.5 lbs. Introduced in 2000.

NIB	EXC.	V.G.	GOOD	FAIR	POOR
1950	1500	-	-	-	-

These post-Model 70 rifles were fitted with redesigned actions and bolt with free-floating barrels, and new style stock with impressed checkering.

NOTE: In 1994, U.S. Repeating Arms reintroduced the pre-1964 Model 70 action on many of its Model 70 rifles. The new action does not affect values but may do so in the future depending on shooter reaction.

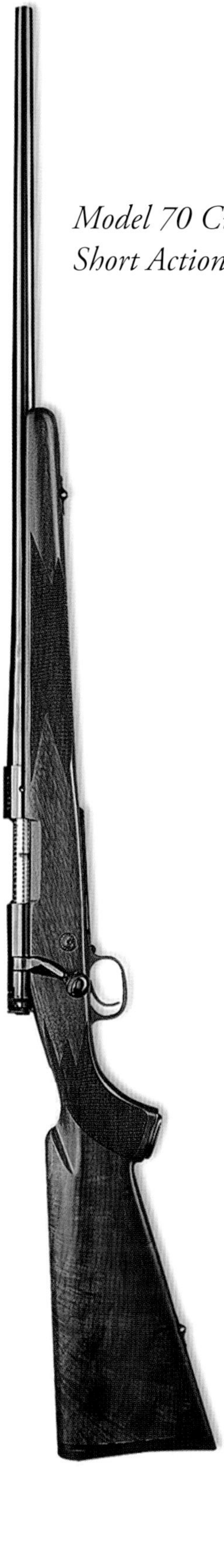

Model 70 Custom Short Action.

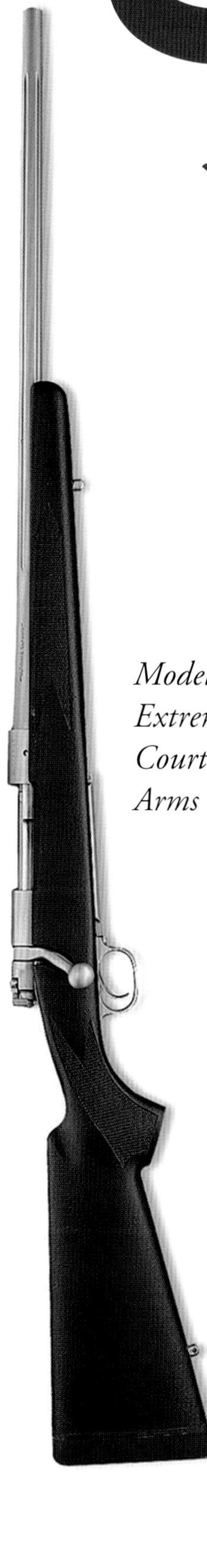

Model 70 Custom Extreme Weather. Photo Courtesy U. S. Repeating Arms Company.

Model 70 Standard Grade, Post-1964.

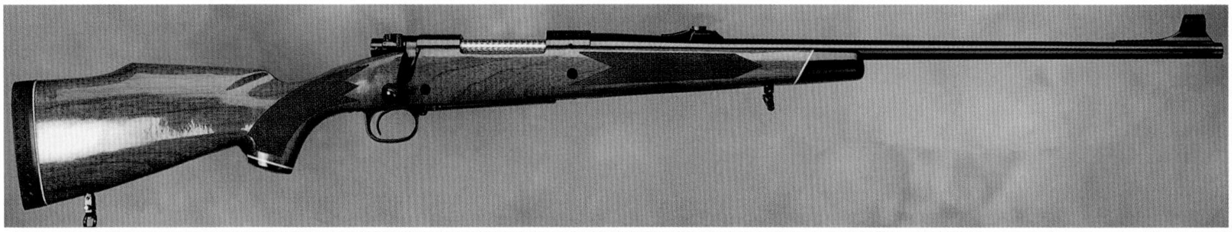

Model 70 African.

MODEL 70 STANDARD GRADE

This is a bolt-action sporting rifle chambered for various popular calibers such as the .22-250, .222 Rem., .243 Win., .270 Win., .30-06, and .308 Win. It features a 22" barrel with open sights and a 5-round, integral box magazine. The finish is blued with a Monte Carlo-type stock furnished with sling swivels. It was manufactured between 1964 and 1971.

EXC.	V.G.	GOOD	FAIR	POOR
350	250	200	150	100

MODEL 70 VARMINT

Chambered for the .22-25, .222 Rem., and .243 Win. cartridges this rifle is fitted with a 24" heavyweight barrel with no sights. Magazine capacity is 5 rounds. Weight is about 9.75 lbs. Built from 1964 to 1971.

EXC.	V.G.	GOOD	FAIR	POOR
400	250	200	150	100

MODEL 70 WESTERNER

This model is chambered for the .264 Win. Magnum and .300 Win. Magnum cartridges. Open sights, 24" barrel. Ventilated recoil pad. Weight is about 7.25 lbs. Built from 1964 to 1971.

EXC.	V.G.	GOOD	FAIR	POOR
400	250	200	150	100

MODEL 70 AFRICAN

Chambered for the .458 Win. Magnum cartridge this rifle is fitted with a 22" barrel with open sights. Magazine capacity is 3 rounds. Weight is about 8.5 lbs. Built from 1964 to 1971.

EXC.	V.G.	GOOD	FAIR	POOR
650	500	350	250	150

MODEL 70 MAGNUM

Chambered for the 7mm Rem. Mag., .300 Win. Mag., and .375 H&H cartridges. Barrel length is 24". Weight is about 7.75 lbs. Built from 1964 to 1971.

EXC.	V.G.	GOOD	FAIR	POOR
500	350	250	200	150

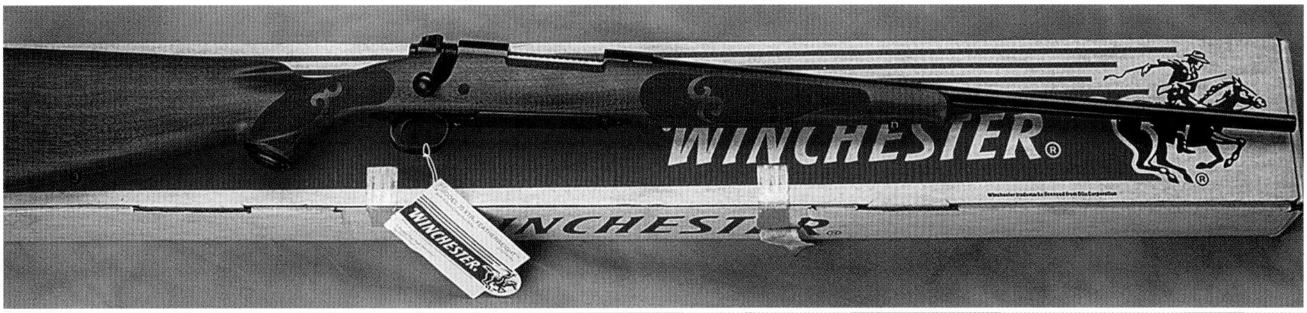

Model 70 XTR Featherweight.

MODEL 70 DELUXE

Built from 1964 to 1971, this rifle features a Monte Carlo stock with hand checkering and ebony forend tip. Offered in .243, .270, .30-06, .300 Win. Mag. Fitted with 22" barrel except magnums, which have 24" barrel. Weight is about 7.5 lbs.

EXC.	V.G.	GOOD	FAIR	POOR
450	300	200	150	100

MODEL 70 MANNLICHER

This is a full-length, Mannlicher-type stocked version of the Model 70 bolt-action rifle that is chambered for the .243, .270, .308, and the .30-06 cartridges. It was introduced in 1969. It features a 19" barrel with open sights. The finish is blued. It was discontinued in 1972. Only 2,401 were produced. Excellent quality.

EXC.	V.G.	GOOD	FAIR	POOR
750	600	500	400	300

MODEL 70 TARGET RIFLE

This version is chambered for the .308 or the .30-06 cartridges. It was offered with a 24" heavy barrel without sights. It is furnished with bases for a target scope. The finish is blued with a heavy walnut target stock with a palm rest. Weight is approximately 10.25 lbs.

EXC.	V.G.	GOOD	FAIR	POOR
650	550	450	350	250

MODEL 70 INTERNATIONAL MATCH ARMY

This version is chambered for the .308 cartridge and has a 24" heavy barrel furnished without sights. It has an adjustable trigger and is blued, with a target-type heavy stock that had an accessory rail and an adjustable butt.

EXC.	V.G.	GOOD	FAIR	POOR
750	650	500	400	300

MODEL 70A

This is a utility version of the bolt-action post-1964 Model 70. It was furnished without a hinged floorplate. The finish is blued, with a walnut stock. It was manufactured between 1972 and 1978.

EXC.	V.G.	GOOD	FAIR	POOR
350	275	225	175	100

MODEL 70 XTR FEATHERWEIGHT

This gun was built after the takeover by the U.S.R.A. Company. It is a bolt-action sporting rifle chambered for various calibers from .22-250 up to the .30-06 cartridges. It has a 22" barrel that is furnished without sights and features either a short- or medium-length action. It has a 5-round, integral magazine. The finish is blued, with a checkered walnut stock. It was introduced in 1981.

NIB	EXC.	V.G.	GOOD	FAIR	POOR
500	400	325	300	250	200

Model 70 Classic Featherweight.

MODEL 70 FIFTIETH ANNIVERSARY MODEL

This is a commemorative version of the post-1964 Model 70 bolt-action rifle. It is chambered for the .300 Win. Mag. and is offered with a 24" barrel. It is engraved and high-gloss blued with a deluxe, checkered walnut stock. There were 500 manufactured in 1987. In order to realize collector potential, it must be NIB with all supplied materials.

NIB	EXC.	V.G.	GOOD	FAIR	POOR
1000	-	-	-	-	-

MODEL 70 XTR SUPER EXPRESS

This is a heavy-duty version of the post-1964 Model 70 chambered for the .375 H&H and the .458 Win. Mag. cartridges. It is offered with a 22" or 24" heavy barrel and a 3-round, integral box magazine. This version has extra recoil lugs mounted in the stock and is blued with a select, straight-grain walnut stock and a recoil pad standard.

NIB	EXC.	V.G.	GOOD	FAIR	POOR
650	500	400	300	200	100

MODEL 70 XTR VARMINT

This version is chambered for the .22-250, .223, and the .243 cartridges. It has a 24" heavy barrel and is furnished without sights. It has a 5-round magazine and is blued with a heavy walnut stock. It was introduced in 1972.

NIB	EXC.	V.G.	GOOD	FAIR	POOR
450	350	300	250	200	100

MODEL 70 WINLIGHT

This version is offered in various calibers between .270 and the .338 Win. Mag. It features a matte-blue finish and a fiberglass stock. It is offered with a 22" or a 24" barrel and a 3- or 4-round magazine. It was introduced in 1986.

NIB	EXC.	V.G.	GOOD	FAIR	POOR
450	350	300	250	200	100

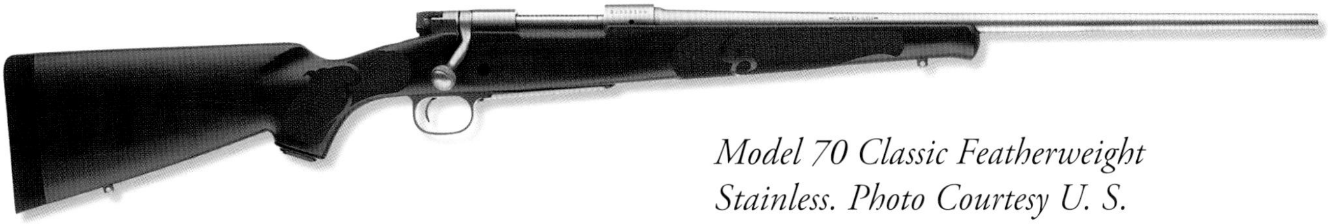

Model 70 Classic Featherweight Stainless. Photo Courtesy U. S. Repeating Arms Company.

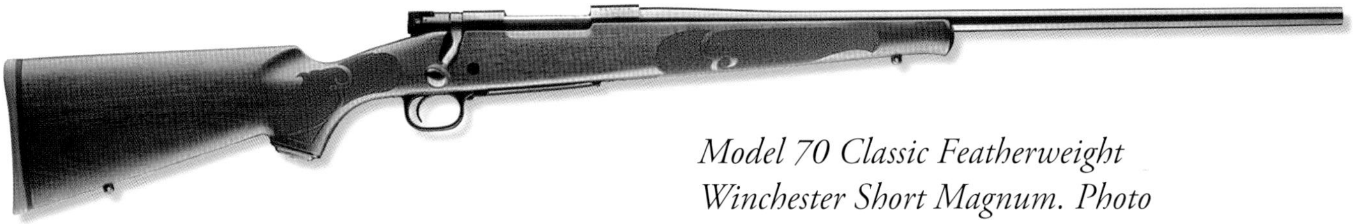

Model 70 Classic Featherweight Winchester Short Magnum. Photo Courtesy U. S. Repeating Arms Company.

MODEL 70 RANGER

This is a utility-grade, bolt-action rifle chambered for the .270 Win., .30-06, and the 7mm Rem. Mag. cartridges. It is offered with a 22" or a 24" barrel with open sights and has a 3- or 4-round box magazine. The finish is blued with a plain hardwood stock.

NIB	EXC.	V.G.	GOOD	FAIR	POOR
400	300	275	225	150	100

MODEL 70 FEATHERWEIGHT CLASSIC

A U.S.R.A. model with 22" barrel, walnut stock, and claw controlled round feeding. The bolt is jeweled and the bolt handle knurled. Comb is straight. Available in .270, .280, and .30-06 calibers. In 1997 this model was offered in the 6.5x55mm Swedish caliber. Rifle weighs about 7.25 lbs. In 2001 this model was offered chambered for the .300 Winchester Short Magnum (WSM) cartridge. In 2005 this model was offered in stainless steel; add 15 percent.

NIB	EXC.	V.G.	GOOD	FAIR	POOR
800	600	400	300	200	100

NOTE: In 2003 a left-hand model was offered. Add $35. For stainless steel model add $60.

MODEL 70 FEATHERWEIGHT CLASSIC ALL-TERRAIN

Introduced in 1996, this model features a weather-resistant stainless steel barrel and action with fiberglass/graphite black synthetic stock. Offered in .270 Win., .30-06, 7mm Rem. Mag., .330 Win. Mag. Weight is about 7.25 lbs. Also offered with the BOSS system.

NIB	EXC.	V.G.	GOOD	FAIR	POOR
800	600	450	300	200	150

NOTE: Add $100 for BOSS.

Model 70 Super Short Magnum. Photo Courtesy U. S. Repeating Arms Company.

MODEL 70 FEATHER-WEIGHT SUPER SHORT

Introduced in 2003 this rifle features a shorter receiver to handle the .223 WSSM and .243 WSSM cartridges. Fitted with a 22" barrel and a checkered walnut stock with solid recoil pad. Weight is about 6 lbs.

NIB	EXC.	V.G.	GOOD	FAIR	POOR
770	600	-	-	-	-

MODEL 70 CLASSIC LAREDO

First offered in 1996, this model features a heavy 26" barrel with pre-1964 action on a gray synthetic stock. Chambered for the 7mm Rem. Mag and the .300 Win. Mag. The forearm is a beavertail. Finish is matte blue. In 1997 this model was offered chambered for the 7mm STW cartridge. In 1998 this model was offered with fluted barrel.

NIB	EXC.	V.G.	GOOD	FAIR	POOR
750	650	550	500	400	300

NOTE: Add $100 for BOSS. Add $125 for fluted barrel.

MODEL 70 CLASSIC COMPACT

Introduced in 1998, this model is a scaled-down version of the Featherweight. It has a length of pull of 12.5" and a 20" barrel. Chambered for .243, .308, and 7mm-08 calibers. Checkered walnut stock. Weight is about 6.5 lbs.

NIB	EXC.	V.G.	GOOD	FAIR	POOR
525	425	-	-	-	-

MODEL 70 CLASSIC SPORTER LT

Introduced in 1999, this model is chambered for a wide variety of calibers from .25-06 to .338 Win. Mag. Fitted with a 24" or 26" barrel depending on caliber and no sights. Walnut stock with butt pad. Blued finish. Also offered in left-hand models from .270 to .338 Win. Mag. Weight is about 8 lbs.

NIB	EXC.	V.G.	GOOD	FAIR	POOR
750	550	-	-	-	-

NOTE: Add $30 for left-hand models.

Model 70 Classic Compact. Photo Courtesy U. S. Repeating Arms Company.

Model 70 Classic Sporter Lightweight. Photo Courtesy U. S. Repeating Arms Company.

MODEL 70 CLASSIC SAFARI EXPRESS

This model is chambered for the .375 H&H Mag, .416 Rem. Mag, and .458 Win. Mag. fitted with a 24" barrel magazine capacity is 4 rounds. Walnut stock with open sights. Left-hand model offered in .375 H&H. Weight is about 8.5 lbs. Introduced in 1999.

NIB	EXC.	V.G.	GOOD	FAIR	POOR
1150	850	-	-	-	-

NOTE: Add $30 for .375 H&H left-hand model.

MODEL 70 SUPER GRADE

Another U.S.R.A. rifle that features a select walnut stock, claw-controlled round feed, a single reinforced cross bolt, 24" barrel shipped with bases and rings. The buttstock has a straight comb with classic cheekpiece and deep-cut checkering. Available in .270, .30-06, 7mm Rem. Mag., .300 Win. Mag., .338 Win. Mag. Rifle weighs approximately 7.75 lbs. Currently in production.

NIB	EXC.	V.G.	GOOD	FAIR	POOR
1000	750	600	500	300	150

MODEL 70 RMEF SUPER GRADE

As above but with stainless steel action and barrel. Chambered for the .300 Win. Mag. cartridge. Fitted with a 26" barrel. Checkered walnut stock with solid recoil pad. Weight is about 8 lbs. Introduced in 2003. Special RMEF (Rock Mountain Elk Foundation) emblem on grip cap. Limited production.

NIB	EXC.	V.G.	GOOD	FAIR	POOR
1180	925	-	-	-	-

MODEL 70 RMEF SUPER GRADE III

This model is chambered for the .325 WSM or .300 WSM calibers and fitted with a 24" stainless steel barrel without sights. Super Grade walnut checkered stock with shadow line cheek piece. Weight is about 7.75 lbs. RMEF grip cap medallion. Introduced in 2005.

NIB	EXC.	V.G.	GOOD	FAIR	POOR
1080	900	-	-	-	-

Model 70 Classic Safari Express. Photo Courtesy U. S. Repeating Arms Company.

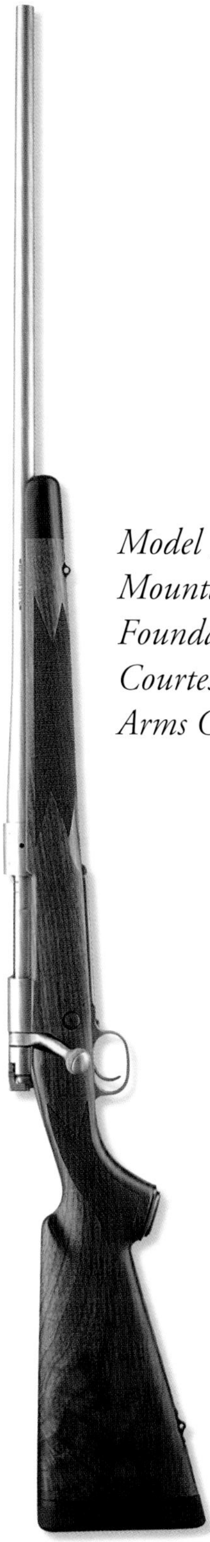

Model 70 Rocky Mountain Elk Foundation. Photo Courtesy U. S. Repeating Arms Company.

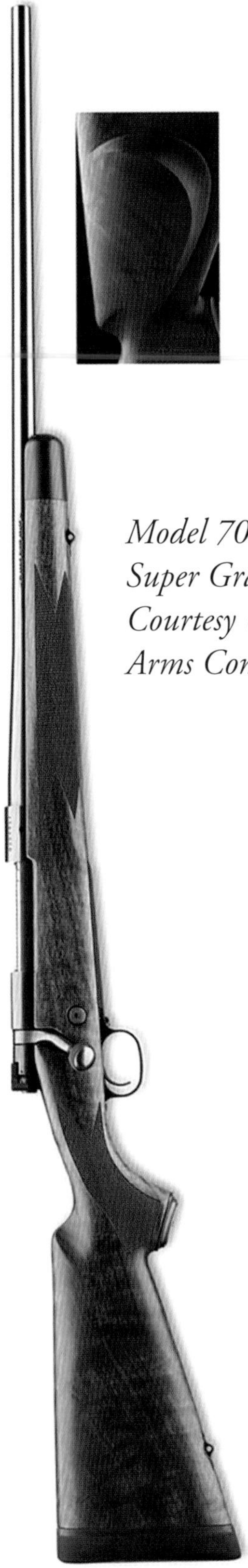

Model 70 Classic Super Grade III. Photo Courtesy U. S. Repeating Arms Company.

MODEL 70 CLASSIC SUPER GRADE III

Similar to the model above but chambered for a variety of short action calibers including WSM calibers. Fitted with a 24" barrel with no sights except for .300 Win. Mag. and .338 Win. Mag. which have 26" barrels. Weight is about 7.75 to 8 lbs. depending on caliber. Introduced in 2005.

NIB	EXC.	V.G.	GOOD	FAIR	POOR
1035	775	-	-	-	-

MODEL 70 SUPER EXPRESS

A U.S.R.A. version of the post-1964 XTR Super Express. Specifications are the same as the earlier model. Rifle weighs 8.5 lbs. Introduced in 1993.

NIB	EXC.	V.G.	GOOD	FAIR	POOR
650	500	400	300	200	100

MODEL 70 HEAVY VARMINT

Introduced by U.S.R.A. in 1993, this rifle features a fiberglass/graphite stock with heavy 26" stainless steel barrel. Offered in .223, .22-250, .243, and .308. In 1997, this model was offered chambered for the .222 Rem. cartridge. Rifle weighs about 10.75 lbs.

NIB	EXC.	V.G.	GOOD	FAIR	POOR
550	475	400	300	200	100

MODEL 70 HEAVY VARMINT-FLUTED BARREL

Introduced in 1997, this model is similar to the above Varmint with the addition of a fluted barrel. Calibers are also the same as the above model.

NIB	EXC.	V.G.	GOOD	FAIR	POOR
600	475	400	-	-	-

MODEL 70 CLASSIC STAINLESS

All-metal parts are stainless steel, including the barrel, with synthetic stock. Available with 24" barrel and chambered for .270, .30-06, 7mm Rem. Mag., .300 Win. Mag., and .338 Win. Mag. Weighs about 7.5 lbs. In 2001 this model was offered chambered for the .300 Winchester Short Magnum (WSM) cartridge.

NIB	EXC.	V.G.	GOOD	FAIR	POOR
550	425	375	300	200	100

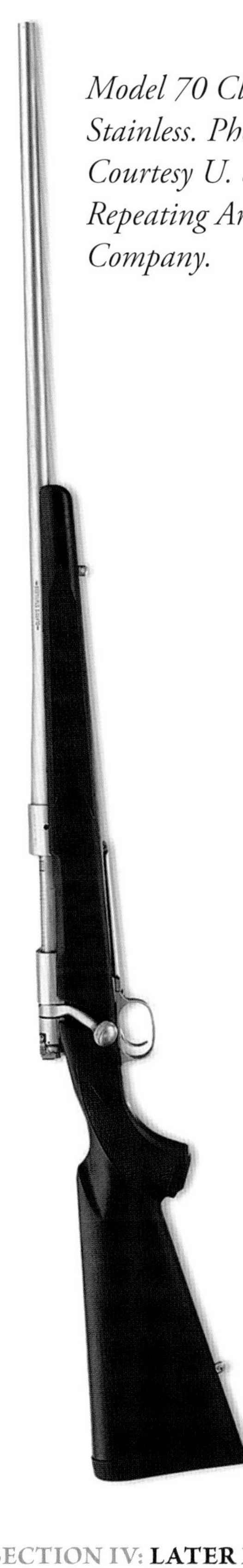

Model 70 Classic Stainless. Photo Courtesy U. S. Repeating Arms Company.

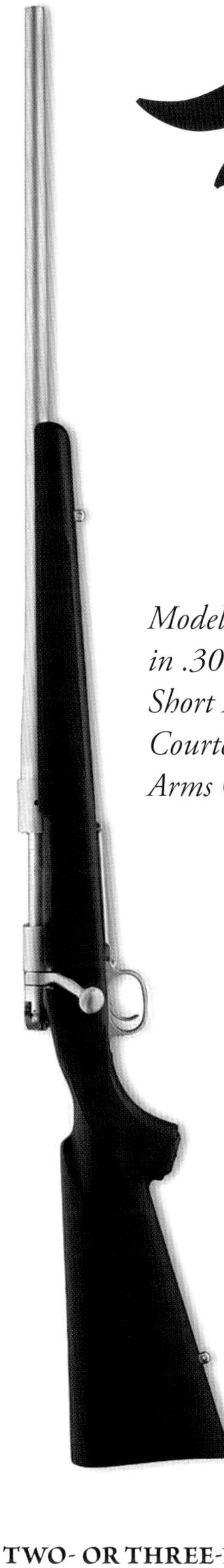

Model 70 Classic Stainless in .300 Winchester Short Magnum. Photo Courtesy U. S. Repeating Arms Company.

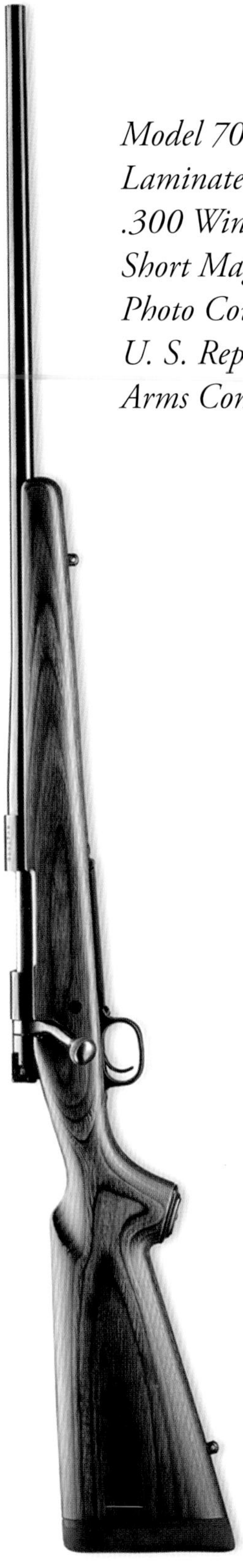

Model 70 Classic Laminated in .300 Winchester Short Magnum. Photo Courtesy U. S. Repeating Arms Company.

MODEL 70 CLASSIC LAMINATED

Introduced in 1998 this model features a laminated stock and and blued or stainless steel barrel and action. Offered in .270, .30-06, 7mm Rem. Mag., .300 Win. Mag., and .338 Win. Mag. Pre-1964 action. Bolt is jeweled and bolt handle is knurled. Barrel lengths are 24" and 26", depending on caliber. Weight is about 8 lbs. In 2001, this model was offered chambered for the .300 Winchester Short Magnum (WSM) cartridge.

NIB	EXC.	V.G.	GOOD	FAIR	POOR
800	600	-	-	-	-

MODEL 70 CLASSIC CAMO

This model features a Sporter-style stock with 24" or 26" barrel and Mossy Oak Treestand camo on the stock. Blued or stainless finish. Chambered for .270 Win., .30-06, 7mm Rem. Mag., and .300 Win Mag. Magazine capacity is 5 rounds. Weight is about 7.5 lbs. Introduced in 1998.

NIB	EXC.	V.G.	GOOD	FAIR	POOR
725	550	-	-	-	-

MODEL 70 SM

This rifle features a synthetic stock with black matte finish. Barrel length is 24". Available in 10 calibers from .223 Rem. to .375 H&H Mag. Depending on caliber, rifle weighs between 7 and 8 lbs. Currently in production.

NIB	EXC.	V.G.	GOOD	FAIR	POOR
525	400	300	200	150	100

MODEL 70 DBM-S

Similar to Model 70 SM but fitted with detachable box magazine. The metal parts are blued and the stock is synthetic. Offered in eight calibers from .223 Rem. to .338 Win. Mag. Furnished with scope bases and rings are open sights. Rifle weighs about 7.25 lbs., depending on caliber. Introduced in 1993.

NIB	EXC.	V.G.	GOOD	FAIR	POOR
550	425	325	225	150	100

Model 70 Black Shadow. Photo Courtesy U. S. Repeating Arms Company.

MODEL 70 VARMINT

Similar to the Model 70 Heavy Varmint but furnished with a traditional walnut stock and 26" medium-heavy barrel. Offered in .223 Rem., .22-250, .243, and .308. Weighs 9 lbs.

NIB	EXC.	V.G.	GOOD	FAIR	POOR
500	400	300	200	150	100

MODEL 70 DBM

DBM stands for detachable box magazine. Fitted with a straight-comb walnut stock. Jeweled bolt with blued receiver. Shipped with scope bases and rings or open sights. Rifle offered in eight calibers from .223 Rem. to .300 Win. Mag. Rifle weighs about 7.35 lbs., depending on caliber. Introduced in 1993.

NIB	EXC.	V.G.	GOOD	FAIR	POOR
525	425	325	225	150	100

MODEL 70 SPORTER

U.S.R.A.'s basic Model 70 offering. Straight-comb walnut stock with checkering, jeweled bolt and blued receiver and barrel are standard. Available in 12 calibers from .223 Rem. to .338 Win. Mag. including .270 Weatherby Mag. and .300 Weatherby Mag. Barrel length is 24" and is available with either scope bases and rings or open sights. Rifle weighs about 7.5 lbs.

NIB	EXC.	V.G.	GOOD	FAIR	POOR
500	400	300	200	150	100

MODEL 70 WINTUFF

Similar to the Sporter except fitted with a laminated hardwood straight-comb stock with cheekpiece. Offered in 24" barrel lengths with a choice of 6 calibers from .270 Win. to .338 Win. Mag. Furnished with scope bases and rings. Rifle weighs about 7.65 lbs., depending on caliber.

NIB	EXC.	V.G.	GOOD	FAIR	POOR
500	400	300	200	150	100

MODEL 70 LIGHTWEIGHT

Similar to the Model 70 Winlight. Offered with straight-comb checkered walnut stock with knurled bolt and blued receiver and barrel. The barrel is 22" without sights. Offered in 5 calibers: .223, .243, .270, .308, and .30-06. Rifle weighs about 7 lbs., depending on caliber.

NIB	EXC.	V.G.	GOOD	FAIR	POOR
450	350	300	200	150	100

MODEL 70 BLACK SHADOW

Chambered for the .270, .30-06, 7mm Rem. Mag., and .300 Win. Mag. and fitted with a 22" or 24" barrel, depending on caliber. Finish is matte black with composite stock. Push-feed action. Weight is 7.25 lbs. Introduced in 1998.

NIB	EXC.	V.G.	GOOD	FAIR	POOR
475	350	300	250	200	-

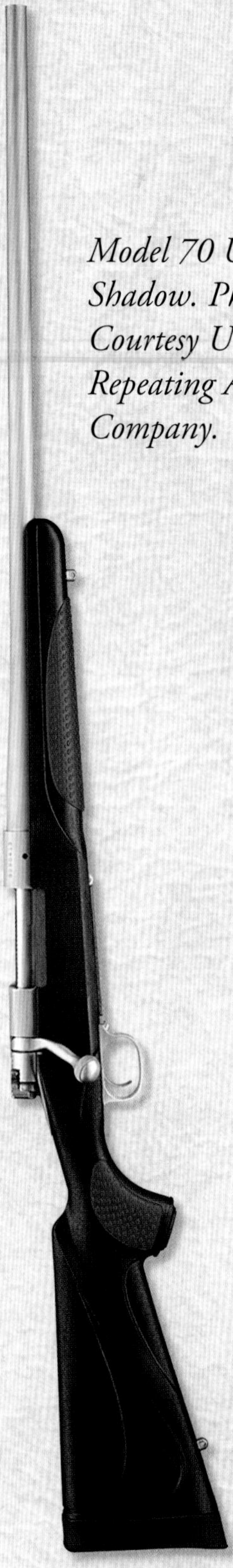

Model 70 Ultimate Shadow. Photo Courtesy U. S. Repeating Arms Company.

MODEL 70 ULTIMATE SHADOW

Introduced in 2003 this bolt-action model features a new black synthetic stock design with improved gripping surfaces and soft recoil pad. This model has a blued action and barrel. Chambered for the .300 WSM, .270 WSM, or the 7mm WSM cartridges. Fitted with a 24" barrel. Weight is about 6.75 lbs. Also offered with stainless action and barrel.

NIB	EXC.	V.G.	GOOD	FAIR	POOR
800	625	-	-	-	-

NOTE: For stainless steel model add $45.

MODEL 70 ULTIMATE SHADOW CAMO

As above but with Mossy Oak New Break-Up camo. Introduced in 2004.

NIB	EXC.	V.G.	GOOD	FAIR	POOR
935	700	-	-	-	-

MODEL 70 SUPER SHADOW SHORT MAGNUM

Similar to the above model but chambered for the .223 WSM or .243 WSM cartridge. Fitted with a 22" barrel and blind magazine. Weight is about 6 lbs. Introduced in 2003.

NIB	EXC.	V.G.	GOOD	FAIR	POOR
545	425	-	-	-	-

Model 70 Ultimate Shadow Camo, Blued Finish. Photo Courtesy U. S. Repeating Arms Company.

Model 70 Super Shadow Short Magnum. Photo Courtesy U. S. Repeating Arms Company.

Model 70 Super Shadow. Photo Courtesy U. S. Repeating Arms Company.

Model 70 Stealth. Photo Courtesy U. S. Repeating Arms Company.

MODEL 70 SUPER SHADOW

Similar to the Ultimate Shadow but fitted with a controlled round push feed bolt. Chambered for the .300 WSM, .270 WSM, or the 7mm WSM cartridge. Fitted with a 22" barrel, composite stock and blind magaziine. Weight is about 6.75 lbs. Introduced in 2003.

NIB	EXC.	V.G.	GOOD	FAIR	POOR
550	425	-	-	-	-

MODEL 70 STEALTH

This is a varmint model with 26" heavy barrel chambered for .223 Rem., .22-250, or .308 Win. It has a push-feed bolt-action. Black synthetic stock. Matte black finish. Weight is approximately 10.85 lbs. In 2004 the .223 WSSM, .243 WSSM and the .25 WSSM calibers were added.

NIB	EXC.	V.G.	GOOD	FAIR	POOR
885	650	475	-	-	-

MODEL 70 COYOTE

This model, introduced in 2000, has a push-feed bolt-action and is chambered for the .223 Rem, .22-250, and .243 Win. calibers. Fitted with a medium-heavy 24" stainless steel barrel with laminated stock and large forend. Weight is about 9 lbs. In 2002 the rifle was offered in .270 WSM, 7mm WSM, and .300 WSM. In 2005 the .325 WSM was added to this model.

NIB	EXC.	V.G.	GOOD	FAIR	POOR
725	500	-	-	-	-

Model 70 Coyote. Photo Courtesy U. S. Repeating Arms Company.

Model 70 Coyote Lite Stainless. Photo Courtesy U. S. Repeating Arms Company.

Model 70 Coyote Light, Blued Finish. Photo Courtesy U. S. Repeating Arms Company.

MODEL 70 COYOTE LITE

Introduced in 2005 this model features a lightweight composite stock with skeletonized aluminum block bedding. Recoil pad. Fluted 24" medium-heavy barrel with no sights. Offered in .223 Rem and all WSSM and WSM calibers.

NIB	EXC.	V.G.	GOOD	FAIR	POOR
870	600	-	-	-	-

NOTE: Add $40 for stainless steel.

MODEL 70 LADIES/ YOUTH RANGER

A scaled-down version of the Ranger. Length of pull is 1" shorter than standard. Rifle weighs 6.5 lbs. Chambered in .243 and .308. In 1997 this model was offered chambered for the .223 Rem. and the 7mm-08 Rem. cartridges.

NIB	EXC.	V.G.	GOOD	FAIR	POOR
450	350	300	200	150	100

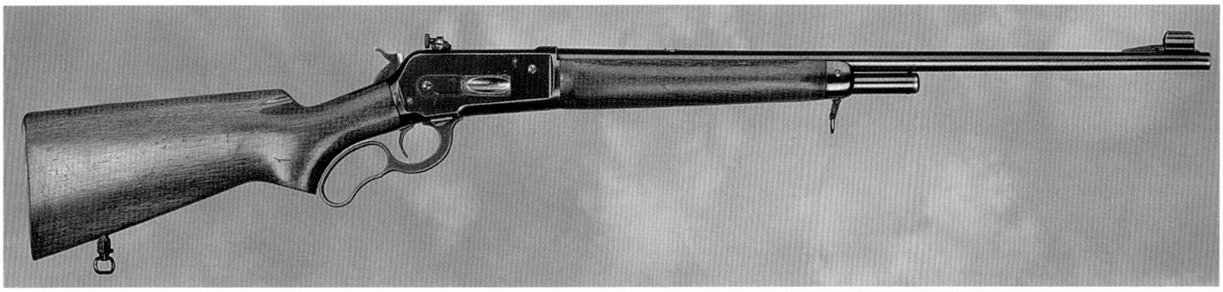

Model 71 Standard Rifle.

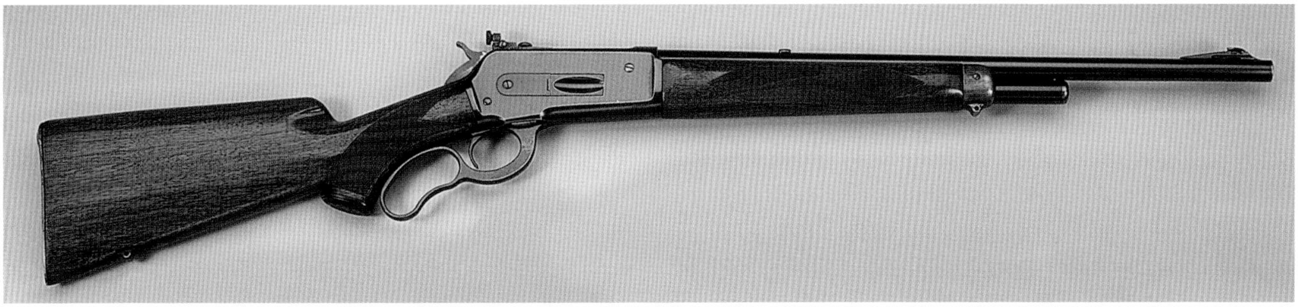

Model 71 Deluxe Carbine.

MODEL 71

When Winchester dropped the Model 1886 from its line in 1935, the company replaced its large-bore lever-action rifle with the Model 71 chambered for the .348 Winchester. The Model 71 is similar in appearance to the Model 1886 with some internal parts strengthened to handle the powerful .348 cartridge. The rifle was available in four basic configurations:

1) Standard Rifle, 24" round barrel, 3/4 magazine, plain walnut pistol-grip stock and semi-beavertail forearm.
2) Standard Rifle (Carbine), 20" round barrel, 3/4 magazine, plain walnut pistol-grip stock and semi-beavertail forearm.
3) Deluxe Rifle, 24" round barrel, 3/4 magazine, checkered walnut pistol-grip stock and checkered semi-beavertail forearm. The frames and barrels were blued on all models of this rifle.
4) Deluxe Rifle (Carbine), 20" round barrel, 3/4 magazine, checkered walnut pistol-grip stock and checkered semi-beavertail forearm. The frames and barrels were blued on all models of this rifle.

The Model 71 was produced from 1935 to 1957 with about 47,000 built.

STANDARD RIFLE

EXC.	V.G.	GOOD	FAIR	POOR
1400	1000	800	400	300

STANDARD RIFLE (CARBINE)

EXC.	V.G.	GOOD	FAIR	POOR
3250	2000	1600	1200	650

DELUXE RIFLE

EXC.	V.G.	GOOD	FAIR	POOR
2500	1800	800	525	425

DELUXE RIFLE (CARBINE)

EXC.	V.G.	GOOD	FAIR	POOR
3750	3000	2000	1250	700

NOTE: For pre-war Model 71s add a premium of 20 percent. The pre-war Model 71 has a longer tang than its post-war equivalent. For a bolt peep sight add 10 percent.

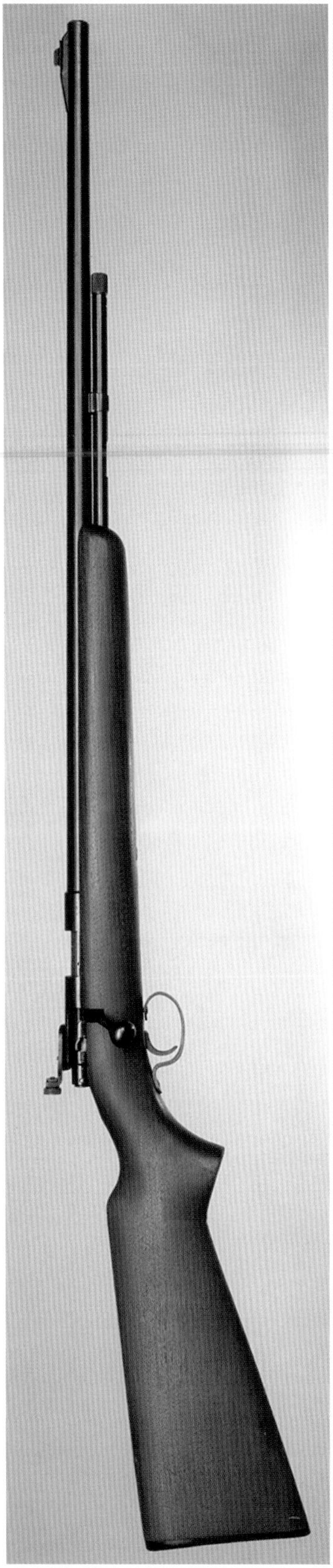

Model 72

MODEL 72

This model is a bolt-action rifle with tubular magazine. It is chambered for the .22 Short, Long, and LR cartridges interchangeably. Early rifles were available with 2-3/4 or 5 power telescopes, but the majority were furnished with either open sights or peep sights. This rifle was available in two different configurations:

1) Sporting Rifle, 25" round barrel, chambered for the .22 Short, Long, and LR cartridges, one-piece plain walnut pistol- grip stock and forend.
2) Gallery Special, 25" round barrel, chambered for .22 Short only, stock same as Sporting Rifle.

This model was not serial numbered. It was built between 1938 and 1959 with about 161,000 rifles sold.

EXC.	V.G.	GOOD	FAIR	POOR
425	350	275	200	125

NOTE: Gallery Special will command a premium of 100 percent. For rifles with factory scopes and no sights add 200 percent depending on condition. Add 25 percent premium for peep sights. Add 20 percent for Model 72A with grooved receiver.

MODEL 74

This was a semi-automatic chambered for either the .22 Short or the .22 LR. The rifle has a tubular magazine in the buttstock and a 24" round barrel. The bolt on this rifle was designed to be easily removed for cleaning or repair. The stock was plain walnut pistol-grip with semi-beavertail forend. A Gallery Special was offered that was chambered for the .22 Short and fitted with a steel shell deflector. This gallery model was also available with chrome trimmings at extra cost.

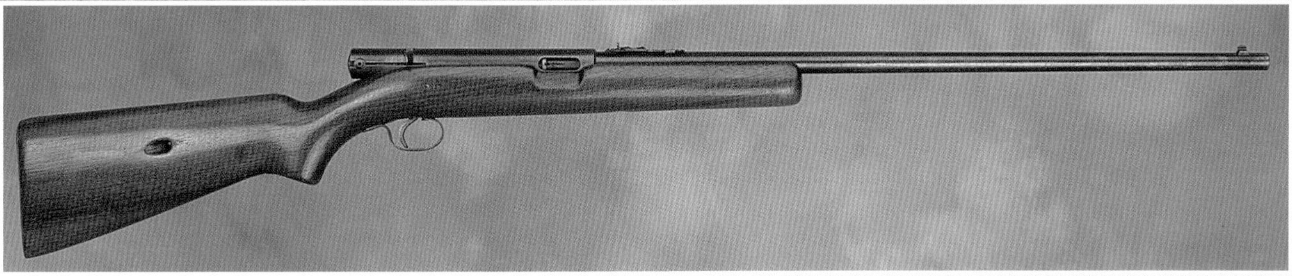

Model 74.

SPORTING RIFLE

EXC.	V.G.	GOOD	FAIR	POOR
400	300	225	150	100

GALLERY SPECIAL-.22 SHORT ONLY

EXC.	V.G.	GOOD	FAIR	POOR
600	450	325	225	150

NOTE: For Gallery models with chrome trimmings, add a premium of 50 percent.

MODEL 75

From a contemporary Winchester advertisement:

"The New Model 75 A MAN-SIZED RIFLE!

The Winchester Model 75 is built man's size with the same length barrel and the same length of trigger pull as the model 52. It is, however, 22 ounces lighter than the Standard grade Model 52.

The action is military type, developed especially for this rifle. A thumb-type lever safety is conveniently placed on the right side. The Standard target clip box type magazine holds five .22 long rifle rim fire cartridges. The barrel is 28" long, with a diameter at the shoulder of approximately 1". At the muzzle it measures approximately 11/16". It comes equipped with the Winchester No. 99A telescope height sight, with quick detachable, covered front sight and interchangeable target post and aperture inserts. The stock is sturdy, one-piece American black walnut."

Available in two styles:

1) Sporting Rifle, 24" round barrel, chambered for .22 LR, select walnut checkered pistol-grip stock and forend. This rifle was furnished with either open rear sights or a Lyman 57 E receiver sight.
2) Target Rifle, 28" round barrel, chambered for .22 LR, plain walnut pistol-grip stock and forend. The Target Rifle was furnished with either a Winchester 8-power telescope or a variety of target sights.

This model was discontinued in 1958 with about 89,000 sold.

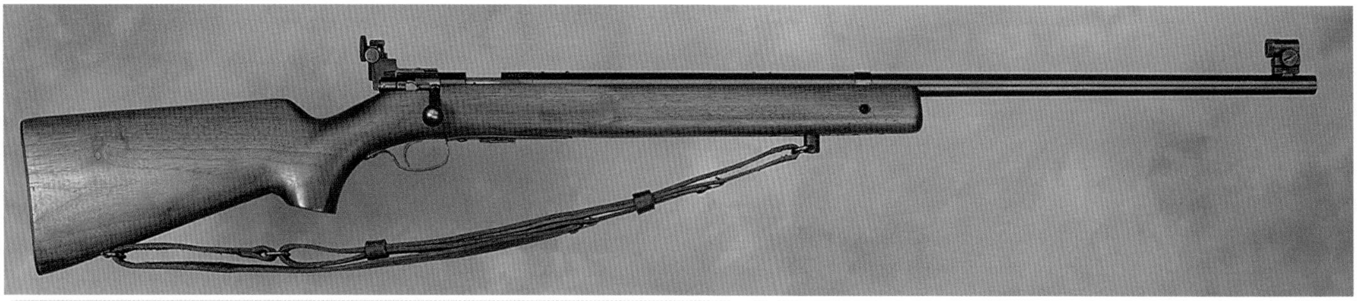

Model 75 Targe

MODEL 75 SPORTER

NIB	EXC.	V.G.	GOOD	FAIR	POOR
1400	900	700	500	350	200

MODEL 75 TARGET

EXC.	V.G.	GOOD	FAIR	POOR
700	600	500	350	200

MODEL 77

This rifle was built on the blow-back design for semi-automatic rifles and is chambered for the .22 LR. It features a 22" round barrel and either a detachable box magazine or under barrel tubular magazine. The rifle has a trigger guard made of nylon. It has a plain walnut pistol-grip stock with semi-beavertail forend and composition buttplate. Built between 1955 and 1963, Winchester sold about 217,000 of these rifles.

STANDARD RIFLE

EXC.	V.G.	GOOD	FAIR	POOR
300	200	150	100	50

DELUXE RIFLE

This variation is very rare, like the standard rifle, but with checkering and sling swivels. The checkering looks like that found on other Winchester rifles of that period, e.g., Model 70s.

EXC.	V.G.	GOOD	FAIR	POOR
450	350	275	175	100

NOTE: Models with tubular magazines will bring a premium of 10 percent to 20 percent.

MODEL 88 "CENTENNIAL MODEL" (1855/1955)

The Model 88 was a modern short-stroke lever-action chambered for the .243, .308, 284, and .358 calibers. It was available in a rifle version with 22" round barrel and a carbine version with 19" round barrel. The carbine model was not chambered for the .358 cartridge. Both were furnished with a detachable box magazine. The stock was a one-piece design with pistol grip and was offered with hand-cut checkering or pressed basket weave checkering after 1964. The rifle was introduced in 1955 and the carbine was first offered in 1968. Both versions were discontinued in 1973 with about 283,000 sold.

RIFLE

EXC.	V.G.	GOOD	FAIR	POOR
850	650	350	250	150

NOTE: Pre-1964 models, with cut checkering, add 25 percent premium. Prices above are for .308 caliber; for .243 add 15 percent, .284 add 200 percent, and for 358 add 300 percent.

This model was offered with no front or rear sights (Gopher Special) for a few years prior to 1962. Add 100% for this variant. Beware of fakes.

CARBINE

Only 28,000 carbines were built, about 1 for every 10 rifles. Rarely encountered.

EXC.	V.G.	GOOD	FAIR	POOR
1000	850	900	650	300

Model 94 Traditional-CW (Checkered Walnut). Photo Courtesy U. S. Repeating Arms Company.

NOTE: Add 25 percent for .243, add 125 percent for .284 calibers. The carbine was not offered in .358 caliber.

POST-1964: MODEL 94 AND VARIATIONS (TO BE DISCTINGUISHED FROM THE MODEL 1894)

Winchester, or U.S. Repeating Arms, closed its doors in New Haven, Connecticut effective March 31, 2006. Collectors and dealers alike have already started to accumulate recently manufactured examples of that Model 94 rifles and carbines. Many of these later weapons have been selling for as much as 50% over retail value. This may represent an opportunity for investment, or for collecting weapons that exist in the marketplace in rather large numbers, but, for the most part, are still very affordable. Beware, production of these rifles may, at some point in time, reoccur, and if it does, it's likely that prices will recede to approximate recent levels.

HIGH GRADE

Engraved receiver with gold accents and select walnut stock.

NIB	EXC.	V.G.	GOOD	FAIR	POOR
1075	850	-	-	-	-

MODEL 94

This is the post-1964 standard lever-action carbine chambered for the .30-30, 7-30 Waters, and the .44 Magnum cartridges. It is offered with a 20" or 24" barrel and has a 6- or 7-round, tubular magazine depending on barrel length. The round barrel is offered with open sights. The forearm is held on by a single barrel band. The finish is blued, with a straight-grip walnut stock. In 1982 it was modified to angle ejection to simplify scope mounting. It was introduced as a continuation of the Model 94 line in 1964. In 2003 a top-tang safety was installed and the .480 Ruger caliber was added.

NIB	EXC.	V.G.	GOOD	FAIR	POOR
325	250	200	150	100	75

§ Add $20 for .44 Magnum caliber, which was discontinued in 1986

§ Add $20 for 7-32 Waters caliber, which is very rare

§ Add $20 for 24 inch barrel, which was discontinued in 1990

MODEL 94 TRADITIONAL-CW

As above but with checkered walnut stock. Chambered for the .30-30, .44 Mag., and the .480 Ruger cartridge.

NIB	EXC.	V.G.	GOOD	FAIR	POOR
550	350	-	-	-	-

NOTE: For .44 Mag. add $20. For the .480 Ruger add $70.

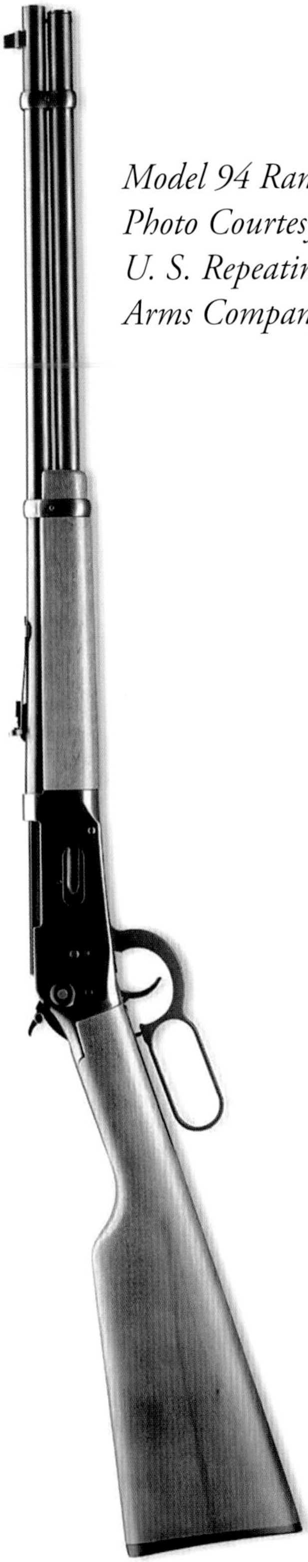

Model 94 Ranger. Photo Courtesy U. S. Repeating Arms Company.

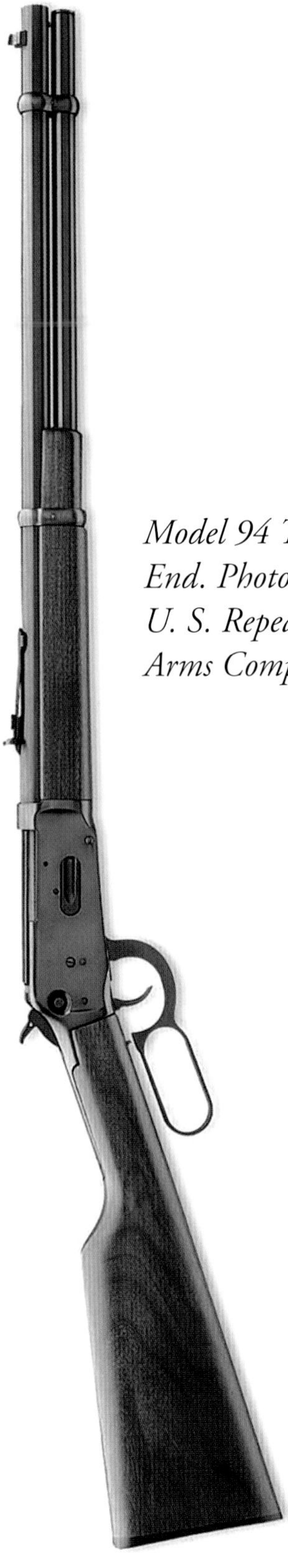

Model 94 Trail's End. Photo Courtesy U. S. Repeating Arms Company.

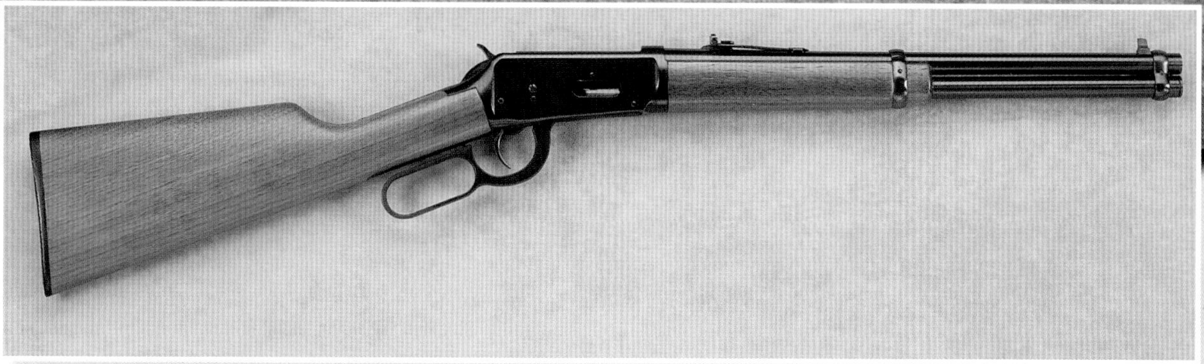

Model 94 Ranger Compact.

MODEL 94 RANGER

Chambered for .30-30 cartridge and fitted with a 20" barrel. Weight is about 6.25 lbs. In 2003 a top-tang safety was installed.

NIB	EXC.	V.G.	GOOD	FAIR	POOR
400	300	225	150	100	75

MODEL 94 RANGER COMPACT

Introduced in 1998 this model features a 16" barrel with 12.5" lop. Chambered for .30-30 or .357 Magnum. Furnished with black recoil pad. Post-style front sight with adjustable rear sight. Hardwood stock. Weight is approximately 5.87 lbs

NIB	EXC.	V.G.	GOOD	FAIR	POOR
350	250	225	200	-	-

MODEL 94 TRAILS END

This model was manufactured in .357 Magnum, .44-40, .44 Mag, or .45 Colt, 11 shot tubular magazine, 20" barrel, round or octagon, standard or large loop lever. Introduced in 1997.

NIB	EXC.	V.G.	GOOD	FAIR	POOR
500	400	300	-		

* Add $40 for large loop lever, which was discontinued in 1998
* Add $100 for takedown model
* Add $100 for case color frame
* Add $200 for both octagon barrel and case color frame, named Trails End Hunter

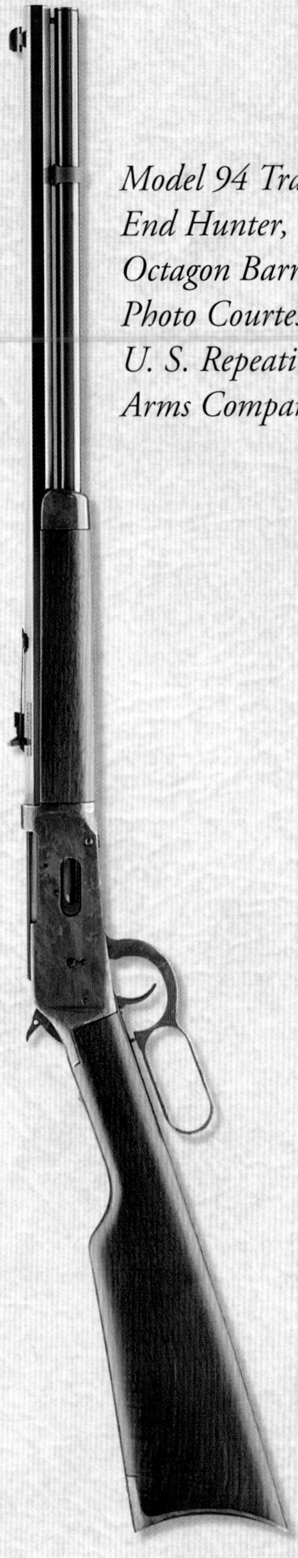

Model 94 Trail's End Hunter, Octagon Barrel. Photo Courtesy U. S. Repeating Arms Company.

MODEL 94 TRAILS END OCTAGON

As above but with 20" octagon barrel and choice of blued or case colored receiver. Crescent butt. Weight is about 6.75 lbs. Introduced in 2004.

NIB	EXC.	V.G.	GOOD	FAIR	POOR
955	750	-	-	-	-

NOTE: Add $60 for case colored receiver.

MODEL 94 TRAILS END HUNTER

Offered in .25-35 Win., .30-30 Win., or .38-55 Win. and fitted with a 20" round or octagon barrel. Plain walnut stock. Blued finish on round barrel model and case colored finish on octagon model. Weight is about 6.5 lbs. Introduced in 2005. Deduct 25 percent for .30-30.

NIB	EXC.	V.G.	GOOD	FAIR	POOR
1500	1350	-	-	-	-

NOTE: Add $290 for octagon barrel model.

MODEL 94 TAKEDOWN SHORT HUNTER

This model was manufactured in .30-30 Winchester, .44 Magnum, or for .450 Marlin; takedown feature, uncheckered, XS ghost rain sight.

NIB	EXC.	V.G.	GOOD	FAIR	POOR
600	500	400	-	-	-

MODEL 94 BLACK SHADOW

This model features a black synthetic stock with nonglare finish and black recoil pad. Offered in .30-30, .44 Magnum, or .44 Special, .444 Marlin caliber. Fitted with a 20" barrel. Weight is about 6.5 lbs. Introduced in 1998.

NIB	EXC.	V.G.	GOOD	FAIR	POOR
350	275	250	225	-	-

* Add $25 for .44 Magnum caliber
* Add $20 for .44 special caliber
* Add $100 for .444 Marlin caliber

Model 94 Trail's End Hunter, Round Barrel. Photo Courtesy U. S. Repeating Arms Company.

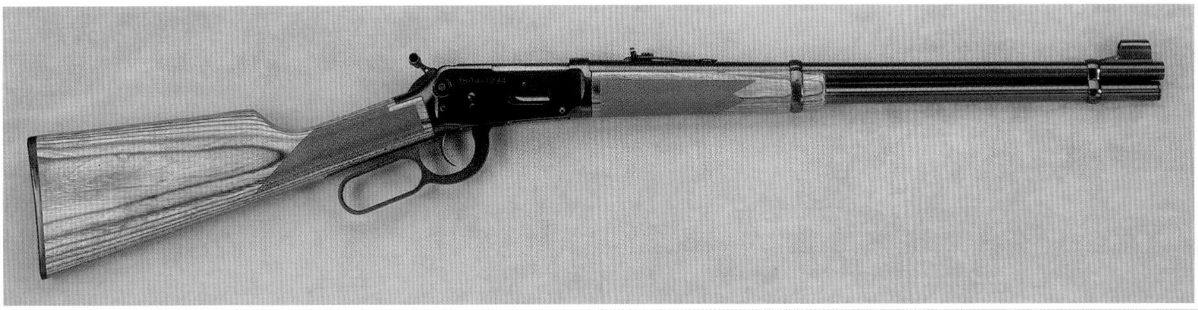

Model 94 WinTuff.

MODEL 94 DELUXE

Checkered stock.

NIB	EXC.	V.G.	GOOD	FAIR	POOR
350	250	200	150	125	100

MODEL 94 WIN-TUFF

Laminated stock.

NIB	EXC.	V.G.	GOOD	FAIR	POOR
350	275	225	165	125	100

MODEL 94 XTR

Select, checkered walnut stock, discontinued 1988.

EXC.	V.G.	GOOD	FAIR	POOR
350	250	165	100	85

MODEL 94 XTR DELUXE

Fancy checkering.

EXC.	V.G.	GOOD	FAIR	POOR
425	325	225	150	110

MODEL 94 TRAPPER

16" barrel. Chambered for the .30-30, .357 Mag., .44 Mag, .44 Special or .45 Colt cartridge. In 2003 a top-tang safety was installed, also option is 12.5 inch LOP.

NIB	EXC.	V.G.	GOOD	FAIR	POOR
500	350	250	150	100	75

- Add $35 for .44 Magnum caliber
- Add $20 for .44 Special caliber
- Add $20 for 12.5" LOP

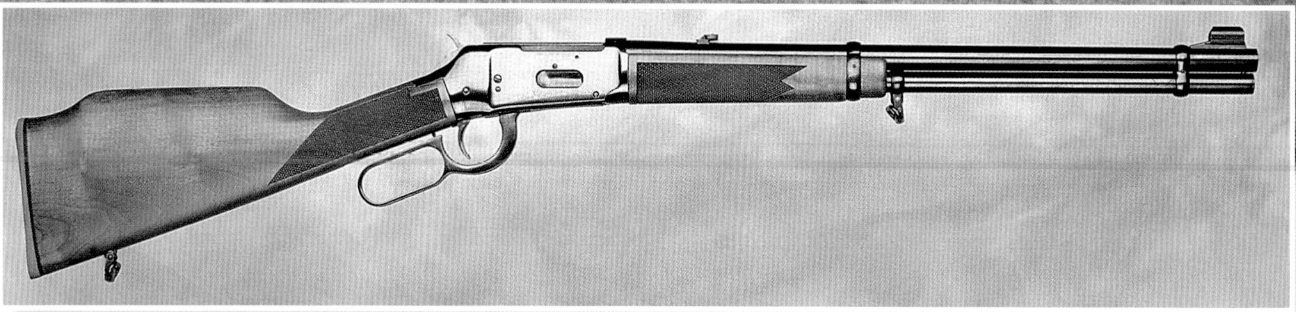

Model 94 XTR Big Bore.

MODEL 94 CLASSIC SERIES, AND SADDLE RING CARBINE

EXC.	V.G.	GOOD	FAIR	POOR
345	275	185		

MODEL 94 XTR BIG BORE

This rifle was available chambered for .308 Winchester, .356 Winchester, or .375 Winchester caliber with 20" checkered walnut stock, sling swivels, and angled ejection port for scope mounting. Introduced in 1983.

EXC.	V.G.	GOOD	FAIR	POOR
1325	850	675	500	400

- Add $200 for .356 or .307 Winchester caliber

MODEL 94 ANTIQUE CARBINE

Gold-plated saddle ring.

EXC.	V.G.	GOOD	FAIR	POOR
325	225	190	125	90

MODEL 94 WRANGLER

.32 Win. Special. Approximately 8000 manufactured.

EXC.	V.G.	GOOD	FAIR	POOR
400	300	190	125	100

MODEL 94 WRANGLER II

manufactured in .32 Winchester special cartridge, or .38-55 caliber, angle ejection port, roll engraved receiver, manufactured in 1983-1985.

NIB	EXC.	V.G.	GOOD	FAIR	POOR
375	300	250	200	150	100

MODEL 94 WRANGLER-LARGE LOOP MODEL

Chambered in .30-30, .44 Magnum or .45 Colt with large loop lever, blue finish, open sights, and uncheckered walnut stock. Manufactured from 1992 to 1999.

NIB	EXC.	V.G.	GOOD	FAIR	POOR
375	300	250	-	-	-

add $30 for 44 Mag or 45 Colt calibers

MODEL 94 LEGACY 20"

This Model 94 is fitted with a 20" barrel and chambered for the .30-30, .357 Magnum, .44 Magnum or .45 Colt. It is fitted with a half pistol-grip stock. Both walnut buttstock and forearm are cut checkered. Weight is 6.5 lbs. In 2003 a top-tang safety was added.

NIB	EXC.	V.G.	GOOD	FAIR	POOR
475	375	250	150	100	75

MODEL 94 LEGACY 24"

Introduced in 2005 this model features a 24" round barrel with full length magazine. Checkered walnut stock with semi- pistol grip. Chambered for the .30-30, .357 Mag., .44 Rem. Mag. or the .45 Colt cartridge. Drilled and tapped for scope mount. Blued finish. Weight is about 6.75 lbs.

NIB	EXC.	V.G.	GOOD	FAIR	POOR
485	375	-	-	-	-

MODEL 94 LEGACY 26"

Similar to the model above but offered in both round and octagon barrel and blue or case colored receiver. Marble's tang sight. Chambered for the .30-30 or .38-55 calibers. Weight is about 7 lbs. Introduced in 2005.

NIB	EXC.	V.G.	GOOD	FAIR	POOR
800	575	-	-	-	-

Add $55 for case colored receiver. Add $100 for octagon barrel.

MODEL 94 CENTENNIAL LIMITED EDITIONS

Introduced in 1994, these models celebrate the 100-year anniversary of the Winchester Model 1894. Offered in three grades, these models are of limited production. The Grade I is limited to 12,000 rifles while the High Grade is limited to 3,000 rifles. Only 94 of the Custom Limited model were produced. Each Limited model has different grades of select walnut and engraving coverage. All are chambered for the .30-30 Winchester cartridge.

GRADE I

NIB	EXC.	V.G.	GOOD	FAIR	POOR
800	700	600	450	300	200

HIGH GRADE

NIB	EXC.	V.G.	GOOD	FAIR	POOR
1200	950	700	500	300	200

CUSTOM HIGH GRADE

NIB	EXC.	V.G.	GOOD	FAIR	POOR
4750	3900	2500	1000	750	450

Model 94 Legacy, Case-Colored with 26" Octagon Barrel. Photo Courtesy U. S. Repeating Arms Company.

Model 94 Heritage 1 of 1000. Photo Courtesy U. S. Repeating Arms Company.

Model 94 1 of 1000, Closeup of Left Receiver. Photo Courtesy U. S. Repeating Arms Company.

MODEL 94 HERITAGE-LIMITED 1 OF 1000

Introduced in 2002 and limited to 1,000 rifles. Fitted with half round/half octagon 26" barrel. Engraved with #3 pattern with gold plate. Fancy walnut stock. Chambered for the .38-55 cartridge.

NIB	EXC.	V.G.	GOOD	FAIR	POOR
1885	1500	-	-	-	-

Model 94 Heritage Custom Edition 1 of 100. Photo Courtesy U. S. Repeating Arms Company.

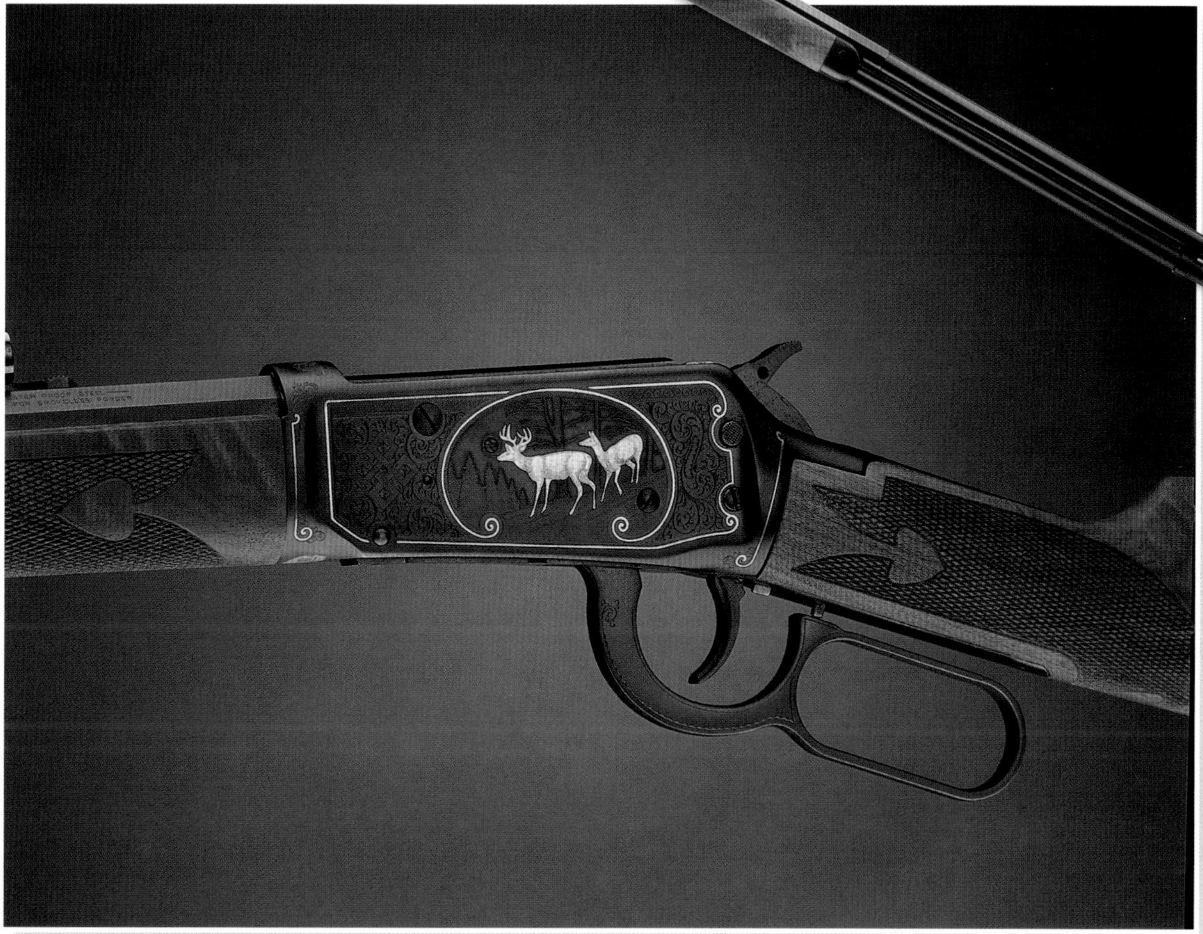

Model 94 1 of 100, Left View. Photo Courtesy U. S. Repeating Arms Company.

MODEL 94 HERITAGE-CUSTOM 1 OF 100

Similar to the above model but with finer wood and engraved with #2 pattern with gold. Limited to 100 rifles. Introduced in 2002.

NIB	EXC.	V.G.	GOOD	FAIR	POOR
$5,000	-	-	-	-	-

Model 94 Timber Scout. Photo Courtesy U. S. Repeating Arms Company.

Model 94 Pack Rifle. Photo Courtesy U. S. Repeating Arms Company.

MODEL 94 TIMBER CARBINE

Introduced in 1999, this model is chambered for the .444 Marlin or .450 Marlin. Barrel is 17.75" long and ported. Hooded front sight. Magazine capacity is 5 rounds. Weight is about 6 lbs. Finish is blue. Walnut stock.

NIB	EXC.	V.G.	GOOD	FAIR	POOR
600	450	350	-	-	-

NOTE: Add $25 for .444 Marlin.

MODEL 94 TIMBER SCOUT

This model, introduced in 2005, features an 18" barrel chambered for the .30-30 Win. or .44 Rem. Mag. cartridges with a quick detachable scope mount attached to the barrel for long eye relief, takedown feature available, new 2006. Plain walnut stock with pistol grip. Blued finish. Weight is about 6 lbs. Scope not included.

NIB	EXC.	V.G.	GOOD	FAIR	POOR
595	450	-	-	-	-

- Add $25 for .44 Magnum
- Add $100 for takedown feature

MODEL 94 PACK RIFLE

This lever-action model features an 18" barrel chambered for the .30-30 or .44 Magnum. It has a walnut stock with pistol grip and no checkering. Magazine is 3/4-style and has a 4-round capacity for the .30-30, and five rounds for the .44 Mag. Open sights. Weight is about 6.25 lbs. Introduced in 2000.

NIB	EXC.	V.G.	GOOD	FAIR	POOR
475	350	-	-	-	-

NOTE: Add $25 for 44 Magnum.

POST-1964 WINCHESTER CUSTOM GUN SHOP MODEL 94

NOTE: There are a number of special order options offered by the Custom shop that will greatly affect price, such as special-order engraving, stock carving, wood, sights, etc. It is strongly suggested that an independent appraisial be secured prior to a purchase.

MODEL 94 CUSTOM LIMITED EDITION NEW GENERATION

This lever-action rifle is stocked with fancy checkered walnut with pistol grip and long nose forend. Custom engraved with gold inlaid moose on right side and gold inlaid buck and doe on the left side. Fitted with tang safety. Barrel is 20" and chambered for the .30-30 cartridge. Introduced in 2003. Weight is about 6.25 lbs.

NIB	EXC.	V.G.	GOOD	FAIR	POOR
2500	1700	-	-	-	-

MODEL 94 CUSTOM LIMITED EDITION

This is essentially a special order Model 94 with choice of engraving and stock carving. Chambered for the .44-40 and fitted with a 24" octagonal barrel. Fancy walnut stock. Limited to 75 rifles. Weight is about 7.75 lbs. Suggest an appraisal prior to a sale.

NIB	EXC.	V.G.	GOOD	FAIR	POOR
2250	1750	-	-	-	-

MODEL 94 LIMITED EDITION CENTENNIAL

.30-30 Winchester caliber, manufactured as a commemorative of the 100th anniversary of the Model 94, in 1994. Features #9 style Winchester engraving pattern, rolled, 12,000 manufactured.

EXC.	V.G.	GOOD	FAIR	POOR
1800	1600	-	-	-

Add 100% for High Grade Model with #6 engraving.

MODEL 94 LIMITED EDITION CENTENNIAL CUSTOM HIGH GRADE RIFLE

#5 style Winchester engraving, only 94 manufactured in 1994.

NIB	EXC.	V.G.	GOOD	FAIR	POOR
9000	-	-	-	-	-

SETS

Complete sets of Model 94 Limited Edition Centennial Rifles with the same serial numbers (only 94 made) are valued at approximately $11,000 per set.

Model 94 Custom Limited Edition, New Generation. Photo Courtesy U. S. Repeating Arms Company.

Model 100 Rifle.

MODEL 100

This rifle is a gas operated semi-automatic and chambered for the .243, .308, and .284 caliber cartridges. The Model 100 was the first commercial Winchester self-loading, centerfire rifle introduced since the Winchester Model 1910. It was available in a rifle version with a 22" round barrel and a carbine version with a 19" barrel. Both were furnished with a detachable box magazine. The stock was a one-piece design with pistol grip and was offered in either hand-cut checkering or pressed basket weave checkering. Rifles were introduced in 1960 and the carbine in 1967. The Model 100 was last produced in 1973 with about 263,000 guns sold.

WARNING: The Model 100 was recalled in 1990. On some examples a faulty firing pin could cause unintended firing. Do not purchase this model without first determining if the problem has been repaired. Call Winchester Product Service for information.

RIFLE

EXC.	V.G.	GOOD	FAIR	POOR
475	400	300	250	200

NOTE: For pre-1964 models add a 15 percent premium. Prices given are for .308 caliber; for .243 add 15 percent; for .284 add 20 percent.

CARBINE

Only about 53,000 carbines were made, about one for every five rifles.

EXC.	V.G.	GOOD	FAIR	POOR
575	475	375	325	225

NOTE: Add 25 percent premium for .243, and 100 percent premium for .284.

MODEL 121

This is a single-shot, bolt-action rifle chambered for the .22 rimfire cartridge. It has a 20.75" barrel with open sights. The finish is blued, with a plain walnut stock. It was manufactured between 1967 and 1973. A youth model with a shorter stock was designated the 121Y and is valued the same.

EXC.	V.G.	GOOD	FAIR	POOR
150	100	80	60	40

MODEL 131

This is a bolt-action repeater chambered for the .22 rimfire cartridge. It has a 20.75" barrel with open sights and a 7-round, detachable magazine. The finish is blued, with a plain walnut stock. It was manufactured between 1967 and 1973. A tubular magazine version was designated the Model 141 and is valued the same.

EXC.	V.G.	GOOD	FAIR	POOR
150	110	90	75	50

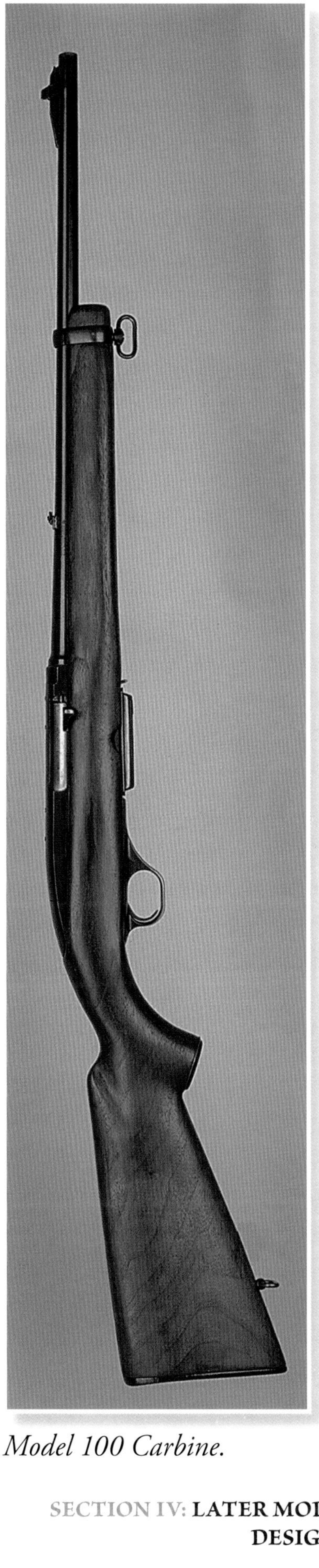

Model 100 Carbine.

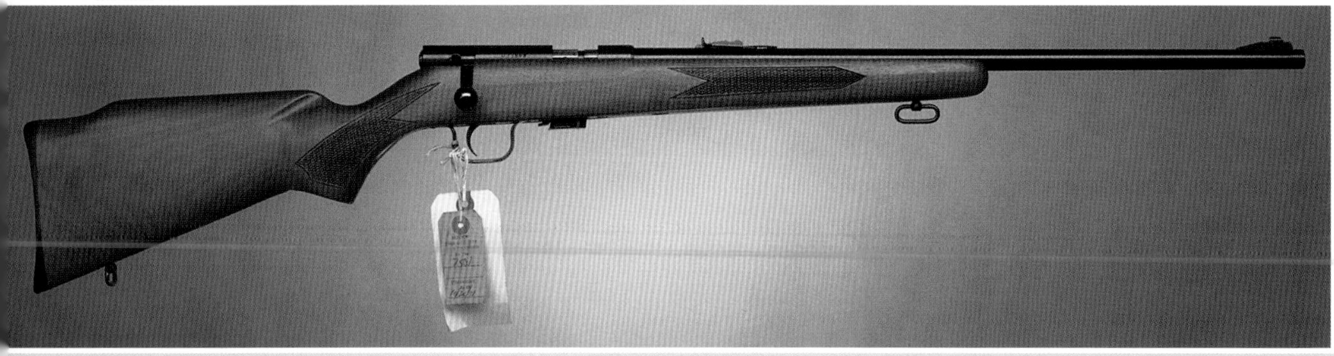

Model 320.

MODEL 310

This is a single-shot, bolt-action rifle chambered for the .22 rimfire cartridge. It features a 22" barrel with open sights. The finish is blued, with a checkered walnut stock. It was manufactured between 1972 and 1975.

EXC.	V.G.	GOOD	FAIR	POOR
250	150	125	100	75

MODEL 320

This is a bolt-action repeating rifle that is similar in configuration to the Model 310 single-shot. It has a 5-round, detachable box magazine. It was manufactured between 1972 and 1974.

EXC.	V.G.	GOOD	FAIR	POOR
400	300	250	175	125

MODEL 250

This is a lever-action repeating rifle with a hammerless action. It is chambered for the .22 rimfire cartridge and has a 20.5" barrel with open sights and a tubular magazine. The finish is blued, with a checkered pistol-grip stock. It was manufactured between 1963 and 1973.

EXC.	V.G.	GOOD	FAIR	POOR
200	125	80	60	40

MODEL 250 DELUXE

This version is similar to the Model 250 and is furnished with select walnut and sling swivels. It was manufactured between 1965 and 1971.

EXC.	V.G.	GOOD	FAIR	POOR
225	150	100	75	50

MODEL 255

This version is simply the Model 250 chambered for the .22 WMR cartridge. It was manufactured between 1964 and 1970.

EXC.	V.G.	GOOD	FAIR	POOR
225	150	100	70	50

MODEL 255 DELUXE

This version was offered with select walnut and sling swivels. It was manufactured between 1965 and 1973.

EXC.	V.G.	GOOD	FAIR	POOR
250	175	125	100	75

MODEL 270

This is a slide-action rifle chambered for the .22 rimfire cartridge. It has a 20.5" barrel and a tubular magazine. The finish is blued, with a checkered walnut stock. It was manufactured between 1963 and 1973.

EXC.	V.G.	GOOD	FAIR	POOR
135	115	85	50	35

MODEL 150

This is a lever action 22 long rifle, with 20.5 inch barrel, tubular magazine, no checkering, sling swivels, manufactured from 1967 to 1974, approximately 48,000 manufactured.

EXC.	V.G.	GOOD	FAIR	POOR
250	175	125	75	50

MODEL 250

This is a lever action 22 Magnum, with 20.5 inch barrel, tubular magazine, checkered pistol grip, manufactured from 1963 to 1973

EXC.	V.G.	GOOD	FAIR	POOR
275	200	135	90	65

MODEL 250-DELUXE

This model is similar to the Model 250, but with sling swivels. (This is relatively a rare model.)

EXC.	V.G.	GOOD	FAIR	POOR
350	250	175	100	65

MODEL 255

This model is very similar to the Model 250, and was manufactured from 1964 to 1970. (This is a relatively rare model.)

EXC.	V.G.	GOOD	FAIR	POOR
325	225	185	110	65

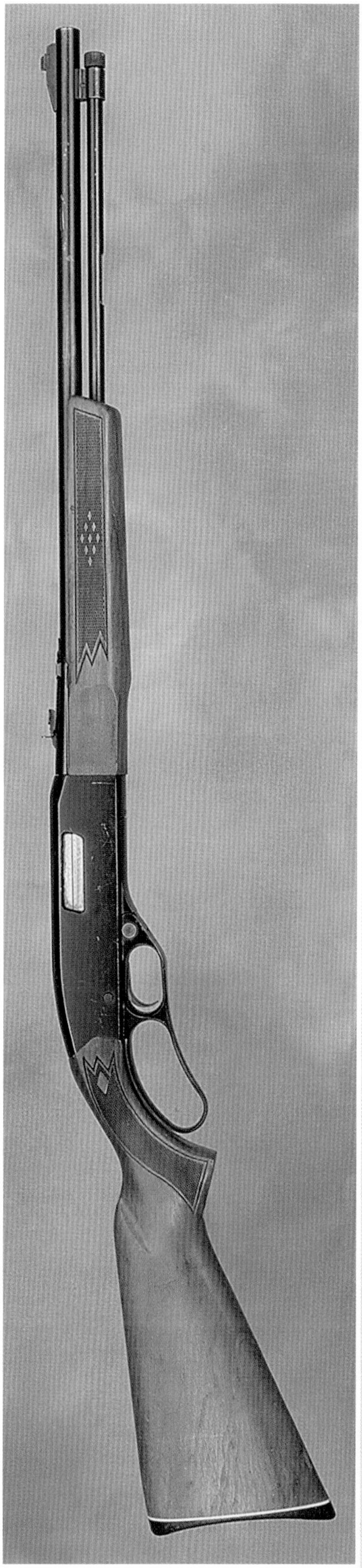

Model 250.

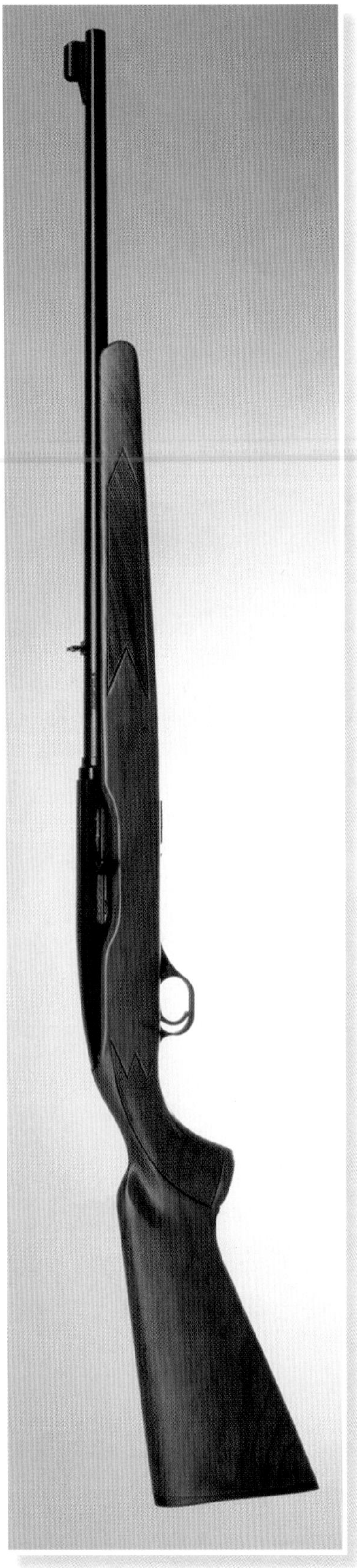

Model 490.

MODEL 490

This is a blowback-operated, semi-automatic rifle chambered for the .22 LR cartridge. It has a 22" barrel with open sights and a 5-round, detachable magazine. The finish is blued, with a checkered stock. It was manufactured between 1975 and 1980.

EXC.	V.G.	GOOD	FAIR	POOR
325	225	165	100	75

MODEL 677

This model looked the same as the Model 67 but was manufactured without iron sights and therefore will have no sight cuts in the barrel. The rifle was furnished with either 2-3/4 power scopes or 5 power scopes. This model was not serial numbered. Introduced in 1937 and discontinued in 1939.

EXC.	V.G.	GOOD	FAIR	POOR
2250	1350	900	600	300

NOTE: Add a 50 percent premium for rifles chambered for .22 WRF.

MODEL 697

The Model 697 was similar in appearance to the Model 69 except it was equipped exclusively for a telescope. Winchester offered either a 2-3/4 or 5-power scope with the bases attached at the factory and the scope packed separately. Built between 1937 and 1941 with small sales, this model was not serial numbered.

EXC.	V.G.	GOOD	FAIR	POOR
2000	1200	800	600	400

NOTE: For factory scopes with no sights add 50 percent.

Wildcat .22 Bolt Action Rifle. Photo Courtesy U. S. Repeating Arms Company.

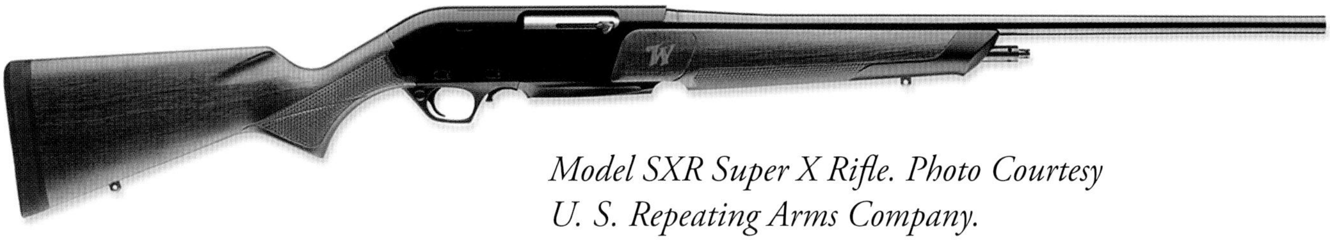

Model SXR Super X Rifle. Photo Courtesy U. S. Repeating Arms Company.

WILDCAT

Bolt-action repeater styled after Mosin-Nagant military sporter. Caliber: .22 LR. Magazine: 5- and 10-round detachable. Stock: checkered walnut with Schnabel. Barrel: 21-inch blued. Weight: 4.5 lbs. Imported. Introduced 2006.

EXC.	V.G.	GOOD	FAIR	POOR
250	225	–	–	–

MODEL SXR SUPER X RIFLE

Gas-operated semi-automatic patterned after Browning BAR ShortTrac and LongTrac. Calibers: .30-06 (4), .300WM (3), .270 WSM (3), .300 WSM (3). Barrel: 22-inch (.30-06), 24-inch. Weight: 7-1/4 lbs. Stock: Two-piece checkered walnut. Introduced 2006.

EXC.	V.G.	GOOD	FAIR	POOR
250	225	–	–	–

EXPRESS RIFLE

This is an Over/Under, double-barreled rifle chambered for the .257 Roberts, .270, 7.7x65R, .30-06, and the 9.3x74R cartridges. It features 23.5" barrels with a solid rib and express sights. It is engraved with game scenes and has a satin-finished receiver. The stock is checkered select walnut. It was manufactured in 1984 and 1985.

EXC.	V.G.	GOOD	FAIR	POOR
2800	1850	1350	1100	750

SECTION V

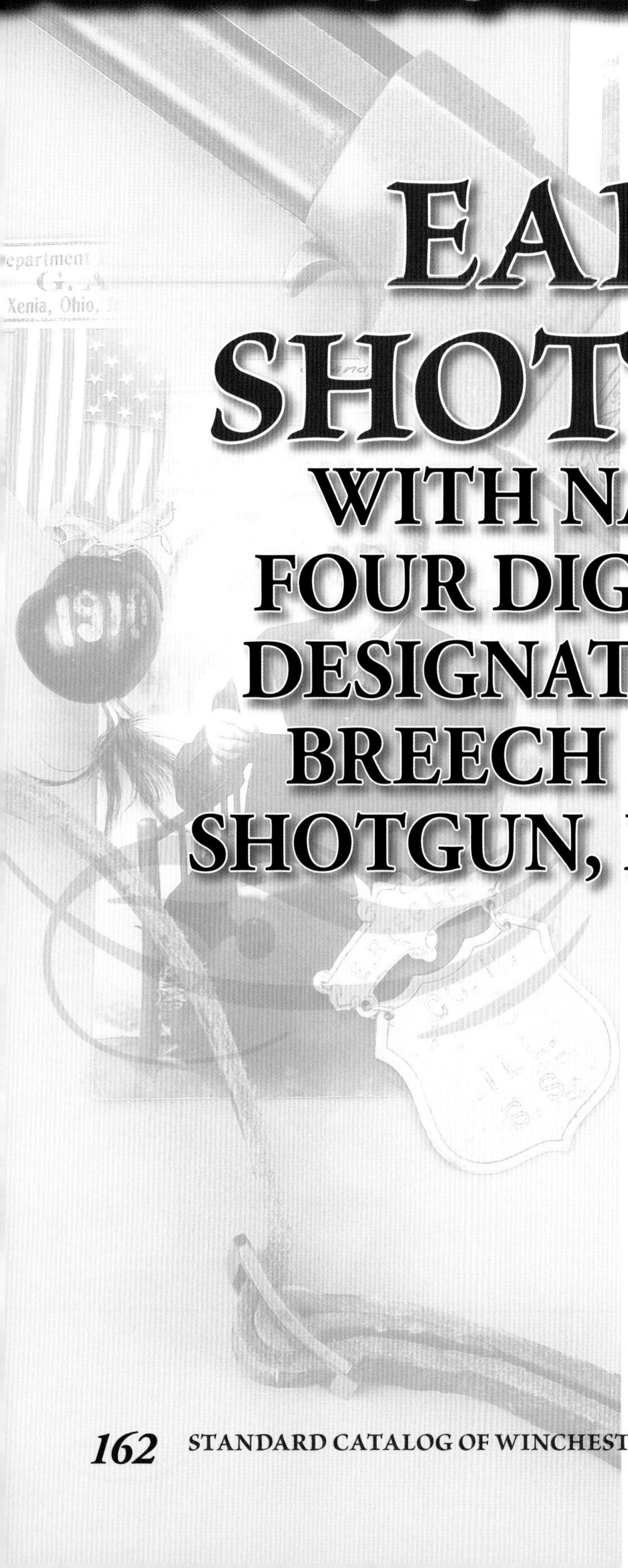

EARLY SHOTGUNS

WITH NAMES OR FOUR DIGIT MODEL DESIGNATIONS: E.G., BREECH LOADING SHOTGUN, MODEL 1897

Editor's Note: Due to semantic and rhetorical considerations, organizing this book into sections of shotguns and rifles is not perfectly straightforward. For example, the Winchester Model 1885 single-shot rifle had a shotgun variation in 20 gauge. Is that a rifle, a shotgun, or something in between? Nevertheless, we have done our best to present the following information in a manner most helpful to the reader.

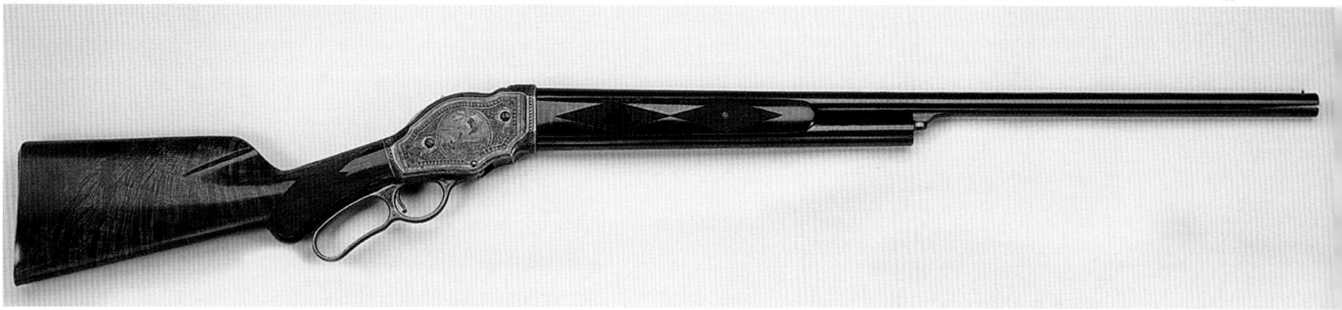

Model 1887 Standard Shotgun Deluxe Grade

BREECHLOADING DOUBLE-BARREL SHOTGUN

Winchester imported an English-made shotgun sold under the Winchester name between 1879 and 1884. The gun was available in 10 and 12 gauge with 30" or 32" Damascus barrels. It was sold in five separate grades referred to as "classes." The lowest grade was the "D" and the best grade was called the "Match Grade." These were marked on the sidelocks. The center rib was stamped "Winchester Repeating Arms Co., New Haven, Connecticut, U.S.A." About 10,000 of these guns were imported by Winchester.

CLASS A, B, C, AND D

EXC.	V.G.	GOOD	FAIR	POOR
2500	2250	1250	850	500

MATCH GUN

EXC.	V.G.	GOOD	FAIR	POOR
2500	2250	1250	850	500

MODEL 1887 SHOTGUN

Winchester enjoyed a great deal of success with its imported English shotgun, and the company decided to manufacture a shotgun of its own. In 1885 it purchased the patent for a lever-action shotgun designed by John M. Browning. By 1887 Winchester had delivered the first model 1887 in 12 gauge and shortly after offered the gun in 10 gauge. Both gauges were offered with 30" or 32" Full choked barrels, with the 30" standard on the 12 gauge and 32" standard on the 10 gauge. A Riot Gun was offered in 1898 both in 10, and 12 gauge with 20" barrels choked cylinder. Both variations of the Model 1887 were offered with plain walnut pistol-grip stocks with plain forend. The frame was case hardened and the barrel blued. Between 1887 and 1901 Winchester sold approximately 65,000 Model 1887 shotguns.

STANDARD SHOTGUN

EXC.	V.G.	GOOD	FAIR	POOR
2500	1500	850	500	300

RIOT SHOTGUN

EXC.	V.G.	GOOD	FAIR	POOR
3000	2000	950	600	400

MODEL 1893

This was the first slide-action repeating shotgun built by Winchester. It featured an exposed hammer and side ejection. Based on a John M. Browning patent, this model was not altogether satisfac-

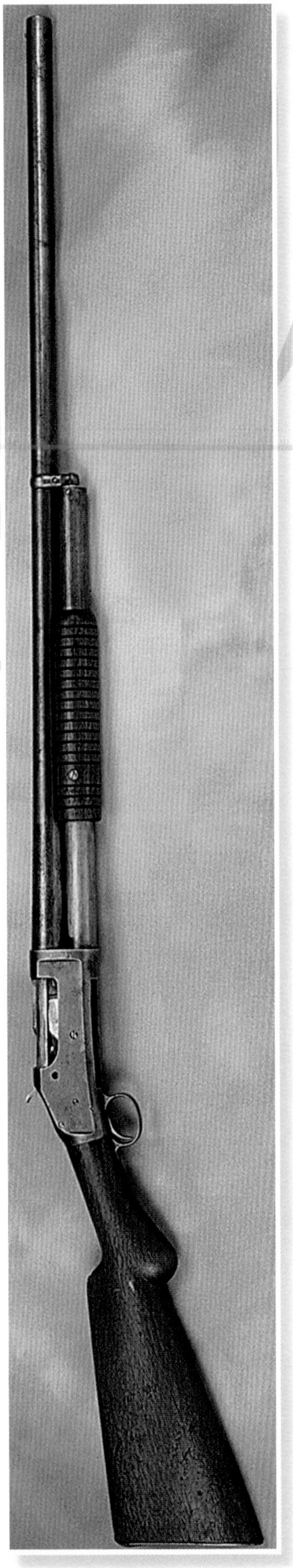

Model 1893.

tory. The action proved to be too weak to handle smokeless loads, even though the gun was designed for black powder. The gun was offered in 12 gauge with 30" or 32" barrels choked Full. Other chokes were available on special order and will command a premium. The stock was plain walnut with a modified pistol grip, grooved slide handle, and hard rubber buttplate. The receiver and barrel were blued. Winchester produced the Model 1893 between 1893 and 1897, selling about 31,000 guns.

STANDARD SHOTGUN

EXC.	V.G.	GOOD	FAIR	POOR
1000	700	600	325	250

MODEL 1897

The Model 1897 replaced the Model 1893, and while similar to the Model 1893, the new model had several improvements such as a stronger frame, chamber made longer to handle 2-3/4" shells, frame top was covered to force complete side ejection, the stock was made longer and with less drop. The Model 1897 was available in 12 or 16 gauge with the 12 gauge offered either in solid or takedown styles and the 16 gauge available in takedown only. The Model 1897 was available with barrel lengths of 20", 26", 28", 30", and 32" and in practically all choke options from full to cylinder. The shotgun could be ordered in several different configurations:

1) Standard Gun, 12 or 16 gauge, 30" barrel in 12 gauge and 28" barrel in 16 gauge, with plain walnut modified pistol- grip stock and grooved slide handle. Steel buttplate standard.
2) Trap Gun 12 or 16 gauge, 30" barrel in 12 gauge and 28" barrel in 16 gauge, fancy walnut stock with oil finish checkered pistol-grip or straight-grip stock with checkered slide handle. Marked "TRAP" on bottom of frame.
3) Pigeon Gun, 12 or 16 gauge, 28" barrel on both 12 and 16 gauge, straight- or pistol-grip stock same as Trap gun, receiver hand engraved.

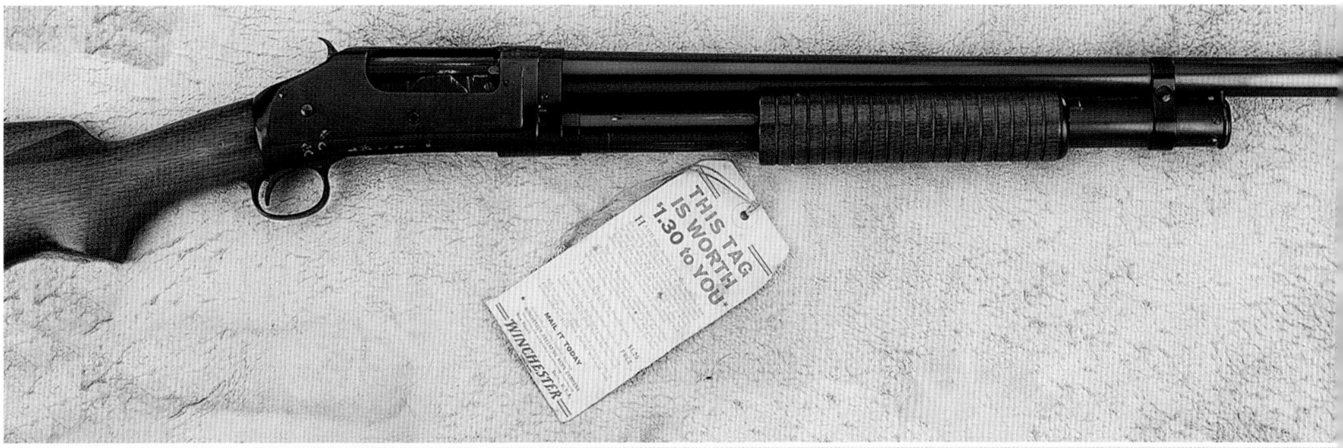

Model 1897, Closeup with Hang Tag.

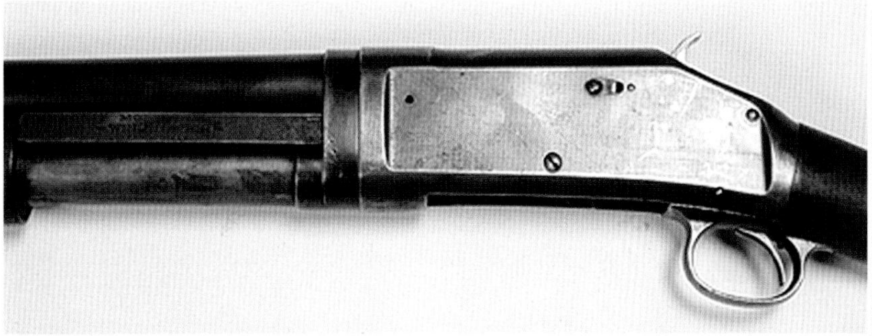

Model 1897. Close-up of receiver..

4) Tournament Gun, 12 gauge only with 30" barrel, select walnut checkered straight-grip stock and checkered slide handle, top of receiver is matted to reduce glare.
5) Brush Gun, 12 or 16 gauge, 26" barrel, Cylinder choke, has a slightly shorter magazine tube than standard gun, plain walnut modified pistol-grip stock with grooved slide handle.
6) Brush Gun, Takedown, same as above with takedown feature and standard length magazine tube.
7) Riot Gun, 12 gauge, 20" barrel bored to shoot buckshot, plain walnut modified pistol-grip stock with grooved slide handle. Solid frame or takedown.
8) Trench Gun, same as Riot Gun but fitted with barrel hand guard and bayonet.

The Winchester Model 1897 was a great seller for Winchester. During its 60-year production span, 1,025,000 guns were sold.

STANDARD GUN

EXC.	V.G.	GOOD	FAIR	POOR
800	650	450	300	200

TRAP GUN

EXC.	V.G.	GOOD	FAIR	POOR
1050	900	600	500	400

PIGEON GUN

EXC.	V.G.	GOOD	FAIR	POOR
3000	2500	1600	1250	1000

TOURNAMENT GUN

EXC.	V.G.	GOOD	FAIR	POOR
1100	900	700	500	400

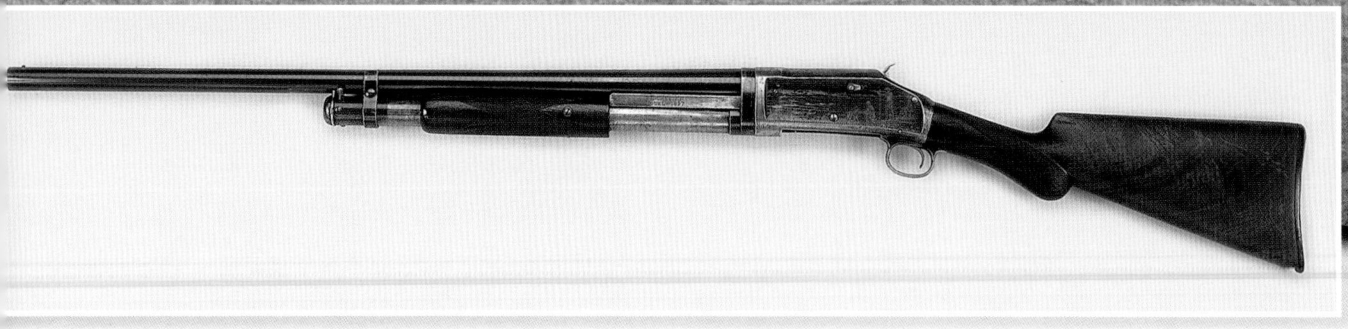

Model 1897 Tournament Gun.

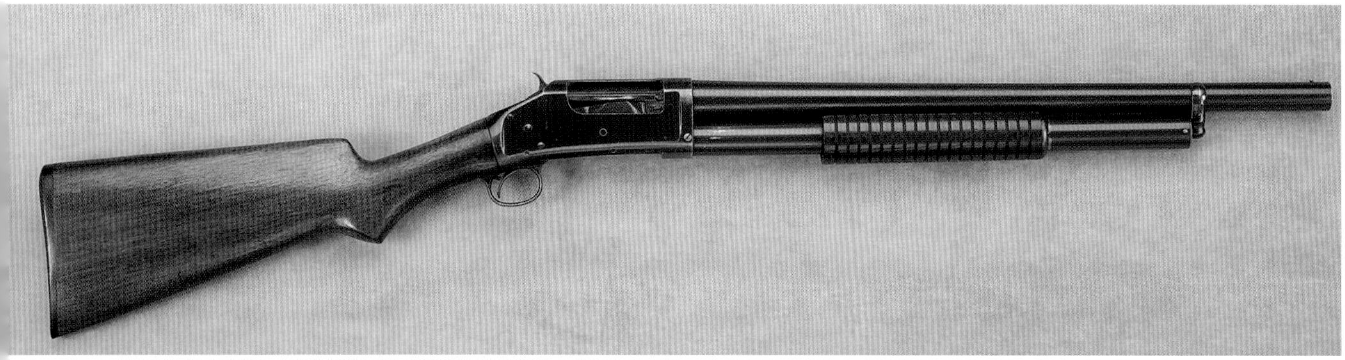

Model 1897 Riot Gun.

BRUSH GUN

EXC.	V.G	GOOD	FAIR	POOR
950	750	600	500	400

RIOT GUN

EXC.	V.G.	GOOD	FAIR	POOR
850	600	500	350	200

TRENCH GUN

EXC.	V.G.	GOOD	FAIR	POOR
2750	2000	1000	500	300

NOTE: Add 25 percent for 16 gauge guns in excellent, very good, and good condition.

MODEL 1901 SHOTGUN

This model is a redesign of the Model 1887 shotgun and was offered in 10 gauge only with a 32" barrel choked Full, Modified, or Cylinder. The barrel was reinforced to withstand the new smokeless powder loads and the frame was blued instead of case hardened. The stock was of plain walnut with a modified pistol and plain forearm. The Model 1901 was built between 1901 and 1920 with about 65,000 guns sold.

STANDARD SHOTGUN

EXC.	V.G.	GOOD	FAIR	POOR
1200	800	600	400	250

MODEL 1912 (SEE MODEL 12 ENTRY IN SECTION IV)

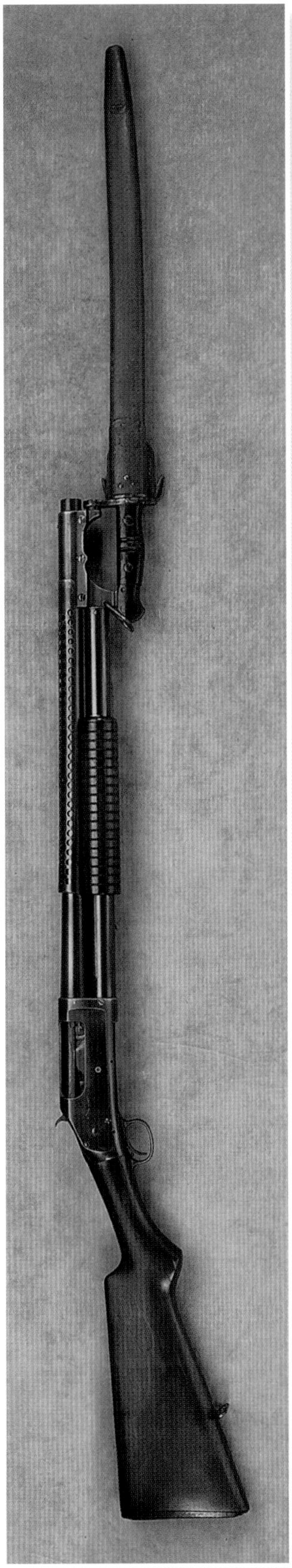

Model 1897 Trench Gun.

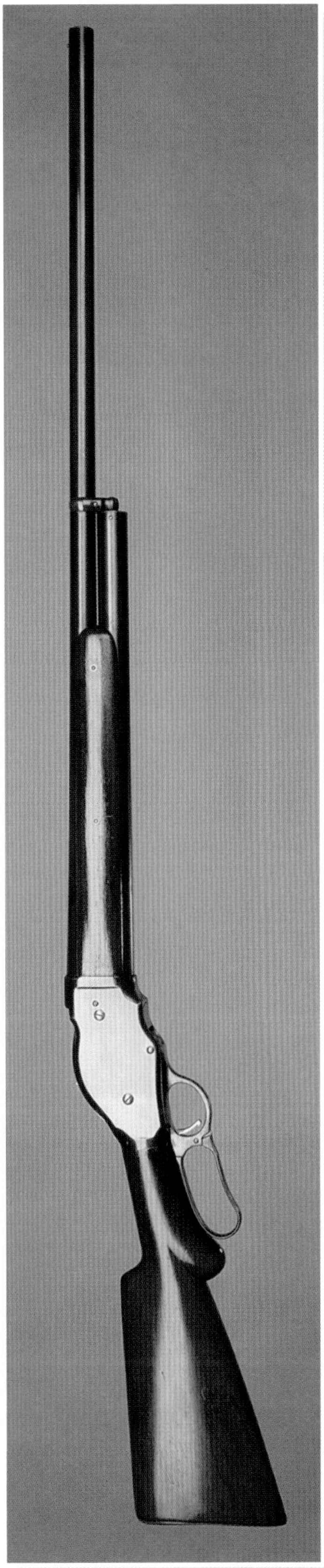

Model 1901 Standard Shotgun.

SECTION VI

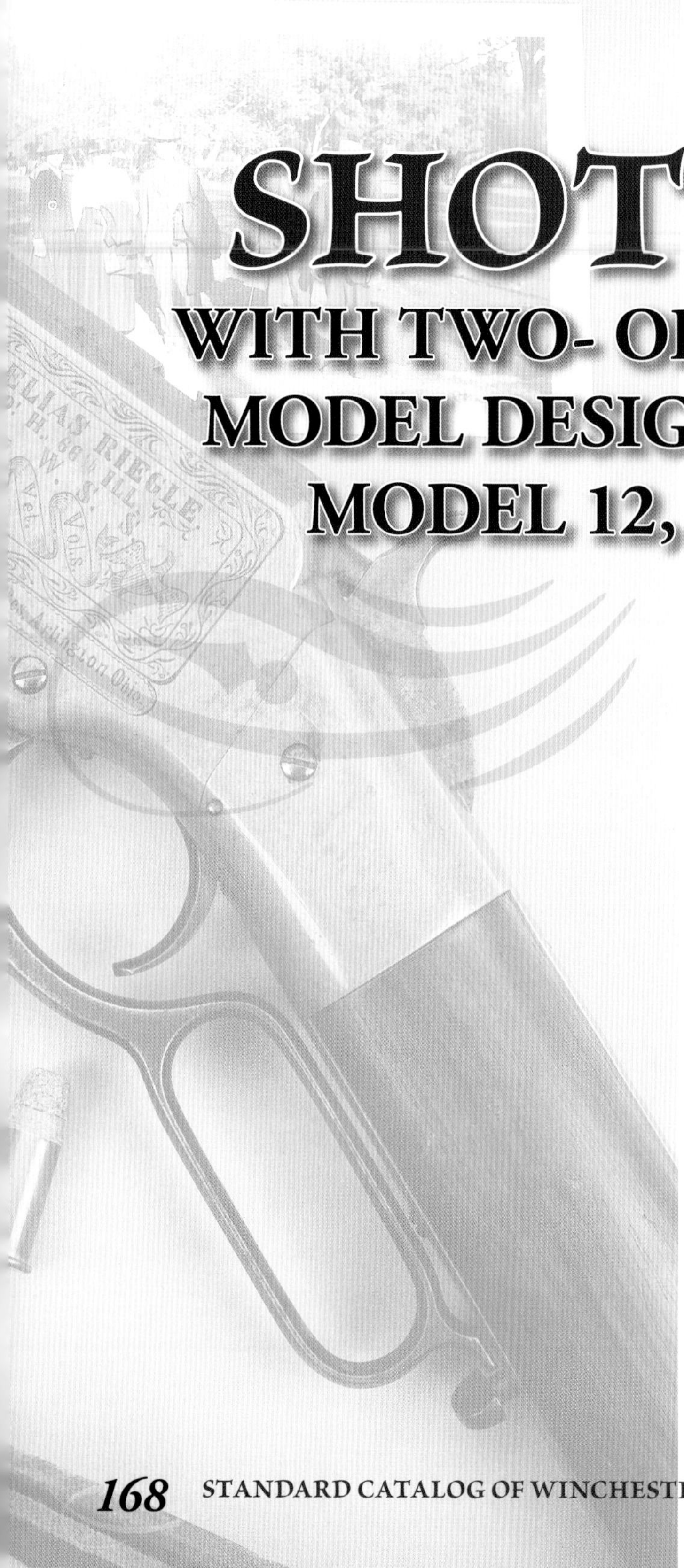

SHOTGUNS

WITH TWO- OR THREE-DIGIT MODEL DESIGNATIONS, E.G. MODEL 12, MODEL 101

MODEL 12

This model was designed by T.C. Johnson and was the first slide-action hammerless shotgun built by Winchester. The Model 12 has enjoyed great success in its 51-year history, and over 1,900,000 were sold. This was a high quality, well-made shotgun that is still in use in the hunting and shooting fields across the country. All Model 12s were of the takedown variety. The Model 12 was dropped from regular product line in 1963, but a special model was produced in the Custom Shop until 1979. In 1972 Winchester resurrected the Model 12 in its regular production line in 12 gauge only and ventilated rib. This reintroduced Model 12 was dropped in 1980. The prices listed are for guns made prior to 1964 or for guns with serial numbers below 1968307. This shotgun was offered in several different styles:

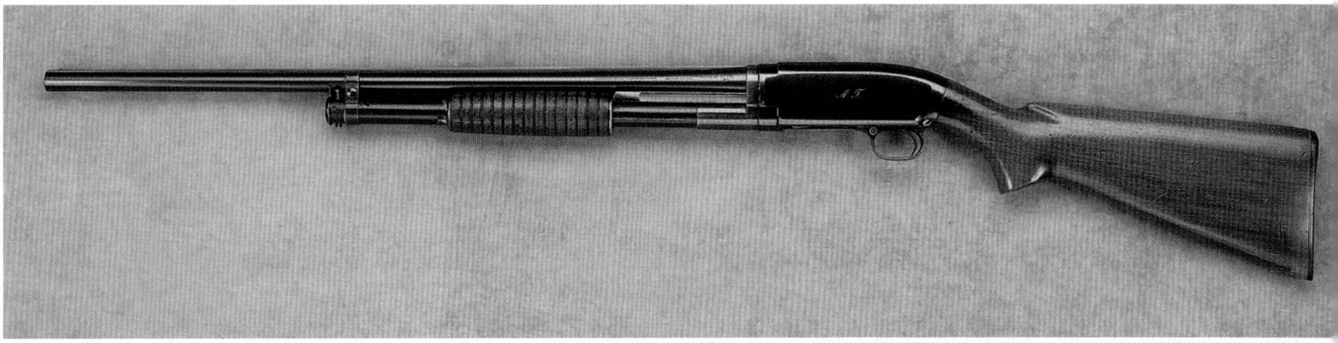

Model 12 in 20 Gauge.

1) Standard Grade, 12, 16, 20, and 28 gauge, with plain, solid rib, or vent rib round barrels of standard lengths (26", 28", 30", 32"), plain walnut pistol-grip stock with grooved slide handle. Built from 1912 to 1963.
2) Featherweight, same as above with lightweight alloy trigger guard. Built between 1959 and 1962.
3) Riot Gun, in 12 gauge only with 20" round choked cylinder, stock same as Standard Grade. Built between 1918 and 1963.
4) Trench Gun, chambered for 12 gauge only with 20" round barrel with ventilated hand guard over barrel, fitted with bayonet lug. All metal surfaces are "Parkerized," and these shotguns should be U.S. marked as a military firearm. Introduced in 1918 and built for U.S. Armed Forces on special order.
5) Skeet Grade, chambered for 12, 16, 20, and 28 gauge with 26" round barrel with solid or ventilated rib, select walnut checkered pistol stock and special checkered extension slide handle (longer than standard). Built from 1933 to 1963.
6) Trap Grade, chambered for 12 gauge only with 30" round barrel with solid rib or ventilated rib, select walnut pistol or straight-grip stock, checkered extension slide handle. Built from 1914 to 1963.
7) Heavy Duck Gun, chambered in 12 gauge only with 30" or 32" round barrel with plain, solid, or ventilated rib, plain walnut pistol-grip stock fitted with Winchester solid red rubber recoil pad, plain grooved slide handle. Built from 1935 to 1963.
8) Pigeon Grade, chambered for 12, 16, 20, and 28 gauges with standard barrel lengths and choice of ribs. This was a special order shotgun and will be seen in many different variations, most of these guns were factory engraved. Built 1914 to 1963.

The Model 12 shotgun will be seen in many different combinations of gauges, barrel lengths, ribs, and stocks, all of which determine value. The more rare a particular combination, the higher the price. The buyer is urged to be extremely cautious before purchasing the more rare combinations, such as a 28 gauge. The best advice is to seek assistance from an expert and get as many opinions as possible. The prices listed are for guns in standard configurations.

STANDARD GRADE

EXC.	V.G.	GOOD	FAIR	POOR
750	400	300	300	200

FEATHERWEIGHT

EXC.	V.G.	GOOD	FAIR	POOR
600	450	350	275	200

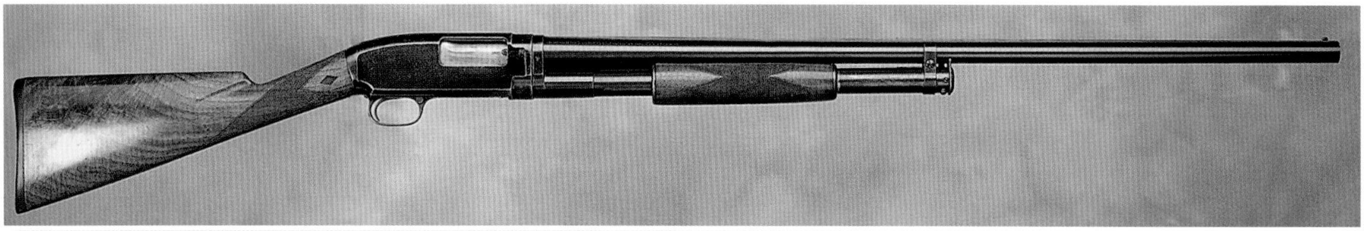

Model 1897 "Black Diamond" Trap Gun.

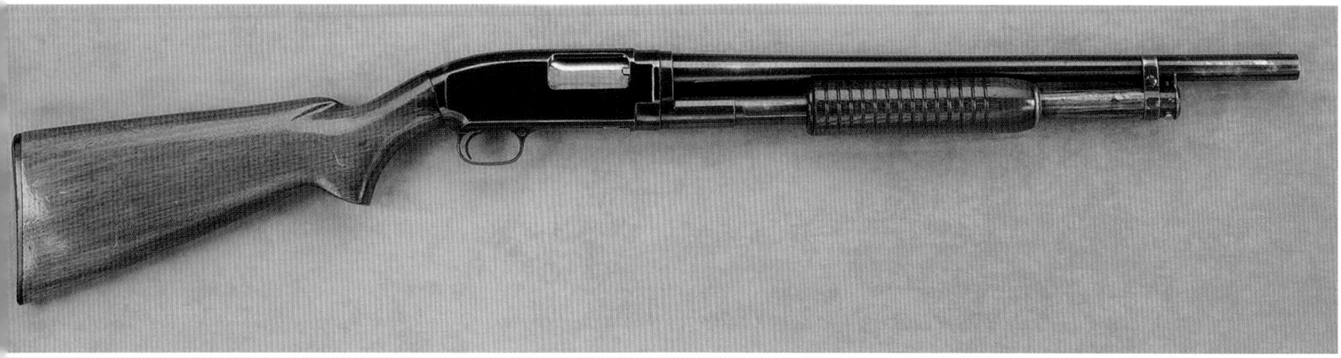

Model 12 Riot Gun.

RIOT GUN

EXC.	V.G.	GOOD	FAIR	POOR
825	650	550	400	250

TRENCH GUN

EXC.	V.G.	GOOD	FAIR	POOR
2750	1750	1100	600	400

SKEET GRADE

EXC.	V.G.	GOOD	FAIR	POOR
1500	850	700	400	350

TRAP GRADE

EXC.	V.G.	GOOD	FAIR	POOR
1000	700	600	450	400

HEAVY DUCK GUN

EXC.	V.G.	GOOD	FAIR	POOR
750	600	450	325	300

NOTE: For Heavy Duck Guns with solid ribs add 25 percent premium.

PIGEON GRADE

EXC.	V.G.	GOOD	FAIR	POOR
2500	1500	1250	650	500

NOTE: For 16 gauge deduct 10 percent. For 20 gauge add 20 percent. For 28 gauge add 600 percent. For guns with solid rib add 20 percent. For guns with Winchester Special ventilated rib add 30 percent. For guns with milled rib add 40 percent. Add 20 percent for 32" barrels on any Model 12 model. Add 30 percent premium for original box and papers.

POST-1964: MODEL 12

POST-1964 SHOTGUNS:
MODEL 12 "Y" SERIES

MODEL 12 FIELD GRADE

This is a later version of the slide-action Model

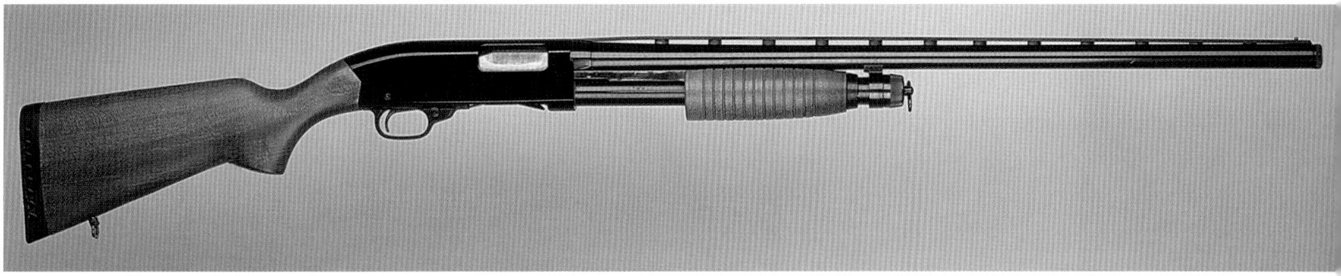

Model 120 Ranger.

12, chambered for 12 gauge only. It was offered with a 26", 28", or 30" vent rib barrel with various chokes. The finish is blued with a jeweled bolt and a hand-checkered, select walnut stock. This version is easily recognizable as it has the letter Y serial number prefix. It was manufactured between 1972 and 1976.

EXC.	V.G.	GOOD	FAIR	POOR
650	550	400	350	275

MODEL 12 SUPER PIGEON GRADE

This is a deluxe version that features extensive engraving and fancy checkering. It was offered with a turned action and select, fancy-grade walnut. It was a limited-production item produced between 1964 and 1972. It was briefly reintroduced in 1984 and discontinued again in 1985.

EXC.	V.G.	GOOD	FAIR	POOR
3000	2500	1850	1400	950

MODEL 12 SKEET

This version is similar to the Field Grade but is offered with a 26", vent rib, skeet-bored barrel. The finish is blued, with a skeet-type stock and recoil pad. It was manufactured between 1972 and 1975.

EXC.	V.G.	GOOD	FAIR	POOR
750	650	550	350	300

MODEL 12 TRAP GRADE

This version features a 30" vent rib barrel with a Full choke. It is blued with a trap-type, standard, or Monte Carlo stock with a recoil pad. It was manufactured between 1972 and 1980.

EXC.	V.G.	GOOD	FAIR	POOR
700	600	500	300	200

MODEL 12 (LIMITED EDITION)

Available in 20 gauge only. Furnished with a 26" vent rib barrel choked Improved Cylinder. The walnut stock is checkered with pistol grip. Introduced in 1993 and available in three different grades.

GRADE 1

4,000 guns.

NIB	EXC.	V.G.	GOOD	FAIR	POOR
700	600	450	350	200	100

GRADE IV

1,000 guns, gold highlights.

NIB	EXC.	V.G.	GOOD	FAIR	POOR
1150	900	650	400	200	100

DUCKS UNLIMITED MODEL

Available through Ducks Unlimited chapters. An independent appraisal is suggested.

MODEL 120 RANGER

An no-frills variant of the Model 1200 slide action. Offered in 12, 16 and 20 gauge.

NIB	EXC.	V.G.	GOOD	FAIR	POOR
225200		165	140	85	50

MODEL 140 RANGER

An no-frills variant of the Model 1400 semi-auto. Offered in 12, 16 and 20 gauge.

NIB	EXC.	V.G.	GOOD	FAIR	POOR
225	200	165	140	85	50

"The Model 21 was Winchester's finest effort with regard to quality, reliability, and strength."

MODEL 20

In order to utilize the expanded production facilities left over from WWI, Winchester introduced a series of three different models of single-shot shotguns; the Model 20 was the first of the three. This model has a visible hammer and a top lever frame. It was the first Winchester to have this type of breakdown action. It was chambered for the .410, 2-1/2" shell. The barrel is 26" round choked full, plain walnut pistol-grip stock with hard rubber buttplate. The forend has a small lip on the front end. The Model 20 was dropped from the product line in 1924 having sold about 24,000 guns.

EXC.	V.G.	GOOD	FAIR	POOR
700	500	350	200	150

MODEL 21

The Model 21 was Winchester's finest effort with regard to quality, reliability, and strength. Developed in the late 1920s the introduction of this fine side-by-side shotgun was delayed by the company's financial troubles. When Winchester was purchased by the Olin family, the Model 21 was assured the attention it richly deserved due to John M. Olin's love for the gun. Despite the Model 21 being offered as a production gun it was, in fact, a hand-built custom-made shotgun. Almost each Model 21 built has a personality of its own because each shotgun is slightly different with regard to chokes, barrel lengths, stock dimensions, and embellishments. The gun was introduced in 1931. From 1931 to 1959 the Model 21 was considered a production line gun and about 30,000 were sold. In 1960, when the Custom Shop was opened, the Model 21 was built there using the same procedures. Sales during the Custom Shop era were about 1,000 guns. Winchester changed the name of some of the Model 21 styles but the production methods stayed the same. In 1981 Winchester sold its firearms division to U.S. Repeating Arms Company including the right to build the Model 21. Again the production procedures stayed the same

as did many of the former employees. U.S. Repeating Arms expanded and changed some of the style designations for the Model 21. Production was discontinued in about 1991. No sales figures are available for this time period. Collectors and shooters will be given the price breakdown for all three eras of production separately.

NOTE: There were eight 28 gauge Model 21s built during this period and five .410 bores built. These guns obviously command a large premium. Factory letters are available on these guns.

MODEL 21-1931 TO 1959

The Model 21 was available in several different styles and configurations:

1) Standard Grade, chambered in 12, 16, and 20 gauge with barrel length from 26", 28", 30", and 32" with matted rib or ventilated rib, select walnut checkered pistol- or straight-grip stock with checkered beavertail forend. Built from 1931 to 1959.
2) Tournament Grade, same as above with special dimension stock. Marked "TOURNAMENT" on bottom of trigger plate. Built from 1933 to 1934.
3) Trap Grade, same as above with slightly better-grade wood and stock made to customers' dimensions. Marked "TRAP" on trigger plate. Built from 1932 to 1959.
4) Skeet Grade, same as above with the addition of the 28 gauge, stock furnished with checkered butt. Marked "SKEET" on trigger plate. Built from 1936 to 1959.
5) Duck Gun, chambered for 12 gauge 3" magnum shells, 30" or 32" barrels, Standard Grade stock except for shorter length of pull. Marked "DUCK" on trigger plate. Built from 1940 to 1952.
6) Magnum Gun, chambered for 3" 12 or 20 gauge, same stock as Duck Gun. Not marked on trigger plate. Built from 1953 to 1959.
7) Custom Built/Deluxe Grade, chambered for 12, 16, 20, 28, and .410, barrel lengths from 26" to 32", stock built to customer's specifications using fancy walnut. Marked "CUSTOM BUILT" on top of rib or "DELUXE" on trigger plate. These grades are frequently but not always engraved. Built from 1933 to 1959.

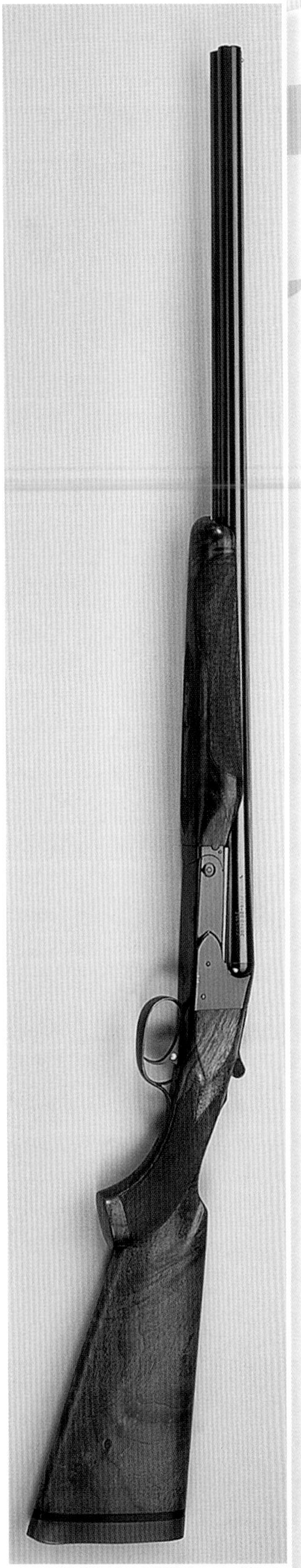

Model 21 Standard Grade in 20 Gauge.

NOTE: Some early Model 21s were furnished with double triggers, extractors, and splinter forends. This combination reduces the price of the gun regardless of grade. Deduct about 25 percent.

STANDARD GRADE

EXC.	V.G.	GOOD	FAIR	POOR
12 gauge				
5500	4700	3800	3300	3000
16 gauge				
6900	6200	5400	4700	4200
20 gauge				
7000	6500	5700	5100	4700

TOURNAMENT GRADE

EXC.	V.G.	GOOD	FAIR	POOR
12 gauge				
5500	4700	3900	3500	3300
16 gauge				
7500	6700	5800	5000	4500
20 gauge				
7700	6900	6000	5400	4800

TRAP GRADE

EXC.	V.G.	GOOD	FAIR	POOR
12 gauge				
5800	4800	4000	3800	3600
16 gauge				
7500	6800	5900	5300	4900
20 gauge				
7700	7000	6300	5800	5300

SKEET GRADE

EXC.	V.G.	GOOD	FAIR	POOR
12 gauge				
5500	4500	3700	3400	3200
16 gauge				
6900	5800	5200	4900	4400
20 gauge				
6900	5900	5200	4800	4200

DUCK/MAGNUM GUN

EXC.	V.G.	GOOD	FAIR	POOR
5600	4600	4200	4000	3800

NOTE: Add 30 percent for 20 gauge Magnum. Factory ventilated ribs command a premium of about $1,800 on 12 gauge guns and $2,500 on 20 and 16 gauge guns. Models 21s with factory furnished extra barrels will bring an additional premium of about $2,500. Refinished and restored Model 21s are in a somewhat unique category of American-made collectible shotguns. A gun that has been professionally refinished by a master craftsman will approximate 90 percent of the value of factory original guns.

CUSTOM BUILT/DELUXE GRADE

The prices paid for guns of this grade are determined by gauge, barrel and choke combinations, rib type, stock specifications, and engraving.

EXC.	V.G.	GOOD	FAIR	POOR
12 gauge				
7000	6500	5500	4500	4000
16 gauge				
8000	7500	6500	5500	4500
20 gauge				
8500	8000	7000	6000	5000

It is best to secure a factory letter from the Cody Firearms Museum. With respect to such letter, it is important to note that these records are incomplete and may be inaccurate in a few cases. Records for Model 21s built during the 1930s may be missing. Special-order guns may have incomplete records. In such cases, a written appraisal from an authoritative collector or dealer may be helpful.

CUSTOM BUILT .410 BORE

EXC.	V.G.	GOOD	FAIR	POOR
45000	35000	30000	26000	22000

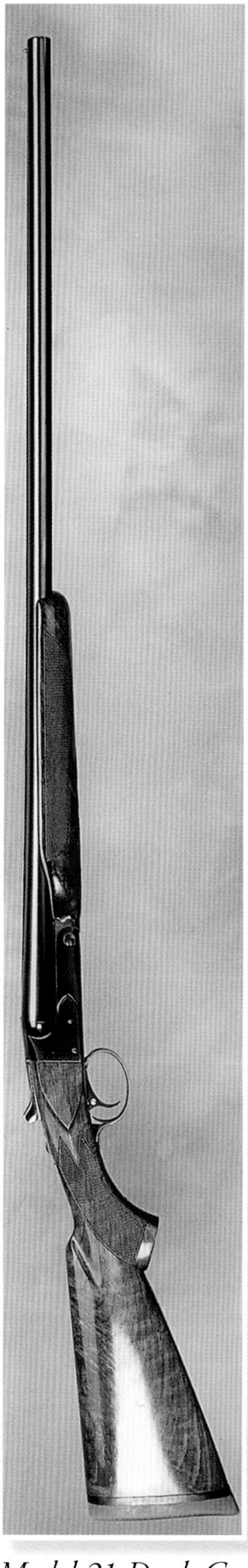

Model 21 Duck Gun.

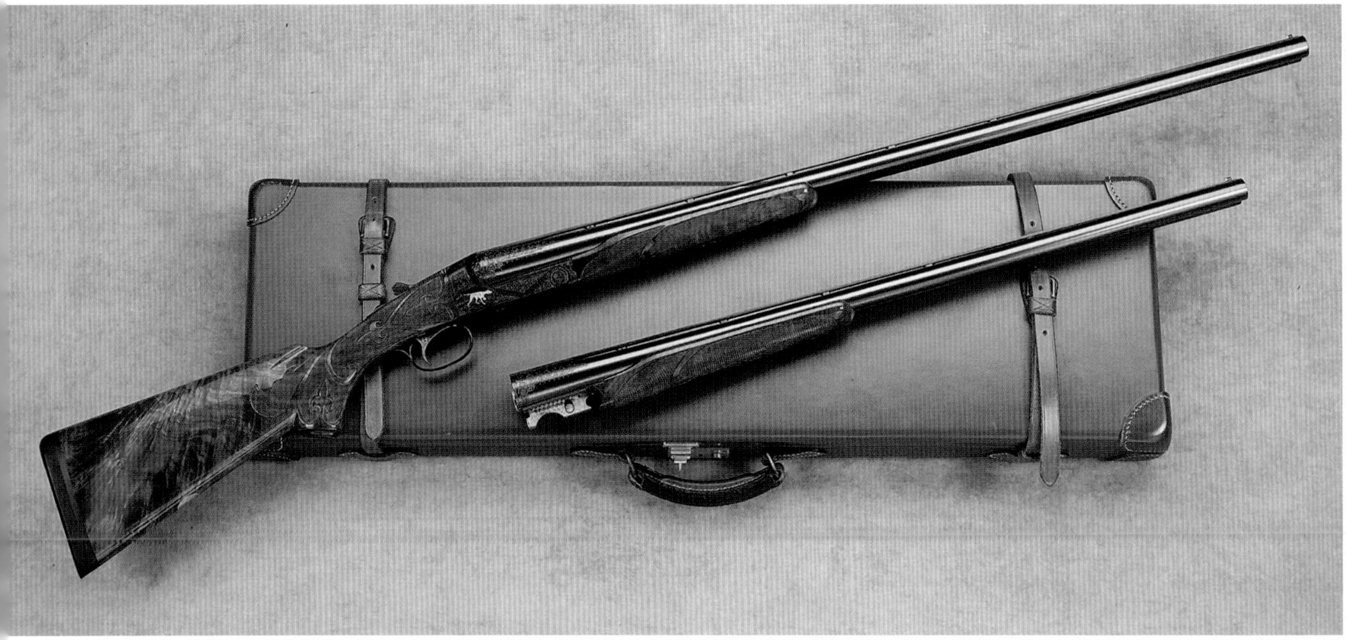

Model 21 Grand American Two-Barrel Set.

CUSTOM SHOP MODEL 21S-1960 TO 1981

When Winchester moved the production of the Model 21 into the Custom Shop, the number of styles was greatly reduced. There were now three distinct styles:

1) Custom Grade, chambered in 12, 16, 20, 28 gauge, and .410 bore in barrel lengths from 26" to 32". Matted rib, fancy walnut checkered pistol- or straight-grip stock with checkered forend. Guns with pistol grips furnished with steel grip cap. A small amount of scroll engraving was provided on the frame of this grade.
2) Pigeon Grade, same chambers and barrel lengths as above with the addition of choice of matted or ventilated rib, leather-covered recoil pad, style "A" carving on stock and forend, and gold engraved pistol grip cap. The frame was engraved with the 21-6 engraving pattern.
3) Grand American Grade, same chambers and barrel lengths as Pigeon Grade with the addition of "B" carving on the stock and forend, 21-6 engraving with gold inlays, extra set of interchangeable barrels with extra forend. All of this was enclosed in a leather trunk case.

CUSTOM GRADE-12 GAUGE

EXC.	V.G.	GOOD	FAIR	POOR
9800	7500	6800	6000	5200

NOTE: Add $4,000 for 16 gauge. Add $3,000 for 20 gauge.

PIGEON GRADE-12 GAUGE

EXC.	V.G.	GOOD	FAIR	POOR
18000	15000	12000	10000	8000

NOTE: Add $6,000 for 16 gauge. Add $5,000 for 20 gauge.

GRAND AMERICAN-12 GAUGE

EXC.	V.G.	GOOD	FAIR	POOR
26000	20000	16000	14000	13000

NOTE: Add $15,000 for 16 gauge (extremely rare). Add $5,000 for 20 gauge.

ENGRAVED MODEL 21S

Winchester catalogued a number of special-order engraving patterns which ranged from a small amount of scroll (#1) to full- coverage game scene and scroll (#6). In addition, there were a few guns engraved on special order to the customer's request. Engraved guns are extremely rare, and the value added will vary with the rarity of the gauge and the date of manufacture. The following table represents

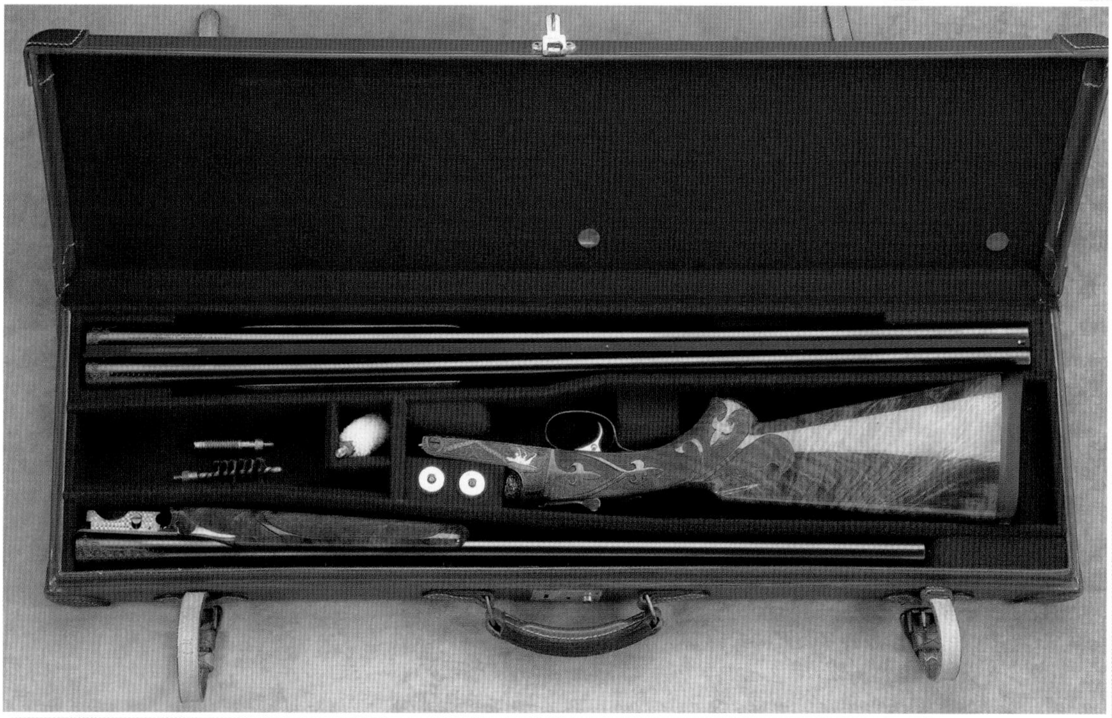

Model 21 Grand American, Cased.

Model 21 Grand American, Closeup of Receiver.

the value added for various standard engraving patterns on 12 gauge guns for the "Custom Shop" (1960-1982) and "Pre-Custom Shop" (1932-1959) periods. However, it is advisable to seek the opinion of an authoritative collector or dealer prior to a sale.

Engraving Pattern	*Pre-Custom Shop*	*Custom Shop*
#1	30 percent	20 percent
#2	40 percent	30 percent
#3	60 percent	45 percent
#4	70 percent	50 percent
#5	90 percent	70 percent
#6	100 percent	80 percent

CUSTOM SHOP MODEL 21S 1982 TO PRESENT

When U.S. Repeating Arms Company took over the production of the Model 21, the Pigeon Grade was dropped from the line. The Grand American Grade was retained with all the features of its predecessor but with the addition of a small-bore set featuring a 28 gauge and .410 bore set of barrels. Two new grades were introduced in 1983: the Standard Custom Grade and the Special Custom Built. In addition to these grades, the factory would undertake to build for its customers whatever was desired. Due to the unique nature of these guns, it is advised that an expert appraisal be sought to establish a value. While the changeover from Winchester to U.S. Repeating Arms was a transfer of business assets and the craftsmen and personnel remained the same, collectors are reluctant to assign the same values to U.S. Repeating Arms Model 21s as those produced by Winchester. No official production figures are available for U.S.R.A. Model 21s, but the number is most likely small; perhaps around 200 guns.

STANDARD CUSTOM BUILT

NIB	EXC.	V.G	GOOD	FAIR	POOR
8000	6500	5500	5000	4500	4000

GRAND AMERICAN

NIB	EXC.	V.G.	GOOD	FAIR	POOR
18000	13000	10000	8500	6000	5000

GRAND AMERICAN SMALL GAUGE SET-28 OR .410 BORE

NIB	EXC.	V.G.	GOOD	FAIR	POOR
60000	45000	35000	27000	22000	20000

MODEL 22

Introduced in 1975 this side-by-side shotgun was manufactured by Laurona in Spain to Winchester's specifications for the European market. It had an oil-finished stock with checkered pistol grip semi-beavertail forearm and hand engraved receiver. The finish was black chrome. The gun was fitted with double triggers, matted rib and offered in 12 gauge only with 28" barrels. It weighs 6-3/4 lbs.

NIB	EXC.	V.G.	GOOD	FAIR	POOR
1250	950	700	550	400	200

MODEL 23 SERIES

MODEL 23 XTR

This is a side-by-side, double-barrel shotgun chambered for 12 or 20 gauge. It is offered with 25.5", 26", 28", or 30" vent rib barrels with 3" chambers and various choke combinations. It is a boxlock gun that features a single trigger and automatic ejectors. It is scroll-engraved with a coin-finished receiver, blued barrels, and a checkered, select walnut stock. It was introduced in 1978. This model is available in a number of configurations that differ in the amount of ornamentation and the quality of materials and workmanship utilized in their construction. These models and their values are listed.

GRADE I

Discontinued.

EXC.	V.G.	GOOD	FAIR	POOR
1325	1100	900	725	450

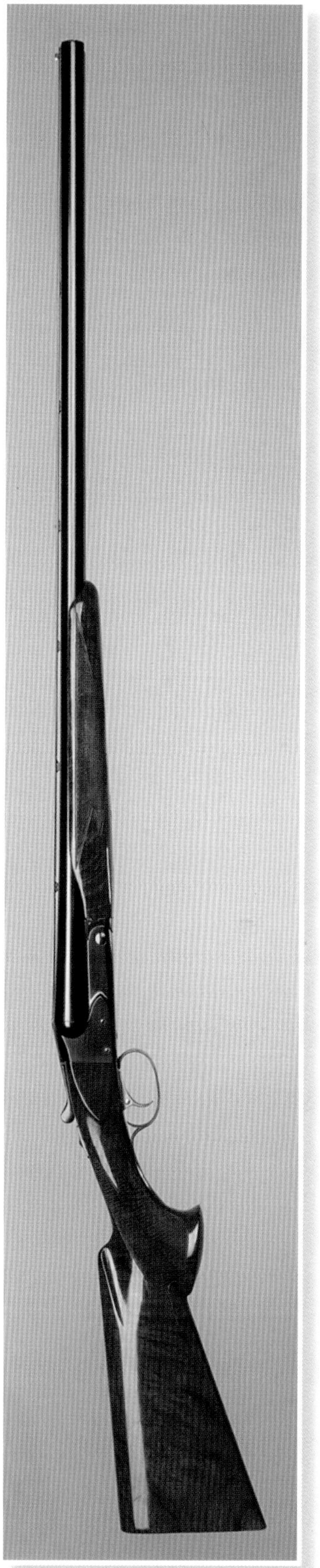

Model 23 Grade I.

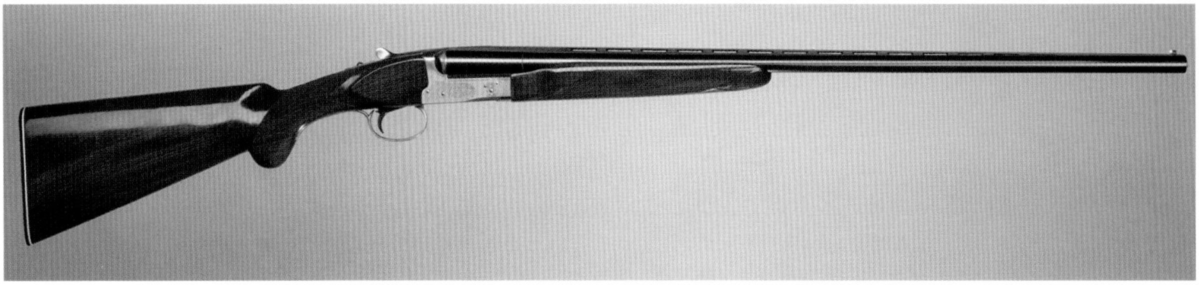

Model 23 Pigeon Grade.

Model 23 Golden Quail.

PIGEON GRADE

With WinChokes.

EXC.	V.G.	GOOD	FAIR	POOR
1450	1200	1075	900	550

PIGEON GRADE LIGHTWEIGHT

Straight stock.

EXC.	V.G.	GOOD	FAIR	POOR
1850	1450	1250	950	650

GOLDEN QUAIL

This series was available in 28 gauge and .410, as well as 12 or 20 gauge. It features 25.5" barrels that are choked improved cylinder/modified. It features a straight-grip, English-style stock with a recoil pad. The .410 version would be worth approximately 10 percent more than the values given. This series was discontinued in 1987.

EXC.	V.G.	GOOD	FAIR	POOR
2150	1800	1500	1100	850

MODEL 23 LIGHT DUCK

This version is chambered for 20 gauge and was offered with a 28" Full and Full-choked barrel. There were 500 manufactured in 1985.

EXC.	V.G.	GOOD	FAIR	POOR
1500	1250	1100	850	750

MODEL 23 HEAVY DUCK

This version is chambered for 12 gauge with 30" Full and Full-choked barrels. There were 500 manufactured in 1984.

EXC.	V.G.	GOOD	FAIR	POOR
1500	1250	1100	850	750

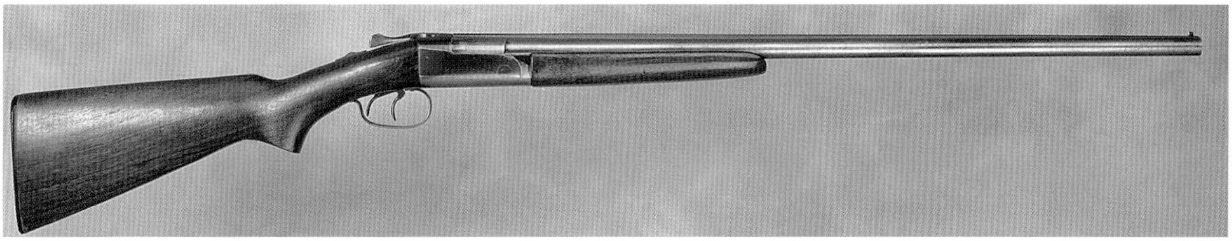

Model 24.

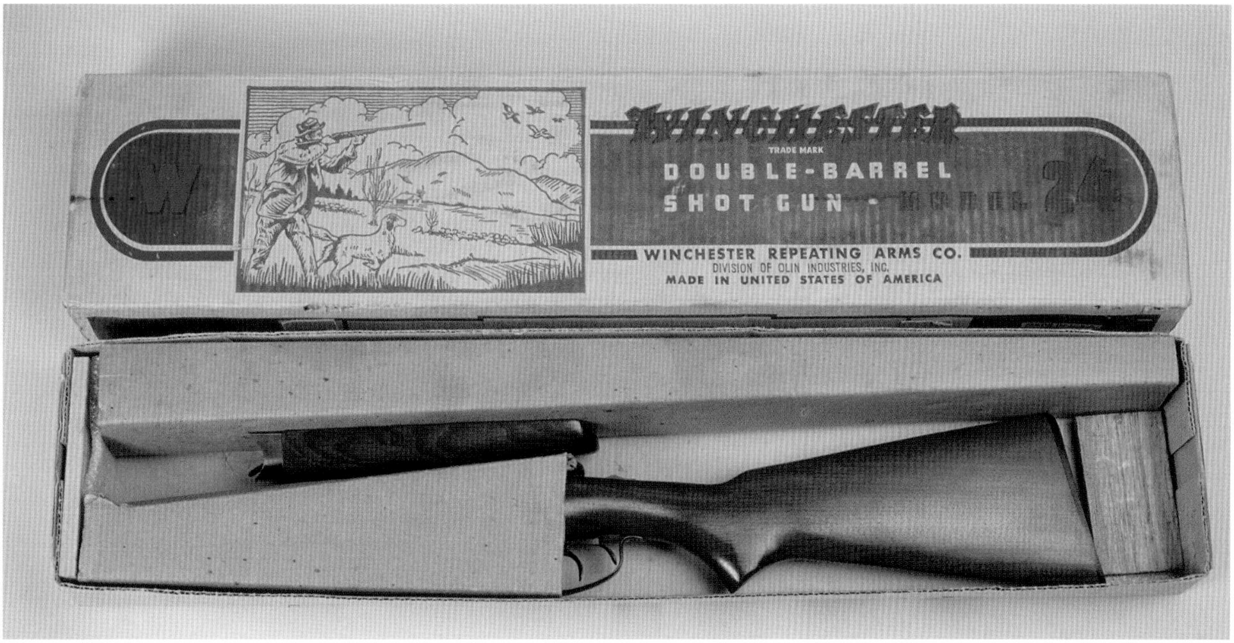

Model 24 in Factory Box.

MODEL 24

The Model 24 was Winchester's attempt to develop a medium-priced double-barrel shotgun. Like the Model 21, it was a top lever breakdown model that was available in 12, 16, and 20 gauge in various barrel lengths from 26" to 30". Offered in a Standard model only with double triggers, raised matted rib, plain walnut pistol- or straight-grip stock with semi-beavertail forend, the Model 24 was introduced in 1939 and was discontinued in 1957 with about 116,000 guns sold.

EXC.	V.G.	GOOD	FAIR	POOR
650	500	400	250	200

NOTE: Add 10 percent for 16 gauge. Add 25 percent for 20 gauge.

MODEL 25

This model is similar in appearance to the Model 12 but does not have the takedown feature. All guns were solid frame. The Model 25 was furnished in 12 gauge with 26" or 28" plain round barrel, plain walnut pistol-grip stock with grooved slide handle. This was an attempt by Winchester to introduce a less expensive version of the Model 12. Introduced in 1949 it was dropped from the product line in 1954 having sold about 88,000 guns.

EXC.	V.G.	GOOD	FAIR	POOR
350	250	200	150	100

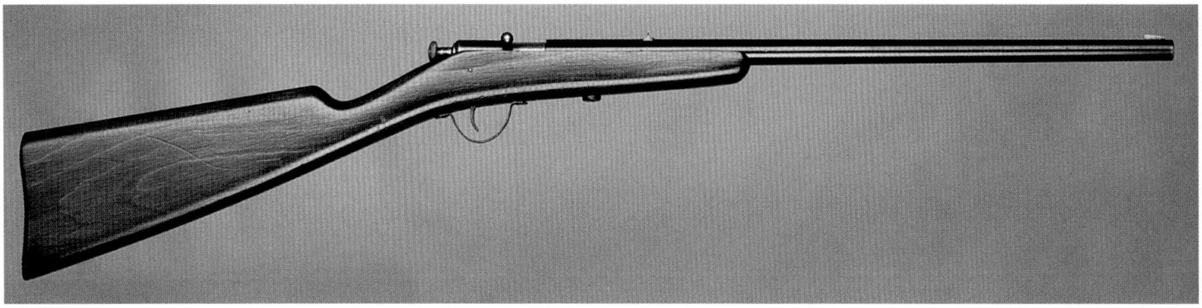

Model 36.

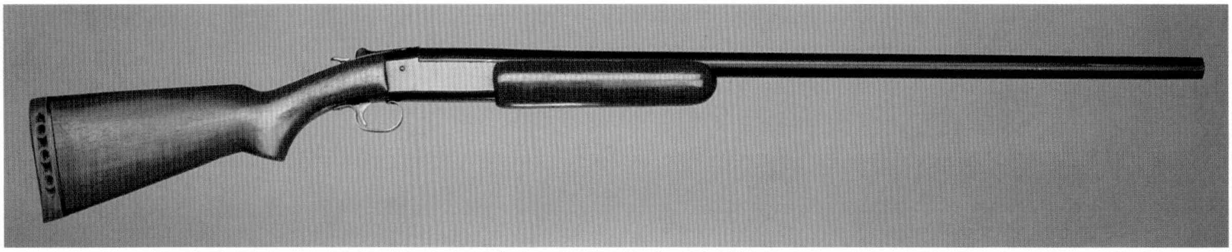

Model 37.

MODEL 36

The Model 36 was the second of the single-shot shotguns to be introduced in 1920. This model features a bolt-action that is cocked by pulling the firing pin head to the rear. It is fitted with an 18" round barrel, chambered for the 9mm Long Shot, 9mm Short Shot, and 9mm Ball interchangeably, plain gumwood straight-grip stock with special metal pistol grip trigger guard. Winchester referred to this model as the "Garden Gun" for use against birds and pests around the house and barn. This model was not serial numbered. It was dropped from the product line in 1927 having sold about 20,000 guns.

EXC.	V.G.	GOOD	FAIR	POOR
750	475	375	300	225

MODEL 37

This model was developed to keep pace with Winchester's competitors in the low-price single-barrel exposed-hammer shotgun market. The shotgun was available in 12, 16, 20, 28 gauge, and .410 bore with barrel lengths from 26" to 30". The stock was plain walnut with pistol grip and semi-beavertail forend. This model was not serial numbered. Introduced in 1936 it stayed in the company line until 1963, having sold slightly over 1,000,000 guns.

NOTE: Do not confuse this model with the Model 37A.

EXC.	V.G.	GOOD	FAIR	POOR
12 gauge				
350	300	250	150	50
16 gauge				
450	400	350	300	75
20 gauge				
600	525	500	425	100
28 gauge				
2500	2000	1150	850	450
.410 bore				
1000	850	500	300	100

YOUTH MODEL

26" Modified choke barrel, Winchester red factory pad.

EXC.	V.G.	GOOD	FAIR	POOR
20 GAUGE	550	450	350	250
125				

NOTE: For 12 and 16 gauge guns add a 50 percent premium for 32" barrels. Use caution for 28 gauge guns. Many fakes are seen for sale.

MODEL 37A

Introduced in 1973. It is single-shot shotgun with exposed hammer. Offered in 12, 16, 20, and 28 gauge as well as .410 bore. All guns choked Full except youth model choked Modified. Walnut finish on hardwood stock. Pistol-grip cap with white spacer. Weight is about 6 lbs. About 395,000 were produced until 1980.

EXC.	V.G.	GOOD	FAIR	POOR
325	225	200	150	100

MODEL 40

This model represents Winchester's second attempt to build a self-loading long recoil-operated repeating shotgun. This shotgun was a hammerless tubular magazine gun without the hump at the rear of the receiver. Available in 12 gauge only with barrel lengths from 28" to 30". The Standard Grade had plain walnut pistol-grip stock and forend. The Skeet Grade was fitted with select walnut checkered pistol-grip stock and checkered forend. The Model 40 suffered from the same design problems as the Model 11, and sales were small. Introduced in 1940 and discontinued in 1941, Winchester sold about 12,000 guns.

STANDARD GRADE

EXC.	V.G.	GOOD	FAIR	POOR
600	500	400	275	200

SKEET GRADE

EXC.	V.G.	GOOD	FAIR	POOR
800	600	500	300	250

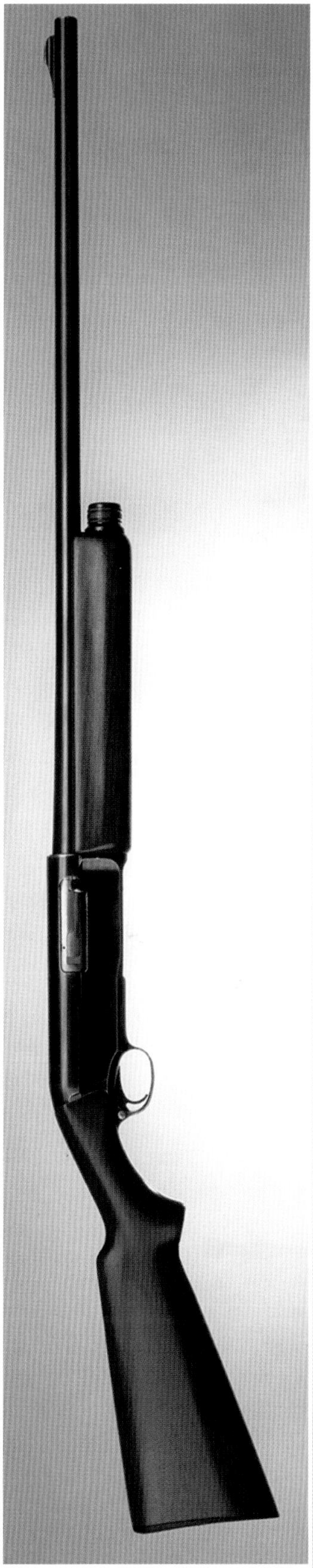

Model 40 Standard Grade.

MODEL 41

This was the third of the low-priced single-shot shotguns to be announced in 1920. Like the Model 36, the Model 41 was a bolt-action arrangement but of much stronger construction and design. It features a 24" round barrel, chambered for the .410 2-1/2" shell, plain walnut pistol-grip stock and forend. Straight-grip stock was furnished at no extra charge. This model was not serial numbered. It was discontinued in 1934 having sold about 22,000 guns.

EXC.	V.G.	GOOD	FAIR	POOR
600	500	350	300	200

MODEL 42

This was the first slide-action shotgun ever developed exclusively for the .410 bore. Invented by William Roemer, the Model 42 was in effect, at least in outward appearance, a miniature Model 12. This shotgun was a quality-built, fast-handling, racy looking shotgun that many refer to as "Everybody's Sweetheart." The Model 42 was the first American .410 bore chambered for the new 3" shell as well as the 2.5" shell. The Model 42 was offered in several different configurations throughout its production. These configurations will greatly influence value:

1) Standard Grade, 26" or 28" plain or solid rib barrel, plain walnut pistol-grip stock with grooved slide handle, fitted with composition buttplate. A straight grip was offered on the Standard Grade on a special order basis, but it is extremely rare. Built from 1933 to 1963.
2) Skeet Grade, 26" or 28" plain, solid rib, or ventilated rib barrel, select walnut checkered pistol or straight-grip stock with checkered extension slide handle. The Skeet Grade was offered in Full, Modified, Improved Cylinder, Cylinder as well as Skeet chokes. Built from 1933 to 1963.
3) Trap Grade, 26" or 28" plain or solid rib barrel, fancy walnut special checkered pistol or straight-grip stock with special checkered extension slide handle. The Trap Grade checkering pattern has one closed diamond on each side of the pistol grip or, in the case of the straight grip, the diamond is located on the underside of the grip. The extension slide handle has two uncut diamonds on each side. Most were stamped "TRAP" on the bottom of the receiver under the serial number. Built from 1934 to 1939.
4) Deluxe Grade, a continuation of the Trap Grade, available with ventilated rib in 1954. Some early models stamped "DELUXE" on bottom of receiver. This stamping is sel-

dom seen and was probably discontinued around 1949. Built from 1940 to 1963.

5) Pigeon Grade, same as above Deluxe Grade but engraved with a pigeon on the lower magazine tube. Very few of this grade were built by Winchester, and the majority were done in the late 1940s. Authentic Pigeon Grade 42s appear to have been built between 1945 and 1949. Some estimate that less than 50 were produced. this is a rare Model 42. Seek an expert opinion before a sale.

NOTE: Engraved Model 42s will occasionally be seen. Collectors are urged to seek expert advice on these rare and expensive guns. The Model 42 was produced from 1933 to 1963. About 164,000 were sold. Factory service and repair for this model were discontinued in February of 1972.

Extra Barrels: Winchester offered extra interchangeable barrels for its Model 42s at the customer's request beginning in 1934. These extra sets of barrels are a rare option. Both barrels should have the same barrel markings and matching serial numbers before originality can be considered. Values are difficult to determine, but as a general rule add 60 percent to the price of a Model 42 if it has a factory-original extra barrel.

Editor's Comment: Contrary to traditional views, Winchester did install factory ventilated ribs on its Model 42. Former employees and factory drawings substantiate this fact. However, the subject of what is a factory rib and what is not has been covered in great detail in an excellent book on the Model 42. Seek expert advice before selling or purchasing any Model 42 with a ventilated rib.

STANDARD GRADE

NIB	EXC.	V.G.	GOOD	FAIR	POOR
2000	1200	950	700	500	250

NOTE: For Standard Grade guns with solid ribs add 50 percent. For pre-war guns add 30 percent.

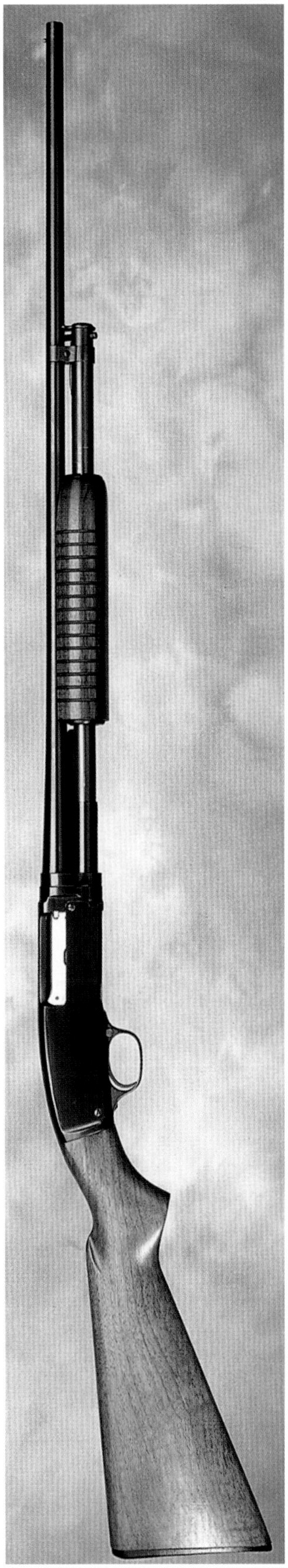

Model 42, Standard Grade.

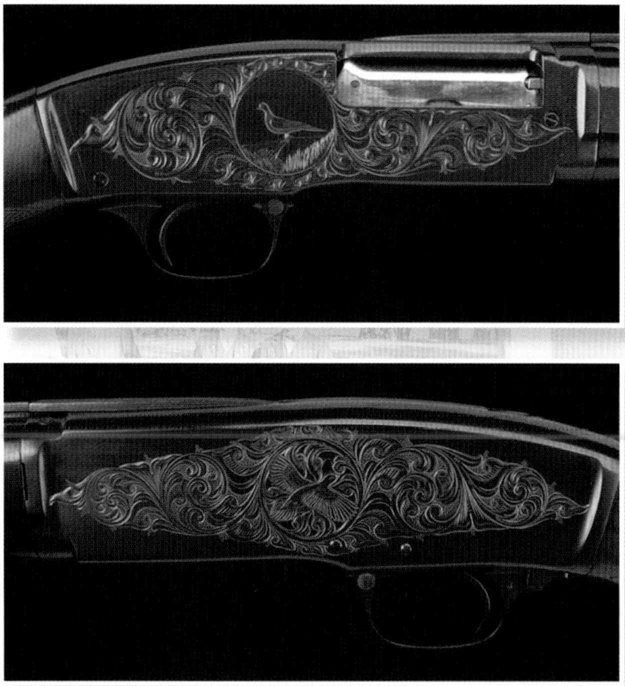

Model 42, Engraved.

SKEET GRADE-SOLID RIB

NIB	EXC.	V.G.	GOOD	FAIR	POOR
4000	3000	2500	1650	850	500

NOTE: Add 25 percent guns chambered for 2-1/2" shells. For pre-war guns add 30 percent. For Skeet Grade guns with no rib deduct 25 percent.

SKEET GRADE-VENTILATED RIB

NIB	EXC.	V.G.	GOOD	FAIR	POOR
5000	4000	3250	1500	900	650

NOTE: Add 25 percent for guns chambered for 2-1/2" shells.

TRAP GRADE

EXC.	V.G.	GOOD	FAIR	POOR
8500	6000	4250	2500	900

DELUXE GRADE-SOLID RIB

EXC.	V.G.	GOOD	FAIR	POOR
6000	4000	2750	950	600

DELUXE GRADE-VENTILATED RIB

EXC.	V.G.	GOOD	FAIR	POOR
7500	5000	2500	950	600

NOTE: For Pigeon Grade Model 42s with documentation on expert authentication add 100 percent.

Cutts Compensator Guns: Approximately 66 original Cutts Compensator guns were produced in the factory, making this one of the rarest options on the Model 42. These original guns will have no choke markings, and were only offered with a vent rib. Add 25 percent for original Cutts guns, deduct 50 percent for non-original Cutts guns.

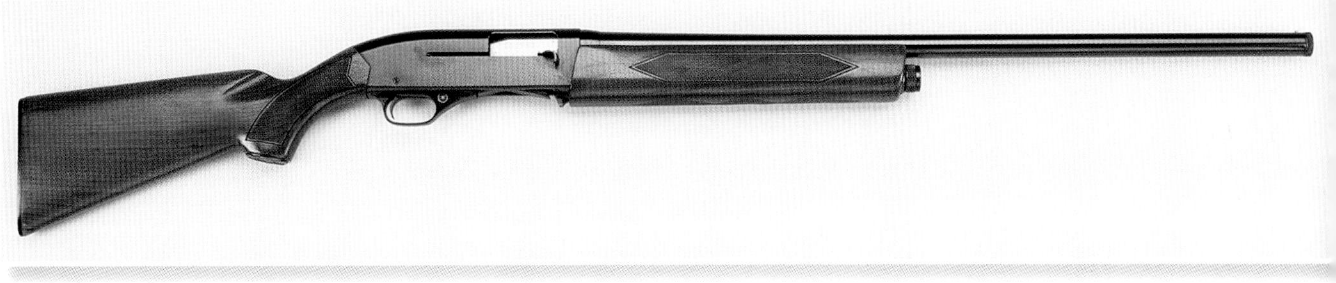

Model 50, Standard Grade.

MODEL 42 (LIMITED EDITION)

A reproduction of the famous Winchester Model 42 .410 bore slide-action shotgun. Furnished with a 26" ventilated rib barrel choked Full. The receiver is engraved with gold border. Introduced in 1993 and limited to 850 guns.

NIB	EXC.	V.G.	GOOD	FAIR	POOR
1250	900	600	400	300	150

MODEL 50

The Model 50 was the company's third attempt to produce a satisfactory self-loading repeating shotgun. Winchester went to the short recoil system, utilizing a floating chamber design. This model was available in several different styles:

1) Standard Grade, 12 or 20 gauge with plain or ventilated rib in lengths from 26" to 30", plain walnut checkered pistol- grip stock and forend.
2) Skeet Grade, 12 or 20 gauge with 26" ventilated rib barrel. Walnut checkered pistol-grip stock and forend.
3) Trap Grade, 12 gauge with 30" ventilated rib barrel, walnut checkered Monte Carlo stock and forend.
4) Pigeon Grade, 12 or 20 gauge with barrel lengths to customers' specifications. Fancy walnut checkered stock and forend. Made on special orders only.
5) Featherweight, a lighter version of all the above except Trap Grade.

This model begins with serial number 1000. This model was successful and was built between 1954 and 1961. Winchester sold about 200,000 guns.

STANDARD GRADE

EXC.	V.G.	GOOD	FAIR	POOR
500	400	300	200	150

SKEET GRADE

EXC.	V.G.	GOOD	FAIR	POOR
600	500	350	250	200

TRAP GRADE

EXC.	V.G.	GOOD	FAIR	POOR
600	500	350	250	200

PIGEON GRADE

EXC.	V.G.	GOOD	FAIR	POOR
1250	900	750	450	250

FEATHERWEIGHT

EXC.	V.G.	GOOD	FAIR	POOR
500	400	325	225	150

NOTE: Add 10 percent for 20 gauge. Add 20 percent for vent rib on standard grade guns.

MODEL 59

The fourth and final pre-1964 Winchester self-loading shotgun featured a steel and fiberglass barrel with aluminum alloy receiver. The gun was available in 12 gauge only with barrel lengths from 26" to 30" with a variety of chokes. In 1961 Winchester introduced the "Versalite" choke tube, which gave

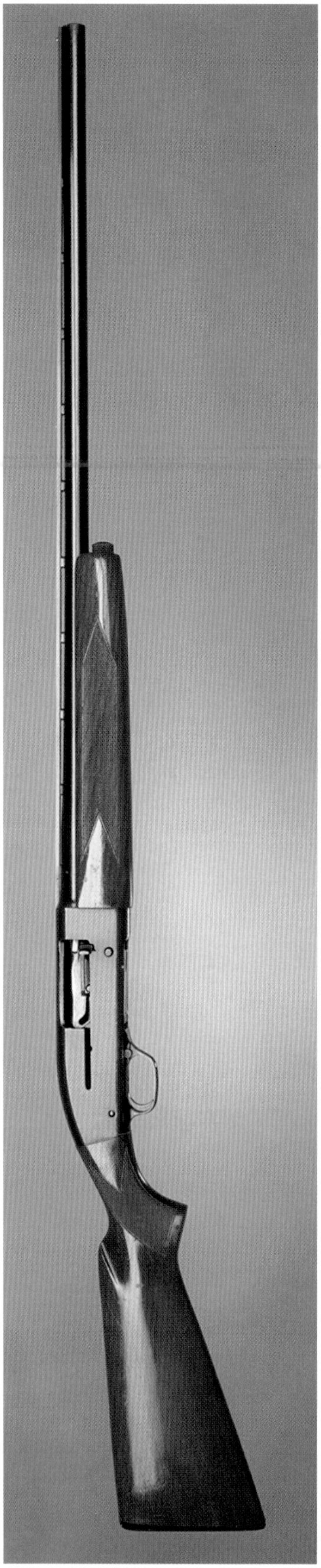

Model 59, Standard Grade.

the shooter a choice of Full, Modified, or Improved Cylinder chokes in the same barrel. This model was available in two different styles:

1) Standard Grade, plain walnut checkered pistol-grip stock and forend.
2) Pigeon Grade, select walnut checkered pistol-grip and forend.

Winchester sold about 82,000 of these guns between 1960 and 1965.

NOTE: This shotgun was also made in 10 gauge (very rare), 20 gauge, and 14 gauge. If any of these very low production or prototype guns are encountered, use extreme caution and seek an expert appraisal.

STANDARD GRADE

EXC.	V.G.	GOOD	FAIR	POOR
650	550	450	350	250

PIGEON GRADE

EXC.	V.G.	GOOD	FAIR	POOR
1500	1100	850	600	300

NOTE: Add 40 percent premium for barrels with three Versalite chokes and wrench. Add 20 percent premium for original box and papers.

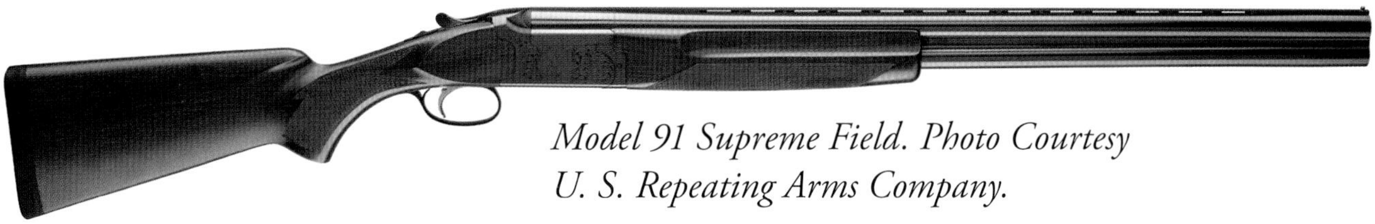

Model 91 Supreme Field. Photo Courtesy U. S. Repeating Arms Company.

Supreme Sporting. Photo Courtesy U. S. Repeating Arms Company.

MODEL 91 SUPREME SERIES

MODEL 91 SUPREME FIELD

Introduced in 2000, this over-and-under gun is chambered for the 12 gauge 3" shell and fitted with 28" vent rib barrels with Invector chokes. Walnut stock with pistol grip and blued engraved receiver. Weight is about 7.5 lbs.

NIB	EXC.	V.G.	GOOD	FAIR	POOR
1240	975	-	-	-	-

MODEL 91 SUPREME SPORTING

Similar to the above model but fitted with a choice of 28" or 30" barrels chambered for 12 gauge 2.75" shells. Barrels are ported. Adjustable trigger. Polished silver receiver with blued barrels. Weight is about 7.5 lbs. Introduced in 2000.

NIB	EXC.	V.G.	GOOD	FAIR	POOR
1400	1000	-	-	-	-

MODEL 91 SUPREME ELEGANCE

Introduced in 2003 this over-and-under model is chambered for the 12 gauge 3" shell. Choice of 26" or 28" vent rib barrels with three choke tubes. Grayed receiver with scroll and bird scenes. Weight is about 7 lbs. depending on barrel length.

NIB	EXC.	V.G.	GOOD	FAIR	POOR
1985	1550	1150	850	-	-

MODEL 101

This is an Over/Under, double-barrel shotgun made in Japan for Winchester and chambered for 12, 20, and 28 gauge, as well as .410. It was offered with 26", 28", or 30" vent rib barrels with various choke combinations. Since 1983 screw-in chokes have been standard, and models so furnished would be worth approximately $50 additional. This is a boxlock gun with a single-selective trigger and automatic ejectors. The receiver is engraved; the finish, blued with a checkered walnut stock. It was manufactured between 1963 and 1987.

EXC.	V.G.	GOOD	FAIR	POOR
875	700	550	425	300

NOTE: 28 gauge add 40 percent; .410 add 50 percent.

WATERFOWL MODEL

This version of the Model 101 is chambered for 12 gauge with 3" chambers. It has 30" or 32" vent rib barrels and a matte finish.

EXC.	V.G.	GOOD	FAIR	POOR
1250	1000	850	650	500

Model 101 Quail in Case.

MODEL 101 MAGNUM

This version is similar to the Field Grade, chambered for 12 or 20 gauge with 3" Magnum chambers. It was offered with 30" barrels with various chokes. The stock is furnished with a recoil pad. It was manufactured between 1966 and 1981.

EXC.	V.G.	GOOD	FAIR	POOR
900	750	575	450	325

MODEL 101 SKEET GRADE

This version was offered with 26" skeet-bored barrels with a competition rib and a skeet-type walnut stock. It was manufactured between 1966 and 1984.

EXC.	V.G.	GOOD	FAIR	POOR
1200	925	825	550	400

MODEL 101 THREE-GAUGE SKEET SET

This combination set was offered with three barrels, chambered for 20 and 28 gauge, as well as .410. It was furnished with a fitted case and manufactured between 1974 and 1984.

EXC.	V.G.	GOOD	FAIR	POOR
2150	1600	1100	800	650

MODEL 101 TRAP GRADE

This version is chambered for 12 gauge only and was offered with 30" or 32" competition ribbed barrels, choked for trap shooting. It is furnished with a competition-type stock. It was manufactured between 1966 and 1984.

EXC.	V.G.	GOOD	FAIR	POOR
1400	1100	925	700	500

MODEL 101 PIGEON GRADE

This is a more deluxe-engraved version of the Model 101, chambered for 12, 20, or 28 gauge, as well as .410. It features a coin-finished receiver with a fancy checkered walnut stock. It was introduced in 1974.

EXC.	V.G.	GOOD	FAIR	POOR
2000	1600	1300	975	750

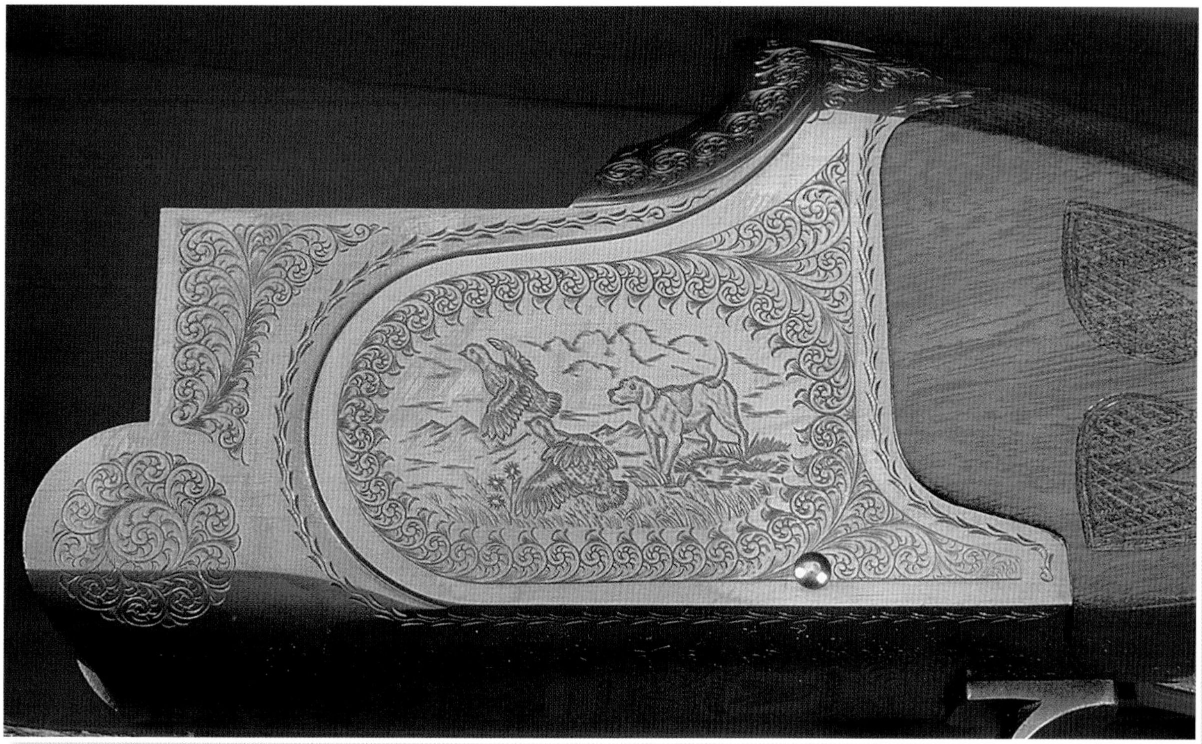

Model 101 Quail, Closeup of Receiver.

SUPER PIGEON GRADE

This is a deluxe version of the Model 101, chambered for 12 gauge. It is heavily engraved with several gold inlays. The receiver is blued, and it features a high-grade walnut stock with fleur-de-lis checkering. It was imported between 1985 and 1987.

EXC.	V.G.	GOOD	FAIR	POOR
4500	3750	2950	2200	1650

QUAIL SPECIAL

Similar to Super Pigeon above, but with quail receiver engraving and fitted case. Limited edition.

EXC.	V.G.	GOOD	FAIR	POOR
4500	3750	2950	2200	1650

MODEL 101 DIAMOND GRADE

This is a competition model, chambered for all four gauges. It was offered in either a trap or skeet configuration with screw- in chokes, an engraved matte-finished receiver, and a select checkered walnut stock. The skeet model features recoil-reducing muzzle vents.

EXC.	V.G.	GOOD	FAIR	POOR
1900	1550	1200	850	650

MODEL 501 GRAND EUROPEAN

This is an Over/Under, double-barrel shotgun chambered for 12 or 20 gauge. It was available in trap or skeet configurations and was offered with a 27", 30", or 32" vent rib barrel. It is heavily engraved and matte-finished, with a select checkered walnut stock. It was manufactured between 1981 and 1986.

EXC.	V.G.	GOOD	FAIR	POOR
1650	1300	1000	750	550

MODEL 501 PRESENTATION GRADE

This is a deluxe version chambered in 12 gauge only. It is ornately engraved and gold-inlaid. The stock is made out of presentation-grade walnut. It was furnished with a fitted case. It was manufactured between 1984 and 1987.

EXC.	V.G.	GOOD	FAIR	POOR
3400	2750	2200	1600	1250

SECTION VII

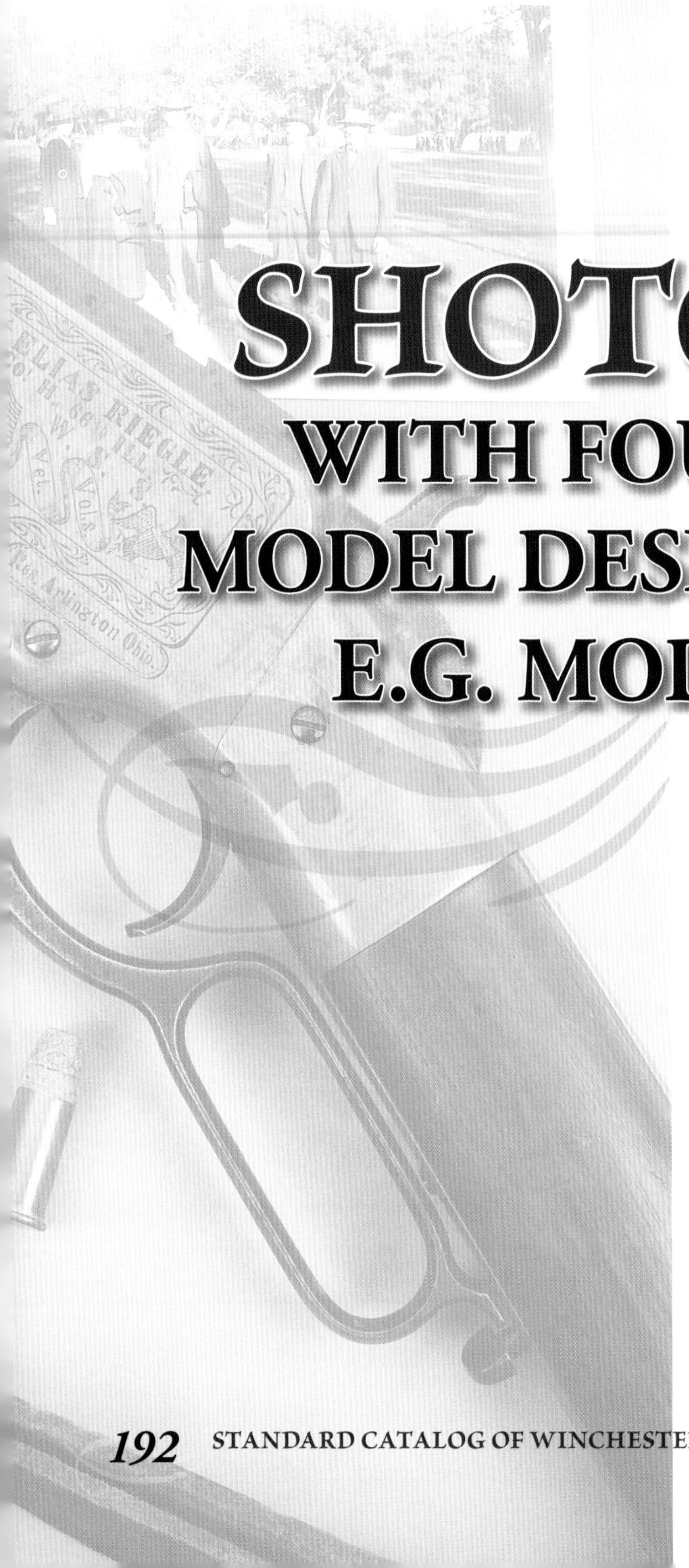

SHOTGUNS WITH FOUR-DIGIT MODEL DESIGNATIONS, E.G. MODEL 1001

MODEL 1001 FIELD

A new addition to the U.S.R.A. product line for 1993. This Over/Under shotgun is available in 12 gauge only, with a 28" ventilated rib barrel furnished with WinPlus choke tubes. A walnut checkered pistol stock is standard. The finish is blued with scroll engraving on the receiver. The receiver top has a matte finish. The gun weighs 7 lbs.

NIB	EXC.	V.G.	GOOD	FAIR	POOR
875	750	650	500	300	150

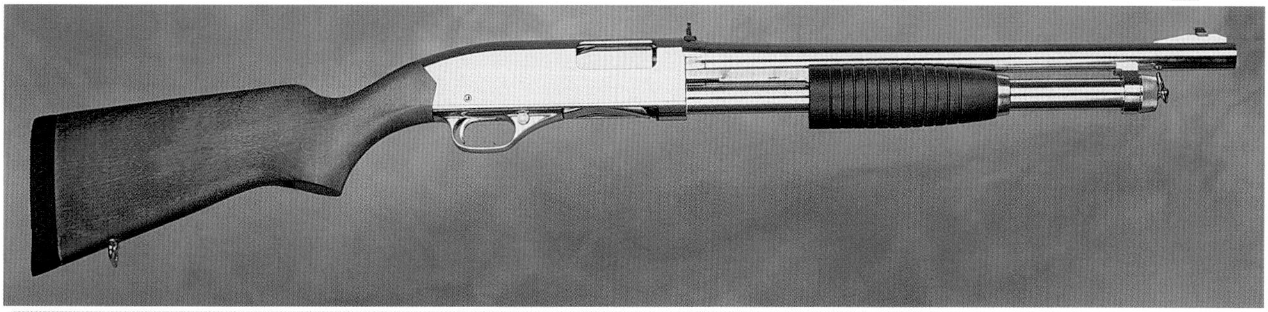

Model 1200 Stainless Marine.

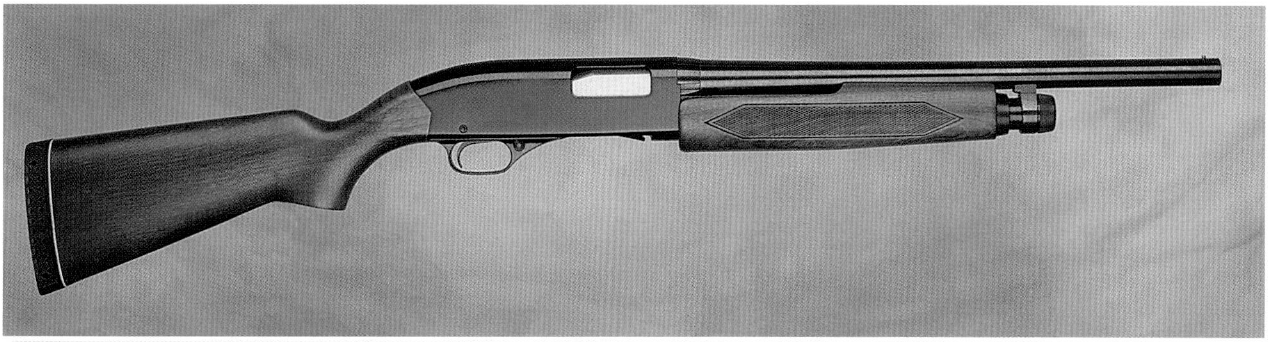

Model 1200 Riot Gun.

MODEL 1001 SPORTING CLAYS I & II

This model features different stock dimensions, a fuller pistol grip, a radiused recoil pad, and a wider vent rib fitted on a 28" barrel (Sporting Clays I model, the Sporting Clays II features a 30" barrel). Comes complete with choke tubes. The frame has a silver nitrate finish and special engraving featuring a flying clay target. Introduced in 1993. Gun weighs 7.75 lbs.

NIB	EXC.	V.G.	GOOD	FAIR	POOR
1000	800	700	550	300	150

MODEL 1200

This is a slide-action shotgun chambered for 12, 16, or 20 gauge. It was offered with a 26", 28", or 30", vent rib barrel with various chokes. It has an alloy receiver and is blued, with a checkered walnut stock and recoil pad. It was manufactured between 1964 and 1981. This model was offered with the plastic Hydrocoil stock, and this would add approximately 35 percent to the values given. Add 25% for "Stainless Marine" variant. Add 50% for riot version.

EXC.	V.G.	GOOD	FAIR	POOR
275	175	150	100	75

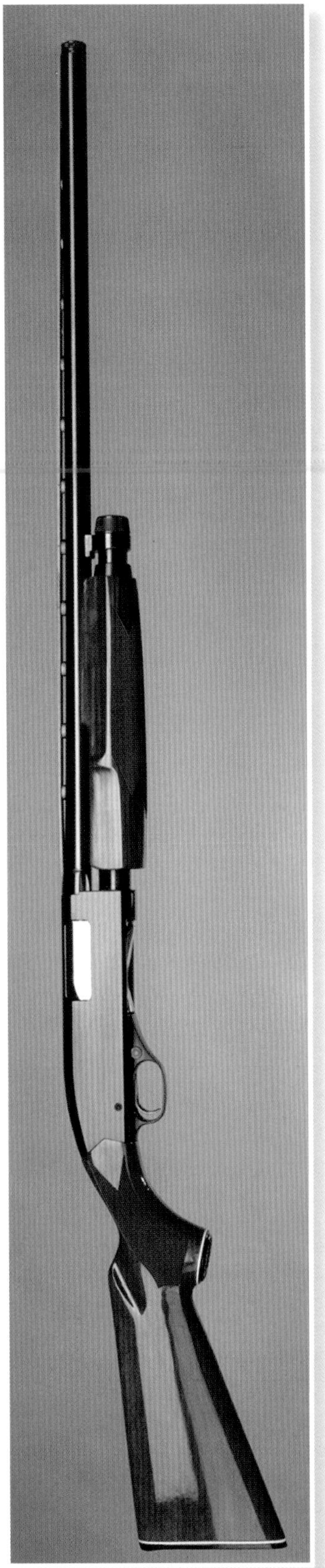

Early Model 1300 XTR.

MODEL 1300 SERIES

MODEL 1300 XTR

The last slide-action shotgun offered by Winchester. It was chambered for 12 and 20 gauge with 3" chambers. It is a takedown gun that is offered with various-length vent rib barrels with screw-in choke tubes. It has an alloy frame and is blued with a walnut stock. It was introduced in 1978.

EXC.	V.G.	GOOD	FAIR	POOR
350	250	200	150	100

MODEL 1300 WATERFOWL

This version is chambered for 12 gauge, 3" only. It has a 30" vent rib barrel with screw-in choke tubes. It is matte-blued, with a satin-finished walnut stock and a recoil pad. It was introduced in 1984. A laminated WinTuff stock was made available in 1988 and would add $10 to the value.

NIB	EXC.	V.G.	GOOD	FAIR	POOR
400	300	250	200	150	100

MODEL 1300 NEW SHADOW GRASS

Introduced in 2004 this 12 gauge 3" gun is fitted with either a 26" or 28" vent rib barrel with choke tubes. Composite stock has New Shadow Grass camo pattern. Weight is about 7 lbs.

NIB	EXC.	V.G.	GOOD	FAIR	POOR
470	370	-	-	-	-

MODEL 1300 WINCAM TURKEY GUN

This version is similar to the Model 1300 Turkey Gun, with a green, laminated hardwood stock. It was introduced in 1987. A WinTuff version is also available and would add $20 to the values given.

NIB	EXC.	V.G.	GOOD	FAIR	POOR
425	325	250	200	150	125

MODEL 1300 STAINLESS SECURITY

This version is chambered for 12 or 20 gauge and is constructed of stainless steel. It has an 18" cylinder-bore barrel and a 7- or 8-shot tubular magazine. It is available with a pistol-grip stock, which would add approximately 50 percent to the values given.

NIB	EXC.	V.G.	GOOD	FAIR	POOR
350	250	225	165	125	100

MODEL 1300 TURKEY

This slide-action model features a 22" vent rib barrel chambered for 3" 12 gauge shells. Supplied with choke tubes. Gun weighs 7.25 lbs.

NIB	EXC.	V.G.	GOOD	FAIR	POOR
400	300	250	200	150	100

MODEL 1300 REALTREE TURKEY

Introduced in 1994, this model features a synthetic stock camouflaged with Realtree. The receiver and 22" barrel are matte finish.

NIB	EXC.	V.G.	GOOD	FAIR	POOR
375	275	225	200	150	100

Model 1300 New Shadow Grass.

Model 1300 Mossy Oak Break-up Turkey.

Model 1300 Black Shadow Turkey.

MODEL 1300 MOSSY OAK BREAK-UP TURKEY

Same as above but with Mossy Oak Break-Up camo stock and gun. Introduced in 2000.

NIB	EXC.	V.G.	GOOD	FAIR	POOR
450	325	-	-	-	-

MODEL 1300 BLACK SHADOW TURKEY

This model was also introduced in 1994 and features a black composite stock with a nonglare finish on the barrel, receiver, bolt, and magazine. Barrel has vent rib and is 22" in length.

NIB	EXC.	V.G.	GOOD	FAIR	POOR
325	225	190	165	125	100

MODEL 1300 NATIONAL WILD TURKEY FEDERATION SERIES III

Engraved receiver, camo stock, open sights on a 22" plain barrel, and all metal and wood parts are nonglare. Comes with a quick detachable sling. Offered in 12 gauge only. Gun weighs 7.25 lbs.

NIB	EXC.	V.G.	GOOD	FAIR	POOR
425	320	250	200	150	100

MODEL 1300 NATIONAL WILD TURKEY FEDERATION SERIES IV

Introduced in 1993, this model is similar to the Series II with the addition of a 22" vent rib barrel. Stock is black laminated. Comes with quick detachable sling. Gun weight 7 lbs.

NIB	EXC.	V.G.	GOOD	FAIR	POOR
400	320	250	200	150	100

Model 1300 NWTF Short Turkey.

Model 1300 Buck and Tom.

MODEL 1300 NWTF SHORT TURKEY

This 12 gauge gun is fitted with an 18" barrel with extended choke tubes. Fiber Optic sights. Mossy Oak camo stock. NWTF medallion on pistol grip cap. Weight is about 6.5 lbs. Introduced in 2005.

NIB	EXC.	V.G.	GOOD	FAIR	POOR
505	375	-	-	-	-

MODEL 1300 WHITETAILS UNLIMITED SLUG HUNTER

This slide-action model features a full-length rifle barrel chambered for 3" 12 gauge shells. Barrel is choked Cylinder. Fitted with a checkered walnut stock with engraved receiver. Receiver is drilled and tapped for bases and rings, which are included. Comes equipped with camo sling. Weighs 7.25 lbs.

NIB	EXC.	V.G.	GOOD	FAIR	POOR
400	300	250	200	150	100

MODEL 1300 SLUG HUNTER

Similar to the Whitetails Unlimited model, but without the engraved receiver.

NIB	EXC.	V.G.	GOOD	FAIR	POOR
400	300	250	200	150	100

MODEL 1300 BUCK AND TOM

Introduced in 2002 for both deer and turkey. Camo stock. Fitted with a 22" barrel with choke tubes for both deer and turkey. Receiver drilled and tapped for scope mount. Weight is about 6.75 lbs.

NIB	EXC.	V.G.	GOOD	FAIR	POOR
525	400	-	-	-	-

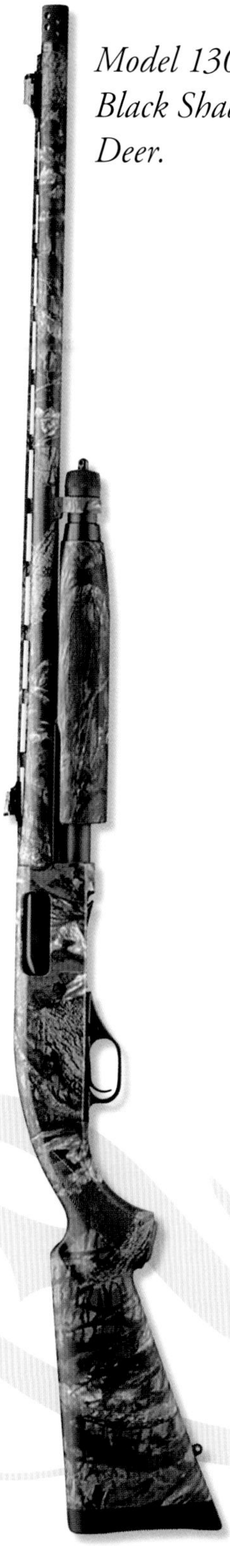

Model 1300 Black Shadow Deer.

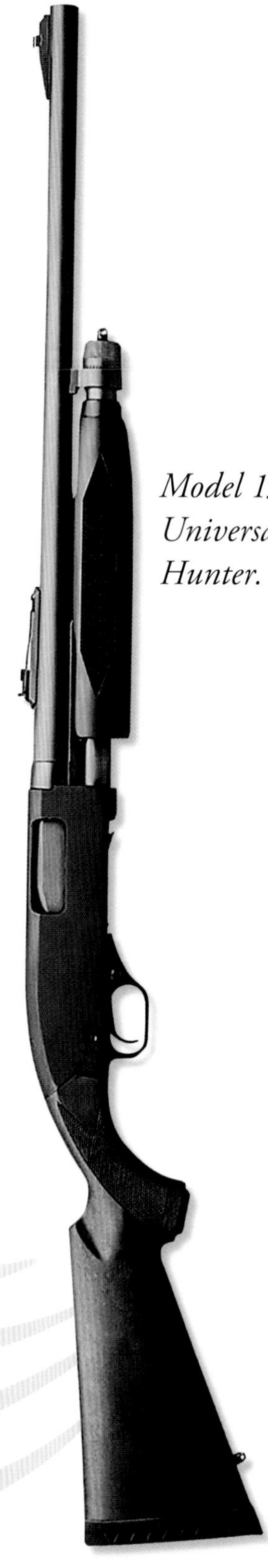

Model 1300 Universal Hunter.

MODEL 1300 UNIVERSAL HUNTER

Introduced in 2002, this model features a camo stock with 26" vent rib barrel. Choke tubes. Weight is about 7 lbs.

NIB	EXC.	V.G.	GOOD	FAIR	POOR
550	425	-	-	-	-

MODEL 1300 BLACK SHADOW DEER

Introduced in 1994, this 12 gauge Model 1300 features a black composite stock with nonglare finish on the bolt, barrel, receiver, and magazine. Barrel is 22" with ramp front sight and adjustable rear sight. In 2000 this model was offered with a rifled barrel for shooting sabot slugs. Add 15% for cantilever scope mount version.

NIB	EXC.	V.G.	GOOD	FAIR	POOR
350	250	175	150	125	100

NOTE: Add $25 for rifled barrel.

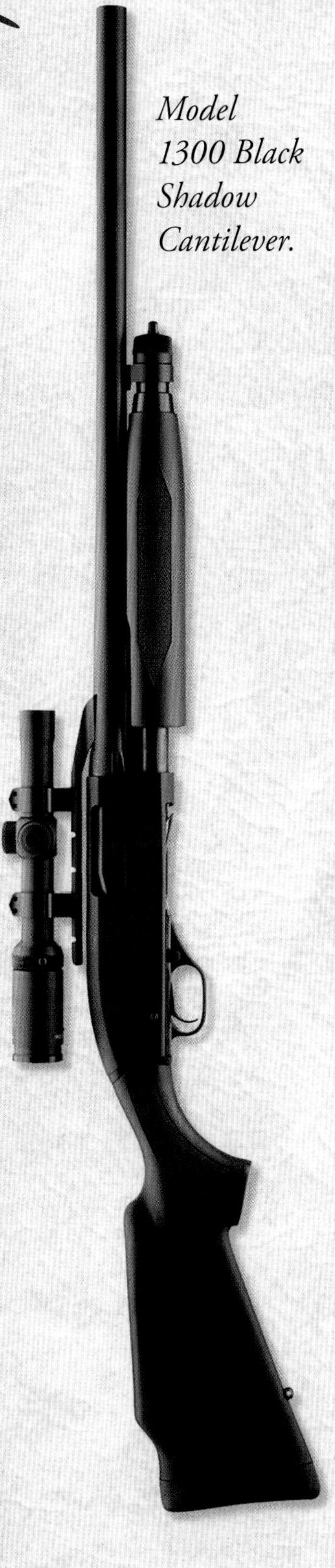

Model 1300 Black Shadow Cantilever.

Model 1300 Black Shadow Field.

MODEL 1300 BLACK SHADOW FIELD

Same as above but fitted with a 26" or 28" vent rib barrel chambered for 3" Mag. shells. Weight is about 7 lbs.

NIB	EXC.	V.G.	GOOD	FAIR	POOR
325	225	200	150	100	80

MODEL 1300 SPORTING/FIELD

This 12 gauge gun has a 28" vent rib barrel with five choke tubes. Checkered walnut stock. Black recoil pad. Weight is about 7.5 lbs. Introduced in 2002.

NIB	EXC.	V.G.	GOOD	FAIR	POOR
450	350	275	200	150	-

MODEL 1300 SPORTING/FIELD COMPACT

As above but with 24" barrel and 1" shorter length of pull. Introduced in 2002.

NIB	EXC.	V.G.	GOOD	FAIR	POOR
450	350	275	200	150	-

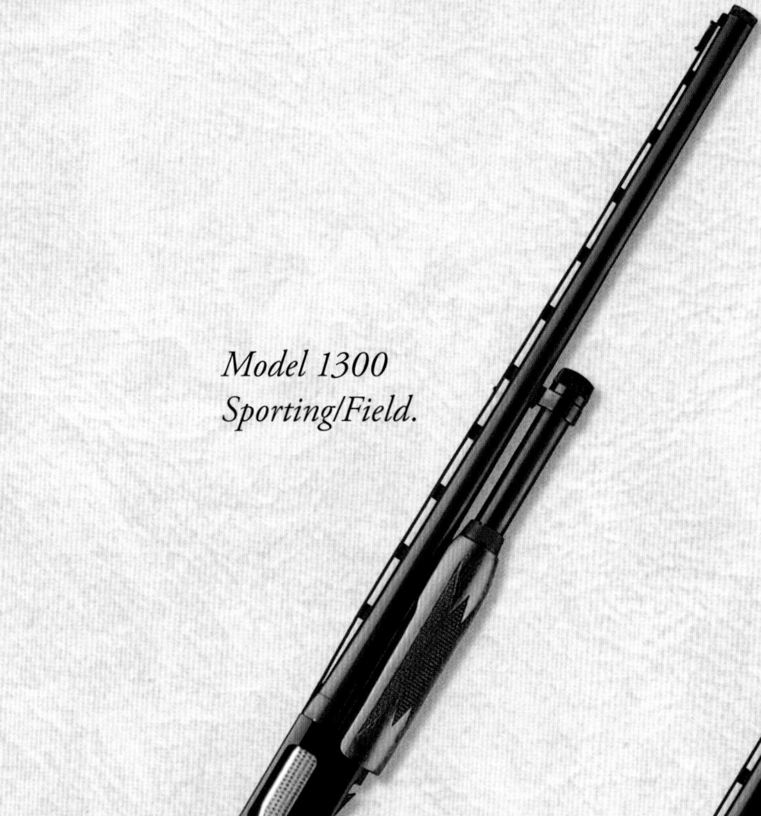

Model 1300 Sporting/Field.

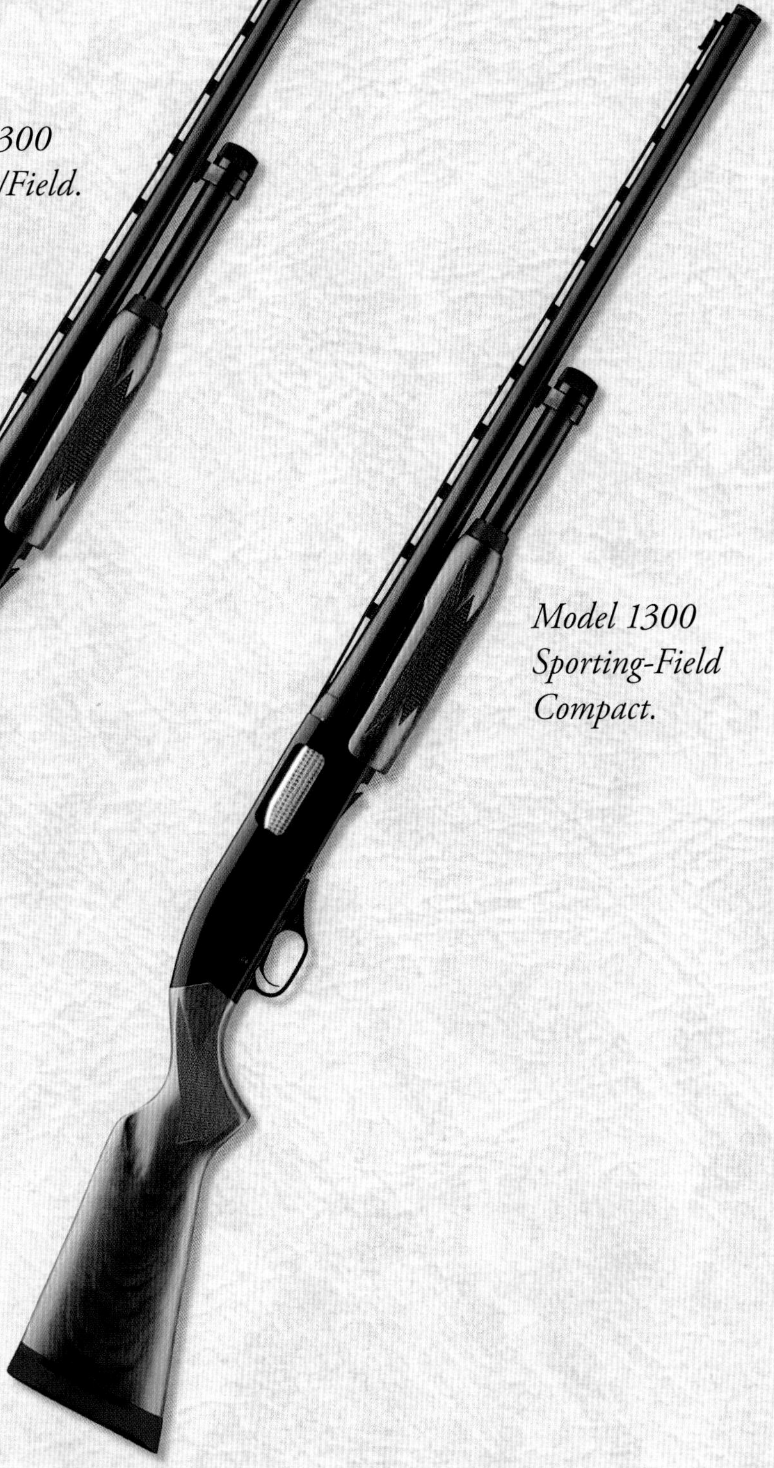

Model 1300 Sporting-Field Compact.

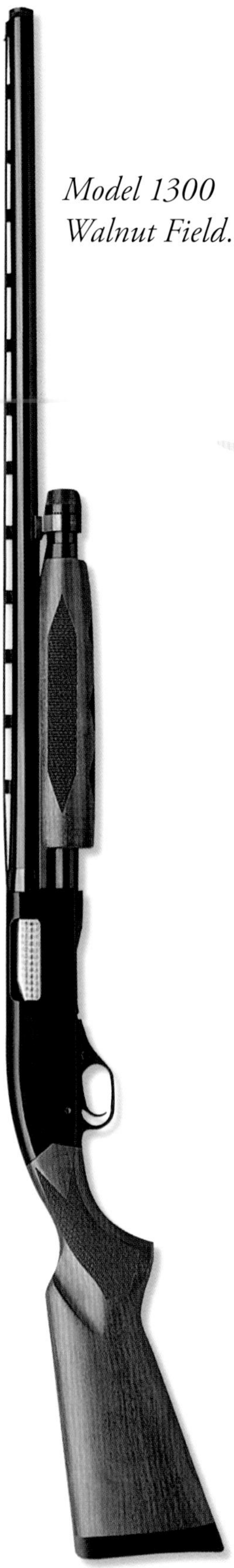

Model 1300 Walnut Field.

Model 1300 Upland Special.

MODEL 1300 WALNUT FIELD

This 12 gauge 3" gun is fitted with either 26" or 28" vent rib barrels with choke tubes. Checkered walnut stock with recoil pad. Weight is about 7.25 lbs. Introduced in 2004.

NIB	EXC.	V.G.	GOOD	FAIR	POOR
440	340	275	-	-	-

MODEL 1300 SLUG HUNTER SABOT (SMOOTHBORE)

Similar to the Slug Hunter but furnished with a smoothbore barrel with a special extended screw-in choke tube that is rifled.

NIB	EXC.	V.G.	GOOD	FAIR	POOR
350	250	200	175	150	100

MODEL 1300 UPLAND SPECIAL

This 12 gauge slide-action shotgun is fitted with a 24" vent rib barrel and straight-grip walnut stock. Weight is about 7 lbs. Introduced in 1999. In 2000 this model was offered in 20 gauge with 24" vent rib barrel.

NIB	EXC.	V.G.	GOOD	FAIR	POOR
375	275	200	-	-	-

MODEL 1300 UPLAND SPECIAL FIELD

This model, introduced in 2004, features a choice of 12 or 20 gauge 3" guns with 24" vent rib barrel with choke tube. Checkered walnut stock with straight grip. Weight is about 6.75 lbs.

NIB	EXC.	V.G.	GOOD	FAIR	POOR
440	340	-	-	-	-

MODEL 1300 RANGER

This slide-action shotgun is a lower-cost version of the Model 1300. Furnished with a hardwood stock and available in 12 or 20 gauge with 26" or 28" vent rib barrel. WinChokes are included.

NIB	EXC.	V.G.	GOOD	FAIR	POOR
300	225	190	165	125	100

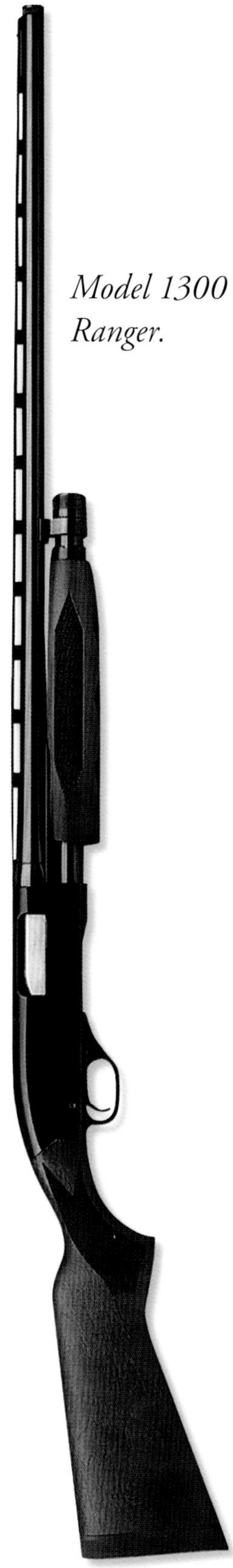

Model 1300 Ranger.

Model 1300 Ranger Deer Compact

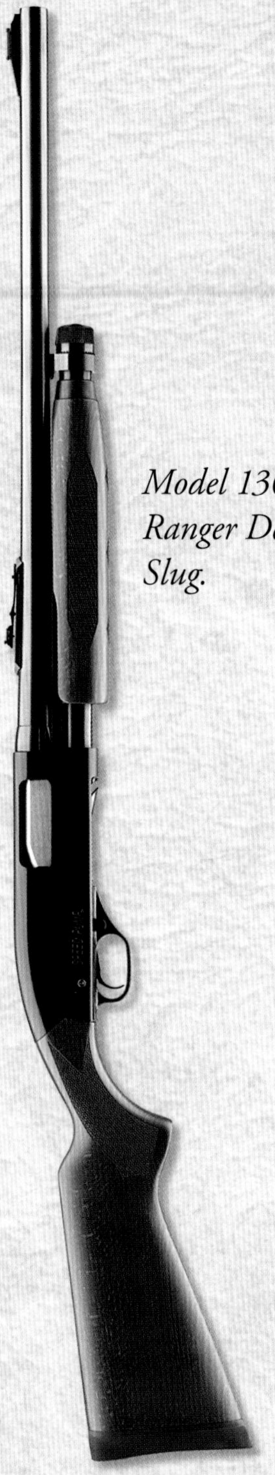

Model 1300 Ranger Deer Slug.

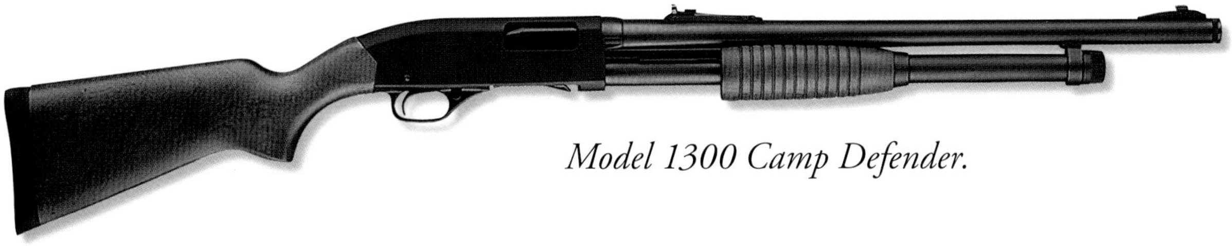

Model 1300 Camp Defender.

MODEL 1300 RANGER LADIES/YOUTH-COMPACT

Available in 20 gauge only this model has a 1" shorter than standard length of pull and a 22" vent rib barrel. Choke tubes are included. Gun weighs 6.75 lbs.

NIB	EXC.	V.G.	GOOD	FAIR	POOR
300	225	190	165	125	100

MODEL 1300 RANGER DEER COMPACT

Similar to above but with smoothbore barrel and iron sights.

NIB	EXC.	V.G.	GOOD	FAIR	POOR
300	225	190	165	125	100

MODEL 1300 RANGER DEER SLUG

Comes in two principal configurations: a 12 gauge 22" smooth barrel with Cylinder choke; and a 12 gauge 22" rifled barrel. Both are chambered for 3" shells and weigh 6.75 lbs.

NIB	EXC.	V.G.	GOOD	FAIR	POOR
300	200	175	150	125	100

MODEL 1300 RANGER DEER COMBO

The Model 1300 Ranger Deer Combos are available in three different configurations. One: 12 gauge 22" smooth barrel and 28" vent rib barrel with WinChokes. Two: 12 gauge 22" rifled barrel with 28" vent rib barrel with WinChokes. Three: 20 gauge 22" smooth barrel with 28" vent rib barrel with WinChokes.

12 GAUGE COMBO

NIB	EXC.	V.G.	GOOD	FAIR	POOR
375	275	225	190	165	100

20 GAUGE COMBO

NIB	EXC.	V.G.	GOOD	FAIR	POOR
375	275	225	190	165	100

MODEL 1300 DEFENDER COMBO

This personal defense slide-action shotgun features an 18" Cylinder choked barrel and a 28" vent rib barrel with modified WinChoke and an accessory pistol grip. A hardwood stock comes fitted to the gun.

NIB	EXC.	V.G.	GOOD	FAIR	POOR
350	250	200	175	150	100

MODEL 1300 DEFENDER 5-SHOT

Same as above but furnished with a hardwood stock only and 18" barrel.

NIB	EXC.	V.G.	GOOD	FAIR	POOR
300	200	175	150	125	100

MODEL 1300 CAMP DEFENDER

Introduced in 1999, this 12 gauge model features a 22" barrel and walnut stock. Magazine capacity is five rounds. Barrel fitted with rifle sights. Weight is about 7 lbs. Comes with Cylinder choke tube.

NIB	EXC.	V.G.	GOOD	FAIR	POOR
350	275	-	-	-	-

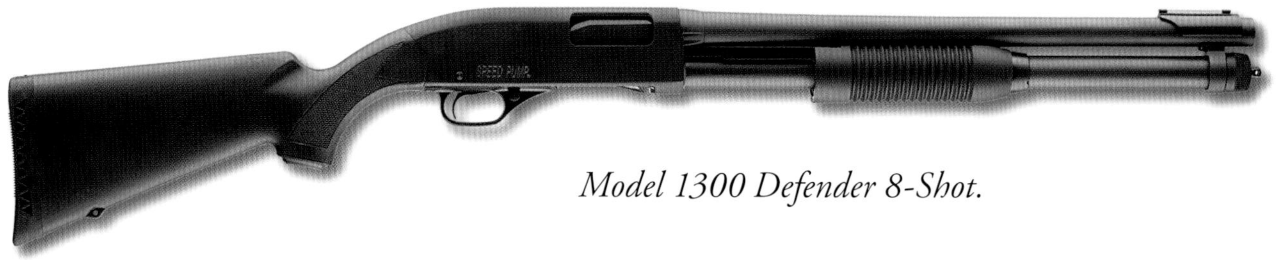

Model 1300 Defender 8-Shot.

Model 1300 Stainless Marine.

MODEL 1300 DEFENDER 8-SHOT

Same as above but furnished with an 18" barrel with extended magazine tube.

NIB	EXC.	V.G.	GOOD	FAIR	POOR
300	200	175	150	125	100

MODEL 1300 DEFENDER SYNTHETIC STOCK

Same as above but fitted with a black synthetic full stock. Available in either 12 or 20 gauge.

NIB	EXC.	V.G.	GOOD	FAIR	POOR
300	200	175	150	125	100

MODEL 1300 DEFENDER PISTOL GRIP

Same as above but fitted with a black synthetic pistol grip and extended magazine tube.

NIB	EXC.	V.G.	GOOD	FAIR	POOR
300	200	175	150	125	100

MODEL 1300 LADY DEFENDER

Chambered for the 20 gauge shell, this model features an 18" barrel with 8-round capacity. Pistol-grip stock. Introduced in 1997.

NIB	EXC.	V.G.	GOOD	FAIR	POOR
300	225	175	125	90	90

MODEL 1300 STAINLESS MARINE (AKA COASTAL MARINE)

This 12 gauge slide-action shotgun comes with a black synthetic full stock with all metal parts chrome plated. Barrel is 18" and magazine tube holds 7 rounds. Gun weighs 6.75 lbs.

NIB	EXC.	V.G.	GOOD	FAIR	POOR
425	325	275	225	165	100

MODEL 1300 STAINLESS MARINE WITH PISTOL GRIP

Same as above with black synthetic pistol grip in place of full buttstock. Gun weighs 5.75 lbs.

NIB	EXC.	V.G.	GOOD	FAIR	POOR
400	300	250	200	150	100

MODEL 1400

This is a gas-operated, semi-automatic shotgun chambered for 12, 16, or 20 gauge. It was offered with a 26", 28", or 30" vent rib barrel, or plain barrel, with various chokes. The finish is blued, with a checkered walnut stock. It was manufactured between 1964 and 1981. The Hydrocoil plastic stock was available on this model and would add approximately 35 percent to the values given.

EXC.	V.G.	GOOD	FAIR	POOR
325	225	200	150	100

Add 250% for Custom High Grade, special order weapon from the Custom Shop, manufactured 1991 to 1992, rare gun

- Add $100 for skeet grade, manufactured 1965 to 1973
- Add $25 for trap grade, manufactured 1965 to 1973
- Subtract $50 for Deer Gun, 22" barrel with sights, manufactured 1965 to 1973
- Add $25 for Slug Hunter, 22 inch barrel, tapped for scope

NEW MODEL 1400

This is a gas-operated, semi-automatic shotgun chambered for 12 or 20 gauge. It is offered with a 22" or 28" vent rib barrel with screw-in chokes. The finish is blued, with a checkered walnut stock. It was introduced in 1989.

NIB	EXC.	V.G.	GOOD	FAIR	POOR
450	350	300	250	200	125

MODEL 1400 RANGER

This is a utility-grade, gas-operated, semi-automatic shotgun chambered for 12 or 20 gauge. It is offered with a 28" vent rib barrel with screw-in chokes, as well as a 24" slug barrel with rifle sights. The finish is blued, with a checkered stock. A combination two-barrel set that includes the deer barrel would be worth approximately 20 percent additional. This model was introduced in 1983.

NIB	EXC.	V.G.	GOOD	FAIR	POOR
400	300	250	200	150	100

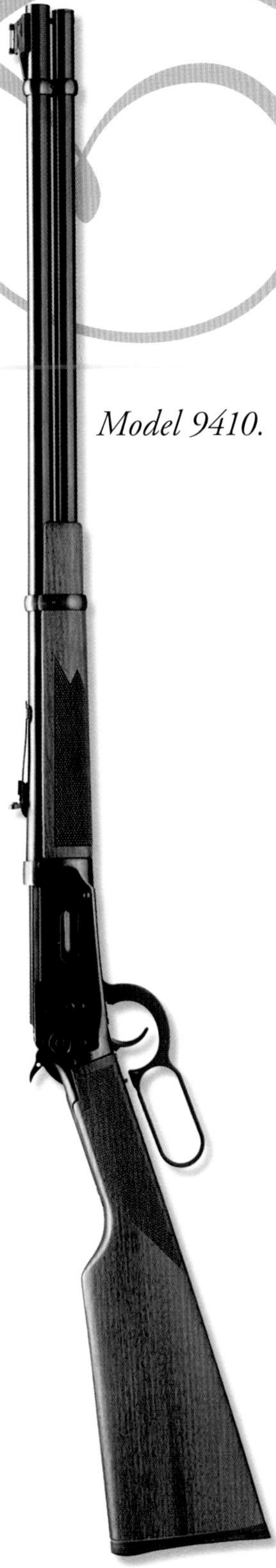

Model 9410.

MODEL 1400 QUAIL UNLIMITED

This 12 gauge semi-automatic shotgun model was introduced in 1993. It features compact engraved receiver with 26" vent rib barrel supplied with WinChoke tubes. Stock is checkered walnut. Gun weighs 7.25 lbs.

NIB	EXC.	V.G.	GOOD	FAIR	POOR
400	300	250	200	150	100

MODEL 1400 RANGER DEER COMBO

This model features a 12 gauge 22" smooth barrel and a 28" vent rib barrel with three WinChokes.

NIB	EXC.	V.G.	GOOD	FAIR	POOR
400	300	250	200	150	100

MODEL 1500 XTR

This is a gas-operated, semi-automatic shotgun chambered for 12 or 20 gauge, with a 28" vent rib barrel with screw-in chokes. The finish is blued, with a walnut stock. It was manufactured between 1978 and 1982.

EXC.	V.G.	GOOD	FAIR	POOR
350	250	225	175	125

MODEL 1911

This was Winchester's first self-loading shotgun and was developed by T.C. Johnson in order to keep pace with the Remington Auto-Loading Shotgun Model 11, which was developed by John M. Browning with help from T.C. Johnson. Because of the delays involved in developing a brand new design, the Model 1911 was introduced on October 7, 1911. The shotgun was a recoil operated mechanism, had a tubular magazine and had the takedown feature. The shotgun was available in two styles:

- Plain Model 1911, 26" or 28" barrel, 12 gauge, choked full, modified, or cylinder, plain birch laminated pistol-grip stock and forend with hard rubber buttplate.

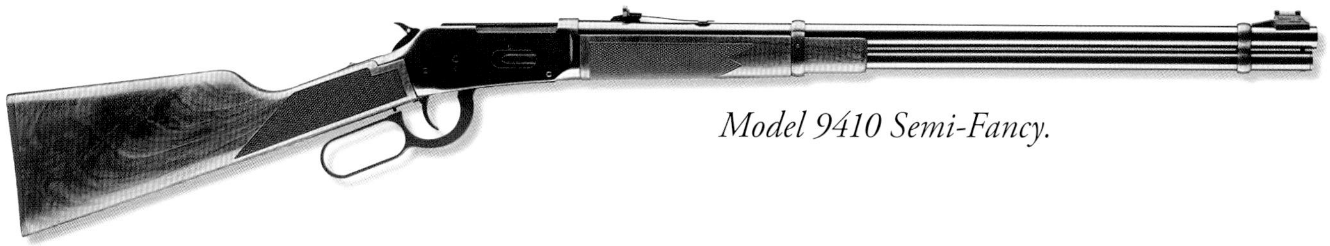

Model 9410 Semi-Fancy.

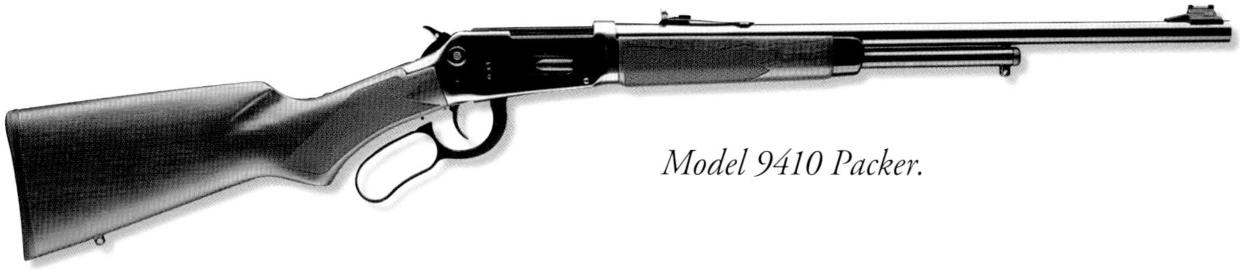

Model 9410 Packer.

- Fancy Model 1911, same as above with fancy birch laminated stock.

Because of the hurry in getting the model ready for production, the shotgun demonstrated design weaknesses and never proved satisfactory. It was discontinued in 1925 with about 83,000 guns sold.

MODEL 1911-PLAIN

EXC.	V.G.	GOOD	FAIR	POOR
550	375	300	250	200

MODEL 1911-FANCY

EXC.	V.G.	GOOD	FAIR	POOR
800	500	400	300	250

MODEL 9410

Introduced in 2001 this model features a .410 shotgun in a lever-action configuration. Barrel length is 24" and is smoothbore with Cylinder choke. Chambered is 2.5". Magazine capacity is nine rounds. Tru-Glo front sight. Weight is about 6.75 lbs. In 2003 a top-tang safety was installed. The Model 9410 has been discontinued along with the rest of the Model 94 line.

NIB	EXC.	V.G.	GOOD	FAIR	POOR
550	400	-	-	-	-

MODEL 9410 SEMI-FANCY

As above but with semi-fancy walnut stock with checkering. Introduced in 2004.

NIB	EXC.	V.G.	GOOD	FAIR	POOR
790	625	-	-	-	-

MODEL 9410 PACKER

Introduced in 2002 this model features a 20" barrel with 3/4 magazine and pistol-grip stock. Weight is about 6.5 lbs.

NIB	EXC.	V.G.	GOOD	FAIR	POOR
575	425	-	-	-	-

Model 9410 Packer Compact.

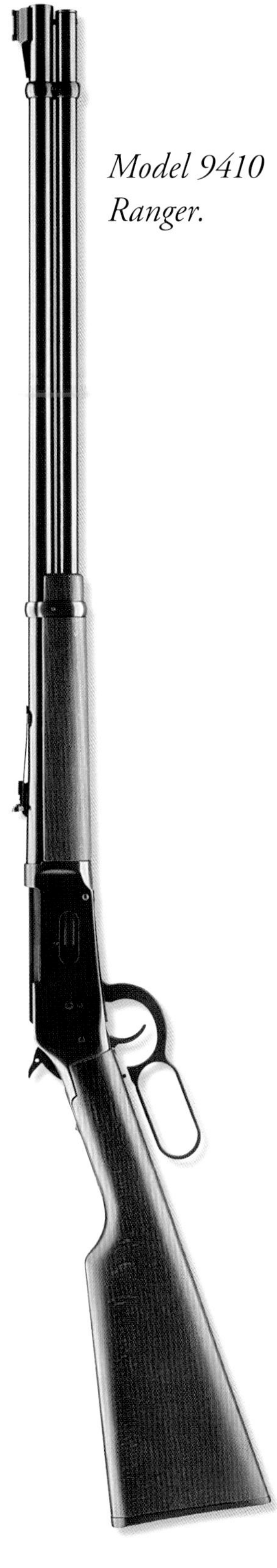

Model 9410 Ranger.

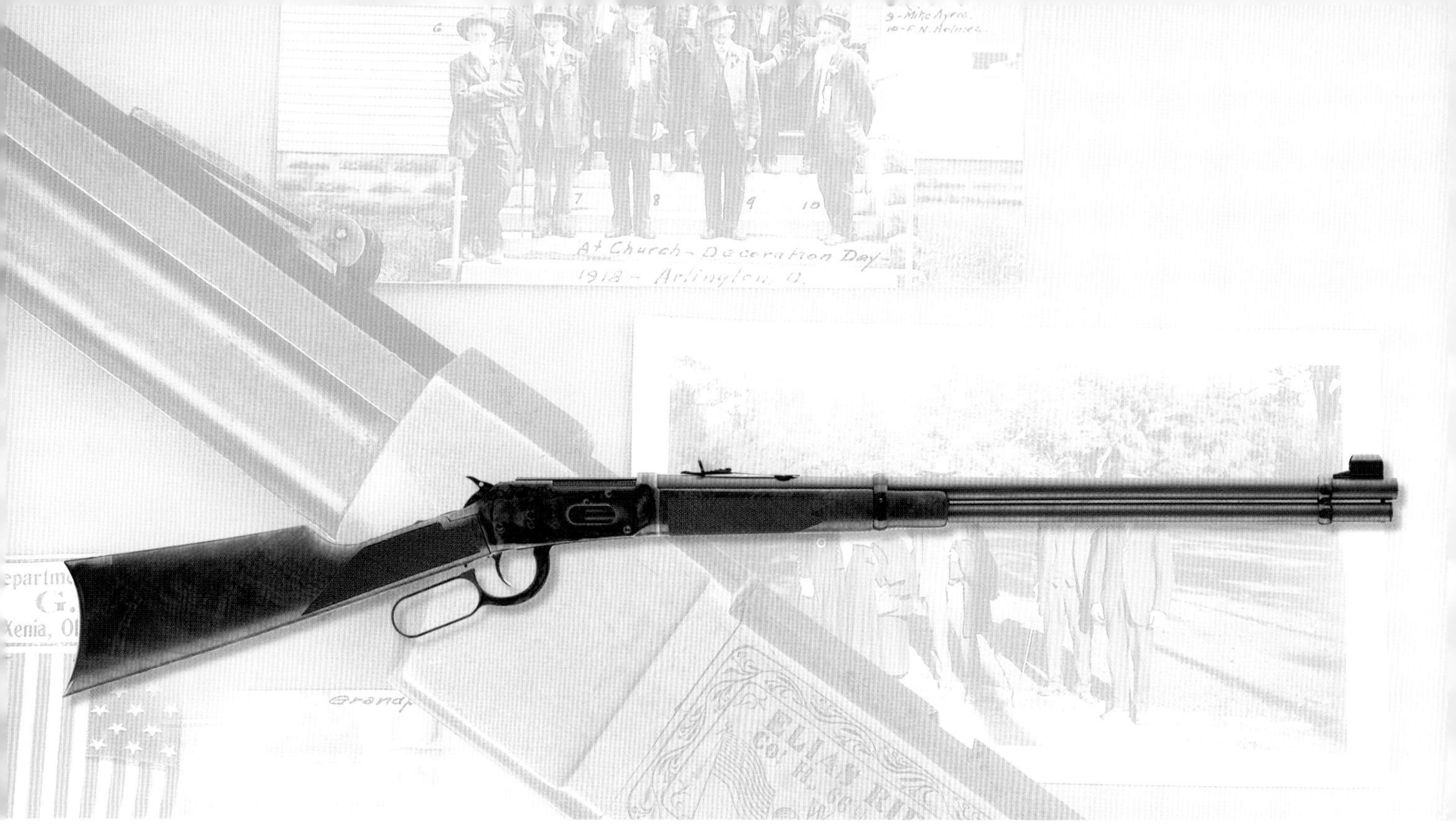

Model 9410 Custom.

MODEL 9410 PACKER COMPACT

Introduced in 2003 this model features a reduced length of pull to 12-1/2". Fitted with Invector chokes. Weight is about 6.25 lbs.

NIB	EXC.	V.G.	GOOD	FAIR	POOR
655	525	-	-	-	-

MODEL 9410 RANGER

This version is the same as the standard or traditional Model 9410 but hardwood stock without checkering. Weight is about 6.75 lbs. Fitted with top-tang safety. Introduced in 2003.

NIB	EXC.	V.G.	GOOD	FAIR	POOR
540	425	-	-	-	-

MODEL 9410 CUSTOM

Introduced in 2005, this .410 shotgun is fitted with a 24" round barrel and full length magazine. Case colored receiver with semi-fancy checkered walnut stock. Weight is about 7 lbs.

NIB	EXC.	V.G.	GOOD	FAIR	POOR
1400	1100	-	-	-	-

SECTION VIII

SHOTGUNS WITH NAMES FOR MODEL DESIGNATIONS: E.G., SELECT, SUPREME

SELECT OVER/ UNDER SERIES

This series of over-and-under shotguns was introduced into the Winchester line in 2004. The series features a low-profile receiver with unique engraving, lightweight barrels, and contoured walnut stocks with distinctive checkering patterns.

PARKER REPRODUCTION

Ultra high-grade shotgun commissioned by Winchester as a reproduction of the original Parker DHE and VHE. 12-or 20-gauge side-by-side with splinter forend and single selective trigger. Made in Japan. Discontinued.

NIB	EXC.	V.G.	GOOD	FAIR	POOR
1985	1550	1150	850	-	-

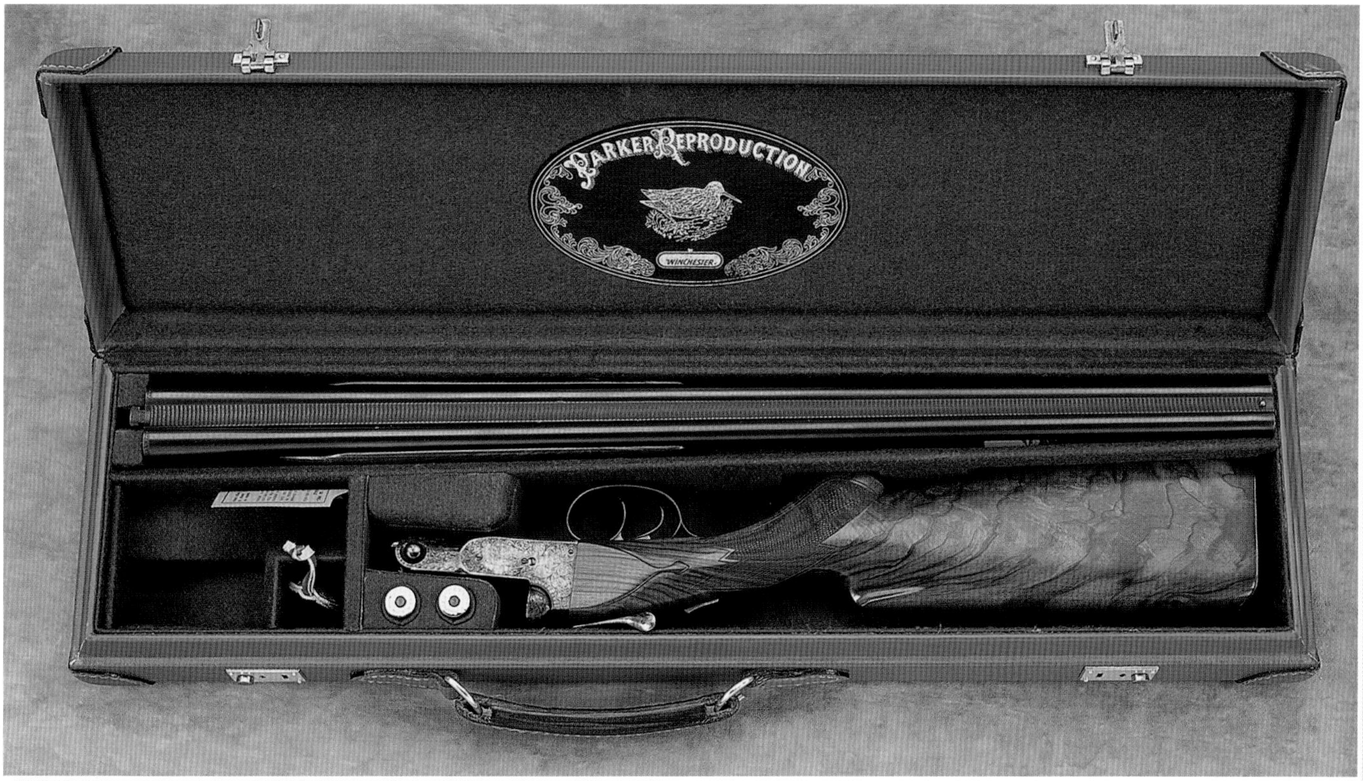

Parker VHE Reproduction.

SELECT ENERGY SPORTING

Chambered for the 12 gauge 2.75" shell and offered with a choice of 28", 30", or 32" vent rib barrels with choke tubes and porting. Truglo front sight. Adjustable trigger shoe. Walnut stock with recoil pad. Weight is about 7.62 lbs. Adjustable comb available.

NIB	EXC.	V.G.	GOOD	FAIR	POOR
1870	1400	-	-	-	-

NOTE: Add $150 for adjustable comb.

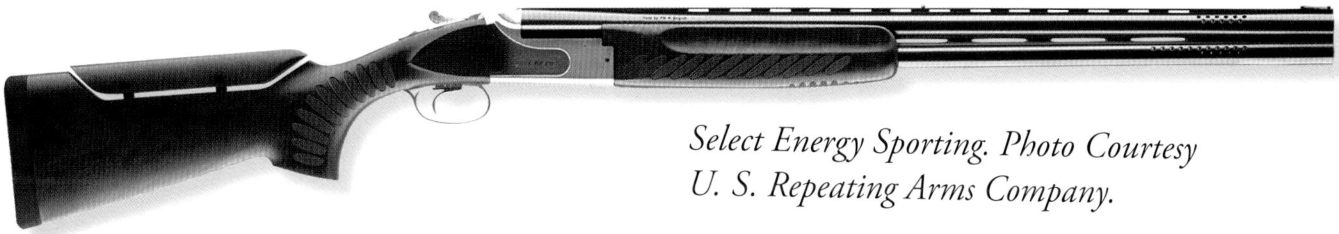

Select Energy Sporting. Photo Courtesy U. S. Repeating Arms Company.

Select Energy Trap. Photo Courtesy U. S. Repeating Arms Company.

Select Extreme Elegance. Photo Courtesy U. S. Repeating Arms Company.

SELECT ENERGY TRAP

This 12 gauge model is fitted with a choice of 30" or 32" back-bored ported barrels. Wide vent rib. Choke tubes. Walnut stock with Monte Carlo comb. Weight is about 7.8 lbs. Adjustable comb available.

NIB	EXC.	V.G.	GOOD	FAIR	POOR
1870	1400	-	-	-	-

NOTE: Add $150 for adjustable comb.

SELECT EXTREME ELEGANCE

This 12 gauge gun features full coverage engraving with game scenes. Choice of 26" or 28" vent rib barrels with choke tubes. Walnut stock with unique checkering pattern. Weight is about 7 lbs.

NIB	EXC.	V.G.	GOOD	FAIR	POOR
2350	1650	-	-	-	-

SELECT FIELD

This 12 gauge 3" gun is fitted with a choice of 26" or 28" vent ribs barrels with choke tubes. Engraved receiver with oval checkering pattern. Weight is about 7 lbs.

NIB	EXC.	V.G.	GOOD	FAIR	POOR
1500	1050	-	-	-	-

SELECT TRADITIONAL ELEGANCE

Similar to the Extreme Elegance but with traditional checkering pattern. Add 25% for ultra high-grade Platinum version.

NIB	EXC.	V.G.	GOOD	FAIR	POOR
2350	1650	-	-	-	-

SELECT MODEL 101 FIELD

This Belgian-made version of Winchester's popular Model 101 was introduced in 2007. It features Grade II/III walnut, 26" or 28" barrels and deep-relief engraving on the blued receiver that mimics the original 101. Classic white line spacer and vented recoil pad. Three choke tubes. Weight is about 7.2 lbs. Introduced in 2007.

NIB	EXC	V.G.	GOOD	FAIR	POOR
2061	-	-	-	-	-

SELECT MODEL 101 SPORTING

Similar to Field model plus competition features such as a wider rib, adjustable trigger, white mid-bead and five extended Signature choke tubes. Ported barrels are 28", 30" or 32".

NIB	EXC	V.G.	GOOD	FAIR	POOR
2328	-	-	-	-	-

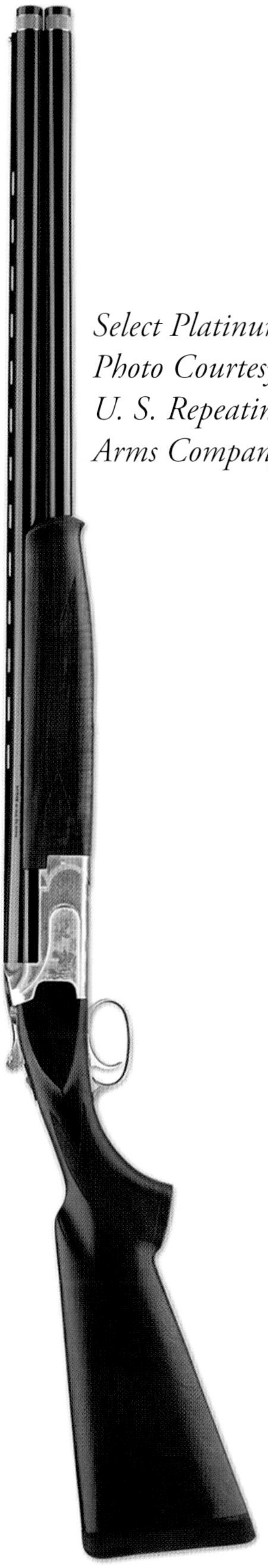

Select Platinum. Photo Courtesy U. S. Repeating Arms Company.

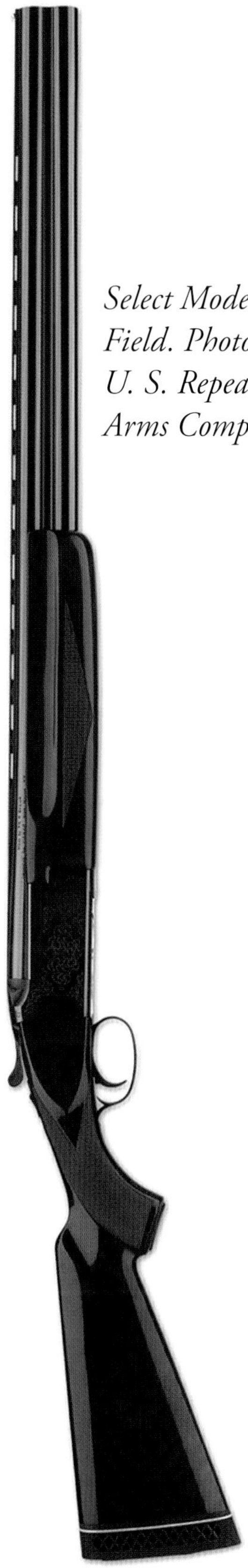

Select Model 101 Field. Photo Courtesy U. S. Repeating Arms Company.

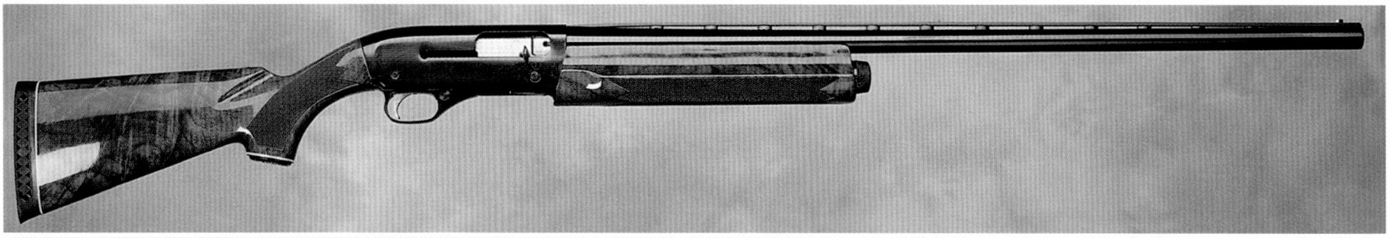

Super X Model 1.

MODEL SUPER X-1 SERIES

SUPER X MODEL I

This is a self-compensating, gas-operated, semi-automatic shotgun chambered for 12 gauge. It was offered with a 26", 28", or 30" vent rib barrel with various chokes. It features all-steel construction and is blued, with a checkered walnut stock. It was manufactured between 1974 and 1981.

EXC.	V.G.	GOOD	FAIR	POOR
500	375	300	250	150

SUPER X MODEL 1 CUSTOM COMPETITION

This is a custom-order trap or skeet gun that features the self compensating, gas-operated action. It is available in 12 gauge only from the Custom Shop. It is offered with a heavy degree of engraving on the receiver and a fancy, checkered walnut stock. Gold inlays are available and would add approximately 50 percent to the values given. This model was introduced in 1987.

NIB	EXC.	V.G.	GOOD	FAIR	POOR
1450	1100	925	775	650	500

SUPER X2 3" MAGNUM COMPOSITE

Gas-operated design chambered for 3" 12 gauge shells. Fitted with a black synthetic stock and choice of 24", 26", or 28" vent rib barrels. Invector chokes. Magazine capacity is five rounds. Weight is about 7.5 lbs. depending on barrel length. Matte black finish.

NIB	EXC.	V.G.	GOOD	FAIR	POOR
725	675	575	-	-	-

SUPER X2 3.5" MAGNUM COMPOSITE

Introduced in 1999, this model is a gas-operated design chambered for 3.5" 12 gauge shells. Fitted with a black synthetic stock and choice of 24", 26", or 28" vent rib barrels. Invector chokes. Magazine capacity is five rounds. Weight is about 7.5 lbs. depending on barrel length. Matte black finish.

NIB	EXC.	V.G.	GOOD	FAIR	POOR
850	675	-	-	-	-

SUPER X2 TURKEY

Similar to the X2 Magnum but with 24" vent rib barrel with truglo sights. Extra-Full choke. Weight is about 7.25 lbs. Black synthetic stock. Introduced in 1999.

NIB	EXC.	V.G.	GOOD	FAIR	POOR
860	675	-	-	-	-

SUPER X2 TURKEY MOSSY OAK BREAK-UP

Same as above but with Mossy Oak Break-Up camo on stock and gun. Introduced in 2000.

NIB	EXC.	V.G.	GOOD	FAIR	POOR
1025	750	-	-	-	-

Super X2 3.5" Composite. Photo Courtesy U. S. Repeating Arms Company.

Super X2 3" Magnum Composite. Photo Courtesy U. S. Repeating Arms Company.

Super X2 NWTF Turkey Black. Photo Courtesy U. S. Repeating Arms Company.

SUPER X2 NWTF TURKEY

Introduced in 2005 this 3.5" 12 gauge gun is fitted with a 24" vent rib barrel with extra full extended choke tubes. Three dot TRUGLO sights. Mossy Oak camo or black synthetic stock. A brass NWTF medallion on the pistol grip cap. Weight is about 7.5 lbs.

NIB	EXC.	V.G.	GOOD	FAIR	POOR
1235	950	-	-	-	-

SUPER X2 UNIVERSAL HUNTER

Similar to the Super X2 Turkey but with a 26" barrel with Extra-Full choke tube. Weight is about 7.75 lbs. Introduced in 2002.

NIB	EXC.	V.G.	GOOD	FAIR	POOR
1100	850	-	-	-	-

SUPER X2 WATERFOWL

Chambered for 12 gauge 3.5" shells and fitted with a 28" vent rib barrel, this model features a Mossy Oak camo finish. Weight is about 8 lbs. Introduced in 1999. In 2004 a New Shadow Grass camo pattern was added.

NIB	EXC.	V.G.	GOOD	FAIR	POOR
1140	850	650	-	-	-

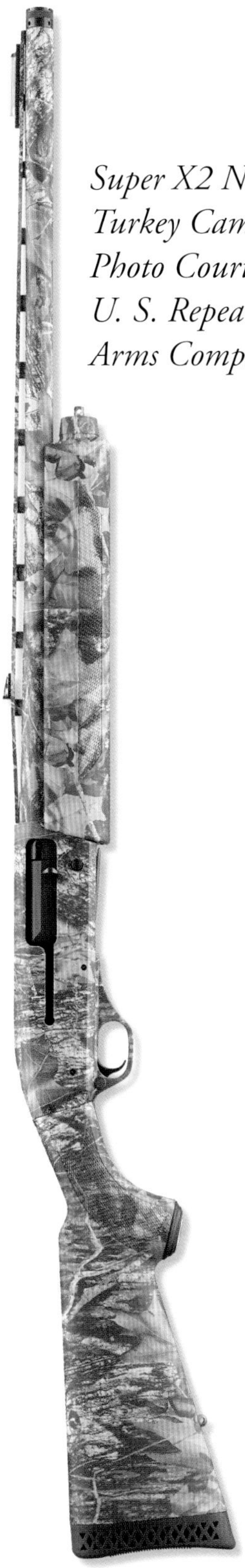

Super X2 NWTF Turkey Camo. Photo Courtesy U. S. Repeating Arms Company.

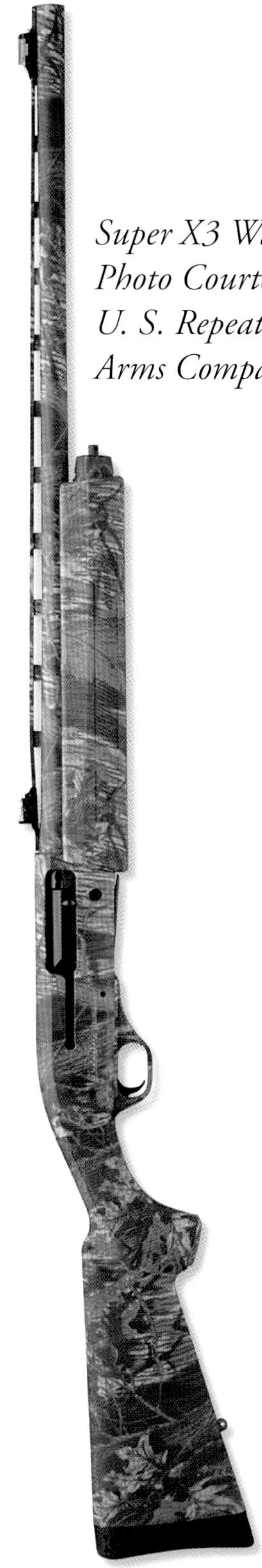

Super X3 Waterfowl. Photo Courtesy U. S. Repeating Arms Company.

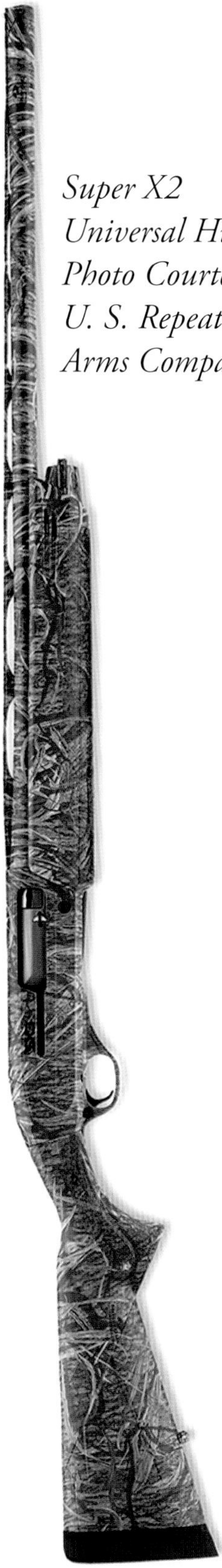

Super X2 Universal Hunter. Photo Courtesy U. S. Repeating Arms Company.

Super X2 Magnum Greenhead. Photo Courtesy U. S. Repeating Arms Company.

Super X2 Field, Walnut Stock. Photo Courtesy U. S. Repeating Arms Company.

SUPER X2 MAGNUM GREENHEAD

Introduced in 2002, this model is chambered for the 12 gauge 3.5" shell and has a composite stock that is green in color. Fitted with 28" barrel. Weight is about 8 lbs.

NIB	EXC.	V.G.	GOOD	FAIR	POOR
995	750	-	-	-	-

SUPER X2 MAGNUM FIELD

This model is chambered for the 12 gauge 3" shell and is offered with either a walnut stock or black synthetic stock. Choice of 26" or 28" vent rib barrel with invector chokes. Weight is about 7.25 lbs. Introduced in 1999.

NIB	EXC.	V.G.	GOOD	FAIR	POOR
800	625	-	-	-	-

SUPER X2 LIGHT FIELD

Checkered walnut stock with choice of 26" or 28" vent rib barrel with choke tubes are featured on this 12 gauge gun. Weight is about 6.5 lbs. Introduced in 2005.

NIB	EXC.	V.G.	GOOD	FAIR	POOR
945	700	-	-	-	-

Super X2 Light Field. Photo Courtesy U. S. Repeating Arms Company.

Super X2 Cantilever Deer.

SUPER X2 CANTILEVER DEER

This 12 gauge model has a 22" fully rifled barrel with fold-down rear sight and scope mount. Black composite stock. Weight is about 7.25 lbs. Introduced in 2002.

NIB	EXC.	V.G.	GOOD	FAIR	POOR
860	650	-	-	-	-

SUPER X2 PRACTICAL

Introduced in 2002, this model is designed for competition shooting. Fitted with a 22" barrel with ghost ring sight and 8-round magazine. Black composite stock. Weight is about 8 lbs.

NIB	EXC.	V.G.	GOOD	FAIR	POOR
1065	800	-	-	-	-

SUPER X2 SPORTING CLAYS

Introduced in 2001, this model is a 12 gauge gun with choice of 28" or 30" barrels with high post rib. Barrels are back bored with Invector chokes. Adjustable comb. Weight is about 8 lbs.

NIB	EXC.	V.G.	GOOD	FAIR	POOR
1200	950	-	-	-	-

Super X2 Practical. Photo Courtesy U. S. Repeating Arms Company.

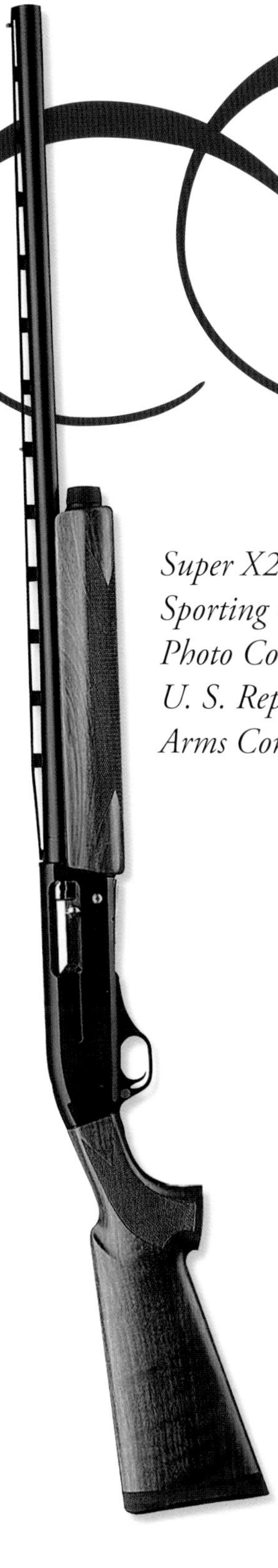

Super X2 Sporting Clays. Photo Courtesy U. S. Repeating Arms Company.

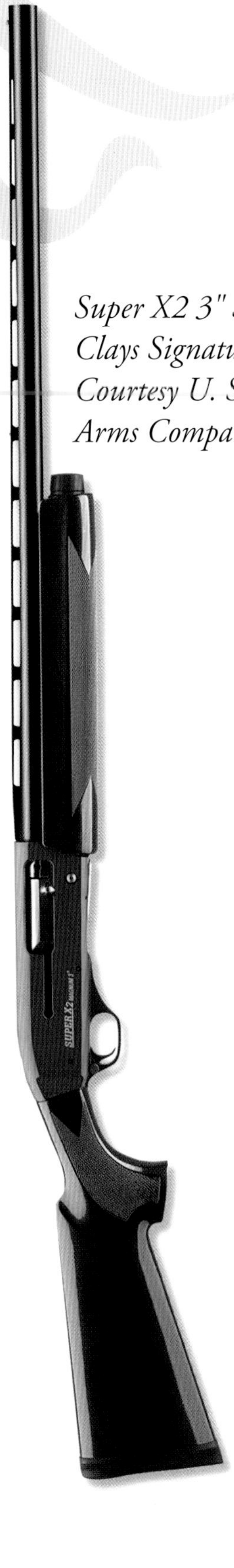

Super X2 3" Sporting Clays Signature II. Photo Courtesy U. S. Repeating Arms Company.

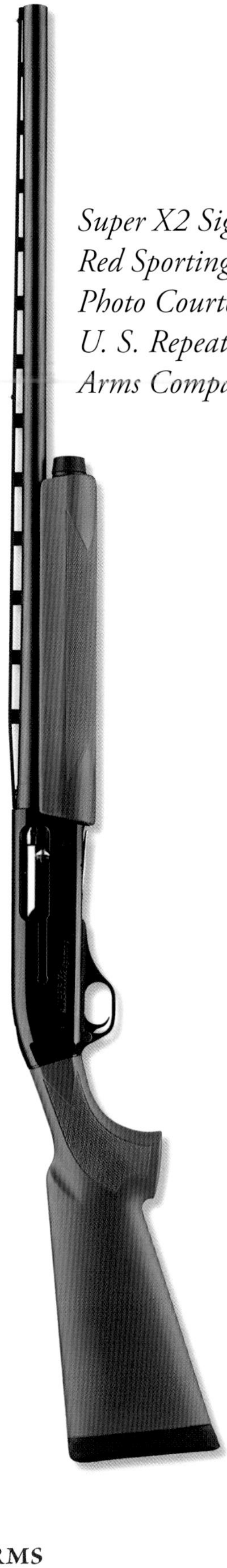

Super X2 Signature Red Sporting. Photo Courtesy U. S. Repeating Arms Company.

SUPER X2 SPORTING CLAYS SIGNATURE II

This 3" 12 gauge gun is fitted with a 30" barrel with choke tubes. The hardwood stock is painted black metallic. The receiver is a red anodized alloy. Weight is about 8.25 lbs. Introduced in 2005.

NIB	EXC.	V.G.	GOOD	FAIR	POOR
1015	800	-	-	-	-

SUPER X2 SIGNATURE RED SPORTING

This 12 gauge 3" shell model features a hardwood stock with red Dura-Touch coating. Fitted with a 30" vent rib barrel with five choke tubes. Weight is about 8 lbs. Introduced in 2003.

NIB	EXC.	V.G.	GOOD	FAIR	POOR
955	750	-	-	-	-

SUPER X3 SERIES

Introduced in 2006, The Super X3 12 gauge features weight and recoil reducing features and a .742" back-bored barrel. It is available in a variety of configurations weighing under 7 lbs. in the 3" Field model and about 7.5 lbs. in composite, camo and 3.5" models. All models except Cantilever Deer included three choke tubes.

SUPER X3 FIELD

Walnut stock and 26" or 28" barrel.

NIB	EXC.	V.G.	GOOD	FAIR	POOR
955	750	-	-	-	-

Super X3 Field. Photo Courtesy U. S. Repeating Arms Company.

Super X3 Composite. Photo Courtesy U. S. Repeating Arms Company.

SUPER X3 COMPOSITE

Matte black stock and forend. Available in 26" or 28" barrel and 3" or 3.5" chamber. Add 100 for 3.5" model.

NIB	EXC.	V.G.	GOOD	FAIR	POOR
925	725	-	-	-	-

SUPER X3 CAMO

Composite camo stock with 3.5" chamber. Available in various camo patterns with 26" and 28" barrel.

NIB	EXC.	V.G.	GOOD	FAIR	POOR
1100	950	-	-	-	-

SUPER X3 CANTILEVER DEER

Slug gun with 22" barrel with cantilever scope mount and 3" chamber.

NIB	EXC.	V.G.	GOOD	FAIR	POOR
955	750	-	-	-	-

COMBINATION GUN

This is an Over/Under rifle/shotgun combination chambered for 12 gauge over .222, .223, .30-06, and the 9.3x74R cartridges. It features 25" barrels. The shotgun tube has a screw-in choke. It is engraved in the fashion of the Model 501 Grand European and features a select checkered walnut stock. It was manufactured between 1983 and 1985.

EXC.	V.G.	GOOD	FAIR	POOR
2500	2200	1950	1450	1000

Super X3 Camo. Photo Courtesy U. S. Repeating Arms Company.

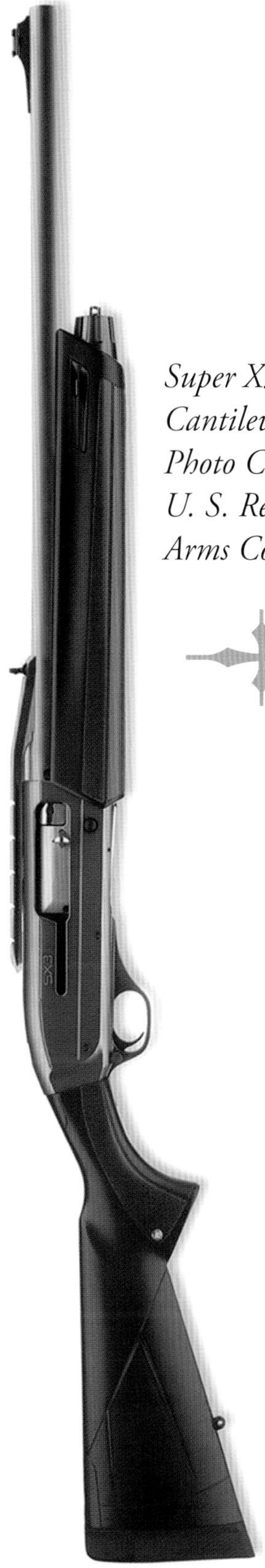

Super X3 Cantilever Deer. Photo Courtesy U. S. Repeating Arms Company.

SECTION IX

WINCHESTER COMMEMORATIVES

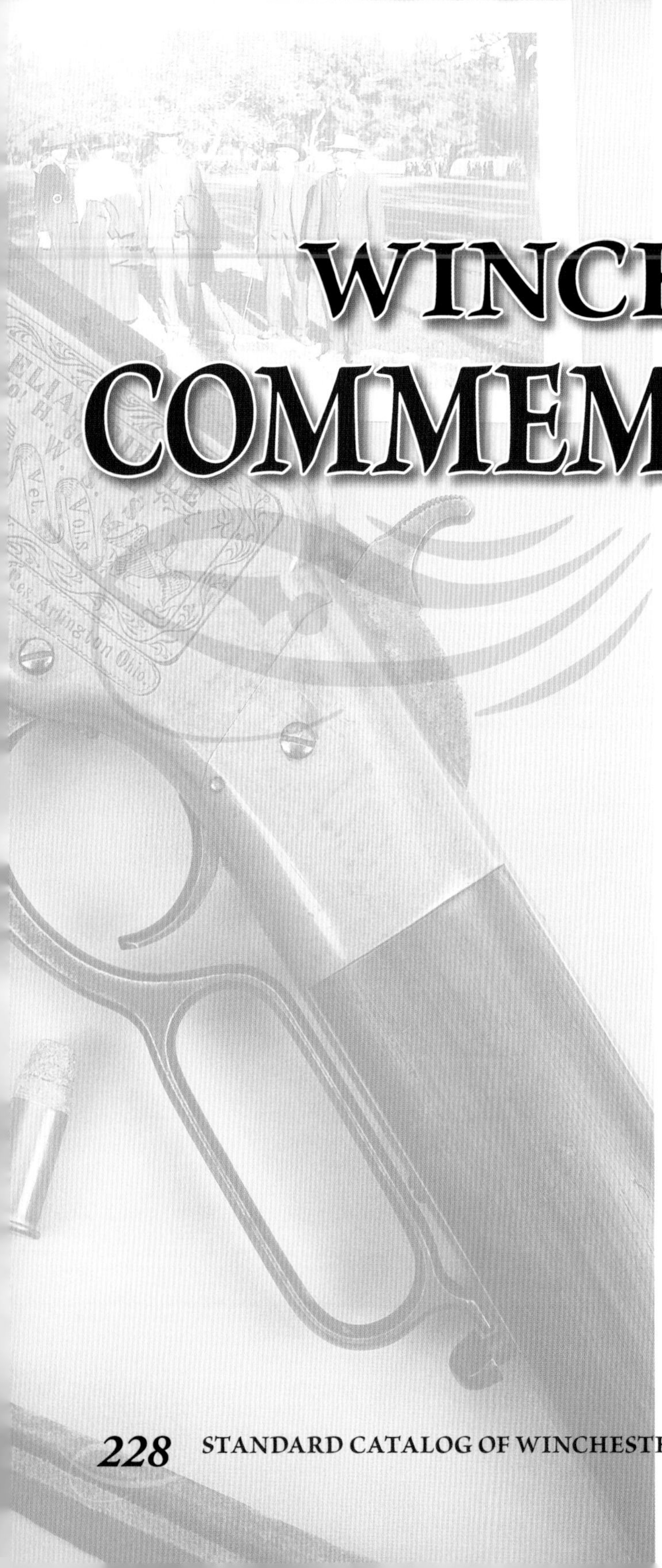

Since the early 1960s, Winchester has produced a number of special Model 1894 rifles and carbines that commemorated certain historic events, places, or individuals. In some cases they are slightly embellished and in others are quite ornate. The general liquidity of these commemoratives has not been as good as would be expected. In some cases they were produced in excessive amounts and could not, in all honesty, be considered limited-production items. In any case, in our opinion one should purchase weapons of this nature for their enjoyment factor as the investment potential is not sufficient reason for their purchase. As with all commemoratives, in order to realize the collector potential they must be NIB with all supplied

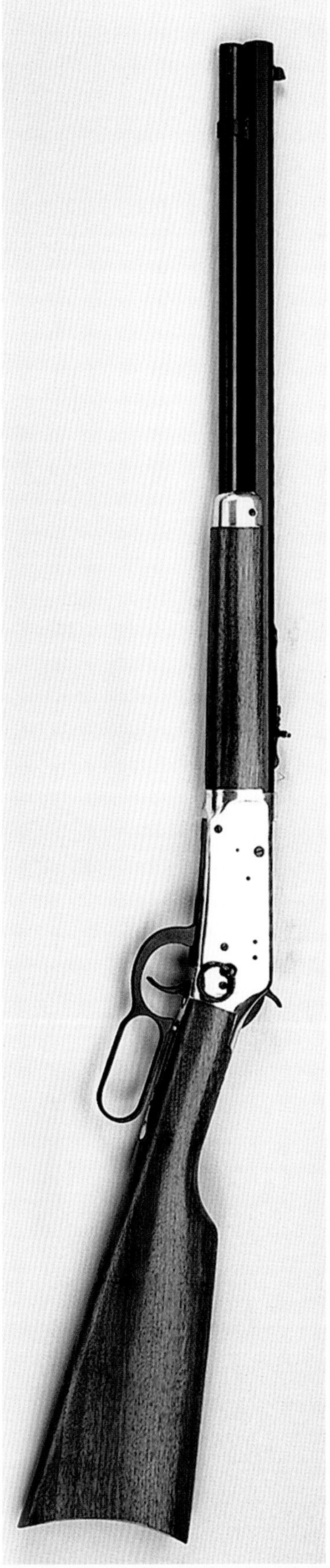

1966 Centennial Carbine Commemorative.

materials including, in the case of Winchester, the colorful outer sleeve that encased the factory carton. If a Winchester commemorative rifle has been cocked leaving a line on the hammer or the lever, many collectors will show little or no interest in its acquisition. If they have been fired, they will realize little premium over a standard, Post-1964 Model 94. A number of commemoratives have been ordered by outside concerns and are technically not factory issues. Most have less collectibility than the factory-issued models. There are a number of concerns that specialize in marketing the total range of Winchester commmemorative rifles. Listed are the factory-issue commemoratives with their current value, their issue price, and the number manufactured.

1964 WYOMING DIAMOND JUBILEE-CARBINE

NIB	ISSUE	AMT. MFG.
795	100	1,500

1966 CENTENNIAL-RIFLE

NIB	ISSUE	AMT. MFG.
495	125	102,309

1966 CENTENNIAL-CARBINE

NIB	ISSUE	AMT. MFG.
475	125	102,309

1966 NEBRASKA CENTENNIAL-RIFLE

NIB	ISSUE	AMT. MFG.
795	100	2,500

1967 Canadian Centennial Rifle Commemorative.

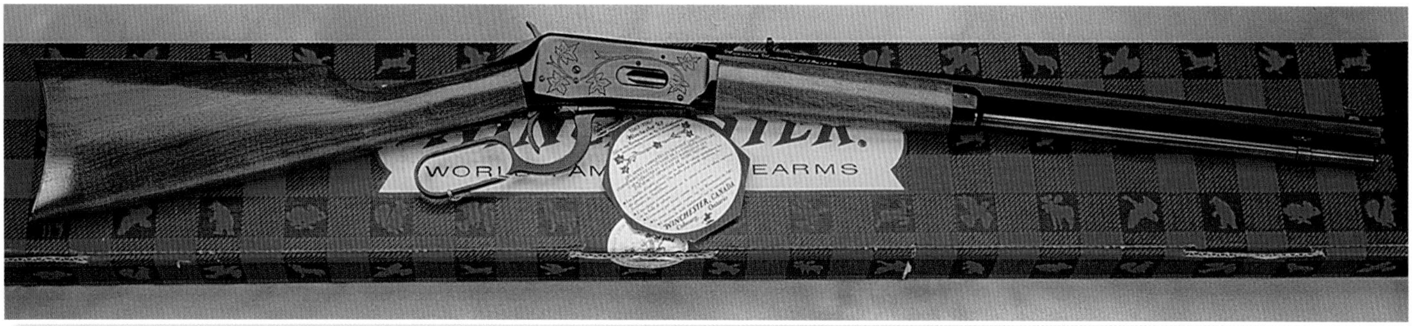

1967 Canadian Centennial Carbine Commemorative.

1967 CANADIAN CENTENNIAL-RIFLE

NIB	ISSUE	AMT. MFG.
495	125	-

1967 CANADIAN CENTENNIAL-CARBINE

NIB	ISSUE	AMT. MFG.
475	125	90,301

1967 ALASKAN PURCHASE CENTENNIAL-CARBINE

NIB	ISSUE	AMT. MFG.
795	125	1,500

1968 ILLINOIS SESQUICENTENNIAL-CARBINE

NIB	ISSUE	AMT. MFG.
395	110	37,648

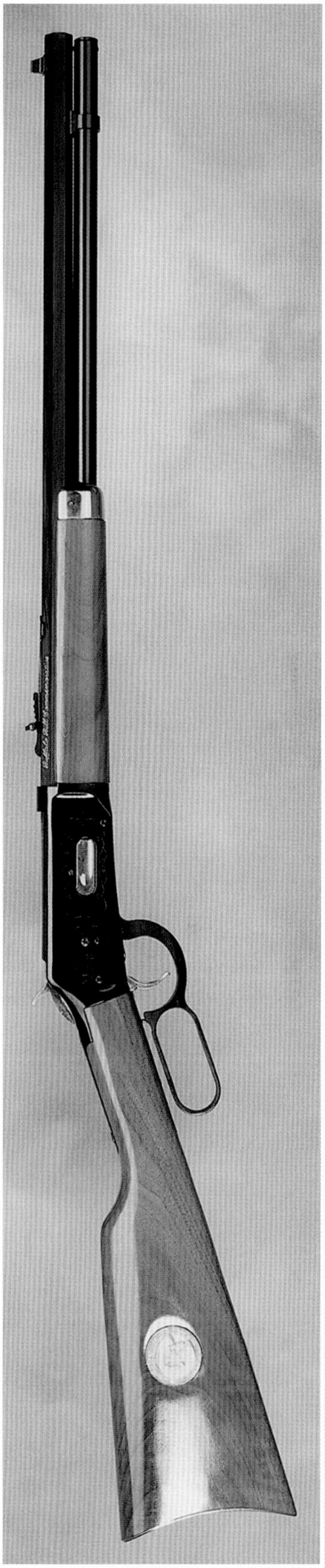

1968 Buffalo Bill Carbine Commemorative.

1968 BUFFALO BILL-CARBINE

NIB	ISSUE	AMT. MFG.
475	130	112,923

1968 BUFFALO BILL-RIFLE

NIB	ISSUE	AMT. MFG.
495	130	-

1968 BUFFALO BILL "1 OR 300"-RIFLE

NIB	ISSUE	AMT. MFG.
2750	1000	300

1969 THEODORE ROOSEVELT-RIFLE

NIB	ISSUE	AMT. MFG.
495	135	-

1969 THEODORE ROOSEVELT-CARBINE

NIB	ISSUE	AMT. MFG.
475	135	52,386

1969 GOLDEN SPIKE CARBINE

NIB	ISSUE	AMT. MFG.
495	120	69,996

1970 COWBOY COMMEMORATIVE CARBINE

NIB	ISSUE	AMT. MFG.
450	125	27,549

1970 COWBOY CARBINE "1 OF 300"

NIB	ISSUE	AMT. MFG.
2750	1000	300

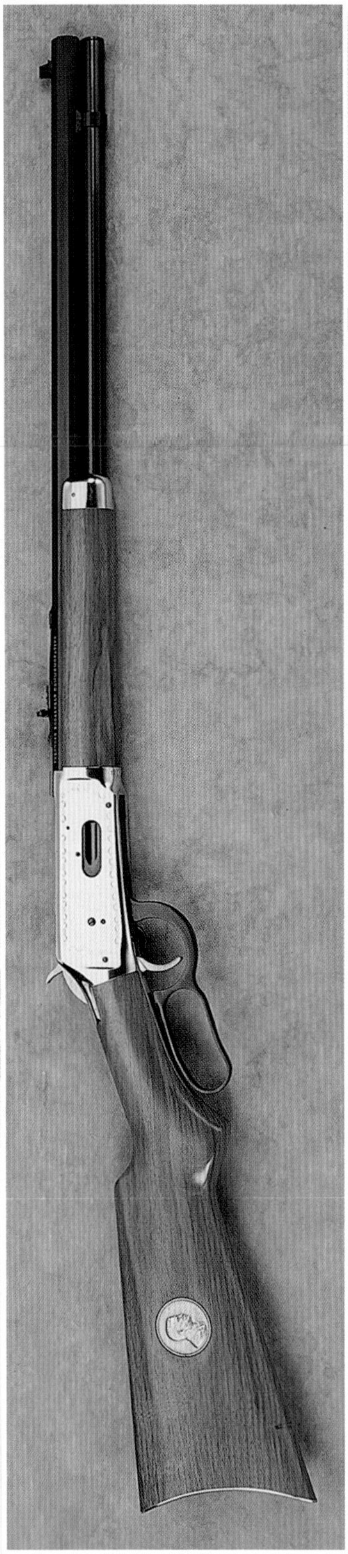

1969 Theodore Roosevelt Carbine Commemorative.

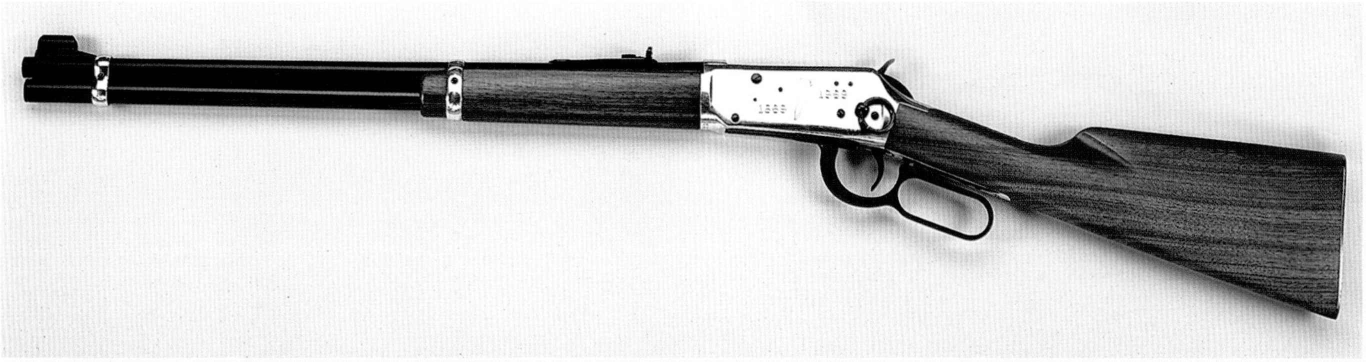

1969 Golden Spike Carbine Commemorative.

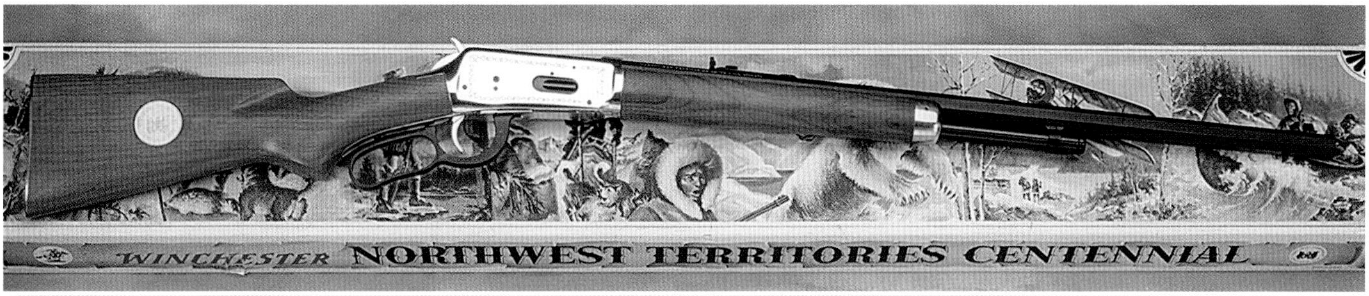

1970 Northwest Territory (Canadian) Commemorative.

1970 NORTHWEST TERRITORIES (CANADIAN)

NIB	ISSUE	AMT. MFG.
850	150	2,500

1970 NORTHWEST TERRITORIES DELUXE (CANADIAN)

NIB	ISSUE	AMT. MFG.
1100	250	500

1970 LONE STAR-RIFLE

NIB	ISSUE	AMT. MFG.
495	140	-

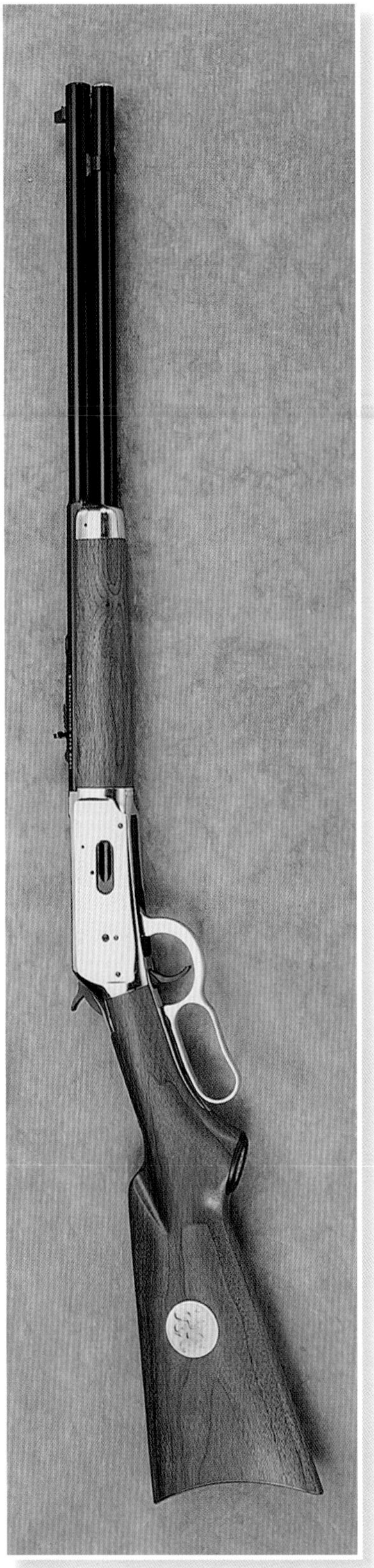

1970 Lone Star Carbine Commemorative.

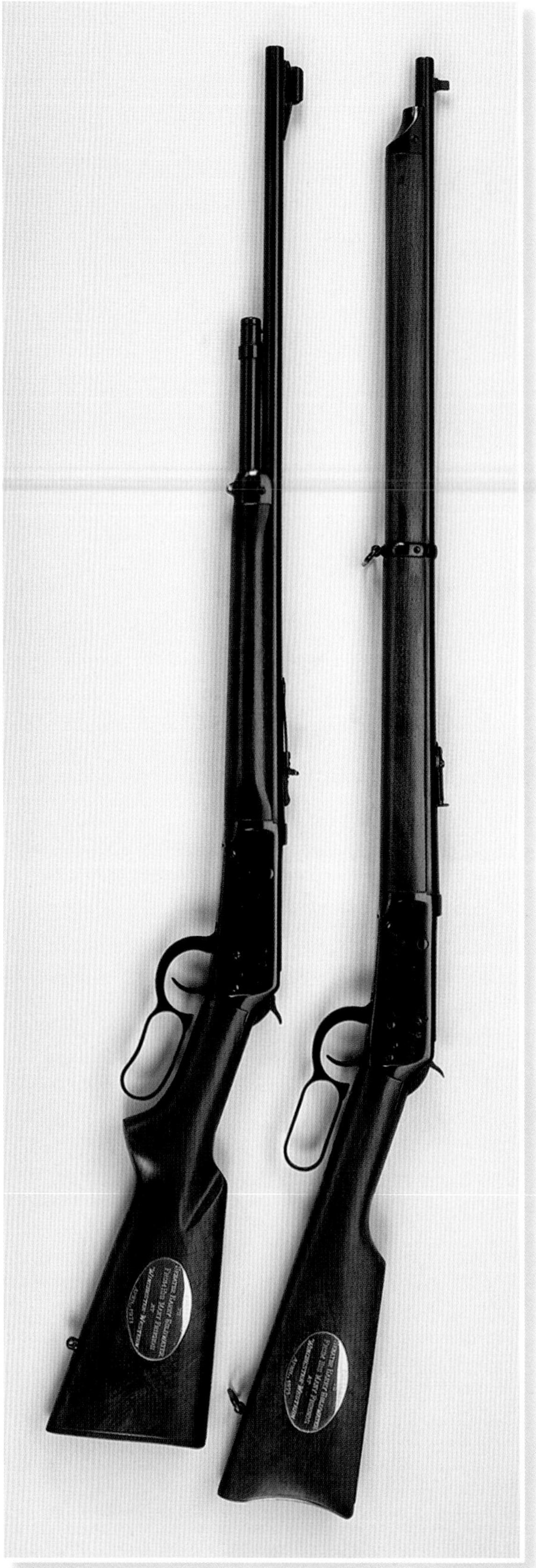

1979 NRA Centennial Commemorative Rifle & Musket Set.

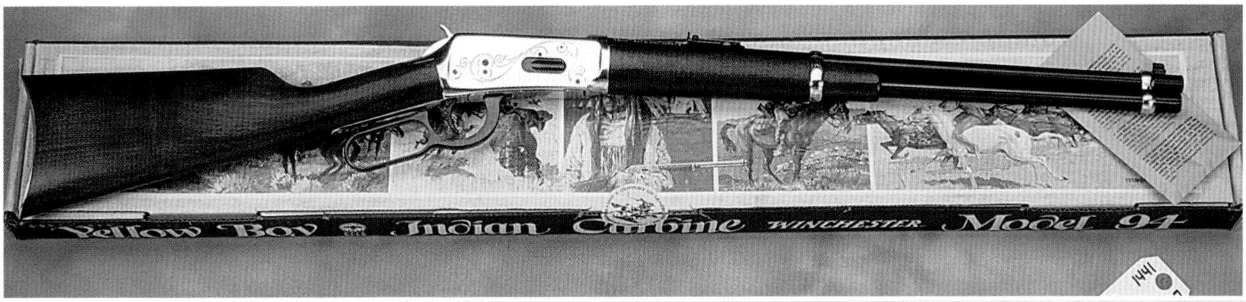

1971 Yellow Boy (European) Commemorative.

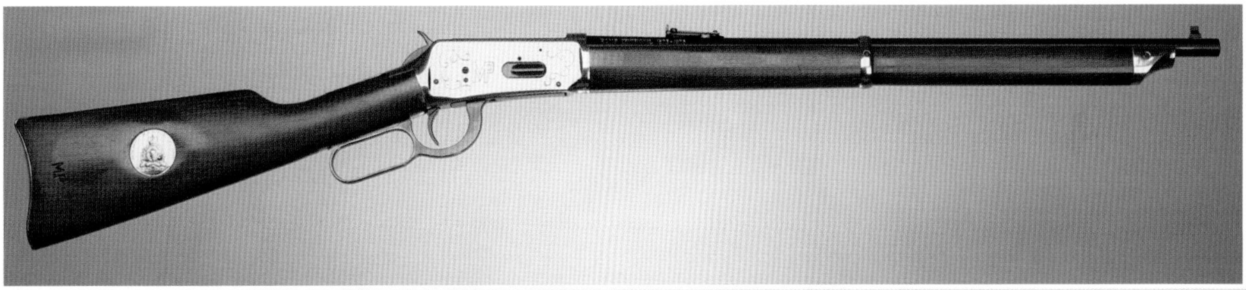

1971 Royal Canadian Mounted Police Musket Commemorative.

1970 LONE STAR-CARBINE

NIB	ISSUE	AMT. MFG.
475	140	38,385

1971 NRA CENTENNIAL-RIFLE

NIB	ISSUE	AMT. MFG.
950	150	21,000

1971 NRA CENTENNIAL-MUSKET

NIB	ISSUE	AMT. MFG.
950	150	23,400

1971 YELLOW BOY (EUROPEAN)

NIB	ISSUE	AMT. MFG.
1150	250	500

1971 ROYAL CANADIAN MOUNTED POLICE (CANADIAN) MUSKET

NIB	ISSUE	AMT. MFG.
795	190	9,500

1971 MOUNTED POLICE (CANADIAN)

NIB	ISSUE	AMT. MFG.
795	190	5,100

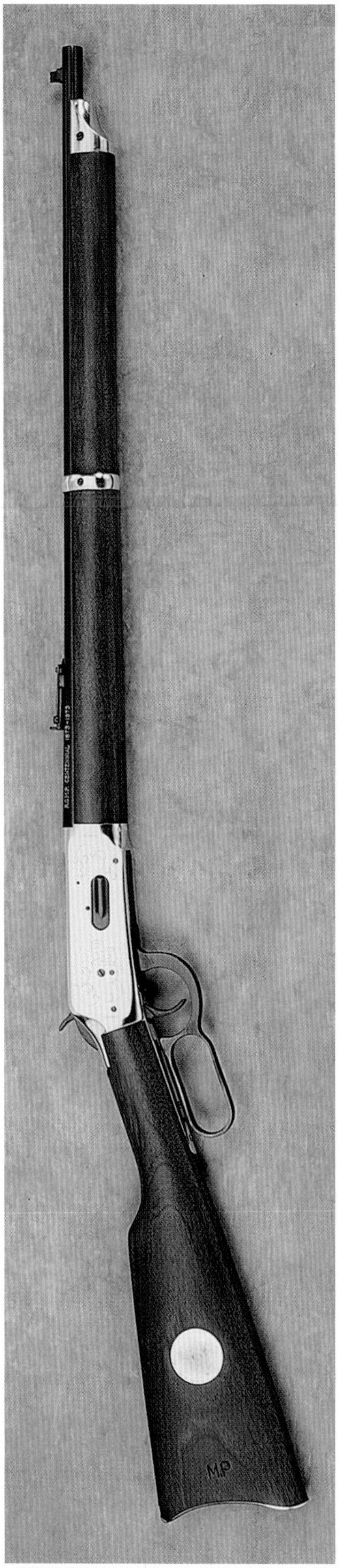

1971 Mounted Police, Presentation Grade Commemorative.

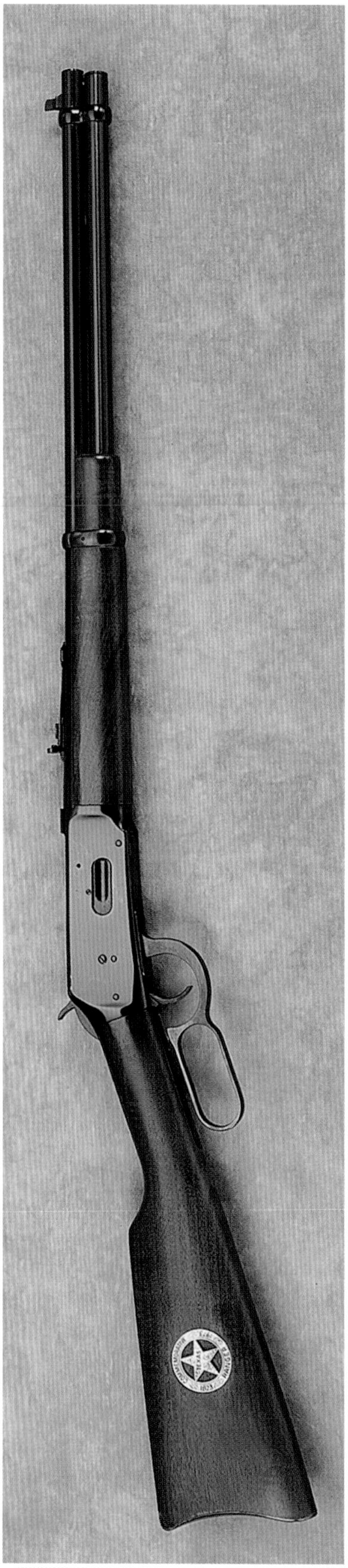

1974 Texas Ranger Carbine Commemorative.

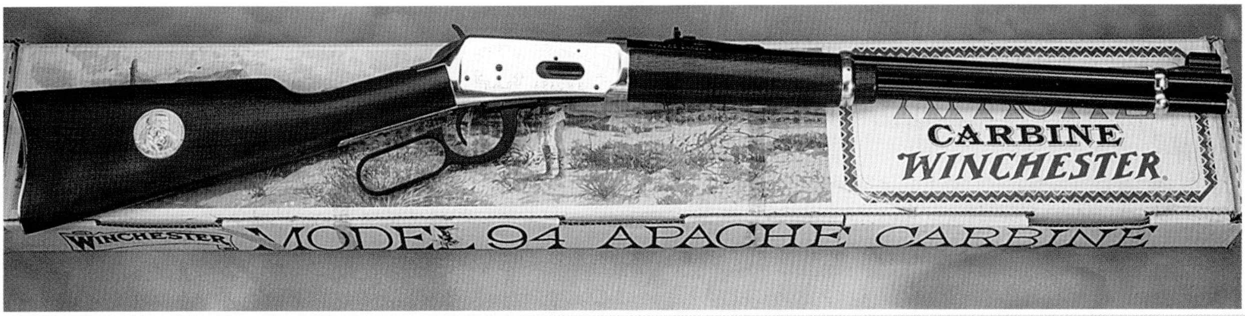

1974 Apache (Canadian) Commemorative.

1974 Comanche (Canadian) Commemorative.

1971 MOUNTED POLICE, PRESENTATION

NIB	ISSUE	AMT. MFG.
9995	-	10

1974 TEXAS RANGER-CARBINE

NIB	ISSUE	AMT. MFG.
695	135	4,850

1974 TEXAS RANGER PRESENTATION

NIB	ISSUE	AMT. MFG.
2750	1000	150

1974 APACHE (CANADIAN)

NIB	ISSUE	AMT. MFG.
795	150	8,600

1974 COMMANCHE (CANADIAN)

NIB	ISSUE	AMT. MFG.
795	230	11,500

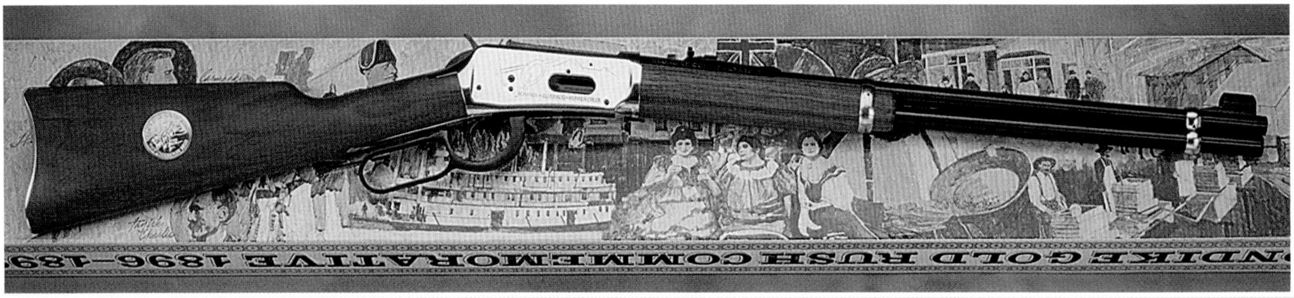

1974 Klondike Gold Rush (Canadian) Commemorative.

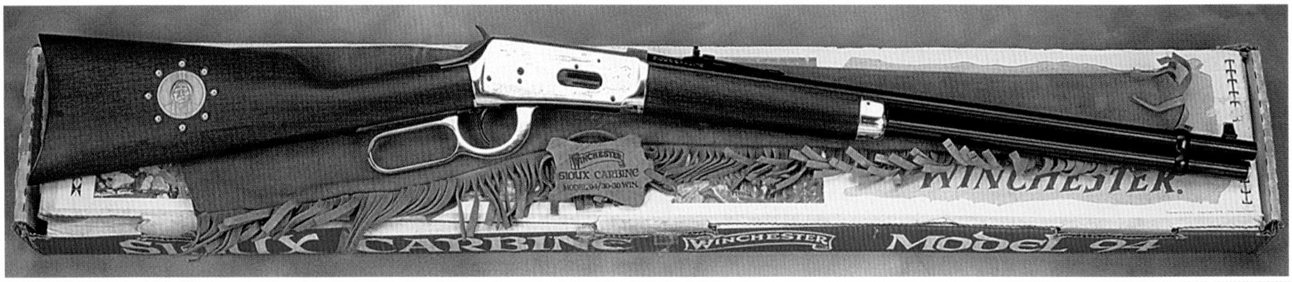

1976 Sioux (Canadian) Commemorative.

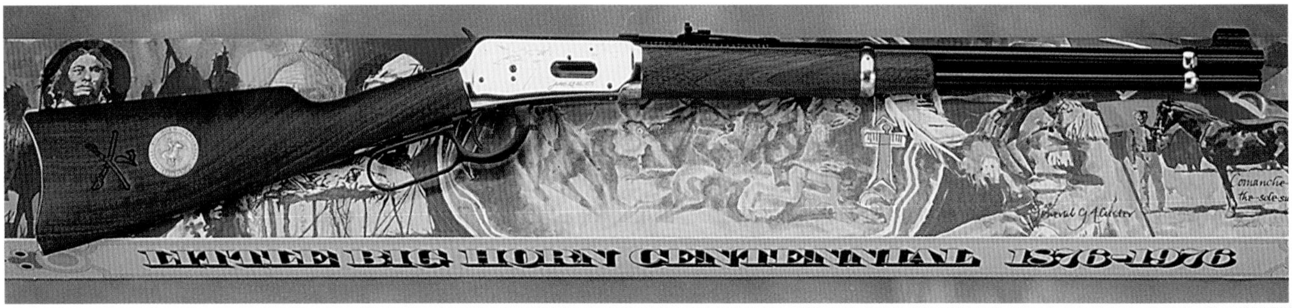

1976 Little Bighorn (Canadian) Commemorative.

1974 KLONDIKE GOLD RUSH (CANADIAN)

NIB	ISSUE	AMT. MFG.
795	240	10,500

1975 KLONDIKE GOLD RUSH-DAWSON CITY ISSUE (CANADIAN)

NIB	ISSUE	AMT. MFG.
8500	-	25

1976 SIOUX (CANADIAN)

NIB	ISSUE	AMT. MFG.
795	280	10,000

1976 LITTLE BIGHORN (CANADIAN)

NIB	ISSUE	AMT. MFG.
795	300	11,000

1976 U.S. BICENTENNIAL CARBINE

NIB	ISSUE	AMT. MFG.
595	325	19,999

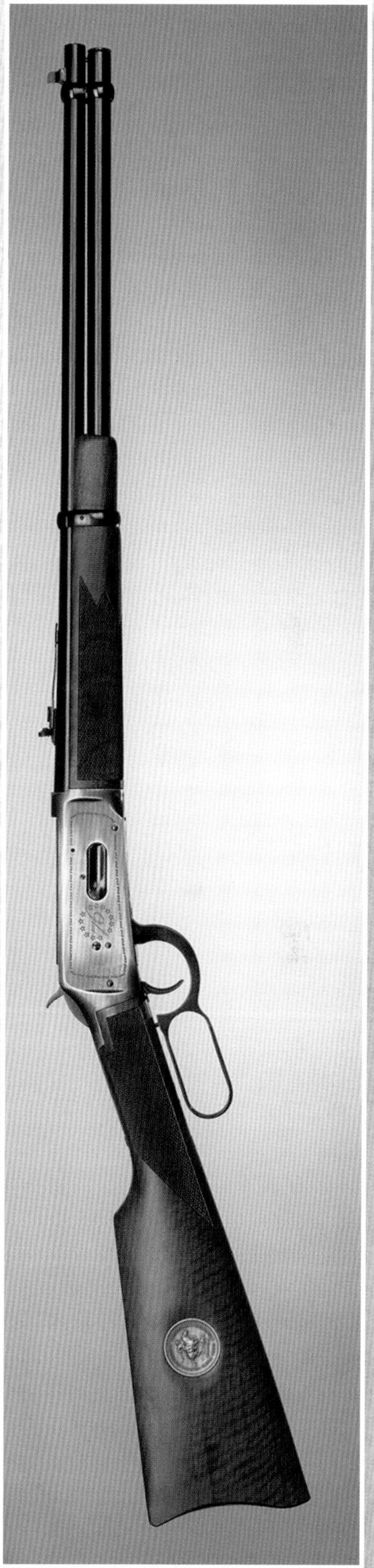

1976 US Bicentennial Carbine Commemorative.

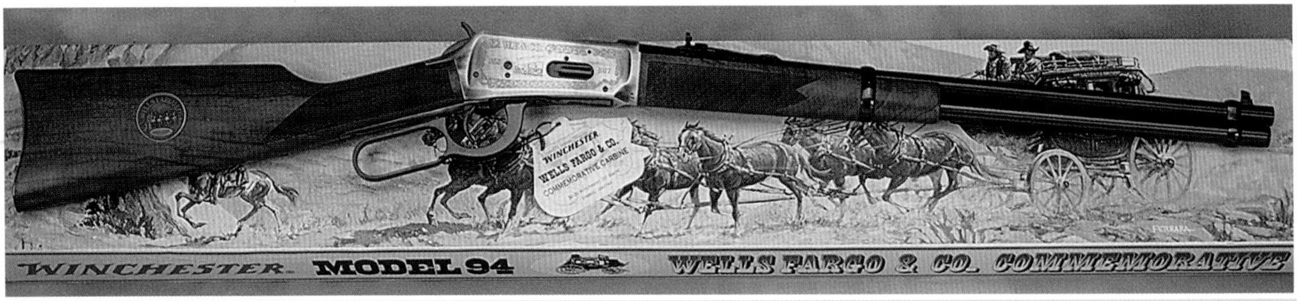

1977 Wells-Fargo Commemorative.

1977 Legendary Lawmen Earp Brothers Commemorative, Closeup of Left Receiver.

1977 WELLS FARGO

NIB	ISSUE	AMT. MFG.
495	350	19,999

1977 LEGENDARY LAWMAN

NIB	ISSUE	AMT. MFG.
495	375	19,999

1977 Legendary Lawmen Earp Brothers Commemorative, Closeup of Right Receiver.

1977 Legendary Lawmen Commemorative.

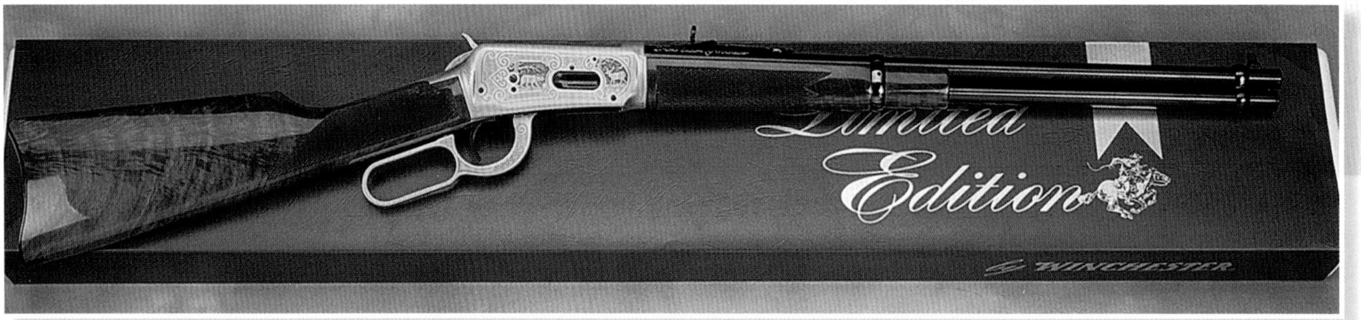

1977 Limited Edition Commemorative.

1977 Cheyenne 22 Commemorative.

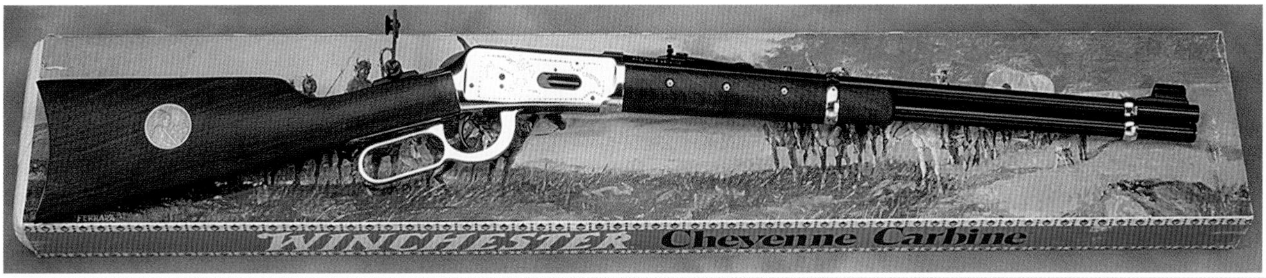

1977 Cheyenne 44-40 Commemorative.

1977 Cherokee 30-30 Commemorative.

1977 LIMITED EDITION I

NIB	ISSUE	AMT. MFG.
1395	1500	1,500

1977 CHEYENNE-.22 CAL. (CANADIAN)

NIB	ISSUE	AMT. MFG.
750	320	5,000

1977 CHEYENNE-.44-40 CAL. (CANADIAN)

NIB	ISSUE	AMT. MFG.
795	300	11,225

1977 CHEROKEE-.22 CAL. (CANADIAN)

NIB	ISSUE	AMT. MFG.
750	385	3,950

1977 CHEROKEE-.30-30 CAL. (CANADIAN)

NIB	ISSUE	AMT. MFG.
795	385	9,000

1978 "ONE OF ONE THOUSAND" (EUROPEAN)

NIB	ISSUE	AMT. MFG.
7500	5000	250

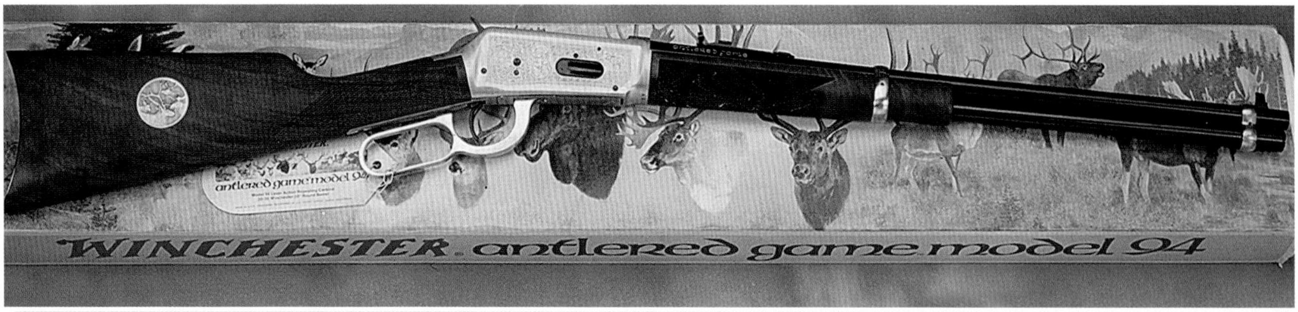

1978 Antler Game Commemorative Carbine.

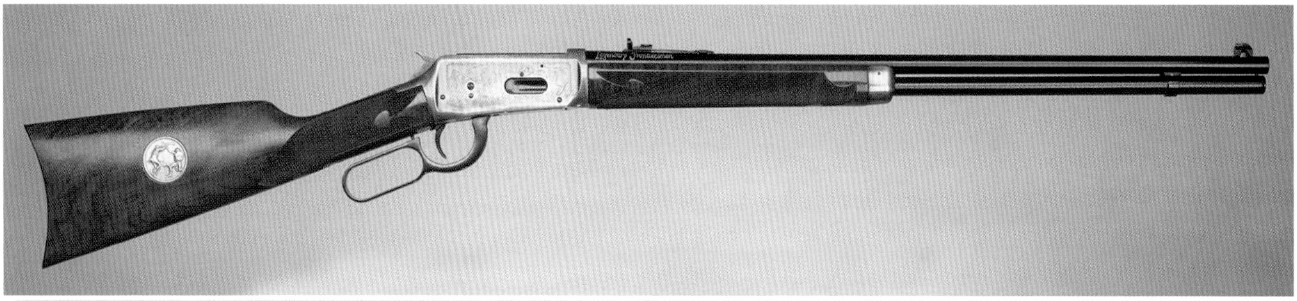

1979 Legendary Frontiersman Rifle Commemorative.

1978 ANTLER GAME CARBINE

NIB	ISSUE	AMT. MFG.
550	375	19,999

1979 LIMITED EDITION II

NIB	ISSUE	AMT. MFG.
1395	1500	1,500

1979 LEGENDARY FRONTIERSMAN RIFLE

NIB	ISSUE	AMT. MFG.
550	425	19,999

1979 MATCHED SET OF 1,000

NIB	ISSUE	AMT. MFG.
2250	3000	1,000

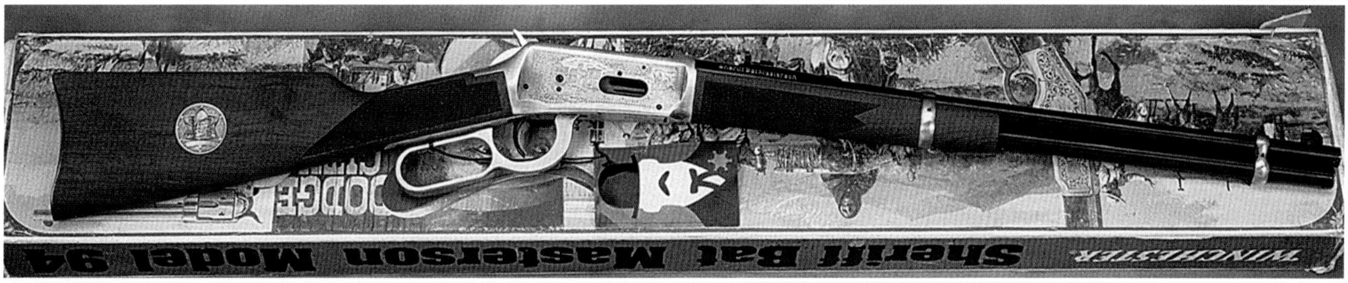

1979 Bat Masterson (Canadian Commemorative).

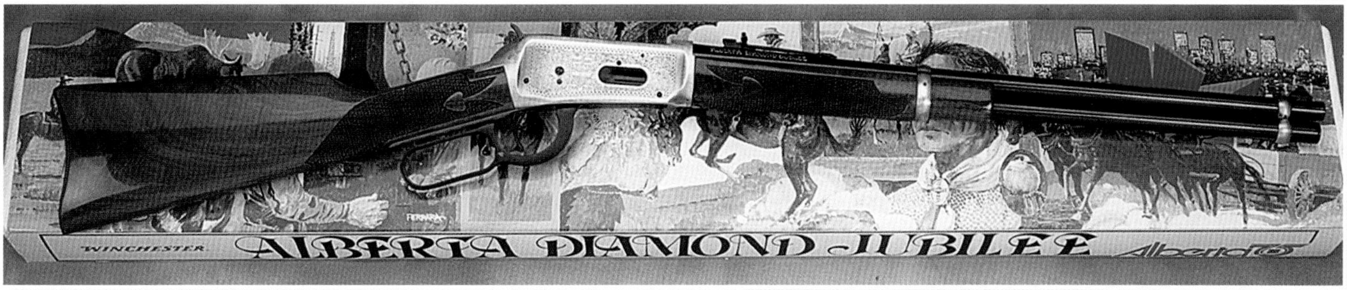

1980 Alberta Diamond (Canadian) Commemorative.

1979 BAT MASTERSON (CANADIAN)

NIB	ISSUE	AMT. MFG.
795	650	8,000

1980 ALBERTA DIAMOND JUBILEE (CANADIAN)

NIB	ISSUE	AMT. MFG.
795	650	2,700

1980 ALBERTA DIAMOND JUBILEE DELUXE (CANADIAN)

NIB	ISSUE	AMT. MFG.
1495	1900	300

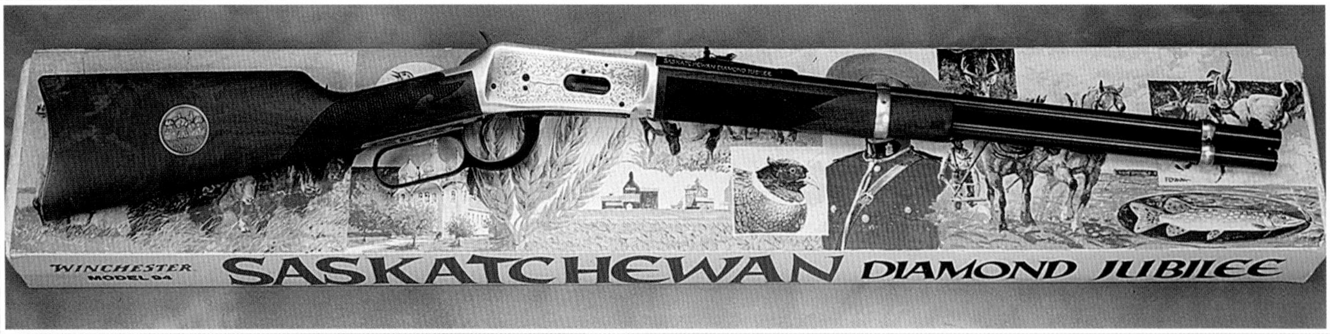

1980 Saskatchewan Diamond Anniversary (Canadian) Commemorative.

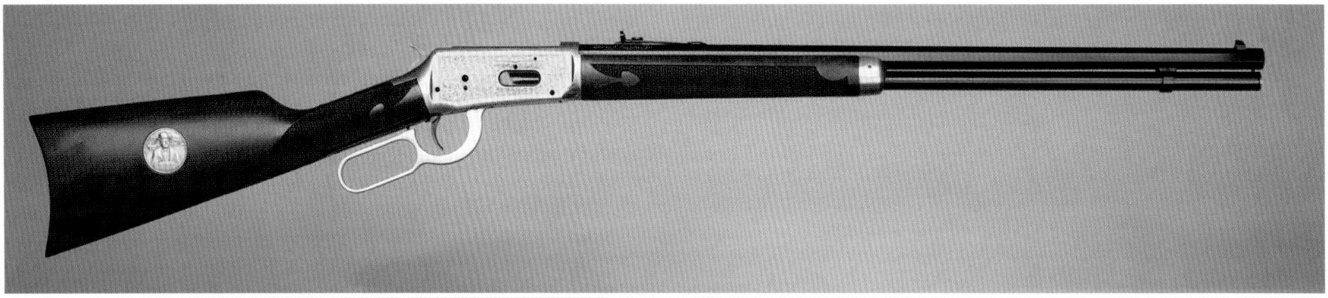

1980 Oliver Winchester Commemorative.

1981 Canada Pacific Centennial (Canadian) Commemorative.

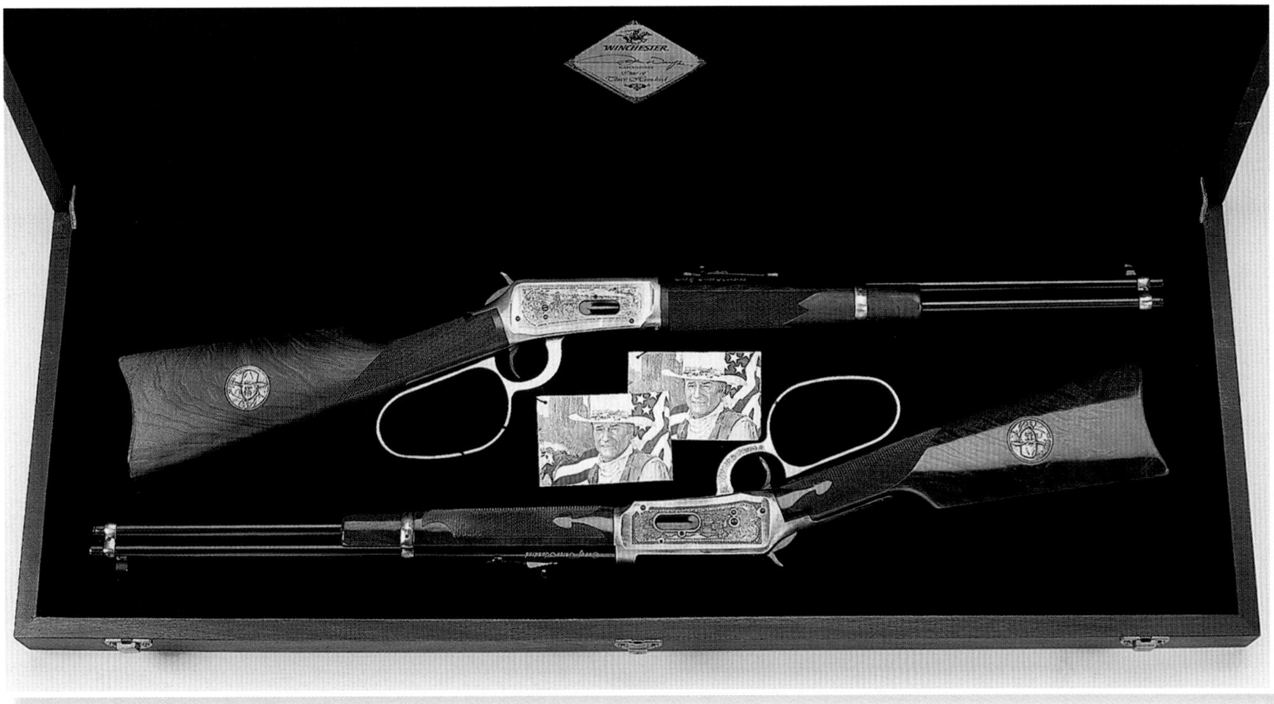

1981 John Wayne Commemorative Matched Set.

1980 SASKATCHEWAN DIAMOND JUBILEE (CANADIAN)

NIB	ISSUE	AMT. MFG.
795	695	2,700

1980 SASKATCHEWAN DIAMOND JUBILEE DELUXE (CANADIAN)

NIB	ISSUE	AMT. MFG.
1495	1995	300

1980 OLIVER WINCHESTER

NIB	ISSUE	AMT. MFG.
695	375	19,999

1981 U.S. BORDER PATROL

NIB	ISSUE	AMT. MFG.
595	1195	1,000

1981 U.S. BORDER PATROL-MEMBER'S MODEL

NIB	ISSUE	AMT. MFG.
595	695	800

1981 CALGARY STAMPEDE (CANADIAN)

NIB	ISSUE	AMT. MFG.
1250	2200	1,000

1981 CANADIAN PACIFIC CENTENNIAL (CANADIAN)

NIB	ISSUE	AMT. MFG.
550	800	2,000

1981 CANADIAN PACIFIC CENTENNIAL PRESENTATION (CANADIAN)

NIB	ISSUE	AMT. MFG.
1100	2200	300

1981 CANADIAN PACIFIC EMPLOYEE'S MODEL (CANADIAN)

NIB	ISSUE	AMT. MFG.
550	800	2,000

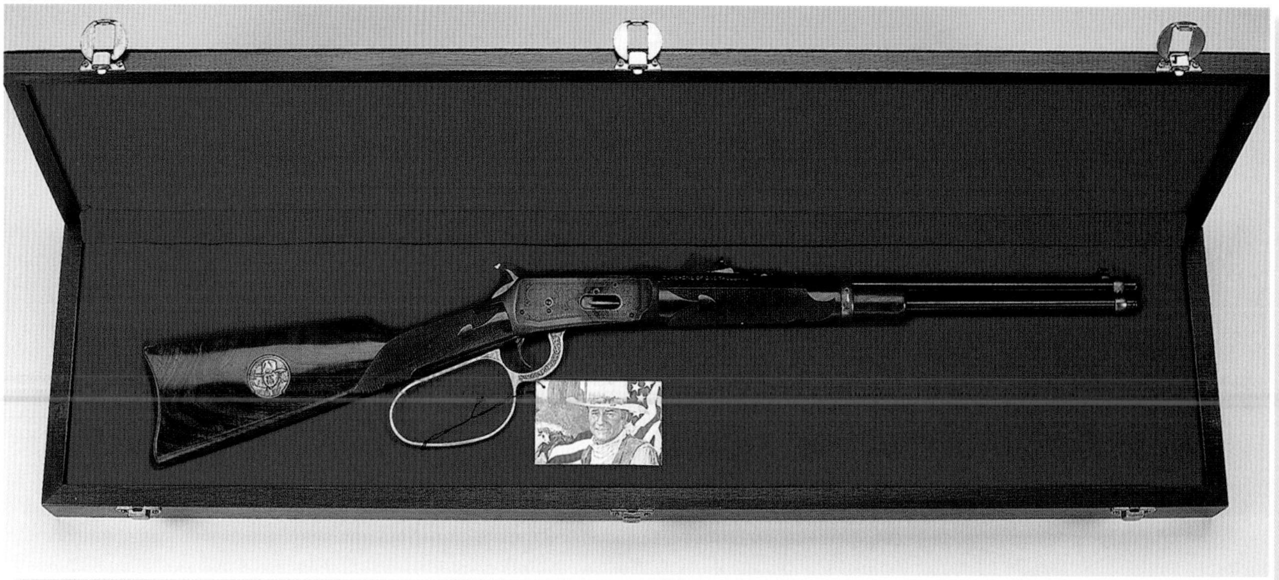

1981 John Wayne "The Duke" Commemorative

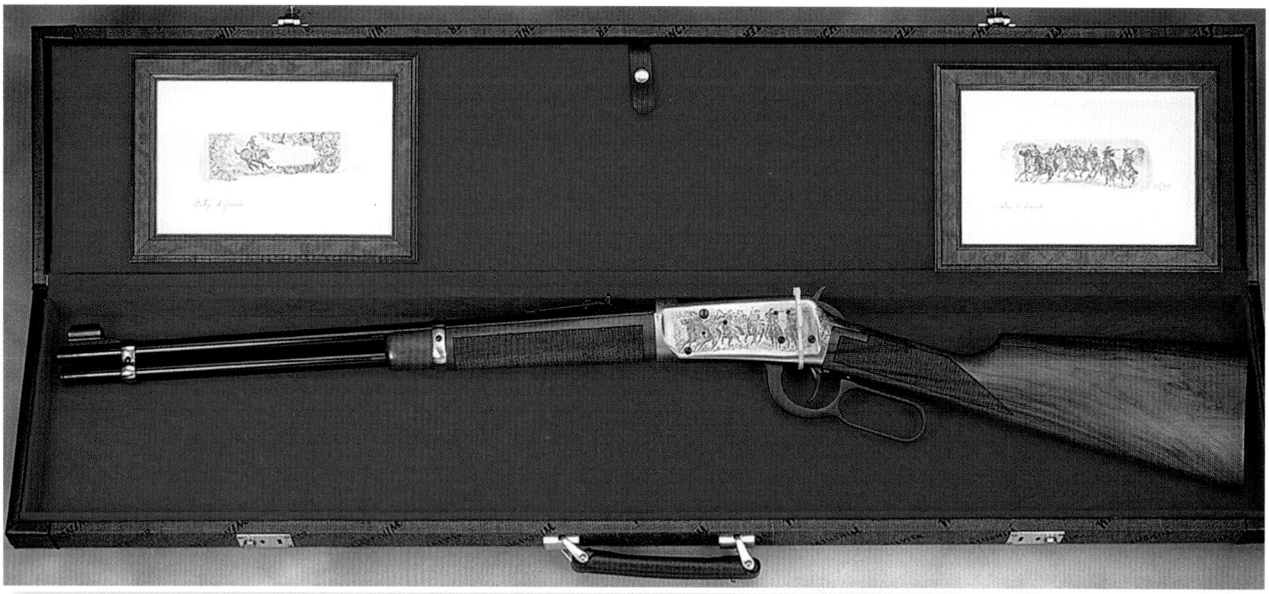

1982 Great Western Artist II Commemorative.

1981 JOHN WAYNE (CANADIAN)

NIB	ISSUE	AMT. MFG.
1495	995	1,000

1981 JOHN WAYNE

NIB	ISSUE	AMT. MFG.
1395	6 00	49,000

1981 DUKE

NIB	ISSUE	AMT. MFG.
3500	2250	1,000

1981 JOHN WAYNE "1 OF 300" SET

NIB	ISSUE	AMT. MFG.
6500	10000	300

1982 GREAT WESTERN ARTIST I

NIB	ISSUE	AMT. MFG.
1295	2200	999

1982 GREAT WESTERN ARTIST II

NIB	ISSUE	AMT. MFG.
1295	2200	999

1982 ANNIE OAKLEY

NIB	ISSUE	AMT. MFG.
795	699	6,000

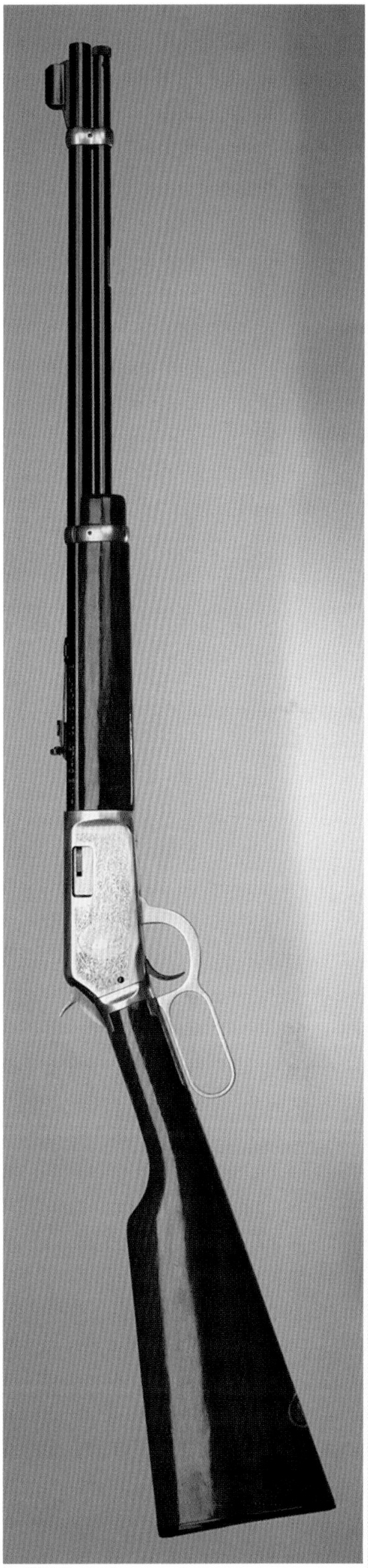

1982 Annie Oakley
9422 Commemorative.

1983 Chief Crazy Horse Commemorative.

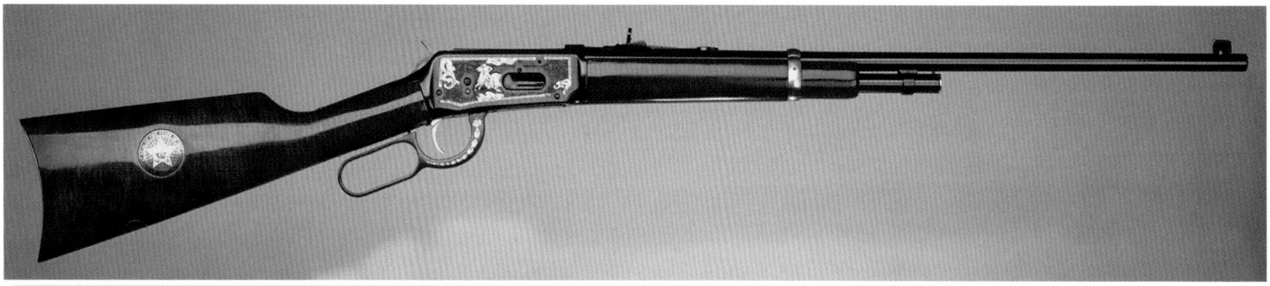

1983 Oklahoma Diamond Jubilee Commemorative.

1983 CHIEF CRAZY HORSE

NIB	ISSUE	AMT. MFG.
695	600	19,999

1983 AMERICAN BALD EAGLE

NIB	ISSUE	AMT. MFG.
595	895	2,800

1983 AMERICAN BALD EAGLE-DELUXE

NIB	ISSUE	AMT. MFG.
4000	2995	200

1983 OKLAHOMA DIAMOND JUBILEE

NIB	ISSUE	AMT. MFG.
1395	2250	1,001

1984 WINCHESTER-COLT COMMEMORATIVE SET

NIB	ISSUE	AMT. MFG.
2250	3995	2,300

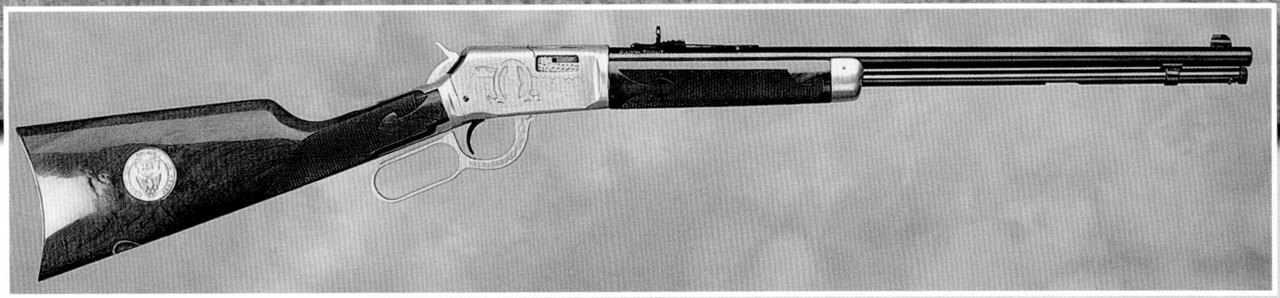

1985 Boy Scout 75th Anniversary Commemorative.

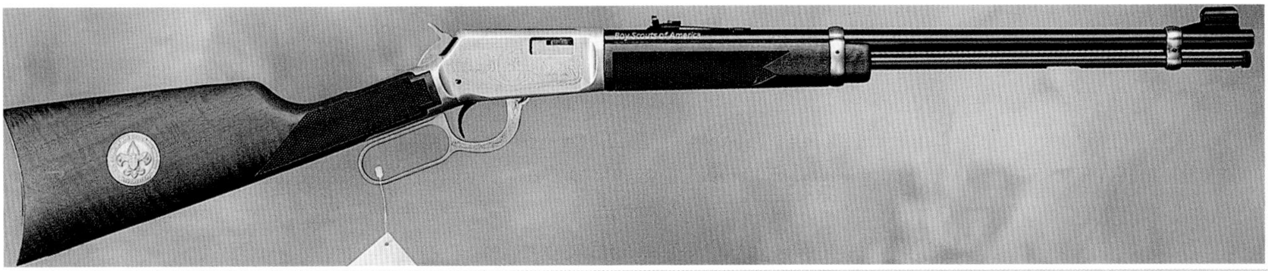

1985 Boy Scout 75th Anniversary Eagle Scout Commemorative.

1985 BOY SCOUT 75TH ANNIVERSARY .22 CAL.

NIB	ISSUE	AMT. MFG.
750	615	15,000

1985 BOY SCOUT 75TH ANNIVERSARY-EAGLE SCOUT

NIB	ISSUE	AMT. MFG.
4500	2140	1,000

TEXAS SESQUICENTENNIAL MODEL-RIFLE .38-55 CAL.

NIB	ISSUE	AMT. MFG.
2400	2995	1,500

TEXAS SESQUICENTENNIAL MODEL-CARBINE .38-55 CAL.

NIB	ISSUE	AMT. MFG.
695	695	15,000

TEXAS SESQUICENTENNIAL MODEL SET WITH BOWIE KNIFE

NIB	ISSUE	AMT. MFG.
6250	7995	150

1986 MODEL 94 DUCKS UNLIMITED

NIB	ISSUE	AMT. MFG.
650	-	2,800

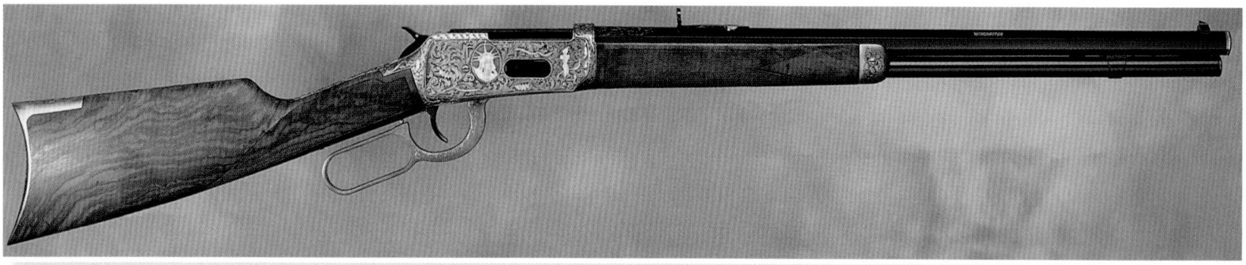

1986 Statue of Liberty Commemorative, Full View.

1986 Statue of Liberty Commemorative, Closeup of Right Receiver.

1986 STATUE OF LIBERTY

NIB	ISSUE	AMT. MFG.
7500	6500	100

1986 120TH ANNIVERSARY MODEL-CARBINE .44-40 CAL.

NIB	ISSUE	AMT. MFG.
895	995	1,000

1986 EUROPEAN 1 OF 1,000 SECOND SERIES (EUROPEAN)

NIB	ISSUE	AMT. MFG.
7000	6000	150

1987 U.S. CONSTITUTION 200TH ANNIVERSARY 44-40

NIB	ISSUE	AMT. MFG.
14000	12000	17

1990 WYOMING CENTENNIAL-30-30

NIB	ISSUE	AMT. MFG.
1495	895	500

1986 Statue of Liberty Commemorative, Closeup of Left Receiver.

1986 Statue of Liberty Commemorative, Closeup of Buttplate.

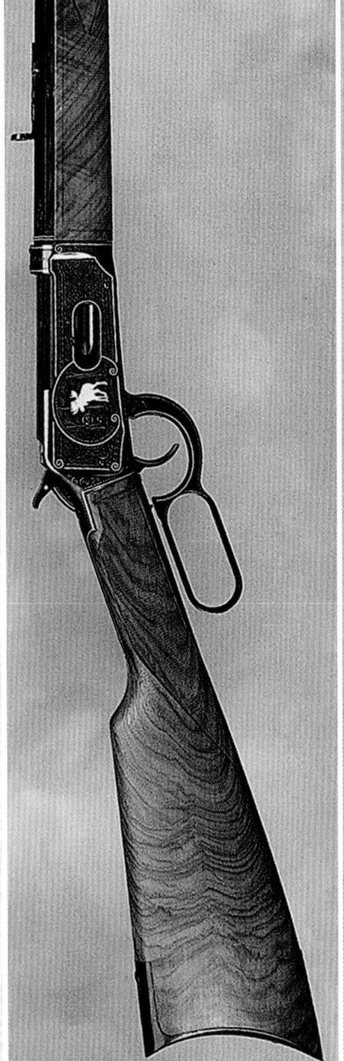

1991 Winchester 125th Anniversary Commemorative, Full View.

1991 WINCHESTER 125TH ANNIVERSARY

NIB	ISSUE	AMT. MFG.
5750	4995	61

1992 ARAPAHO-30-30

NIB	ISSUE	AMT. MFG.
1495	895	500

1992 ONTARIO CONSERVATION-30-30

NIB	ISSUE	AMT. MFG.
1495	1195	400

1991 Winchester 125th Anniversary Commemorative, Closeup of Left Receiver.

1991 Winchester 125th Anniversary Commemorative, Closeup of Right Receiver.

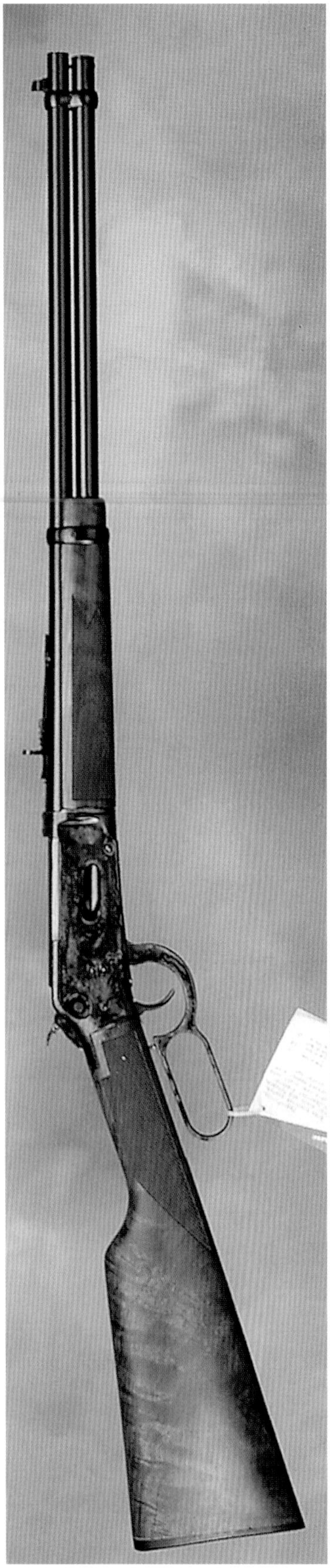

1992 Kentucky Bicentennial Commemorative.

1992 KENTUCKY BICENTENNIAL-30-30

NIB	ISSUE	AMT. MFG.
1495	995	500

1993 NEZ PERCE-30-30

NIB	ISSUE	AMT. MFG.
1495	995	600

1995 FLORIDA SESQUICENTENNIAL CARBINE

NIB	ISSUE	AMT. MFG.
1495	1195	360

1996 WILD BILL HICKOK CARBINE

NIB	ISSUE	AMT. MFG.
1495	1195	350

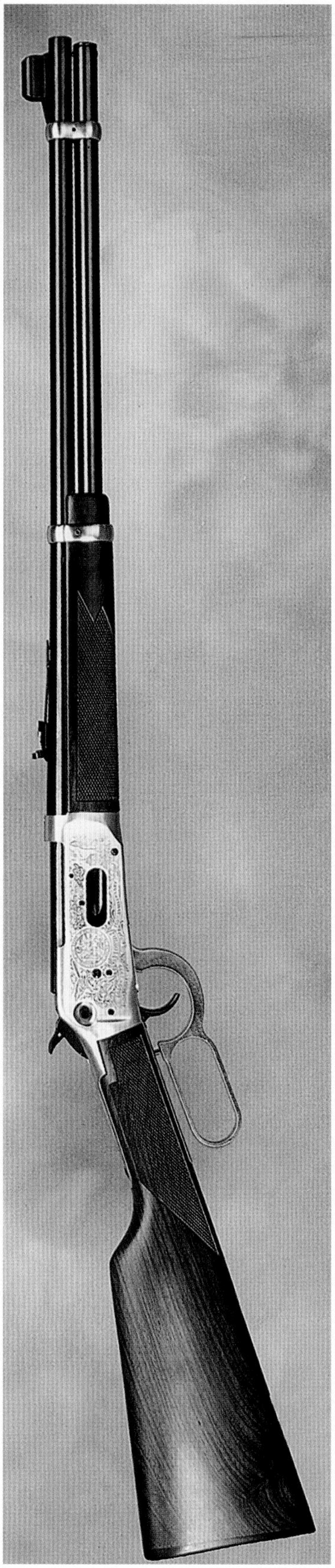

1995 Florida Sesquicentennial Carbine Commemorative.

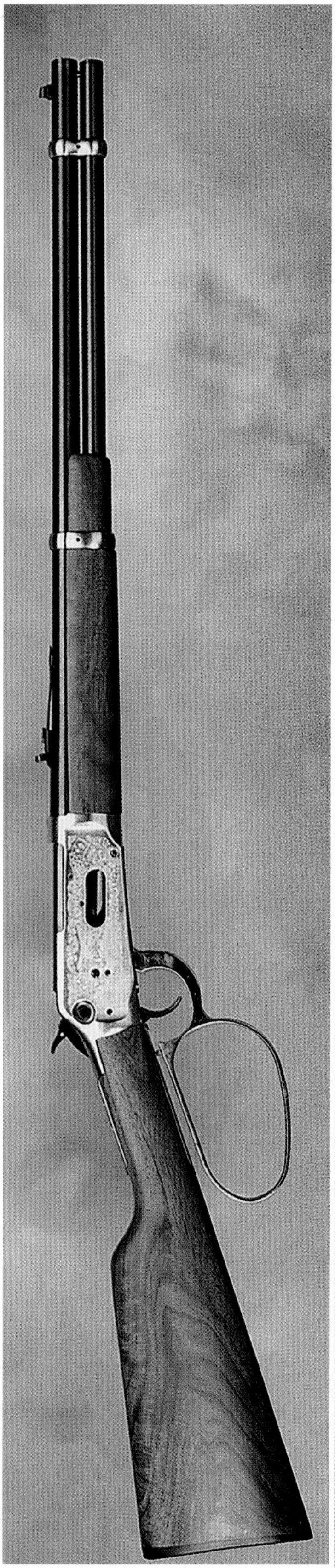

1996 Wild Bill Hickock Carbine Commemorative.

SECTION X

GOVERNMENT PURCHASED WINCHESTERS

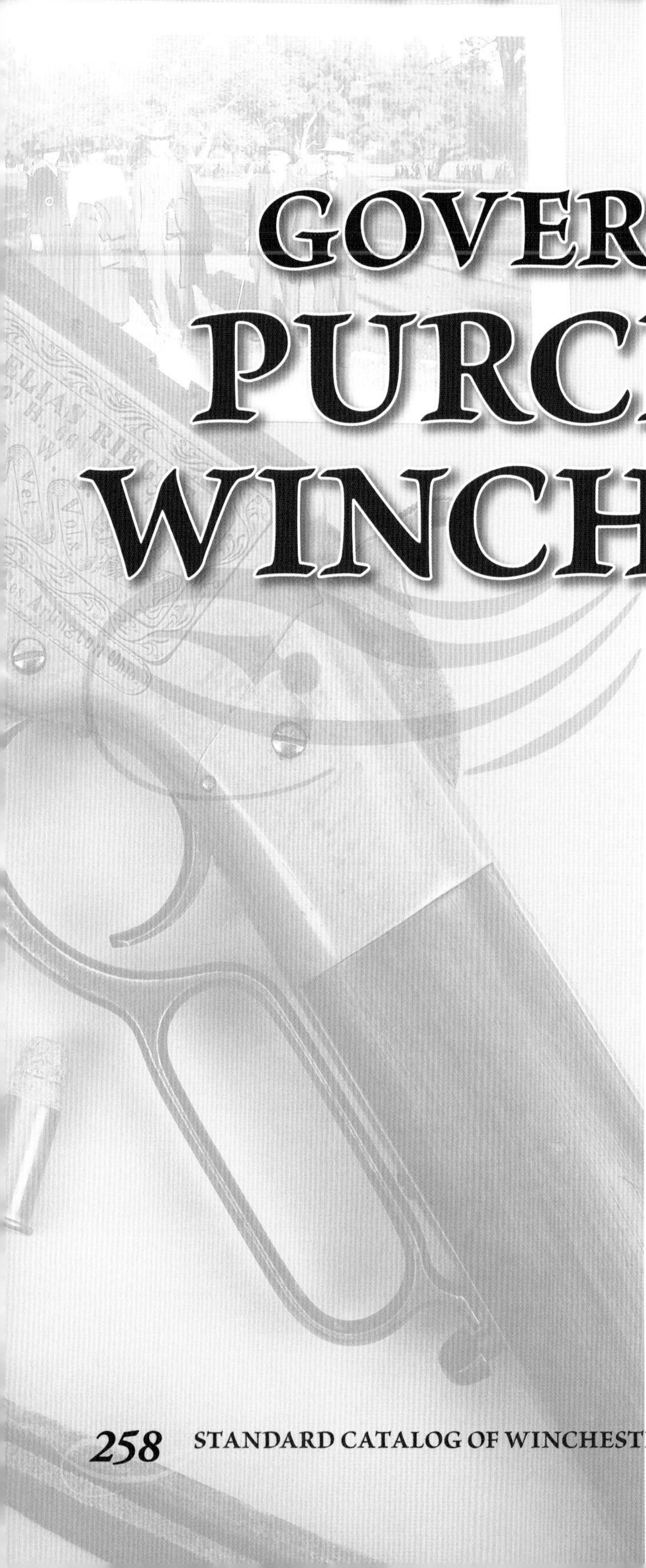

The U.S. government purchased many different Winchester rifles over the years for a wide variety of purposes. During World War I, the Model 1894 carbine was purchased by the government as well as small numbers of the Model 1907 and the Model 1910 self loading rifles. There is evidence that the U.S. Coast Guard purchased several thousand of Model 1906 .22 caliber rifles for use during World War I. The Model 52 bolt action rifle was first designed by Winchester in hopes of a government contract as a military training rifle, but the end of World War I precluded that goal. During World War II, the U.S. government purchased the Winchester Model 74 .22 caliber rifles from 1941 to 1943. It is possible that many Winchester rifles were purchased by the U.S. military for assorted purposes from guard duty to pest control. Many of these rifles will be martially marked and their value has increased over the standard civilian rifle.

Bibliographical *Note:* For more historical information, technical data, and photos see Bruce Canfield's A Collector's Guide to Winchesters in the Service. Also Thomas Henshaw, The History of Winchester Firearms, 1866-1992, Winchester Press, 1995, and George Madis, The Winchester Book, 1985.

MARTIALLY INSPECTED HENRY RIFLES

Beginning in 1863 the Federal Government ordered 1,730 Henry Rifles for use in the Civil War. Most of these government- inspected rifles fall into serial number range 3000 to 4000 while the balance are close to this serial-number range. They are marked "C.G.C." for Charles G. Chapman, the government inspector. These Henry rifles were used under actual combat conditions and for that reason it is doubtful that there are any rifles that would fall into the excellent condition category. Therefore no price is given.

NOTE: There are many counterfeit examples of these rifles. It is strongly advised that an expert in this field be consulted prior to a purchase.

EXC.	V.G.	GOOD	FAIR	POOR
-	-	60000	25000	12000

MODEL 1866

In 1866 the New Haven Arms Company changed its name to the Winchester Repeating Arms Company. The first firearm to be built under the Winchester name was the Model 1866. This first Winchester was a much-improved version of the Henry. A new magazine tube developed by Nelson King, Winchester's plant superintendent, was a vast improvement over the slotted magazine tube used on the Henry and its predecessor. The old tube allowed dirt to enter through the slots and was weakened because of it. King's patent, assigned to Winchester, featured a solid tube that was much stronger and reliable. His patent also dealt with an improved loading system for the rifle. The rifle now featured a loading port on the right side of the receiver with a spring-loaded cover. The frame continued to be made from brass. The Model 1866 was chambered for the .44 caliber Flat Rimfire or the .44 caliber Pointed Rimfire. Both cartridges could be used interchangeably.

The barrel on the Model 1866 was marked with two different markings. The first, which is seen on early guns up to serial number 23000, reads "HENRY'S PATENT-OCT. 16, 1860 KING'S PATENT-MARCH 29, 1866." The second marking

"The Model 1866 Musket was not adopted by the U.S. military. It was sold to Mexico and Prussia."

reads, "WINCHESTER'S-REPEATING-ARMS. NEW HAVEN, CT. KING'S-IMPROVEMENT-PATENTED MARCH 29, 1866 OCTOBER 16, 1860." There are three basic variations of the Model 1866:

1) Sporting Rifle round or octagon barrel. Approximately 28,000 were produced.
2) Carbine round barrel. Approximately 127,000 were produced.
3) Musket round barrel. Approximately 14,000 were produced.

The rifle and musket held 17 cartridges, and the carbine had a capacity of 13 cartridges. Unlike the Henry, Model 1866s were fitted with a walnut forearm. The Model 1866 was discontinued in 1898 with approximately 170,000 guns produced. The Model 1866 was sold in various special order configurations, such as barrels longer or shorter than standard, including engraved guns. The prices listed below represent only standard-model 1866s. For guns with special-order features, an independent appraisal from an expert is highly recommended.

NOTE: The Model 1866 Musket was not adopted by the U.S. military. It was sold to Mexico and Prussia. A large order of 46,000 muskets was delivered to the Turkisk governemnt in 1870 and 1871. A few muskets, about 3,000, were sold to France.

THIRD MODEL

The third style's most noticeable characteristic is the more moderately curved receiver shape at the rear of the frame. The serial number is now stamped in block numerals behind the trigger, thus allowing the numbers to be seen for the first time without removing the stock. The barrel marking is stamped with the Winchester address. The Third Model is found between serial numbers 25000 and 149000. For the first time, a musket version was produced in this serial-number range.

MUSKET

EXC.	V.G.	GOOD	FAIR	POOR
-	11000	8000	3500	2500

FOURTH MODEL

The fourth style has an even less pronounced drop at the top rear of the frame, and the serial number is stamped in script on the lower tang under the lever. The Fourth Model is seen between serial number 149000 and 170100 with the late guns having an iron buttplate instead of brass.

MUSKET

EXC.	V.G.	GOOD	FAIR	POOR
-	12000	9000	3500	2500

MODEL 1866 IRON FRAME RIFLE MUSKET

Overall length 54-1/2"; barrel length 33-1/4"; caliber .45 c.f. Walnut stock with case hardened furniture, barrel burnished bright, the receiver case hardened. The finger lever catch mounted within a large bolster at the rear of the lever. Unmarked except for serial numbers that appear externally on the receiver and often the buttplate tang. Approximately 25 made during the early autumn of 1866. Prospective purchasers are strongly advised to secure an expert appraisal prior to acquisition. Due to the recent identification of this model pricing schedules have yet to be established.

EXC.	V.G.	GOOD	FAIR	POOR
N/A	-	-	-	-

MODEL 1866 IRON FRAME SWISS SHARPSHOOTERS RIFLE

As above, but in .41 Swiss caliber and fitted with a Scheutzen style stock supplied by the firm of Weber Ruesch in Zurich. Marked Weber Ruesch, Zurich on the barrel and serial numbered externally. Approximately 400 to 450 manufactured in 1866 and 1867. This musket was most likely built for Swiss military trials. Prospective purchasers are strongly advised to secure an expert appraisal prior to acquisition. Due to the recent identification of this model pricing schedules have yet to be established.

EXC.	V.G.	GOOD	FAIR	POOR
N/A	-	-	-	-

MODEL 1873 MUSKET

This rifle was fitted with a 30" round barrel and chambered for a variety of calibers at the customer's request. Nominal calibers are: .44-40, .38-40, and .32-20. Magazine capacity was 17 rounds. Muskets were fitted with almost full length wooden stocks with cleaning rod and bayonet fittings. Many of these muskets were sold under contract to foreign governments. Survival rate is very low.

1ST MODEL

EXC.	V.G.	GOOD	FAIR	POOR
-	-	8500	4000	1000

2ND MODEL

The dust cover on the Second Model operates on one central guide secured to the receiver with two screws. The checkered oval finger grip is still used, but on later Second Models this is changed to a serrated finger grip on the rear of the dust cover. Second Models are found in the 31000 to 90000 serial number range.

EXC.	V.G.	GOOD	FAIR	POOR
7500	4000	2000	1250	9000

3RD MODEL

The central guide rail is still present on the Third Model, but it is now integrally machined as part of the receiver. The serrated rear edges of the dust cover are still present on the Third Model.

EXC.	V.G.	GOOD	FAIR	POOR
6000	3500	1250	850	500

MODEL 1876

Musket, 32" round barrel with full-length forearm secured by one barrel band and straight grip stock. Stamped on the barrel is the Winchester address with King's patent date. The caliber marking is stamped on the bottom of the receiver near the magazine tube and the breech end of the barrel.

FIRST MODEL

As with the Model 1873, the primary difference in model types lies in the dust cover. The First Model has no dust cover and is seen between serial number 1 and 3000.

MUSKET

EXC.	V.G.	GOOD	FAIR	POOR
15000	12000	6500	3000	1500

SECOND MODEL

The Second Model has a dust cover with guide rail attached to the receiver with two screws. On the early Second Model an oval finger guide is stamped on top of the dust cover while later models have a serrated finger guide along the rear edge of the dust cover. Second Models range from serial numbers 3000 to 30000.

MUSKET

EXC.	V.G.	GOOD	FAIR	POOR
-	-	9500	4000	1500

NORTHWEST MOUNTED POLICE CARBINE

The folding rear sight is graduated in meters instead of yards.

EXC.	V.G.	GOOD	FAIR	POOR
15000	9000	4500	2000	1250

NOTE: Deduct 50 percent from prices if factory records do not confirm NWP use. A Model 1876 NWP in excellent condition is very rare. Proceed with caution.

MUSKET

EXC.	V.G.	GOOD	FAIR	POOR
18000	9000	5000	1750	1000

THIRD MODEL

The dust cover guide rail on Third Model 76s is integrally machined as part of the receiver with a serrated rear edge on the dust cover. Third Model will be seen from serial numbers 30000 to 64000.

MUSKET

EXC.	V.G.	GOOD	FAIR	POOR
9500	4750	3000	1250	1000

MODEL 1886

Based on a John Browning patent, the Model 1886 was one of the finest and strongest lever actions ever utilized in a Winchester rifle. Winchester introduced the Model 1886 in order to take advantage of the more powerful centerfire cartridges of the time.

Musket, 30" round barrel, musket style forearm with one barrel band. Military style sights. About 350 Model 1886 Muskets were produced. This is the most rare variation of all Winchester lever action rifles.

MUSKET

EXC.	V.G.	GOOD	FAIR	POOR
-	18000	9000	3500	1500

MODEL 1895 U.S. ARMY MUSKET

U.S. Army Musket, 28" round barrel chambered for the .30-40 Krag. Came equipped with or without knife bayonet. These muskets were furnished to the U.S. Army for use during the Spanish-American War and are "US" marked on the receiver.

EXC.	V.G.	GOOD	FAIR	POOR
-	3000	1500	850	450

MODEL 1895 RUSSIAN MUSKET

Russian Musket, similar to standard musket but fitted with clip guides in the top of the receiver and with bayonet. Chambered for the 7.62x54mm R cartridge. Approximately 294,000 Model 1895 Muskets were sold to the Imperial Russian Government between 1915 and 1916. The first 15,000 Russian Muskets had 8" knife bayonets, and the rest were fitted with 16" bayonets. Some of these rifles went to Spain in its Civil War in 1936-1939.

EXC.	V.G.	GOOD	FAIR	POOR
4000	2500	1000	500	250

MODEL 1885 (SINGLE SHOT)

The High Wall musket most often had a 26" round barrel chambered for the .22 caliber cartridge. Larger calibers were available as were different barrel lengths. The High Wall Musket featured an almost full length forearm fastened to the barrel with a single barrel band and rounded buttplate.

The Low Wall musket is most often referred to as the Winder Musket named after the distinguished marksman, Colonel C.B. Winder. This model features a Lyman receiver sight and was made in .22 caliber.

U.S. and Ordnance markings will appear on rifles purchased by the government.

HIGH WALL MUSKET

EXC.	V.G.	GOOD	FAIR	POOR
4000	3000	2000	1500	900

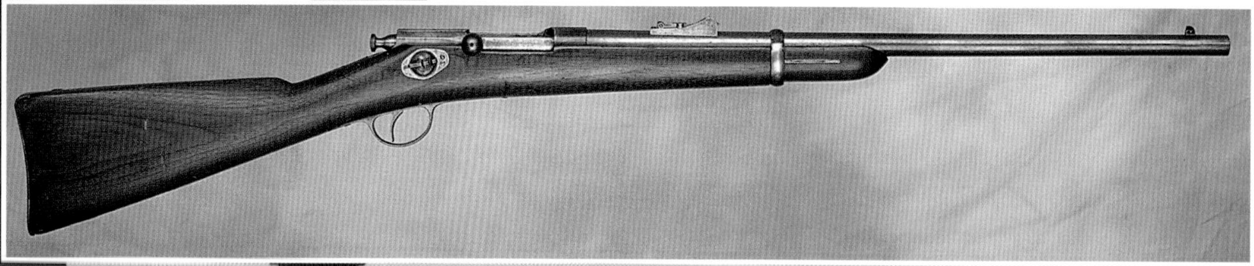

1st Model Hotchkiss.

LOW WALL MUSKET (WINDER MUSKET)

EXC.	V.G.	GOOD	FAIR	POOR
3500	2000	1200	750	400

WINCHESTER HOTCHKISS BOLT ACTION RIFLE

This model is also known as the Hotchkiss Magazine Gun or the Model 1883. This rifle was designed by Benjamin Hotchkiss in 1876, and Winchester acquired the manufacturing rights to the rifle in 1877. In 1879, the first guns were delivered for sale. The Hotchkiss rifle was a bolt-action firearm designed for military and sporting use. It was the first bolt-action rifle made by Winchester. The rifle was furnished in .45-70 Government, and although the 1884 Winchester catalog lists a .40-65 Hotchkiss as being available, no evidence exists that such a chamber was ever actually furnished. Two different types of military configurations will be seen:

1) Carbine, 24" round or 22-1/2" round barrel with military style straight grip stock. Chambered for the 45-55 cartridge.
2) Musket, 32" or 28" round barrel with almost full length military-style straight grip stock. Winchester produced the Model 1883 until 1899, having built about 85,000 guns. Chambered for the 45-70 cartridge.

FIRST MODEL

This model has the safety and a turn button magazine cut-off located above the triggerguard on the right side. The carbine has a 24" round barrel with a saddle ring on the left side of the stock. The musket has a 32" round barrel with two barrel bands, a steel forearm tip, and bayonet attachment under the barrel. The serial number range for the First Model is between 1 and about 6419.

ARMY RIFLE

These Army models are marked with the inspector stamping of "esa/1878" on the left side of the stock. Production total of 513 rifles.

EXC.	V.G.	GOOD	FAIR	POOR
-	6000	3500	900	500

CARBINE

501 carbines produced.

EXC.	V.G.	GOOD	FAIR	POOR
-	5000	2750	900	500

NAVY RIFLE

1,474 produced.

EXC.	V.G.	GOOD	FAIR	POOR
-	4500	2250	900	500

MUSKET

EXC.	V.G.	GOOD	FAIR	POOR
-	3000	1500	700	300

2nd Model Hotchkiss.

3rd Model Hotchkiss.

SECOND MODEL

On this model the safety is located on the top left side of the receiver, and the magazine cutoff is located on the top right side of the receiver to the rear of the bolt handle. The carbine has a 22-1/2" round barrel with a nickeled forearm cap. The musket now has a 28" barrel. Serial number range for the Second Model runs from 6420 to 22521.

CARBINE

400 produced.

EXC.	V.G.	GOOD	FAIR	POOR
-	6000	3000	900	500

MUSKET

EXC.	V.G.	GOOD	FAIR	POOR
-	3500	1750	750	350

THIRD MODEL

The Third Model is easily identified by the two-piece stock separated by the receiver. The carbine is now fitted with a 20" barrel with saddle ring and bar on the left side of the frame. The musket remains unchanged from the Second Model with the exception of the two-piece stock. Serial numbers of the Third Model range from 22552 to 84555.

ARMY RIFLE

EXC.	V.G.	GOOD	FAIR	POOR
-	3500	1750	750	350

MUSKET

EXC.	V.G.	GOOD	FAIR	POOR
-	3500	1750	750	350

Winchester-Lee Straight-Pull US Navy Musket with Bayonet and Scabbard.

WINCHESTER-LEE STRAIGHT PULL RIFLE

This rifle was a military firearm that Winchester built for the U.S. Navy in 1895. The Navy version was a musket type with a 28" round barrel and musket style forearm and plain walnut pistol grip stock. In 1897, Winchester offered a commercial musket version for public sale as well as a Sporting Rifle. All of these guns were chambered for the 6mm Lee (.236 Caliber) cartridge. The Sporting Rifle featured a 24" round barrel with plain walnut pistol grip stock and finger grooves in the forearm. Built from 1895 to 1905, Winchester sold about 20,000 Lee rifles; 15,000 were sold to the U.S. Navy, 3,000 were sold in the commercial version, and 1,700 were Sporting Rifles.

NOTE: Commercial and Sporting rifles will not have martial markings, inspector markings, or bayonet fittings.

U.S. NAVY MUSKET

EXC.	V.G.	GOOD	FAIR	POOR
-	3000	1500	700	500

NOTE: Some of these muskets were stored on the U.S. battleship Maine. Records of serial numbers exist to authenicate these muskets. Add a premium of 50 percent for these examples.

MODEL 1917 (P17)

In 1917, when the United States entered WWI, there was a distinct rifle shortage. There were production facilities set up for the British pattern 1914 rifle. This "Enfield" rifle was redesigned to accept the .30-06 cartridge and was pressed into service as the U.S. rifle Model 1917. This rifle appears similar to the British pattern 1914 rifle. In fact, they are so similar that in WWII, when over a million were sold to Britain for use by their Home Guard, it was necessary to paint a 2" stripe around the butt so that the caliber was immediately known. The barrel length is 26", and it has a 6-round integral box magazine. The finish is matte-blue, with a walnut stock. Towards the end of production parkerized parts were added. The breech is marked "U.S. Model 1917." This was a robust and heavy-duty rifle, and many are used in the manufacture of large-bore custom rifles to this day. There were approximately 2,200,000 manufactured by Remington, Winchester, and Eddystone between 1917 and 1918. The majority were produced at Eddystone, Pennsylvania.

During World War II all parts were parkerized, and barrels were supplied by the Johnson Automatics Company as a result of the rebuild.

NOTE: Add 30 percent for Winchester and Remington models.

EXC.	V.G.	GOOD	FAIR	POOR
800	600	400	200	150

Winchester-Lee Straight-Pull US Navy Musket.

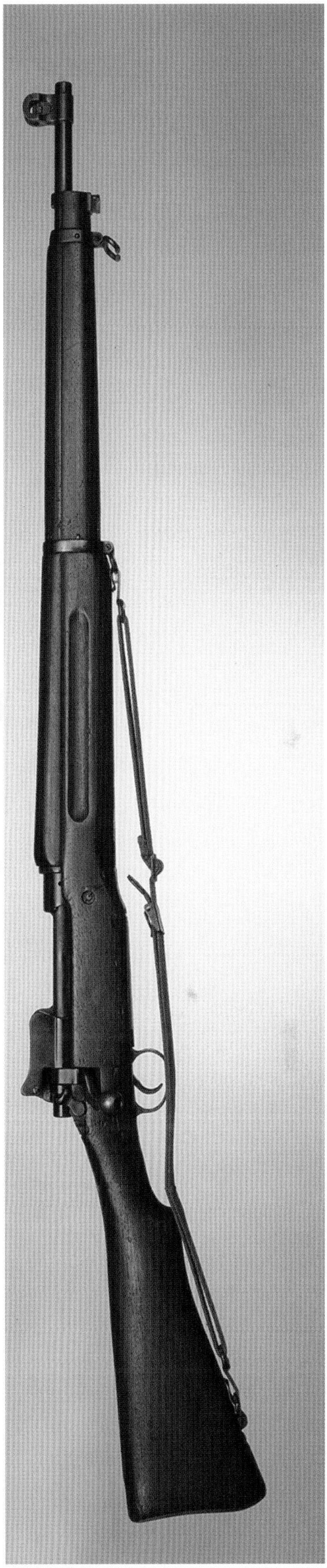

US P17 Manufactured by Winchester.

U.S. M14/M14E2

Based on the famous M1 Garand design this select fire rifle is chambered for the 7.62x51mm cartridge. It has a 21.8" barrel and a 20-round magazine. It weighs approximately 11.2 lbs. Rate of fire is about 750 rounds per minute. Marked "us rifle 7.62mm m14" on the rear top of the receiver. Production began in 1957 and ceased in 1963. Produced by Harrington & Richardson (537,512 total production) stamped "HRA," Springfield (167,172 total production) stamped "SA," Winchester (356,510 total production) stamped "66118" or "OM," and TRW (319,163 total production) stamped "TRW." The M14E2 version is a light machine gun variant with bipod, folding forward hand grip, and muzzle compensator.

NOTE: A sniper version of this rifle was designated the M21 and fitted with a Leatherwood telescope sight. See that listing.

PRE-1968

EXC.	V.G.	FAIR
8500	8000	7500

PRE-1986 CONVERSIONS (OR U.S. MANUFACTURE/M1A SPRINGFIELD ARMORY)

EXC.	V.G.	FAIR
4500	4250	4000

PRE-1986 DEALER SAMPLES

EXC.	V.G.	FAIR
N/A	N/A	N/A

U.S. M1 CARBINE

Introduced in 1941, this is a semiautomatic, gas operated carbine with a 18" barrel and a magazine capacity of 15 or 30 rounds. Half stocked with upper handguard and single barrel band. Bayonet bar located on barrel. Flip up rear sight. Chambered for the .30 U.S. Carbine cartridge. Weight is about 5.25 lbs. Widely used by U.S. military forces during World War II.

NOTE: Prices are for carbines in World War II factory original configuration. Any M1 Carbine with the earliest features sucha as "I" oiler cut stock, high wood, flip rear sight, and narrow barrel band will bring more than the later variations.

WINCHESTER-MANUFACTURED

EXC.	V.G.	GOOD	FAIR	POOR
2000	1400	700	450	375

U.S. RIFLE, CAL. M1 (GARAND) (U.S. M1 RIFLE)

Bibliographical *Note:* For further information, technical, and photos see Bruce Canfield, Complete Guide to the M1 Garand and the M1 Carbine. Andrew Mowbray, Inc.

An Introduction to the U.S. M1 Rifle

by Simeon Stoddard

Adopted in 1936, the M1 remained the standard issue rifle of the United States until it was replaced by the M14 in 1957. It was designed by John C. Garand, who worked for Springfield Armory from 1919 until his retirement in 1953. During this time, Garand concentrated his efforts on the development of a semiautomatic shoulder weapon for general issue to the U.S. armed forces. The M14 rifle, the replacement for the M1, was a compilation of his design work as well.

With the exceptions noted, all values given are for rifles which are in original, as produced condition. Development of the M1 was an ongoing project until it was replaced, as Garand never finished perfecting his basic design. Over 5,400,000 M1 rifles were built, with the majority of them going through a rebuilding process at least once during their service life. During rebuilding, rifles were inspected and unserviceable parts replaced. Parts used for replacement were usually of the latest revision available or what was on hand.

Major assemblies and parts were marked with a government drawing size/part number. This number is often followed with the revision number (see photo above). Barrels were marked, with the exception of early Springfield Armory and all Win-

chester production, with the month and year of manufacture. It must be remembered that this date only refers to when the barrel was produced, and has nothing to do with when the receiver was produced or the rifle was assembled. This barrel date on "original as produced" rifles should be from 0 to 3 months, before the receiver was produced.

Restored rifles, defined as ones with parts added or replaced, to more closely match what they might have been originally, are worth less money than "original as produced" rifles. This difference should be on the order of 30-40 percent of the values shown, and is due to the low number of rifles of this type. When in doubt, get an appraisal. To tell what parts should be correct, study chapters 5 & 6 of "The M1 Garand: WWII" and chapters 7 & 8 of "The M1 Garand: Post WWII" by Scott A. Duff.

REBUILT RIFLE, ANY MANUFACTURE

Value shown is for rifles with a majority of its parts mixed/replaced. Depending on the type of rebuilding that a rifle went through, rifles could be completely disassembled with no attempt to put parts together for the same rifle. Valued mainly for shooting merits. Bore condition, gauging and overall appearance are important factors.

EXC.	V.G.	GOOD
900	550	425

NOTE: Rifles built by Winchester will bring a small premium.

WINCHESTER PRODUCTION

Winchester produced around 513,000 M1 rifles during WWII. Their first contract was an educational order in 1939. This contract was for 500 rifles and the gauges and fixtures to produce the rifles. Winchester's second contract was awarded during 1939 for up to 65,000 rifles. Winchester M1's are typified by noticeable machine marks on their parts, and did not have the higher grade finish that is found on Springfield Armory production. Watch for fake barrels, and barrels marked "Winchester" which were produced in the 1960s as replacement barrels.

WINCHESTER EDUCATIONAL CONTRACT SN: 100000-100500

EXC.	V.G.	GOOD	FAIR	POOR
10000	6000	4500	3000	2000

WINCHESTER SN: 100501-165000

Rifles of this serial number range were produced from Jan. 1941 until May 1942.

EXC.	V.G.	GOOD	FAIR	POOR
6500	4500	2000	1500	750

WINCHESTER SN: 1200000-1380000

Rifles in this serial number range were produced from May 1942 until Aug. 1943.

EXC.	V.G.	GOOD	FAIR	POOR
4500	2500	1800	1000	750

NOTE: Add a premium of $1,000 for earlier rifles.

WINCHESTER SN: 2305850-2536493

Rifles in this serial number range were produced from Aug. 1943 until Jan. 1945.

EXC.	V.G.	GOOD	FAIR	POOR
3000	2000	1250	900	550

NOTE: Add a premium of $500 for earlier rifles.

WINCHESTER SN: 1601150-1640000

Rifles in this serial number range were produced from Jan. 1945, until June 1945. These are often referred to as "Win-13's" because of the revision number of the right front receiver leg.

EXC.	V.G.	GOOD	FAIR	POOR
3500	2500	2000	1500	850

MODEL 1897 TRENCH GUN (MODEL 1917)

Slide action hammer gun 12 gauge, 20" barrel bored to shoot buckshot, plain walnut modified pistol grip stock with grooved slide handle. Solid frame (WWI) or takedown (WWII). Fitted with barrel hand guard and bayonet. This model was furnished to the U.S. Army for trench work in World War I. It was not listed in Winchester catalogs until 1920. This model was also used in large numbers in WWII, Korea, and Vietnam. Prices below are for U.S. marked guns.

MODEL 97 SOLID FRAME-WORLD WAR I

EXC.	V.G.	GOOD	FAIR	POOR
5000	3500	2000	1000	700

MODEL 97 TAKE DOWN-WORLD WAR II

EXC.	V.G.	GOOD	FAIR	POOR
4500	3000	1800	800	650

NOTE: Add about $200 for Winchester marked bayonet.

MODEL 12 TRENCH GUN

Slide action hammerless gun 12 gauge, 20" barrel bored to shoot buckshot, plain walnut modified pistol grip stock with grooved slide handle. Solid frame or takedown. Fitted with barrel hand guard and bayonet. Finish is blued. This model was furnished to the U.S. Army for trench work in World War I and World War II. Prices below are for U.S. marked guns.

EXC.	V.G.	GOOD	FAIR	POOR
5000	3500	2000	800	650

NOTE: Add about $200 for Winchester marked bayonet.

MODEL 1200

In 1968 and 1969 the U.S. military purchased a quantity of Model 1200 shotguns with 20" cylinder bored barrels, Type W bayonet adapter for the Model 1917 bayonet. Stocks were plain and uncheckered with oil finish.

EXC.	V.G.	GOOD	FAIR	POOR
2500	1750	1200	600	300

MODEL 1400

The U.S. military purchased a small quantity of Model 1400 semiautomatic shotguns. these were fitted with a plain 20" barrel and choked cylinder. Scarce.

EXC.	V.G.	GOOD	FAIR	POOR
N/A	-	-	-	-

BROWNING M2/M2HB .50

This is an air-cooled .50 caliber machine first produced in 1933. It has a 44.5" barrel and weighs about 84 lbs. Its rate of fire is 500 rounds per minute. It is belt fed. Marked "browning machine gun cal 50 m2" on the left side of the receiver. Approximately three million were produced. The gun was produced by Colt, FN, Ramo, Saco, and Winchester.

It is one of the most widely used and successful heavy machines ever produced. Besides being utilized as an aircraft, ground and vehicle weapon, the M2 is also used as an antiaircraft gun in single, twin, and four-barrel configurations. The M2 was additionally configured as a water-cooled gun for sustained fire. The commercial designation for this

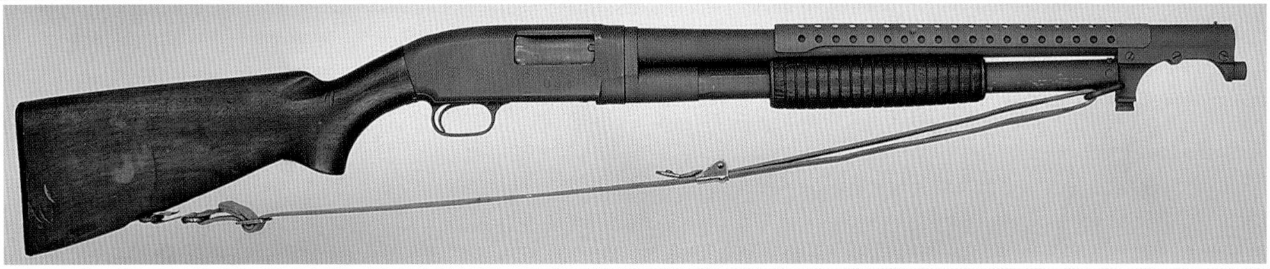

Model 1200 US Military Shotgun.

model was the MG 52A. Widely used throughout the world and is still in use today and still in production in the UK, USA, and Belgium.

The .50 caliber cartridge was first adopted in 1923 after extensive research by John M. Browning, Winchester, and Colt. The cartridge, like many with military applications, has a wide variety of variations.

PRE-1968

EXC.	V.G.	FAIR
30000	27500	25000

BROWNING AUTOMATIC RIFLE (BAR)

This is gas-operated machine gun chambered for the .30-06 cartridge. Fitted with a 23.8" barrel and a 20-round magazine, it weighs about 16 lbs. Its rate of fire is 500 rounds per minute. Marked "browning bar m1918 cal 30" on receiver it was produced from 1917 until 1945, but saw service in the Korean War.

This Browning-designed rifle was built by Colt, Marlin, and Winchester. It has several variations from the original M1918 design. About 50,000 Model 1918 BARs saw service in Europe during World War I. The M1918A1 was first built in 1927 and has the buttplate hinged shoulder support. The bipod has spiked feet and is attached to the gas cylinder. It too is select fire. Weight for the M1918A1 is 18.5 lbs. The M1918 A2 was first built in 1932 and is fitted with a bipod with skid feet attached to the flash hider. There is a monopod beneath the buttstock. The rear sight is from a Browning M1919A4 machine gun and is adjustable for windage. This version has a rate of fire regulator that sets the rate between 450 and 650 rounds per minute. Weight for this variation is 19.5 lbs. During World War II approximately 188,000 Model 1918A2 BARs were produced. The last version is called the M1922 and was built in limited numbers. It is similar to the M1918 but with a heavy finned barrel. The bipod is attached to the barrel. Barrel length is 18" with rate of fire of 550 rounds per minute.

PRE-1968

EXC.	V.G.	FAIR
30000	28000	26000

APPENDIX

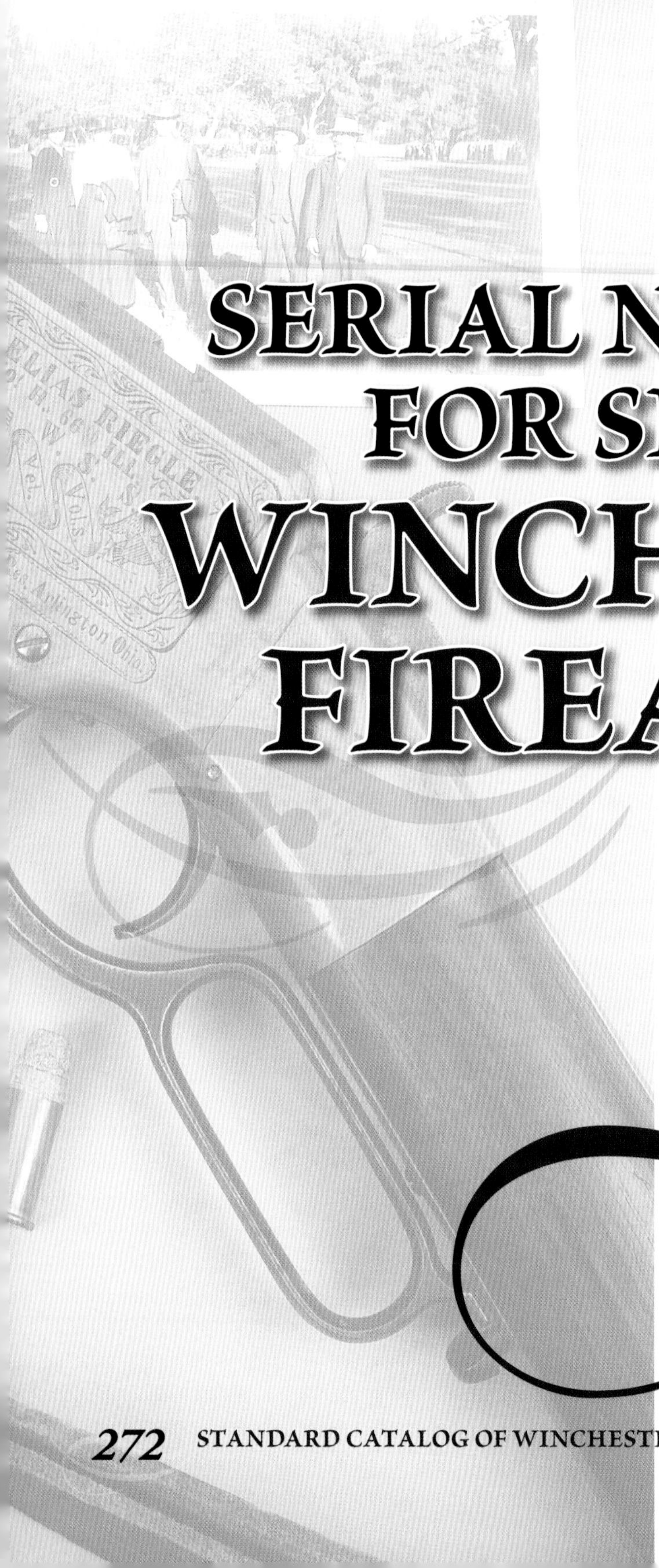

SERIAL NUMBERS FOR SELECT WINCHESTER FIREARMS

Records at the factory indicate the following serial numbers were assigned to guns at the end of the calendar year.

MODEL 100

1961 -1 to 32189	1968 -210053
62 -60760	69 -A210999
63 -78863	70 -229995
64 -92016	71 -242999
65 -135388	72 -A258001
66 -145239	73 -A262833
67 -209498	

MODEL 88

1955 -1 to 18378	1965 -162699
56 -36756	66 -192595
57 -55134	67 -212416
58 -73512	68 -230199
59 -91890	69 -H239899
60 -110268	70 -H258229
61 -128651	71 -H266784
62 -139838	72 -H279014
63 -148858	73 -H283718
64 -160307	

MODEL 74

1939 -1 to 30890	1948 -223788
40 -67085	49 -249900
41 -114355	50 -276012
42 -128293	51 -302124
43 –None	52 -328236
44 -128295	53 -354348
45 -128878	54 -380460
46 -145168	55 -406574
47 -173524	

MODEL 71

1935 - 1 to 4	1947 -25758
36 -7821	48 -27900
37 -12988	49 -29675
38 -14690	50 -31450
39 -16155	51 -33225
40 -18267	52 -35000
41 -20810	53 -37500
42 -21959	54 -40770
43 -22048	55 -43306
44 -22051	56 -45843
45 -22224	57 -47254
46 -23534	

MODEL 70

1935 - 1 to 19	1950 - 173150
36 -2238	51 -206625
37 -11573	52 -238820
38 -17844	53 -282735
39 -23991	54 -323530
40 -31675	55 -361025
41 -41753	56 -393595
42 -49206	57 -425283
43 -49983	58 -440792
44 -49997	59 -465040
45 -50921	60 -504257
46 -58382	61 -545446
47 -75675	62 -565592
48 -101680	63 -581471
49 -131580	

All post-1964 Model 70s began with the serial number 700000.

1964 -740599	1973 - G1128731
65 -809177	74 -G1175000
66 -833795	75 -G1218700
67 -869000	76 -G1266000
68 -925908	77 -G1350000
69 -G941900	78 -G1410000
70 -G957995	79 -G1447000
71 -G1018991	80 -G1490709
72 -G1099257	81 -G1537134

MODEL 63

1933 -1 to 2667	1946 -61607
34 -5361	47 -71714
35 -9830	48 -80519
36 -16781	49 -88889
37 -25435	50 -97259
38 -30934	51 -105629
39 -36055	52 -114000
40 -41456	53 -120500
41 -47708	54 -127000
42 -51258	55 -138000
43 -51631	56 -150000
44 -51656	57 -162345
45 -53853	58 -174692

MODEL 62

1932 - 1 to 7643	1946 - 183756
33 -10695	47 -219085
34 -14090	48 -252298
35 -23924	49 -262473
36 -42759	50 -272648
37 -66059	51 -282823
38 -80205	52 -293000
39 -96534	53 -310500
40 -116393	54 -328000
41 -137379	55 -342776
42 -155152	56 -357551
43 -155422	57 -383513
44 -155425	58 -409475
45 -156073	

MODEL 61

1932 - 1 to 3532	1948 - 115281
33 -6008	49 -125461
34 -8554	50 -135641
35 -12379	51 -145821
36 -20615	52 -156000
37 -30334	53 -171000
38 -36326	54 -186000
39 -42610	55 -200962
40 -49270	56 -215923
41 -57493	57 -229457
42 -59871	58 -242992
43 -59872	59 -262793
44 -59879	60 -282594
45 -60512	61 -302395
46 -71629	62 -322196
47 -92297	63 -342001

This model was discontinued in 1963. For some unknown reason there are no actual records available from 1949 through 1963. The serial number figures for these years are arrived at by taking the total production figure of 342,001, subtracting the last known number of 115281, and dividing the difference equally by the number of remaining years available, (15).

MODEL 55 CENTERFIRE

1924 - 1 to 836	1929 - 12258
25 -2783	30 -17393
26 -4957	31 -18198
27 -8021	32 -19204
28 -10467	33 -Clean-up 20580

MODEL 54

1925 - 1 to 3140	1931 - 36731
26 -8051	32 -38543
27 -14176	33 -40722
28 -19587	34 -43466
29 -29104	35 -47125
30 -32499	36 -50145

MODEL 53

In the case of the Model 53 the following list pertains to the number of guns produced each year rather than a serial number list.

The Model 53 was serially numbered concurrently with the Model 92.

1924 - 1488
25 -286130 -920
26 -253131 -621
27 -229732 -206
28 -1958
1929 - 1733

This model was discontinued in 1932; however, a clean-up of production continued for nine more years with an additional 486 guns. Total production approximately-15,100.

1920 -None indicated	1950 - 70766
21 -397	51 -73385
22 -745	52 -76000
23 -1394	53 -79500
24 -2361	54 -80693
25 -3513	55 -81831
26 -6383	56 -96869
27 -9436	57 -97869
28 -12082	58 -98599
29 -14594	59 -98899
30 -17253	60 -102200
31 -21954	61 -106986
32 -24951	62 -108718
33 -26725	63 -113583
34 -29030	64 -118447
35 -32448	65 -120992
36 -36632	66 -123537
37 -40419	67 -123727
38 -43632	68 -123917
39 -45460	69 -E124107
40 -47519	70 -E124297
41 -50317	71 -E124489
42 -52129	72 -E124574
43 -52553	73 -E124659
44 -52560	74 -E124744
45 -52718	75 -E124828
46 -56080	76 -E125019
47 -60158	77 -E125211
48 -64265	78 -E125315
49 -68149	

This model was discontinued in 1978. A small clean-up of production was completed in 1979 with a total of 125,419.

MODEL 50

1954 - 1 to 24550	1958 - 122750
55 -49100	59 -147300
56 -73650	60 -171850
57 -98200	61 -196400

MODEL 42

1933 - 1 to 9398	1949 - 81107
34 -13963	50 -87071
35 -17728	51 -93038
36 -24849	52 -99000
37 -30900	53 -108201
38 -34659	54 -117200
39 -38967	55 -121883
40 -43348	56 -126566
41 -48203	57 -131249
42 -50818	58 -135932
43 -50822	59 -140615
44 -50828	60 -145298
45 -51168	61 -149981
46 -54256	62 -154664
47 -64853	63 -159353
48 -75142	

MODEL 24

1939 - 1 to 8118	1944 - 33683
40 -21382	45 -34965
41 -27045	46 -45250
42 -33670	47 -58940
43 -None recorded	48 -64417

There were no records kept on this model from 1949 until its discontinuance in 1958. The total production was approximately 116,280.

MODEL 12

1912 - 5308	1938 - 779455
13 -32418	39 -814121
14 -79765	40 -856499
15 -109515	41 -907431
16 -136412	42 -958303
17 -159391	43 -975640
18 -183461	44 -975727
19 -219457	45 -990004
20 -247458	46 -1029152
21 -267253	47 -1102371
22 -304314	48 -1176055
23 -346319	49 -1214041
24 -385196	50 -1252028
25 -423056	51 -1290015
26 -464564	52 -1328002
27 -510693	53 -1399996
28 -557850	54 -1471990
29 -600834	55 -1541929
30 -626996	56 -1611868
31 -651255	57 -1651435
32 -660110	58 -1690999
33 -664544	59 -1795500
34 -673994	60 -1800000
35 -686978	61 -1930029
36 -720316	62 -1956990
37 -754250	63 -1962001

A clean-up of production took place from 1964 through 1966 with the ending serial number 70875.

NEW STYLE MODEL 12

1972 -Y200010
73 -Y2015662
74 -Y2022061
75 -Y2024478
76 -Y2025482
77 -Y2025874
78 -Y2026156
79 -Y2026399

MODEL 1911 S.L.

1911 - 1 to 3819	1919 - 57337
12 -27659	20 -60719
13 -36677	21 -64109
14 -40105	22 -69132
15 -43284	23 -73186
16 -45391	24 -76199
17 -49893	25 -78611
18 -52895	

The model 1911 was discontinued in 1925. However, guns were produced for three years after that date to clean up production and excess parts. When this practice ceased there were approximately 82,774 guns produced.

MODEL 1910

1910 - 1 to 4766	1924 - 17030
11 -7695	25 -17281
12 -9712	26 -17696
13 -11487	27 -18182
14 -12311	28 -18469
15 -13233	29 -18893
16 -13788	30 -19065
17 -14255	31 -19172
18 -14625	32 -19232
19 -15665	33 -19281
20 -Not Available	34 -19338
21 -15845	35 -19388
22 -16347	36 -19445
23 -16637	

A clean-up of production continued into 1937 when the total of the guns were completed at approximately 20786.

MODEL 1907

1907 - 1 to 8657	1933 -44806
08 -14486	34 -44990
09 -19707	35 -45203
10 -23230	36 -45482
11 -25523	37 -45920
12 -27724	38 -46419
13 -29607	39 -46758
14 -30872	40 -47296
15 -32272	41 -47957
16 -36215	42 -48275
17 -38235	43 -None
18 -39172	44 -None
19 -40448	45 -48281
20 -Not Available	46 -48395
21 -40784	47 -48996
22 -41289	48 -49684
23 -41658**	49 -50662
24 -42029**	50 -51640
25 -42360**	51 -52618
26 -42688**	52 -53596
27 -43226**	53 -54574
28 -43685**	54 -55552
29 -44046**	55 -56530
30 -44357**	56 -57508
31 -44572**	57 -58486
32 -44683	

Actual records on serial numbers stops in 1948. The serial numbers ending each year from 1948 to 1957 were derived at by taking the last serial number recorded (58486) and the last number from 1948, (49684) and dividing the years of production, (9), which relates to 978 guns each year for the nine year period.

MODEL 1906

1906 -1 to 52278	1920 -None
07 -89147	21 -598691
08 -114138	22 -608011
09 -165068	23 -622601
10 -221189	24 -636163
11 -273355	25 -649952
12 -327955	26 -665484
13 -381922	27 -679692
14 -422734	28 -695915
15 -453880	29 -711202
16 -483805	30 -720116
17 -517743	31 -725978
18 -535540	32 -727353
19 -593917	

A clean-up of production took place for the next few years with a record of production reaching approximately 729,305.

MODEL 1905

1905 -1 to 5659	1913 -25559
06 -15288	14 -26110
07 -19194	15 -26561
08 -20385	16 -26910
09 -21280	17 -27297
10 -22423	18 -27585
11 -23503	19 -28287
12 -24602	20 -29113

MODEL 1903

1903 -Not Available	1918 -92617
04 -6944	19 -96565
05 -14865	20 -Not Available
06 -23097	21 -97650
07 -31852	22 -99011
08 -39105	23 -100452
09 -46496	24 -101688
10 -54298	25 -103075
11 -61679	26 -104230
12 -69586	27 -105537
13 -76732	28 -107157
14 -81776	29 -109414
15 -84563	30 -111276
16 -87148	31 -112533
17 -89501	32 -112992

This model was discontinued in 1932, however, a clean up of parts was used for further production of approximately 2,000 guns. Total production was stopped at serial number 114962 in 1936.

MODEL 1901 SHOTGUN

1904 -64856 to 64860

05 -6648314 -73202	
06 -6748615 -73509	
07 -6842416 -73770	
08 -6919717 -74027	
09 -7000918 -74311	
10 -7075319 -74872	
11 -7144120 -77000	
12 -72167	
1913 -72764	

MODEL 1897

1897 -to 32335	1928 -796806
98 -64668	29 -807321
99 -96999	30 -812729
1900 -129332	31 -830721
01 -161665	32 -833926
02 -193998	33 -835637
03 -226331	34 -837364
04 -258664	35 -839728
05 -296037	36 -848684
06 -334059	37 -856729
07 -377999	38 -860725
08 -413618	39 -866938
09 -446888	40 -875945
10 -481062	41 -891190
11 -512632	42 -910072
12 -544313	43 -912265
13 -575213	44 -912327
14 -592732	45 -916472
15 -607673	46 -926409
16 -624537	47 -936682
17 -646124	48 -944085
18 -668383	49 -953042
19 -691943	50 -961999
20 -696183	51 -970956
21 -700428	52 -979913
22 -715902	53 -988860
23 -732060	54 -997827
24 -744942	55 -1006784
25 -757629	56 -1015741
26 -770527	57 -1024700
27 -783574	

Records on this model are incomplete. The above serial numbers are estimated from 1897 through 1903 and again from 1949 through 1957. The actual records are in existence from 1904 through 1949.

MODEL 1895

1895 -1 to 287	1914 -72082
96 -5715	15 -174233
97 -7814	16 -377411
98 -19871	17 -389106
99 -26434	18 -392731
1900 -29817	19 -397250
01 -31584	20 -400463
02 -35601	21 -404075
03 -42514	22 -407200
04 -47805	23 -410289
05 -54783	24 -413276
06 -55011	25 -417402
07 -57351	26 -419533
08 -60002	27 -421584
09 -60951	28 -422676
10 -63771	29 -423680
11 -65017	30 -424181
12 -67331	31 -425132
13 -70823	32 -425825

MODEL 94 (MODEL 1894)

1894 -1 to 14579	1939 -1101051
95 -44359	40 -1142423
96 -76464	41 -1191307
97 -111453	42 -1221289
98 -147684	43 -No Record Avail.
99 -183371	44 -No Record Avail.
1900 -204427	45 -No Record Avail.
01 -233975	46 -No Record Avail.
02 -273854	47 -No Record Avail.
03 -291506	48 -1500000
04 -311363	49 -1626100
05 -337557	50 -1724295
06 -378878	51 -1819800
07 -430985	52 -1910000
08 -474241	53 -2000000
09 -505831	54 -2071100
10 -553062	55 -2145296

11 -599263	56 -2225000
12 -646114	57 -2290296
13 -703701	58 -2365887
14 -756066	59 -2410555
15 -784052	60 -2469821
16 -807741	61 -2500000
17 -821972	62 -2551921
18 -838175	63 -2586000
19 -870762*	1964 -2700000
20 -880627	64 -2797428
21 -908318	65 -2894428
22 -919583	66 -2991927
23 -938539	67 -3088458
24 -953198	68 -3185691
25 -978523	69 -3284570
26 -997603	70 -3381299
27 -1027571	71 -3557385
28 -1054465	72 -3806499
29 -1077097	73 -3929364
30 -1081755	74 -4111426
31 -1084156	75 -4277926
32 -1087836	76 -4463553
33 -1089270	77 -4565925
34 -1091190	78 -4662210
35 -1099605	79 -4826596
36 -1100065	80 -4892951
37 -1100679	81 -5024957
38 -1100915	62 -5103248

- *The post-1964 Model 94 began with serial number 2700000.
- Serial number 1000000 was presented to President Calvin Coolidge in 1927.
- Serial number 1500000 was presented to President Harry S. Truman in 1948.
- Serial number 2000000 was presented to President Dwight D. Eisenhower in 1953.
- Serial numbers 2500000 and 3000000 were presented to the Winchester Gun Museum, now located in Cody, Wyoming.
- Serial number 3500000 was not constructed until 1979 and was sold at auction in Las Vegas, Nevada. Serial number 4000000; whereabouts unknown at this time.
- Serial number 4500000-shipped to Italy by Olin in 1978. Whereabouts unknown.
- Serial number 5000000-in New Haven, not constructed as of March 1983.

MODEL 1892

1892 -1 to 23701	1913 -742675
93 -35987	14 -771444
94 -73508	15 -804622
95 -106721	16 -830031
96 -144935	17 -853819
97 -159312	18 -870942
98 -165431	19 -903649
99 -171820	20 -906754
1900 -183411	21 -910476
01 -191787	22 -917300
02 -208871	23 -926329
03 -253935	24 -938641
04 -278546	25 -954997
05 -315425	26 -973896
06 -376496	27 -990883
07 -437919	28 -996517
08 -476540	29 -999238
09 -522162	30 -999730
10 -586996	31 -1000727
11 -643483	32 -1001324
12 -694752	

MODEL 1890

Records on the Model 1890 are somewhat incomplete. Our records indicate the following serial numbers were assigned to guns at the end of the calendar year beginning with 1908. Actual records on the firearms that were manufactured between 1890 and 1907 will be available from the "Winchester Museum," located at The "Buffalo Bill Historical Center," P.O. Box 1020, Cody, WY 82414.

1908 -330000 to 363850	1920 -None
09 -393427	21 -634783
10 -423567	22 -643304
11 -451264	23 -654837
12 -478595	24 -664613
13 -506936	25 -675774
	26 -687049

14 -531019	27 -698987
15 -551290	28 -711354
16 -570497	29 -722125
17 -589204	30 -729015
18 -603438	31 -733178
19 -630801	32 -734454

The Model 1890 was discontinued in 1932; however, a clean-up of the production run lasted another 8+ years and included another 14,000 to 15,000 guns. Our figures indicate approximately 749,000 guns were made.

MODEL 1887

1887 -1 to 7431	1993 -54367
88 -22408	94 -56849
89 -25673	95 -58289
90 -29105	96 -60175
91 -38541	97 -63952
92 -49763	98 -64855

According to these records no guns were produced during the last few years of this model and it was therefore discontinued in 1901.

MODEL 1886

1886 -1 to 3211	1905 -138838
87 -14728	06 -142249
88 -28577	07 -145119
89 -38401	08 -147322
90 -49723	09 -148237
91 -63601	10 -150129
92 -73816	11 -151622
93 -83261	12 -152943
94 -94543	13 -152947
95 -103708	14 -153859
96 -109670	15 -154452
97 -113997	16 -154979
98 -119192	17 -155387
99 -120571	18 -156219
1900 -122834	19 -156930
01 -125630	20 -158716
02 -128942	21 -159108
03 -132213	22 -159337
04 -135524	

No further serial numbers were recorded until the discontinuance of the model, which was in 1935 at 159994.

MODEL 1885 SINGLE-SHOT

1885 -1 to 375	1900 -88501
86 -6841	01 -90424
87 -18328	02 -92031
88 -30571	03 -92359
89 -45019	04 -92785
90 –None	05 -93611
91 -53700	06 -94208
92 -60371	07 -95743
93 -69534	08 -96819
94 –None	09 -98097
95 -73771	10 -98506
96 -78253	11 -99012
97 -78815	12 -None
98 -84700	13 -100352
99 -85086	

No further serial numbers were recorded until the end of 1923. The last number recorded was 139700.

MODEL 1876

1876 -1 to 1429	1888 -63539
77 -3579	89 -None
78 -7967	90 -None
79 -8971	91 -None
80 -14700	92 -63561
81 -21759	93 -63670
82 -32407	94 -63678
83 -42410	95 -None
84 -54666	96 -63702
85 -58714	97 -63869
86 -60397	98 -63871
87 -62420	

MODEL 1873

1873 -1 to 126	1897 -513421
74 -2726	98 -525922
75 -11325	99 -541328
76 -23151	1900 -554128
77 -23628	01 -557236
78 -27501	02 -564557

79 -41525	03 -573957
80 -63537	04 -588953
81 -81620	05 -602557
82 -109507	06 -613780
83 -145503	07 -None
84 -175126	08 -None
85 -196221	09 -630385
86 -222937	10 -656101
87 -225922	11 -669324
88 -284529	12 -678527
89 -323956	13 -684419
90 -363220	14 -686510
91 -405026	15 -688431
92 -441625	16 -694020
93 -466641	17 -698617
94 -481826	18 -700734
95 -499308	19 -702042
96 -507545	

No last number available: 1920, 21, 22, 23-720609.

MODEL 1866

1866 -12476 to 14813	1883 -162376
67 -15578	84 -163649
68 -19768	85 -163664
69 -29516	86 -165071
70 -52527	87 -165912
71 -88184	88 -167155
72 -109784	89 -167401
73 -118401	90 -167702
74 -125038	91 -169003
75 -125965	92 -None
76 -131907	93 -169007
77 -148207	94 -169011
78 -150493	95 -None
79 -152201	96 -None
80 -154379	97 -169015
81 -156107	98 -170100
82 -159513	99 -Discontinued

EARLY WINCHESTER PRESIDENTS

1) Oliver Winchester (1857-1880)
2) William Wirt Winchester (1880-1881). He was the son of Oliver Winchester.
3) William Converse (1881-1890). He was the husband of Mary A. Pardee.
4) Thomas Gray Bennett (1890-1910). He was the husband of Hannah Jane Winchester.
5) George E. Hodson (1910-1915). He was a partner in the company with Oliver.
6) Winchester Bennett (1915-1918). Son of Thomas Gray Bennett.
7) Thomas Gray Bennett (1918-1919)

NEW DEVELOPMENTS AT WINCHESTER

On August 15, 2006, Olin Corporation, owner of the Winchester trademarks, announced that it had entered into a new license agreement with Browning to make Winchester brand rifles and shotguns, though not at the closed Winchester plant in New Haven; Browning has announced that production of any Winchester designs will be done overseas. Browning, based in Morgan, Utah, and the former licensee, U.S. Repeating Arms Company, are both subsidiaries of FN Herstal.

MODEL INDEX

TWO- OR THREE-DIGIT MODEL DESIGNATIONS, E.G., MODEL 64, MODEL 100, ETC.

NAMES OR FOUR DIGIT MODEL DESIGNATIONS: E.G., BREECH LOADING SHOTGUN,